CIVILIZING THE ENEMY

CIVILIZING THE ENEMY

German Reconstruction and the Invention of the West

Patrick Thaddeus Jackson

THE UNIVERSITY OF MICHIGAN PRESS   *Ann Arbor*

FOR HOLLY, MY TRUE COMPANION

Copyright © by the University of Michigan 2006
All rights reserved
Published in the United States of America by
The University of Michigan Press
Manufactured in the United States of America
⊚ Printed on acid-free paper

2009   2008   2007   2006   4   3   2   1

A CIP catalog record for this book is available from the British Library.

Library of Congress Cataloging-in-Publication Data

Jackson, Patrick Thaddeus, 1972–
    Civilizing the enemy : German reconstruction and the invention of
the West / Patrick Thaddeus Jackson.
        p.   cm.
    Includes bibliographical references and index.
    ISBN-13: 978-0-472-09929-0 (cloth : alk. paper)
    ISBN-10: 0-472-09929-9 (cloth : alk. paper)
    ISBN-13: 978-0-472-06929-3 (pbk. : alk. paper)
    ISBN-10: 0-472-06929-2 (pbk. : alk. paper)
    1. International relations—Social aspects.   2. Rhetoric—Political aspects.
    3. Reconstruction (1939–1951)—Germany.   4. Cold War.
    5. Civilization, Western.   I. Title.

JZ1253.J33   2006
940.53′1440943—dc22   2006001569

Grateful acknowledgment is given for the excerpt from *Winnie-the-Pooh* by A. A. Milne, illustrated by
E. H. Shepard, copyright 1926 by E.P. Dutton, renewed 1954 by A. A. Milne. Used by permission of
Dutton Children's Books, a Division of Penguin Young Readers Group, a Member of Penguin Group
(USA) Inc., 345 Hudson Street, New York, NY 10014. All rights reserved. In the United Kingdom and
the British Commonwealth (excluding Canada), *Winnie-the-Pooh* © A. A. Milne. Published by
Egmont UK Limited, London and used with permission.

ISBN-13 978-0-472-02228-1 (electronic)

Contents

*T*HE USA DOES NOT KNOW EUROPE.... Therefore the USA is inclined not to interest itself in European affairs. And to the contrary, this is completely wrong. If European culture—which has suffered heavily for the past thirty years—completely dies out, this will also be of immense importance for the USA. The danger is great. Asia stands at the Elbe. Only an economically and spiritually healthy western Europe under the leadership of England and France—a western Europe to which the part of Germany not occupied by Russia belongs as a substantial component—can stop the further spiritual and forceful advance of Asia. Help me to disseminate the conviction throughout the USA that the rescue of Europe can only be accomplished with the help of the USA, and that the rescue of Europe is also essential for the USA.

—Konrad Adenauer to William Sollman, 16 March 1946

Preface

$\mathcal{A}$N OP-ED PIECE BY HENRY KISSINGER on tensions within NATO appeared in several American newspapers on 10 February 2003. In it, Kissinger criticized France and Germany for opposing United States–led efforts to disarm Iraq by force, arguing that the likely result of such opposition will be to "confirm the fundamentalist view of the West's psychological collapse" and wreak lasting damage on "the Western alliance." The language is striking, both for its casual assumption that the United States and the countries of Western Europe belong to a community anchored by a common culture (and that they have been attacked by "fundamentalists" on this basis) and for its injured tone at what is understood to be a betrayal of that community by the Europeans. "Alliances do not function because heads of state consult their lawyers," Kissinger declares; "they thrive precisely when they involve moral and emotional commitments beyond legal documents." And "the West," for Kissinger, encapsulates commitments of this sort.

How did notions of community like this become so firmly entrenched in international politics that commentators could deploy them quite unself-consciously? The existence and rhetorical currency of a notion like 'Western Civilization' is far from obvious, considering that the twinned principles of sovereignty and anarchy continue to structure world politics to a significant degree. Despite globalization, sovereign states, acknowledging no higher authority than themselves, continue to claim a monopoly on the legitimate use of force and to reserve to themselves the right to make final decisions about the distribution of resources and the overall shape of global authority. The supposed existence of a community like Western Civilization flies in the face of this traditional notion, and also contradicts the neoliberal assertion that the globalized world is now a world of firms and consumers. The world envisioned by the language of 'Western Civilization' is different from both the world of sovereign states in anarchy and the world of global markets, and the persistence of this language in the face of the manifest institutional realities of these two worlds remains puzzling.

Thinking about the issue historically raises a second puzzle, since the language of 'Western Civilization' has only been current in political debates for about a century. This raises problems for the assertions by scholars that the West is an ancient cultural community: if the community is so ancient, why has it only been noticed recently? Further problems are raised by the fact that those using the notion do not seem to agree on the *content* of the community to which they refer; the precise geographical boundaries of the West, along with the normative foundations of the community, seem to vary from speaker to speaker. A particularly striking example of the ambiguous boundaries of the West can be seen in the case of Germany, which was a dire enemy of the United States and much of Western Europe in the first part of the twentieth century but emerged as a staunch Western ally after the Second World War. The language of 'Western Civilization,' although powerful, is also historically and strategically pliable.

In this book I undertake an exploration of this strange rhetoric, and in particular its implication in the construction of the "postwar settlement" following the Second World War. I concentrate on the reconstruction of Germany for both historical and more contemporary reasons. For one thing, existing accounts of the postwar settlement in both international relations (IR) and diplomatic history do not take public rhetoric seriously. They therefore fail to explain why German reconstruction occurred, why it took place in the way that it did, and why it placed the new West German state on something of an equal footing with its former enemies in a relatively short amount of time. I argue that the *rhetorical* construction of the postwar world and Germany's role in it plays a *causal* role in producing and sustaining the reconstruction of Germany. As I shall demonstrate, the rhetorical commonplace of 'Western Civilization' is central to this construction. 'Western Civilization' functions in both the German and the American contexts as a discursive resource for delegitimating policy options opposed to Germany's incorporation into American-led military and economic institutions. Hence, the *occidentalism* of these postwar reconstruction policies is a critical element of their successful implementation.

My focus on discourse and public rhetoric garners a number of significant analytical advantages over existing approaches. Unlike accounts focusing on military security, I do not have to read the stability of the later Cold War backward into a very confusing and in many ways indeterminate historical period; instead of simply regarding the bipolar division of the world as inevitable, my account elucidates the causal mechanisms whereby this division was produced and naturalized. Unlike accounts focusing on economic interests, I need not reduce human social action to a more or less determinate response to material positionality; agency remains central to my account of events. And unlike many existing IR constructivist works dealing with culture and identity, I refrain from reducing culture to unobservable beliefs inside of heads, or reducing identity to some kind of (social) environmental compulsion; I concentrate on intersubjective, observable articulations that shape possibilities rather than exhaustively determining them. The account that I offer explains postwar German reconstruction without having to adopt such questionable theoretical positions.

In this book, I focus on the public rhetorical contests over the boundaries of legitimate action both in the United States and in the western zones of occupied Germany. I closely examine the debates surrounding the passage and implementation of the two major pillars of postwar German reconstruction—the European Recovery Program (ERP, informally and publicly known as the Marshall Plan) and NATO—with an eye to questions about whether and to what extent a reconstructed German state should participate in these economic and military endeavors. Especially in a democracy, the availability of public rhetorical commonplaces that can be utilized so as to render a given policy acceptable is an indispensable part of the process of public policy-making, particularly for a set of policies as massive as postwar reconstruction. Enormous flows of resources and reconfigurations of political practice require justification, and absent the rhetorical deployments that I analyze, it is unlikely that the resulting policies and institutions would have taken the form that they ultimately did. My account highlights the room for maneuver exploited by various actors, as they took advantage of the inherently ambiguous character of public rhetoric in their efforts to assemble sets of publicly acceptable reasons for their preferred courses of action; the outcome of clashes between various public deployments explains the course of postwar German reconstruction.

Central to my account is the rhetorical commonplace of 'Western Civilization,' the notion that the United States, Canada, and Western Europe participate in a common cultural community with millennia-old roots in classical Greece. The irony that this notion was first voiced in the nineteenth century by conservative German academics was entirely lost on the American liberals who seized on the notion in the early postwar period as a way of delegitimating the unilateralist proposals of their domestic opponents. Conservative German politicians also seized on the notion as a way of advocating *Westbindung* (which involved close, institutionalized cooperation with the United States, Britain, and France, even at the cost of a temporary acceptance of the division of the country in two) and delegitimating the alternatives that were offered by their Social Democratic opponents. In effect, a coalition of liberal Americans and conservative Germans joined forces around a common commitment to preserve a civilizational community; this transnational alliance made postwar German reconstruction possible.

Aside from these historical considerations, there are also more contempo-

rary reasons for reconsidering postwar German reconstruction. The splits between the former allies that culminated in the Cold War were first rehearsed in occupied Germany, as an organized system overtly intended to promote four-power cooperation became the arena for a number of controversies. Germany became the flash point of the postwar world for the simple reason that it was the place where the victorious Allies first proclaimed their institutional solidarity, and hence the place where subsequent tensions and clashes between them were largely played out. There is no better lens for examining the postwar settlement than German reconstruction, as policies enacted in and around Germany set the tone for global relations between the various parties. The occidentalism of German reconstruction was replicated elsewhere, helping to stabilize what we only later came to think of as "the Cold War." Thus an examination of the arena in which these debates were first fought out will enhance our understanding of what we might call the conceptual infrastructure of international politics over the last half century. Inquiring into the origins of the Cold War in this way reveals a startling conclusion: viewed in terms of public legitimation, the Cold War *already was* a "clash of civilizations." This raises profound questions about what kind of order might succeed the Cold War.

The book proceeds in eight chapters. Chapter 1 discusses the recent return of "civilization" and "civilizations" to the conceptual lexicon of mainstream social scientists and argues that although this literature succeeds in putting civilization(s) back on the agenda, it commits a grave theoretical error in treating notions like "Western Civilization" as though they referred to concrete entities with dispositional essences. Instead, we should focus on the *language* of 'Western Civilization,' sidestepping any questions about what the West "really is." In this way, we can begin to appreciate the kind of shaping effect that public debates about identity have on specific policy initiatives, such as those involved in postwar German reconstruction.

Chapter 2 introduces my alternative, a *transactional social constructionism* that concentrates on public rhetoric as an adequate cause of outcomes. I draw on Weber and Wittgenstein as a way of developing the general position and utilize recent work on national identity and social movements to isolate three key causal mechanisms at work in legitimation contests: *specifying,* in which one party tries to redefine a previously introduced rhetorical commonplace; *breaking,* in which one party attempts to disrupt their opponent's position by highlighting inconsistencies in the opposing position; and *joining,* in which one party tries to undermine their opponent's position by linking a central commonplace of the opponent's position to an arrangement pointing in a different policy direction. I argue that the outcome of a legitimation contest is largely a function of how these mechanisms combine in particular public debates.

Chapter 3 begins the empirical analysis of postwar German reconstruction with a sketch of the "rhetorical topography" of the debates in question. I identify the central rhetorical commonplaces in play and show that the opposing sides in the struggles over public policy were largely constituted by different arrangements of similar commonplaces, such as 'the preservation of liberty' and 'anticommunism.' I illustrate the presence and key role of occidentalist appeals to 'Western Civilization' in both the American and the German debates, showing how this commonplace was a central component of legitimation strategies pursued on both sides of the Atlantic. In chapter 4, I engage in genealogical process-tracing in order to show two things: where this commonplace came from (ironically, 'Western Civilization' in its present form came from nineteenth-century debates in the German academy) and how it made its way into the public realm so that it could be deployed by politicians in the early postwar period (the "Western Civ" course that became a prominent part of undergraduate education in the early part of the twentieth century, and the prominence of public intellectuals such as Oswald Spengler, are central pieces of this story). It is the widespread dissemination of the commonplace that makes possible the arguments about defending and acting on behalf of Western Civilization that figure prominently in the postwar debates.

Having thus established the presence and prominence of 'Western Civilization' in the postwar debates, I then engage in a three-chapter account of how the commonplace was deployed in particular rhetorical clashes. Chapter 5 begins with the postwar planning debates in the United States in 1944 and proceeds through the early discussions in the western zones of occupation about the formation of new political parties and clashes in the four-power administrative structure established to run the country; it continues up through Secretary of State James F. Byrnes's famous speech at Stuttgart in September 1946. 'Western Civilization' plays some role in all of these debates but does not really emerge as a dominant theme until the subsequent period and the debates surrounding the ERP and the inclusion of Germany in it; this turning point is the focus of chapter 6. Chapter 7 shows how the justification of the ERP in occidentalist terms, and the use of occidentalist language to deal with German territorial issues such as the Saar problem, laid the rhetorical groundwork for the subsequent formation of the North Atlantic Treaty Organization, as well as legitimating eventual German participation in the organization as an armed member.

Throughout the empirical narrative, I pay close attention to the historically plausible alternative courses of action present in the policy debates: the so-called isolationist option of defending the continental United States without stationing troops in or giving immense economic aid to Western Europe, the "neutralist" option for Germany pursued by Kurt Schumacher's opposition Social Democratic Party, and the various plans to continue wartime cooperation between the United States and the Soviet Union in some form. All of these alternatives, advocates of which were actual participants in these debates, were importantly delegitimated by the use of occidentalist language by those committed to a transatlantic alliance of 'Western' democracies. Considering these alternatives allows me both to demonstrate the causal importance of occidentalist language and to avoid the trap of reading historical outcomes backward into a period of great ambiguity and contestation.

By reminding ourselves of the historical contingency of the Cold War, and of the historical contingency of concepts like 'Western Civilization' that were institutionally enacted as part of it, we may be able to correct one of the central intellectual mistakes of our times: the temptation to take the social world for granted, as though it were immutable. There is no inevitability to the role that 'Western Civilization' played in postwar German reconstruction, and no necessary reason why we should use it now or in the future in evaluating transatlantic relations. Whether or not we wish to base policy on this occidentalist basis is a normative and political question, and is not answerable through mere empirical study. However, empirical study can, and should, serve to remind us that any decision about deploying occidentalist rhetoric cannot be justified on historical grounds alone: just because people once spoke of the United States and Western Europe as belonging to "the West" is not itself a reason that we should continue to do so.

Accordingly, chapter 8 turns to the present day and explores several possible futures for 'Western Civilization,' illustrating both the continuities and the differences involved in the contemporary rearrangement of the conceptual infrastructure forged in the wake of the Second World War. Ultimately, whether 'Western Civilization' endures is contingent on the forms of agency that we exercise, and whether our actions tend to reproduce 'the West' or proceed in a rather different direction.

Before we accept or reject 'the West' as a principle upon which to base political and social relations, we should *linger* over what is assumed in Kissinger's argument, and take time to reflect on the practical and ethical consequences of an occidentalist stance. This book hopes to contribute to that reflection.

Acknowledgments

$\mathcal{R}$HETORICAL COMMONPLACES are always produced out of other, earlier commonplaces; they may not have completely specifiable beginnings, but there are key moments at which elements come together to produce a new configuration. Something similar happens when an individual human being is born and raised; each of us is always in some way a product of our parents and our upbringing. My parents Michael and Mary-Jo Jackson played critical roles in generating the specific configuration that is me, and in encouraging me along the path that eventually led to my writing of this book. For this I will always remain grateful.

One of the threads of my argument in this book involves the importance of ideas that students pick up during their college educations; the process of discovery and self-crafting that enables students to come into contact with novel notions and carry them into the wider world is importantly facilitated by talented and committed professors who seek to craft spaces within which students can really *learn*. I was fortunate to have several such persons playing an important role during my undergraduate years at the James Madison College of Michigan State University: my primary adviser Michael Schechter, Linda Racioppi, Richard Zinman, Norm Graham, Folke Lindahl, and Eric Petrie. I am indebted to all of them for many years of advice, support, and conversation. Outside of JMC, I learned more about the use of textual evidence and about the craft of argument from courses taught by John Coogan (Department of History) and Sheila Teahan (Department of Literature) than from any other courses.

My graduate education in the Department of Political Science at Columbia University was, as graduate education tends to be, less open-ended and exploratory; professional socialization, while not the overwhelming or exclusive point of the exercise, is certainly foregrounded. Ira Katznelson, whose seminar on "the lineages of American political science" I took during my first semester at Columbia, remained my most important adviser and mentor as I wound my way through the program. Ira encouraged my interest in historical processes of social construction and concretely illustrated that a historically sensitive social science was both possible and productive. Along the way, I also benefited from conversations with Jack Snyder, John Ruggie, Charles Tilly, Hendrik Spruyt, Anders Stephanson, Peter Johnson, and Volker Berghahn.

Almost more important than the professors with whom one works in graduate school are one's fellow students; much of the actual learning takes place in conversations over drinks or dinner, or (in the case of Columbia) while riding the subway to someplace in lower Manhattan. My most important interlocutors at graduate school were the members of the informal "relational constructionist group": Sherrill Stroschein, Daniel Nexon, Stacie Goddard, Allyson Ford, and Alex Cooley. Traces of discussions with them undoubtedly show up throughout the book. Mark Blyth, several years ahead of me in the program, was an important early source of peer support and helped to convince me that I wasn't crazy to tackle 'the West' as a dissertation topic. Plus, he knew where all the good bars in the city were—a real help for a first-year Ph.D. student and newcomer to New York.

While at Columbia I was fortunate enough to be able to teach in the Contemporary Civilization program for two years as a preceptor (from the Latin for "you're not a professor so we don't have to pay you as much"); that experience, and especially the weekly preceptor meetings during which we would compare notes and discuss pedagogical strategies, made an invaluable contribution to my development as a teacher. I thank David Johnston for the opportunity, and my fellow preceptors for many stimulating debates and discussions.

One of the most important institutions in academia is the professional conference, as this provides an opportunity to obtain critical feedback on one's work and to make connections to scholars at other institutions. Conferences are also essential for graduate students looking to have their wacky ideas taken seriously, as positions that might be a hard sell in one's home department often fly better in the broader environment of a conference. It's also nice to get out and be related to simply as a fellow scholar, something that is perennially difficult when interacting with faculty members in whose courses one once sat as a student. The first professional conference I attended was the International Studies Association-Northeast conference in 1996; at that meeting, Yale Ferguson and Bob Denemark made me feel extremely welcome in the profession, and their support has remained important to me over the years. At the 1997 ISA-NE conference I met Naeem Inayatullah, whose relentless commitment to not letting me get too comfortable with my analytical tools has decisively improved my scholarship for the better. At the 1998 main ISA conference I got to know Alex Wendt and Iver Neumann, both of whom have remained extremely important interlocutors and collaborators in the ongoing effort to keep social-theoretical considerations at or near the center of mainstream debates in the field.

Conferencing has also enabled me to create and sustain important conversations with a number of other scholars, who commented on various pieces of the project as I presented it in different formats. At the risk of accidentally forgetting someone, let me publicly single out Daniel Green, Jennifer Sterling-Folker, Peter Mandaville, Benjamin Herborth, Thomas Berger, Steve Rosow, Martha Finnemore, Yosef Lapid, Colin Wight, Jacinta O'Hagan, Mark Salter, Mustapha Kemal Pasha, Peter Katzenstein, Colin Elman, Jutta Weldes, Mlada Bukovansky, Friedrich Kratochwil, Jim Mittelman, David Blaney, Patricia Goff, Kevin Dunn, Fred Chernoff, Andrew Oros, Peter Howard, Nick Onuf, Hayward Alker, and—perhaps most significantly—Janice Bially Mattern, whose broad agreement with the contours of my transactional constructionist position enables the kind of detailed discussion of specific nuances that is sometimes difficult to have with other scholars. I am deeply grateful that I can get into arguments with Janice about *precisely* how the power of language operates at the most basic analytical level, and look forward to doing so for years to come.

I have also had wonderful opportunities to present working drafts of sections of this book in a number of places: the Columbia University Forum on the Core, the Norwegian Institute of International Affairs, Johns Hopkins University, Michigan State University, the Council on Comparative Studies at American University, the ISA workshops "Identity and IR" and "Civilization(s) in World Politics," and the Northeast Circle at ISA-Northeast. I would like to thank all of the participants in those occasions for their helpful and critical feedback. Bud Duvall also invited me to present a chapter in the Minnesota International Relations Colloquium; his comments, along with those of Ron Krebs and the other participants in the colloquium, were among the most incisive that I received, and helped me to sharpen the argument considerably.

Students in several of my courses have heard earlier versions of parts of the argument of this book and have often served as the first audience for a half-formed idea—and as some of my most perceptive critics. I would particularly like to thank the students in my "Culture and Identity in World Politics" seminar at New York University (1998–2000), those in my "Borders and Orders" (2002) and "The Conduct of Inquiry in International Relations" (2001–5) courses at American University, and participants in the study-abroad program in Kraków, Poland, during the summer of 2004, with its associated seminar "The Eastern Boundaries of Western Civilization."

Scholarly work does not get accomplished without various kinds of support, ranging from financial to organizational to logistical. For providing a hospitable working environment at American University, I would like to thank Lou Goodman, Nanette Levinson, Renee Marlin-Bennett, and John Richardson. For grants that enabled me to spend months in German archives, I am grateful to the Deutsche Akademische Austauschdienst, the National Endowment for the Humanities, and American University's Faculty Senate. For opening their home to me (and to my family) on multiple occasions, I am grateful to Heinz-Joseph and Ulla Knepper; I am also grateful to Marius Schneider for letting me stay in his apartment. And a special note of thanks to the librarians and archivists at the Konrad-Adenauer-Stiftung, the Archiv für Sozialdemokratie of the Friedrich-Ebert-Stiftung, the Institut für Zeitgeschichte, the Bundespresseamt, the Auswärtiges Amt, and the Council on Foreign Relations for making their collections and facilities available to me.

I have been extremely fortunate to have a plethora of outstanding research assistants over the years; all of them have made invaluable contributions to the book, whether by hunting up obscure documents or by tracking down equally obscure citations. I extend deep gratitude to Amy Pike, Kim Camp, Chandra Dunn, Jennifer Lobasz, Maia Carter Hallward, Kiran Pervez, and Jesse Crane-Seeber for all of their efforts.

It was a chance meeting with Ido Oren at a conference in 2004 that led, more or less directly, to Jim Reische at the University of Michigan Press becoming aware of the book manuscript and sending it out for review; I thank Ido for bringing the book to Jim's attention and Jim, Amy Fuller, and Kevin Rennells for guiding me through the process of getting it published. I should also thank Alex Wendt and one anonymous reviewer for their comments on the manuscript at that stage.

Thanks also to Jake Kawatski and Dianne Grandstrom at Twin Oaks Indexing for preparing the index.

Kiran Pervez, Jesse Crane-Seeber, and Sherrill Stroschein gave the penultimate manuscript a close read and managed to catch a number of ambiguities and awkward moments that had stubbornly persisted through multiple redrafts and versions. The blame for any such moments that remain in the text after their close attention should be laid on my head alone.

Dan Nexon and I have been discussing the theoretical and conceptual issues surrounding a transactional social constructionist approach to world politics for so many years now that I am sometimes unclear which of us came up with a particular point first. In a sense, it doesn't really matter; although the basic philosophical commitment may be virtually the same, what we do with those points in our individual empirical work is rather different. But I would be seriously remiss in not acknowledging a debt of gratitude to Dan for our ongoing theoretical explorations, which have informed this book in so many ways that I couldn't even begin to list them all.

The credits of Hollywood films have recently begun to list "production babies" near the end; in that spirit, I want to acknowledge my two production babies—Quinn and Chloe—whose arrival made things more interesting in a variety of ways. Exogenous shocks—even those that aren't really exogenous because they were planned—can alter a network profoundly, and I have no idea what this book would have looked like or what kind of scholar I'd be had they not come into the world when they did.

My wife Holly has been my truest companion for years, unfailingly supporting and advising my endeavors even when they took me away from her side to dusty archives and chaotic offices. She has helped me to tease out the implications of my philosophical positions for a variety of spheres of life and has kept me from disappearing into the great black abyss of academia during those times when I most needed to be reminded of the world outside of work. She has been and remains my best friend and staunchest confidant—my partner in the truest sense of the word. I cannot imagine having written this book without her at my side, and cannot imagine dedicating it to anyone else.

1 *The West Pole Fallacy*

When the rain began Pooh was asleep. It rained, and it rained, and it rained, and he slept and he slept and he slept. You remember how he discovered the North Pole; well, he was so proud of this that he asked Christopher Robin if there were any other Poles such as a Bear of Little Brain might discover.

"There's a South Pole," said Christopher Robin, "and I expect there's an East Pole and a West Pole, though people don't like talking about them."

Pooh was very excited when he heard this . . .

—A. A. Milne, *The Complete Tales of Winnie-the-Pooh*

ON 7 MAY 1945, Admiral Karl Dönitz, recently appointed Führer of the Third Reich by Hitler's last will and testament, approved the signing of documents accepting an unconditional German surrender (Botting 1985: 89). The following day, three representatives of the German High Command signed an "Act of Military Surrender" in Berlin, bringing the Second World War in Europe formally to a close (Ruhm von Oppen 1955: 28–29).[1] The country was in shambles, having been devastated by Allied strategic bombing and the "scorched earth" policy pursued by the retreating German army, as well as by the damage inflicted by the victorious armies themselves. "Out of a total of 16 million houses" in the occupied areas of Germany, "2.34 million had been completely destroyed and 4 million had sustained 25 percent (or more) damage. . . . In western Germany as a whole 20 million people were homeless. . . . Less than half the locomotives in Germany were in working order and only a third of the coaches were reparable" (Botting 1985: 122–25).

A month later, on 5 June 1945, representatives of the four Allied governments—Eisenhower for the United States, Zhukov for the Soviet Union, Montgomery for the United Kingdom, and de Lattre de Tassigny for the Provisional Government of the French Republic—issued a "Declaration Regarding the Defeat of Germany and the Assumption of Supreme Authority with Respect to Germany," in which they proclaimed:

> There is no central government or authority in Germany capable of accepting responsibility for the maintenance of order, the administration of the country

1. The second surrender signing was necessitated by some controversy about the actual legal status of the document signed on 7 May and by Stalin's strong desire to have Marshal Zhukov accept the German surrender for the Red Army (Botting 1985: 89–100).

and compliance with the requirements of the victorious Powers. . . . The Government of the United Kingdom, the United States of America and the Union of Soviet Socialist Republics, and the Provisional Government of the French Republic, hereby assume supreme authority with respect to Germany, including all the powers possessed by the German Government, the High Command and any state, municipal, or local government or authority. (Ruhm von Oppen 1955: 29–30)

Germany thus ceased to exist as an independent member of international society, with responsibility for and authority over the lands it had occupied being assumed by the victorious Allies (Kelsen 1945).

On 5 May 1955, almost ten years to the day after the unconditional surrender of the Reich, Konrad Adenauer, chancellor of the Federal Republic of Germany (BRD),[2] signed documents officially making the BRD a party to the North Atlantic Treaty and terminating the occupation regime, except for a few residual rights pertaining to the status of Berlin (Ninkovich 1988: 100–11). Shorn of some of its eastern territories, the former enemy state was now a staunch military ally of many of the countries that had been bitterly fighting against it a decade previously, and it was bound by treaty to come to their defense—and vice versa. Unlike the declaration of ten years before, the Soviet Union was not a part of the festivities, except as the implied opponent of both the BRD *and* of the other members of the North Atlantic Alliance, against which the Alliance had been erected. Commenting on that occasion, Adenauer declared,

We had won the friendship of our former opponents. . . . The treaties were a serious commitment for us, and corresponded to our deepest inner conviction that there was only *one* place for us in the world: a place on the side of the free peoples of the world. This also conformed to the sense of German history and the striving, if in vain, of earlier governments to come to a firm friendly relationship with the nations of the West. (1966b: 434)

This is quite a startling transformation, both in the status of Germany as an entity and in the general texture of world politics that surrounded and produced that alteration in status. How should we account for this transformation, whereby the BRD was reconstructed as an actor on the world political stage?[3] *Reconstruction,* as I will use the term, refers to the process by which a

2. Throughout this book I will use the German abbreviation for the Federal Republic: BRD, which stands for Bundesrepublik Deutschland. I do this in order to remain consistent with the abbreviations I will use for the names of the German political parties.

3. In this book I am principally concerned with the reconstruction of the western zones of occupation, which became the BRD in 1949 and joined NATO in 1955. Terminology is complex here, largely because of the contested status of terms such as *German* and *Germany* in the empirical case under analysis. Indeed, the dynamics and outcome of this contestation

nonactor becomes an actor again: how the authority for various governmental functions, particularly for those involving interstate relations, was transferred to West German authorities, who thereby became the authorized representatives of a new actor in interstate relations. In particular, three aspects of this reconstruction stand in need of explanation: Why was a German state rebuilt so soon after the end of the Second World War—a war that had, after all, been fought *against* a German state? Why did the United States take the leading role in this rebuilding of the western zones of occupation? And why was this reconstruction carried out primarily through the Marshall Plan and NATO, placing the BRD on somewhat of an equal footing with the other members of what quite recently had been an *anti-German* coalition?

I believe that the key to explaining these aspects of reconstruction lies in the civilizational language that Adenauer deployed when discussing the Federal Republic's accession to the North Atlantic Treaty: the notion that the BRD belonged firmly within a community of Western nations. It is my contention that West German reconstruction can be satisfactorily explained by a focus on public rhetoric, on the rhetorical commonplaces that were used to render certain policy options legitimate and others unacceptable. The presence of the notion of 'Western Civilization' in the debates about German reconstruction made possible the integration of the western zones of occupied Germany into the institutional structures of what was ordinarily characterized as 'the West.'[4] Absent this rhetorical commonplace, events might well have turned out quite differently.

Civilizations in World Politics

My emphasis on civilizational language participates in a broader intellectual movement within the social sciences that might be characterized as "bringing civilization and civilizations back in." Samuel Huntington's popular best seller (1996), while perhaps the best-known recent work on the subject, by no means exhausts the trend. Indeed, Huntington's "cultural" understanding of civilizations (Schäfer 2001: 310) places him somewhat at odds with many of

---

form the bulk of the empirical narrative in the following chapters, and the fact that two "German" states rather than one were erected in the early postwar period is central to the story of "German" reconstruction. But I am not trying to explain the creation of the Deutsche Demokratische Republik (the German Democratic Republic, popularly known as East Germany and abbreviated DDR), although the creation of the DDR does play an important role in the empirical narrative from time to time.

4. I use 'Western Civilization' and 'the West' interchangeably, as they play analogous roles in the rhetorical strategies that I am discussing in this book. Other locutions, such as 'civilization' (in the sense of "civilization-in-the-singular"—see chapter 4 for an elaboration of this critical distinction) do not play analogous roles and will not be used as synonyms.

the other contemporary civilizational analysts. Be that as it may, Huntington's central thesis—that increasingly, the most significant tensions and conflicts in world politics would be those between members of different civilizations—and the books and articles that he has written exploring it are undoubtedly partially responsible for the recent resurgence of civilizational analysis.

Published only a few years after the dissolution of the Soviet Union, Huntington's book represents part of a broader effort to rethink the study of world politics after the demise of the bipolar balancing dynamic that had captivated analysts for decades. As part of this effort, many scholars looked toward concepts and authors that had largely hovered on the fringes of the social-scientific mainstream during the height of the U.S.-Soviet rivalry. Huntington's deployment of "civilization" as part of a reconceptualization of world politics participated in a broader "return" of culture and identity to center stage in international relations (IR) theory (Lapid 1996), even as Huntington's specific implementation of that return came in for a not insignificant amount of criticism. Some argued that Huntington had inaccurately represented the fluidity and dynamism of civilizations—that his approach rested on theoretical or conceptual misstatements about the character of social identity (O'Hagan 2004: 32–34). Others argued that the primary problem with Huntington's analysis was empirical, in that it misstated the essential core of the civilizations under investigation, particularly Western Civilization. Along these lines, David Gress set out to provide "a fuller and more accurate delineation of Western identity" that divided the history of the West into two phases: "the Old West, identified as the synthesis of classical, Christian, and Germanic cultures, and the New West, the synthesis of reason, liberty, and progress" (Gress 1998: 16). These two phases are not separate, but essentially linked.

> To see the new west as a radical break, begun in the fifteenth and completed in the nineteenth century, was to deny that its roots lay deep in the Old. To progressives and radicals, the secular, rational freedom of modernity was inexplicable as a fruit of the past; it was the original creation of the bold spirits of the Enlightenment and the era of revolution. Such a definition ignored the triple legacy of Western freedom—from the Greeks through the Romans, from Christianity, and from the Germans. (261)

Like Huntington, Gress advanced an argument about the need for the West to mount a vigorous defense of its fundamental values and institutions, while acknowledging the diversity of such values and institutions abroad. For both, civilizational analysis is primarily about conserving traditions, and in particular about ensuring that the United States return to its fundamentally Western heritage in order to ensure that Western Civilization as a whole survives (Gress 1998: 552–55; Huntington 1996: 306–7).

Much of the other contemporary academic work on civilizations rejects this stance. Although the concept of "civilization" had largely vanished from the social-scientific lexicon over the course of the twentieth century (Tiryakian 2001: 282–83), there was a vibrant older tradition of civilizational analysis that had been kept alive by world-systems theorists (Chase-Dunn and Hall 1997; Wallerstein 1974) and by members of the *Annales* historical school (Braudel 1995). This tradition was far more interested in the political economy of civilizations than Huntington had been, and it spent far more time analyzing how networks of interaction affected the dynamics of hegemonic rise and decline (Wilkinson 2000). Scholars influenced by this tradition relax the metahistorical assumption that civilizations are closed cultural systems (Arnason 2001: 397–98) and seek instead to specify the complex interrelationships of factors that affect long-term social change. "Civilizations" are a conceptual tool used to help make sense of such dynamics (Melko 1969: 4).

But for all their invocations of fluidity and flux, these civilizational analysts retain an essential continuity with Huntington inasmuch as they continue to insist that civilizations are *objects* with essentially continuous core features. To engage in civilizational analysis is to treat a civilization as a discrete object, as a "thing-like entity" with "an enduring essence" (Collins 2001: 422). This remains the case even when analysts qualify their specification of a civilization's essential qualities with references to the ambiguity and internal complexity of civilizations; in the end, they return to the position that civilizations are essentially different from one another. Huntington offers perhaps the most revealing qualification.

> Civilizations have no clear-cut boundaries and no precise beginnings and endings. People can and do redefine their identities and, as a result, the composition and shapes of civilizations change over time. The cultures of people interact and overlap. The extent to which the cultures of civilizations resemble or differ from each other also varies considerably. *Civilizations are nonetheless meaningful entities,* and while the lines between them are seldom sharp, they are real. (1996: 43, emphasis added)

The assertion that civilizations are "real," coming on the heels of an ample demonstration of the flexibility and even the fuzziness of the concept, is striking. What does it mean to say that civilizations and the differences between them are "real," even though their boundaries and the precise content of their central cores change over time? If "both Magna Carta and Auschwitz are emblematic of European civilization" (Melleuish 2000: 118), why talk about an entity called "European Civilization" *at all?*

The West Pole Fallacy

There is an important conceptual continuity between the scholarly analyses of civilizations and political pronouncements about civilizations. Although politicians tend to be less nuanced in their specification than scholars are, the basic gesture is almost identical. To give only two examples:

1. In 2004, Gerhard Schröder, Chancellor of the Federal Republic of Germany, accepted an invitation from French President Jacques Chirac to participate in the ceremonies commemorating the anniversary of the invasion of Normandy (D-Day). Schröder's acceptance was especially significant since his predecessor Helmut Kohl had declined a similar invitation two decades previously on the grounds that he did not want to celebrate an event in which many German soldiers were killed. Justifying his decision to participate, Schröder argued that his presence would be "a sign of recognition of the role of Germany, of postwar Germany, as an established democracy and as a part of the Western community of values" (Bernstein and Landler 2004).

2. The same year, U.S. Representative Tom Tancredo (R-Colorado) launched "The Western Civilization Project," an initiative designed to "ensure that the concepts and ideals embodied by Western civilization are effectively taught in public schools" in the United States. Chief among these principles were "democratic institutions and the rule of law, the concept of universal human rights, the development of science and technology, and religious tolerance" (Eagle Forum 2004).

I am not claiming that there are no significant differences between these two political expressions of civilizational loyalty and the existing scholarship on civilizations. Civilizational scholars have a far more precise and careful delineation of what a civilization (like the West) consists of, and ordinarily bring considerable empirical evidence to bear to support their claims. But like civilizational politics, civilizational analysis is an *essentialist* form of social activity. Both civilizational politics and civilizational analysis seek to identify an essential core to the civilizations to which they refer, and to draw conclusions about specific institutions and action from this specification. A civilization is presumed to rest on "continuities in human thought and practices through which different human groups attempt to grapple with their consciousness of present problems" (Cox 2002: 157), and this presumption animates both scholarly and political uses of the concept.

This connection between civilizational politics and civilizational analysis becomes clearer if we consider a basic logical problem iassociated with efforts to precisely define the essence of a civilization. Such exercises become tautological to the extent that they derive the essential character of a community from empirical observation of some subset of humanity and then use that essentialist definition to delineate the empirical extent of the community. Thus, Gress identifies a medieval synthesis of ideals and institutions that he calls "Christian ethnicity"; he opposes this to universalism and argues that the former, not the latter, represents the actual soil from which the modern West grew, and its truest heart (1998: 211–13). In so doing, he condemns most philosophers after Rousseau for abandoning this synthesis, and he critiques many if not most of the social movements of the twentieth century for having followed that false path (Jackson 1999: 146–48). So the logic is: the essence of Western Civilization is X; these people/movements do not uphold X; hence they are not Western. But this conclusion is in no way a surprise, because the exclusion of those people/movements is already built into the definition. Why not simply *redefine* the essence of the West to incorporate these currents of thought and action?[5]

The suspicion grows that efforts to derive an essence of a given civilization, or to proceed with a type of analysis that presumes that a civilization *has* such an essence, are making a conceptual error: they are mistaking an analytical concept for an empirical object. In technical terms, this is known as *reification,* or the fallacy of misplaced concreteness (Handler 1994: 27). There is a world of difference, epistemologically speaking, between using a term like *civilization* as a way of making sense out of a mass of empirical material, on one hand, and treating the material thus organized as though this were more or less the way the world actually *was,* on the other. The social sciences in particular are prone to conflating the two, inasmuch as the concepts with which they operate are often plucked out of the world of everyday practice and transformed into ideal-typical analytical tools. Max Weber was particularly critical of this conflation, which he often observed in studies of religions like Christianity.

> In this sense the ideas are naturally no longer purely *logical* devices, and no longer concepts, with which reality is comparatively *measured.* They are instead ideals by which it is evaluatively *judged.* Here it is *no longer* a matter of a purely theoretical process of *referring* to values empirically, but instead of value-*judgments* which have been taken over into the "concept" of Christianity. *Because* the ideal-type claims empirical *validity,* it towers into the region of the evaluative *interpretation* of Christianity. The ground of empirical science is forsaken; before us stands a profession of faith, and *not* an ideal-typical *conceptual* construct. (1999b: 199)

The problem here is that analysts attempting to specify the essence of a religion (or a civilization) have strayed across the thin but crucial logical boundary separating science from politics. Even though such work is pitched as con-

5. Huntington does something very similar in his recent book on American national identity (2004): having defined an American Creed based on a New England Puritanical reading of Protestant Christianity, he then identifies groups and individuals resistant to that Creed (mainly Catholic Hispanic immigrants and those advocating bilingual education and other forms of multiculturalism) as representing threats to American national identity, instead of as representing transformations of American identity. A broadly similar kind of tautological reasoning seems to be at work here.

sisting of authoritative secondary-source commentaries, claims about the essence of some set of social arrangements are better understood as primary-source attempts to shape those arrangements. An analyst arguing that a particular set of values or norms constitutes the essence of Western Civilization is in this way no different from a politician pronouncing on Western values: both are attempting to actively influence those dynamics in their preferred direction, so as to shore up the essential values that they claim to have identified empirically. This is unobjectionable for politicians, since they are not claiming scientific expertise for their characterizations; but it is quite problematic for social scientists, who *do* make such claims.

In this instance we might refer to the conflation of empirical and normative judgments as the West Pole Fallacy: the presumption that because people *refer to* a civilization like the West, it follows that there *is* an entity called the West to which they are referring—and that therefore there is an empirically correct answer to questions about that entity's essence. This is as unjustified a leap as inferring from the existence and practices of a group of religious believers that the divinity whom they worship must actually exist. The divinity may exist, just as there may actually be a civilizational entity called Western Civilization, but studying social practices referring to "Western Civilization," or to a divinity, will not give us much leverage on determining whether they do or not.

Still less will taking the referent object of a set of social practices over into one's theoretical and conceptual apparatus provide a solution, since this imposes an answer by fiat and makes the analyst complicit in the production and reproduction of the object under investigation. There is a logical gulf between analyzing an "Expotition" (to use Winnie-the-Pooh's endearing terminology) that seeks to discover the West Pole,[6] and participating in such an Expotition. Social science can and should remain firmly on the analytical side of that gulf and avoid converting its concepts and terminology into "political advertisements" and "weapons of war" (Weber [1917/1919] 1994: 14–15). And it should do this for two reasons: *theoretically,* because there is no way to validly leap from the observation of social action to a judgment about the empirical validity of the concepts that orient that action; and *practically,* because there is no need to make such a leap in order to analyze the dynamics

---

6. Technically, Pooh never went on an Expotition to find the West Pole, although he and his companions did set out to find the North Pole—and, as invariably happens in such Expotitions, found something that they pressed into service as the North Pole by hanging a sign on it that declared that this was indeed the North Pole (Milne 1994: 125–27). There is a cautionary lesson here, I think, for scientific realist accounts of how knowledge is constructed through a nominalist "baptism" of phenomena (Wendt 1999: 57–58): how would one ever know whether one was simply entrapped in a fairy tale of one's own making? I take up this point again in chapter 2.

and impacts of social action. Waiting for Godot may have causal effects irrespective of whether Godot exists or not.

> It is a certain form of talked-about-activity, activity talked about as *waiting,*
> which *necessitates* their reference to a Godot, not the existence of a Godot
> which necessitates their waiting. No such Godot (at least in their experience)
> has ever existed. . . . It is an *imagined* Godot which plays a real part in their
> lives. (Shotter 1993a: 82)

From Western Civilization to 'Western Civilization'

How might we avoid the West Pole Fallacy? One way would be to proceed further down the road taken by world-systems theorists, who largely dissolve any essentialist notion of a "civilization" into a complex and overlapping network of social relations. A world-system[7] can be thought of as a set of intersocietal exchange networks and can be bounded empirically by determining where "falloff" occurs: where the effects of any given type of exchange diminish to irrelevance (Chase-Dunn and Hall 1997: 52–55). Although most world-systems theorists display a preference for networks of *material* exchange (perhaps largely on technical grounds, because the movement of goods is easier to track than the movement of norms and ideas; perhaps on ideological grounds, since world-systems work grew out of a broadly Marxist approach to historical study), there is no compelling theoretical reason why systems *need* to be defined materially. Indeed, a case can be made that a focus on the transfer of ideas and information offers a more promising way to cut into the significant shifts in world history (Collins 2001; McNeill 2000). Such a network-structural approach would do without any essentialism about human communities, regarding them instead as emergent local stabilities in social relations produced and sustained by broader systemic factors.

In effect, this would mean abandoning the concept of "civilization" altogether, inasmuch as this concept is taken to refer to an enduring *cultural* continuity over time. Such a move would mean accepting the judgment that essentialist claims are more like politics than they are like science, and abandoning surface-level political controversies in an effort to grasp deeper and more fundamental factors affecting the shape and direction of human history over the long term. Fernand Braudel called for just such an analytical shift in distinguishing between three levels of history and varieties of temporality, with the very long term—the *longue durée*—functioning as the most important analytical level for important historical questions (1958). In this way civi-

---

7. Most scholars in this tradition even avoid the word *civilization,* when they do not explicitly redefine civilizations as world-systems lacking a common culture and defined by their strong social interconnections (Wilkinson 2000: 54).

lization is transformed into "the longest story of all" (1995: 34), but it is a purely *structural* story of forces and dynamics beyond the control of any specific individuals or organizations.

We should keep in mind that such a move bears a specific analytical cost: it renders us unable to say much about specific social and political events, or to analyze them in a rigorous manner. Focusing on a big systemic picture may allow us to apprehend the overall shape of social dynamics, but it is considerably less useful for the understanding of particular outcomes. Consider, for instance, the study of war: international anarchy might serve as a permissive cause in that war remains an ever-present *possibility* for sovereign states acknowledging no temporal superior authority, but this alone does not explain why *particular* wars happen. Other factors must be adduced in order to account for specific events (Waltz 1959: 231–32). Alternatively, consider a sports analogy: large-scale statistical analysis may be a reliable way of assessing a player's performance over the long term, but it does not explain how she or he performed on a *particular* day; nor does it necessarily explain why a player is in the game on any given day, as opposed to resting on the bench.[8] Taking a systemic road means shifting the questions that we can reasonably ask and answer.

The abandonment of "civilization" has another, more pernicious consequence: it means devaluing the content of political debate and disregarding the terms in which concrete social and political actors frame their positions. This amounts to a dismissal of the manifest *content* of such debates as either an epiphenomenal consequence of deeper social forces or as an irrelevant sideshow—albeit one that, as "false consciousness," might obscure the operation of actual structural factors. In other words, *identity* is abandoned as a relevant category for the analysis of human social experience, and the myriad struggles to define ourselves and our relationship to others—so recently restored to the social-scientific lexicon (Goff and Dunn 2004: 2–4; Lapid 1996: 7–8)—disappear from view. After all, if our sense of belonging to some community is produced by machinations of industrial capital (Gellner 1983), or by an objective threat posed to our survival as individuals (Sterling-Folker 2002b), why spend much time worrying about the nuances of the terms in which such a sense of belonging is expressed?

There is, however, another alternative. Following the lead of scholars of

---

8. This gets tricky, because statistics about past performance might be deployed by managers and coaches when determining the day's active roster or lineup. In that case, however, the (proximate) causal factor for the player's being in the lineup or not is the concrete act of deployment, and not the statistics themselves. After all, one does not always put one's best players into every game; at times, the prudent course of action is to rest a player in preparation for a future match. Strategy, whether deliberate or unintentional, invariably intervenes between structure and outcome.

national identity like Rogers Brubaker, we might simultaneously affirm "civilization" as a category of political and social *practice* while denying it a role in our *theoretical apparatus*. Brubaker suggests that we should acknowledge that while concrete social and political actors orient their action in terms of "the nation," this does not imply that nations are real entities or that nationalism is "a 'force' to be measured as resurgent or receding" (1996: 10). Instead, "we should focus on nation as a category of practice, nationhood as an institutionalized cultural and political form, and nationness as a contingent event or happening, and refrain from using the analytically dubious notion of 'nations' as substantial, enduring collectivities" (21). Katherine Verdery concurs, warning scholars not to be "conned by the terms of national ideologies" into thinking that nations *really are* essential, substantial, and enduring things (1993: 39). We can signal this shift typographically, by placing terms like 'nation' and 'civilization' in single quotation marks in order to indicate that we are referring to a term and a concept deployed by concrete social and political actors. We thus shift from the analysis of civilizations—putatively real and substantial objects—to the analysis of 'civilizations'—terms and concepts that occur in the course of specific political and social contests and affect the shape of particular events.

In effect, what I am suggesting is that the analysis of political and social outcomes would be better served if we *give up* "civilizational analysis" in the traditional sense, in much the same way that Brubaker and others urge us to give up "nationalist analysis" in order to better understand how boundaries between 'nations' are established and maintained. Instead, we should shift our focus to what might be called "civilizational identity"—the dynamics and implications associated with claims to belong to a given civilization, and the political and social consequences of debates about what that membership *means* in practice (O'Hagan 2002: 11–14). Robert Cox neatly captures what is at stake in making such a turn.[9]

> It [civilizational identity] refers only to a conscious affirmation of belonging to a civilization. It does not refer to the "common sense" or perceptions of "reality" that characterize particular civilizations and which are to be found at a deeper level of consciousness—a level at which something that has been shaped by the historical development of a people comes to be understood by them as universal and natural. (2002: 163)

This is precisely what I am advocating: a turn away from any putative "deeper level of consciousness" so that we may better grasp the dynamic processes through which a notion like 'Western Civilization' comes to exercise an impact on concrete social and political outcomes.

9. Note that Cox is quite critical of this move, even as he summarizes its logic quite nicely.

'Western Civilization' would thus play a role in postwar German reconstruction *not* by being an essential entity that somehow objectively determined a field of possible outcomes. Rather, it would be the *appeal to* 'the West' that played a critical role. Along the way, the notion of 'the West' would have been fleshed out along particular lines and linked to other notions in particular ways so as to create the *impression* of an essential entity in the name of which postwar German reconstruction was carried out. And if I am right, this is the 'West' that remains with us today and serves as a paradigmatic exemplar both for civilizational scholarship and civilizational politics—both pro- and anti-'Western.' If we give up the futile search for a West Pole, we may be able to appreciate these dynamics more clearly. In the next chapter I will outline a way to do so.

2 The Language of Legitimation

A SUCCESSFUL SOCIAL-SCIENTIFIC account of postwar German reconstruction has to accomplish two tasks. First, it must *causally* account for the victory of the policies actually enacted over other socially plausible alternatives proposed at the time. Second, it must do so while preserving a central role for *human agency*.

The first task derives simply from the definition of the empirical puzzle. We want to know why, for example, the United States spent approximately $3.1 billion[1] building up the infrastructure and capabilities of a formerly powerful enemy, instead of reducing the country to an agricultural subsistence mode of existence (as had originally been proposed by Secretary of the Treasury Henry Morgenthau, and more or less approved as U.S. policy by President Franklin D. Roosevelt in 1944) or simply concluding the military victory and then withdrawing its troops from Europe (as had happened after the First World War and was advocated by so-called isolationists[2] like Senator Robert Taft). Likewise, we want to know why a West German state bound economically and militarily to western Europe and the United States was erected, rather than a militarily neutralized all-German state within either its 1933 or 1937 borders (as was proposed by the Christian Socialist Jakob Kaiser, a one-time rival of Adenauer for leadership of their Christian Democratic Union Party, and later implicitly proposed by Kurt Schumacher, leader of the oppo-

---

1. Dollar figures from ECA 1948–51: ix–x, 152–53, and Federal Government 1953: 23–24. This sum includes both the Federal Republic's share of the funds allotted under the auspices of the ERP during the years 1948–51 (approximately $1.5 billion) and the approximately $1.6 billion spent by the United States under the auspices of the GARIOA (Government and Relief in Occupied Areas) program during the years 1946–50 and does not include the expenses of the military government in 1945, which were a part of the regular army budget. See Arkes 1972: 306–8 and Milward 1984: 94–95.

2. I question the analytical utility of this characterization—along with its paired opposite, "internationalism"—in chapter 3.

sition Social Democratic Party). These and other alternative policies, which will be discussed in detail in the empirical narrative to follow, are not mere imaginative constructions but are drawn from contemporary debates about the shape of the postwar world; a good social-scientific account of German reconstruction must causally explain why these alternatives, posed at the time, did not in fact come to pass.

The other requirement—that a good social-scientific account must preserve the role of human agency—comes from contemporary debates in social theory. Many participants in these debates have drawn important methodological and substantive consequences from the observation that reality is in important ways *socially constructed,* which means simply that social reality has no independent ontological status apart from the activities of human beings (Hacking 1999: 2).[3] In this particular case, this means that without human beings and their social activities there would be no West Germany to reconstruct, no resources to transfer from one state to another, and no political debate about the proper course for policy to follow (and no governments or states to whom that policy could be attributed). This is a trivial point, perhaps, but one that is often ignored in social theory in general and International Relations (IR) theory in particular, where there is an endemic tendency to treat social facts (like state sovereignty, governmental authority, international institutions, and so on) as if they were naturally occurring objects rather than the products of ongoing social processes. But I would argue that a good account of a social phenomenon cannot succumb to such a temptation and likewise cannot forget that "the concept 'society' refers to interdependent people in the plural," and not to something that is external to people and their social actions (Elias 1970: 125).

Existing accounts of postwar German reconstruction in diplomatic history and IR theory fail to accomplish these two tasks adequately. Realist theorists who explain reconstruction as an instance of the imperative to balance power in the anarchic international system (Gaddis 1986; Schweller and Priess 1997; Sheetz 2000) have problems explaining why other strategies would not have served the needs of national security equally well; they also reduce individual actions to more or less efficient throughputs for broader systemic imperatives, thus failing to preserve agency. Liberal and Marxist theorists look to the interests induced by specific patterns of economic relations both within and between states to explain postwar reconstruction (Horowitz 1969; Kindleberger 1974; Lake 1999), but in so doing they encounter similar empirical and conceptual problems. IR constructivists, despite an explicit focus on social identity and dynamic interaction between entities (Wendt 1992), end up in

3. This is not to say that social life is not affected by nonsocial factors, but simply that social acts and practices mediate and shape whatever effects those nonsocial factors exert. The precise dynamics of this process remain the subject of intense controversy among social theorists of virtually all persuasions.

practice relying on shared subjective values to do the heavy lifting in their explanations (Hampton 1995; Risse-Kappen 1996; Schimmelfennig 1998–99) and for that reason encounter much the same problems as other analysts. Empirical problems like these are generated by theoretical weaknesses, and hence a different approach is needed.[4]

I believe that the challenge of accounting for the victory of the reconstruction policies actually enacted while preserving human agency can best be met by a turn to a *transactional social constructionist* conception of social reality: *transactional* because the analytical focus is on social ties and transactions rather than putatively solid and stable actors with relatively fixed interests,[5] and *social constructionist* because the causal mechanisms producing policy outcomes involve the social production and reproduction of patterns of meaning. Such a conception involves a fundamental reorientation in conceptual focus: instead of beginning with stable actors and social patterns and asking how and why they change, transactional social constructionism begins with the analytical presumption of continual flux and seeks to explain how social life is relatively *stabilized* (Jackson and Nexon 1999: 296–99; Shotter 1993a: 178–79).

Although a "structural" explanation in comparison to those individualist explanations that locate key causal mechanisms and factors firmly inside of units and actors, transactional social constructionism is probably best thought of as a kind of *post-structural* approach. Instead of more or less parametric "structures" encompassing and enfolding action, we have spaces of practical activity within which the ongoing stabilization of social relations takes place (Shotter 1993a: 164–65; Tilly 2002: 122) and that generate emergent "figurations" (Elias 1991) or "social arrangements" (Onuf 1998). It is these emergent local stabilizations that are the focus of a transactional social constructionist analytic.[6]

Explaining how policy options are selected involves an investigation of the

4. Theoretical weaknesses are insufficient to ground my overall argument that a focus on rhetorical commonplaces does a better job of accounting for postwar German reconstruction. At appropriate points during the empirical narrative (spanning chapters 5, 6, and 7) I will take up specific empirical issues raised by these alternative explanations and show how my approach does a better job. Thanks to Peter Katzenstein for suggesting this way of organizing the argument.

5. I follow Karl Deutsch (1954: 39) in using the term *transaction* rather than *interaction,* as the former term catches up changes that take place "inside" of social entities as well as those taking place "between" them. See also Emirbayer 1997.

6. This is technically true of all post-structuralisms, which take the structure of a situation seriously without reifying that structure; to the contrary, post-structural analyses analytically dissolve "structure" into a myriad of component mechanisms, processes, and activities (Jackson and Nexon 1999: 317–18; Wellman 1997: 31–40). Post-structuralism is a form of structural analysis, albeit not identical to those essentialist forms of structuralism that place their analytical bets on "objectively" existing parameters constraining social action.

process of *legitimation,* which is the central causal process in my account of policy outcomes.[7] I define legitimation as the process of drawing and (re)establishing boundaries, ruling some courses of action acceptable and others unacceptable. Out of the general morass of public political debate, legitimation contingently stabilizes the boundaries of acceptable action, making it possible for certain policies to be enacted.

Hence, accounting for postwar German reconstruction means explaining how the reconstruction policies concretely pursued were legitimated: how they were made acceptable, and alternative policies made unacceptable, to a variety of audiences. My account preserves human agency by highlighting the role of social activity in forging and sustaining these patterns of legitimating rhetoric. By concentrating on the contours and contents of debates contemporary to the policies enacted, my account also avoids reading the future backward into the past—a questionable analytical strategy often deployed by existing historical accounts in an effort to explain the triumph of one course of action over others in terms of its putative correspondence with a state of affairs (like bipolarity, or a stable international trading system) that only came into being *after* the policy in question was enacted.[8] What matters to an account of legitimation is the language utilized *at the time* to render a policy acceptable, not how well that language foreshadows a future state of affairs or how well it harmonizes with some supposedly "objective" environmental condition, such as the imperatives of anarchy or the preservation of global capitalism.

In the remainder of this chapter I lay out the theoretical foundations of such an approach, fleshing out a concept of legitimation that draws heavily on Max Weber's oft-misunderstood notion. I then briefly discuss how such a concept addresses the theoretical weaknesses of existing approaches.

Legitimation

In investigating the process of legitimation, there is no better starting place than Max Weber's observation that

> no form of rule voluntarily contents itself with only material or only emotional or only value-rational motives as prospects for its continuation. On the contrary, each seeks to awaken and to foster the belief in its "legitimacy." But

---

7. Note that the concept of "legitimation" enjoys a "prosthetic" character, simultaneously revealing and producing the world under investigation (Jackson forthcoming; Shotter 1993b: 19–23). The claim here is not that what was taking place in postwar German reconstruction "really was" legitimation; rather, the claim is the more modest position that the period in question is usefully understood under this analytical description.

8. This can become extremely tautological in cases where the policy in question is also causally implicated in the production of that future state of affairs. Given the ambiguous character of the early postwar period (Eisenberg 1996: 6–7), it seems extremely risky to

according to the kind of legitimacy claimed, the type of obedience, the type of administration designated to guarantee it, and the character of the form of rule exercised all differ fundamentally—along with their effects. (1976: 122)

For Weber, the key problem of legitimation is how some people get other people to obey their commands. The problem of whether those living in a given situation—whether they are in power or not—actually *believe* in the terms of legitimation, or whether they cynically act as if they do in order to advance their own self-interest or other private goals, is neatly sidestepped by Weber, who argues that such questions are, at best, only secondary considerations that are "not decisive for the classification of a form of rule." What is decisive is that "the particular *claim* to legitimacy is, according to its *type*, to a significant degree 'valid,' and that this secures the continuation of the form of rule and designates the chosen means of rule." Indeed, Weber points out, even eschewing explicit claims to public legitimacy is a form of legitimation, as a set of relations based purely on conceptions of self-interest is still a pattern of justification that is "in the highest degree decisive for the structure of a form of rule" (123). There is no escaping the impact of the form and content of different claims to legitimacy.

Two important consequences follow from this definition: the notion of "legitimacy" is made sociologically relative rather than transcendentally absolute, and is linked firmly to the aggregate patterns of social action in a given context rather than to the individual decisions made by people living in that context. Both of these consequences are crucial to a transactional social constructionist notion of legitimation, and vital to an account of postwar German reconstruction that hopes to move beyond the problems of existing accounts. Recent discussions of legitimation—and of processes of social construction more generally—in IR have not taken these two Weberian consequences to heart in a comprehensive fashion, and hence they tend to replicate the problems that they hoped to solve by turning to legitimation in the first place. I will unpack these two Weberian consequences through a critique of this literature, in order to clarify both the implications of a Weberian approach and the differences between this approach and others current in the field.[9]

---

characterize any policy enacted during this time as "anticipating" or "recognizing" something like the Cold War, when it is extremely likely that such policies helped to produce the Cold War as a relatively stable set of social relations. I will return to this point in chapter 8.

9. Here I bracket discussion of approaches to social order and outcomes that engage in an explicit strategy of removing legitimacy and legitimation in favor of some kind of instrumentally rational decision-making procedure (Levi 1988; Przeworski 1985). For a general critique of such approaches, and in particular the strong assumptions about individual rationality on which such approaches depend, see Jackson 2002a and Blyth 2003.

ANALYTICAL, NOT NORMATIVE

A central element of Weber's thought in general is the conceptual distinction between ethical and empirical argument. As noted in the previous chapter, Weber repeatedly warns against integrating value judgments into analytical concepts, as this would mean that "the ground of an experiential science [*Erfahrungswissenschaft*][10] is foresaken" (1999b: 199). This stance is also apparent in his categorical declaration that "the taking of practical political positions and the scientific [*wissenschaftliche*] analysis of political structure and party positions are two different things," the problem being that most academic analysts seem unable to resist taking sides on the issues that they study and therefore convert their words into "political advertisements" and "weapons of war" ([1917/1919] 1994: 14–15). Much of Weber's conceptual work consists in trying to rehabilitate everyday concepts fraught with transcendental normative content and fashion usable analytical tools out of them; "objectivity" and "rationality" are two of the better-known examples of this strategy.[11] Contra the arguments of some interpreters of Weber, "legitimacy" should be understood in the same way.

Weber's desire to strip the notion of "legitimacy" of its transcendental normative content can be clearly seen in the very typography of his initial discussion. Weber places the word "legitimacy" in double quotation marks, a clear sign of distancing from the ordinary-language meaning of the term; he also speaks of "the claim to legitimacy" [*Legitimitätsanspruch*] more often than he speaks of legitimacy per se.[12] It is also apparent in his designation of three ideal-typical patterns of legitimation claims, each with its own set of dynamics and implications. Although the challenging of traditional authority by charismatic leadership and the subsequent routinization[13] of charisma into a more bureaucratized system of succession provides something of a dynamic progression, Weber expresses no clear normative preference for this course of events—despite the efforts of commentators like Jürgen Habermas to discern a normative position in Weber's analysis (Habermas 1984: 179–80). "Legitimacy," for Weber, is simply an empirical component of a political and social order, albeit an indispensable one.

10. The German word *Wissenschaft*, often translated "science," has a broader meaning than the more narrow English term; "systematic inquiry" would be a more exact, if inelegant, translation.

11. "Objectivity" is treated at length in Weber 1999b; on "rationality," see Weber 1976.

12. I emphasize these relatively minor points of usage because they are usually obscured in the English translation (Weber 1968) with which most English-speaking scholars are most familiar.

13. *Veralltäglichung*, literally "making-everyday." This continuity of concern between Weber and the post-structural analysts on whom I draw later should be kept firmly in mind.

Indeed, the object of inquiry for Weber is *not* "legitimacy," understood as the transcendental ethical or normative validity of a policy or course of action, but a quite different social process. There is no sense in Weber that any kind of political order—and by implication, any course of political action—is somehow more *inherently* "legitimate" than any other; at any rate, the question of whether some course of action is or is not valid in this transcendental sense is a separate issue.[14] This is why I prefer the term *legitimation* to describe the process in which Weber is interested: any social "legitimacy" that a policy possesses must be empirically explained, not presumed or transcendentally demonstrated. While this raises problems for political theorists trying to draw a coherent ethical theory from Weber's work (MacIntyre 1984: 26), it should raise no such problems for empirical analysts.

Separating the normative from the analytical does not simply mean separating advocacy for a policy from the analysis of that policy; it also means not building claims about the transcendental normative validity of a policy into the causal mechanism used to explain how that policy came about. While rarely so naive as to regard the transcendental normative validity of a course of action as a sufficient cause for its adoption, many scholars still have recourse to notions of ultimate validity in their explanations in a more indirect way: in attributing the success or failure of some policy to its consistency with some *other* set of notions whose normative validity is unquestioned. The problem with doing so is that such a stance moves all of the crucial explanatory factors into an untheorized "normative structure," which subsequently does the real causal work in the argument and reduces the people involved in the legitimation process into mere throughputs for specific value-orientations.

As an example of this, consider Keck and Sikkink's discussion of the "boomerang pattern" that they observe when a social movement blocked in one state places indirect pressure on that government by activating transnational network allies who place pressure on *their* governments, and subsequently on the original government doing the blocking of the movement (1998: 12–13). This pattern can only work when the issue in question is one that can be used to mobilize transnational support, which means that legitimation, far from being *explained* by this boomerang pattern, is *presumed* in the analysis. Indeed, the authors give little guidance on how particular policies come to be seen as so illegitimate that opposition to them comes to seem legitimate, except for the suggestion that certain types of issues—those involving bodily harm, for example, or those involving legal equality of opportunity

14. People often seem to forget that Weber's distinction between facts and values was first and foremost a logical distinction; Weber never argued that either politics or "science" (*Wissenschaft*) could or should be carried out in complete isolation from value claims embedded in a cultural context. The point is just that the normative practice or evaluation of politics is different from the empirical analysis of it. See Ringer 1997: 137–40.

(27)—seem easier to mobilize populations around. Indeed, it almost appears as if there is something *inherently* illegitimate about policies violating a certain conception of human rights; otherwise, the "committed actor" necessary to bring "human rights violations" to the attention of foreign policy officials (203) would have little success.

This argumentative logic is characteristic of many analysts of transnational social movements: those devoted to the defense of human rights (Klotz 1995), environmental protection (Wapner 1995), promotion of medical care on the battlefield (Finnemore 1996), opposition to land mines (Price 1998), and so on. It is also found in the work of sophisticated rationalists like John Ikenberry, who seeks to explain choices made by major powers after wars in terms of their desire to legitimate their dominance in the international system; multilateral policies, he suggests, will be more effective because they are more democratic, and democratic forms of rule are simply more legitimate (2001: 52–53, 266–67). The basic analytical question—how these notions become "legitimate" in the first place—is left aside, and without an answer to this question analysts are left in the uncomfortable position of presuming, without demonstrating, the transcendental normative validity of some fairly contentious ethical positions.[15]

The difficulties in providing such a justification can be seen in Habermas's long-standing project of trying to derive legitimate norms from transcendental conditions embedded in the very act of speaking itself. This would, if successful, provide a firm normative basis from which to analyze extant social orders and allow scholars to simultaneously explain and critique the adoption of policies (Geuss 1981: 76–77). As Habermas rejects the distinction between analytical and normative claims, his position is not surprising; what is surprising is that some IR analysts believe that they can simply ignore this aspect of Habermas's project when discussing the impact of processes of argumentation on political outcomes (Crawford 2002: 29–35; Risse 2000: 7, 17–19). Habermas is quite clear that he conceptualizes political legitimation as a temporary measure designed to make up for the failings of a capitalist economic system: "a legitimation crisis can be avoided in the long run only if the latent class structures of advanced-capitalist societies are transformed or if the pressure for legitimation to which the administrative system is subject can be removed" (1975: 93). Extant forms of legitimation can *only* be conceptualized as a very

---

15. "Bracketing" normative structure for the purpose of focusing on how agents draw on normative notions in order to pursue their goals, as Finnemore (1996: 25)—following Giddens (1984)—advises, participates in a process of reification that prevents an appreciation of the process character of legitimation. It also ends up denying the structurationist insight at the core of Giddens's work, and ultimately denying human agency. See the following discussion.

subtle form of false consciousness, in which the gap between expectations and outcome is bridged through symbolism (73).

Analysts drawing on Habermasian notions are engaged in a normative evaluation of social relations, whether they are aware of this or not. Unless we wish to presume the correctness of Habermas's position on these issues, it is probably a safer bet to remain with a more *sociological* account of legitimation in which the causal role of public arguments depends on the character of the existing cultural context (Crawford 2002: 80–81). We should also avoid making any strong claims about the transcendental validity of any of the arguments advanced by political and social actors, concentrating instead on the empirical and historical process whereby various notions were made available for concrete deployment (Crawford 2002: 122–23; Doty 1993: 314–16; Laffey and Weldes 1997: 209–13; Ringmar 1996a: 71–74, 79–81). This will allow us to establish the efficacy of a practice of legitimation without straying into a normative evaluation of that practice.[16]

BEYOND BELIEF[17]

While much contemporary work on legitimation does not seem to have taken the first Weberian consequence to heart in a completely clear manner, virtually all of it implicitly rejects the second. The vast majority of references to "legitimacy" in contemporary IR assume that legitimation involves the modification of subjective beliefs in heads, whether these are the heads of elite policymakers or the heads of their citizens. This stance is linked to the notion that the sort of question that legitimation answers is a question about individual decisions, where the acceptability of a course of action becomes one factor figuring into an individual decision-making process. Legitimation is thus understood as a way to answer the question "What motivates states [and other actors] to follow international norms, rules, and commitments?" (Hurd 1999: 379). As I have argued in detail elsewhere, Weber does *not* share this position, even though his strong opposition to it is often obscured by translations of Weber into English that sometimes make him seem like an American liberal individualist (Jackson 2002b). In fact, Weber is trying to direct our analytical attention to the social context out of which policy outcomes arise, rather than to the reductionist causal mechanisms characteristic of much contemporary social science.

Weber's stance is thus quite different from that adopted by most contem-

16. Naturally, Habermasians and other critical theorists will disagree with me on this issue. But in order to do so consistently they would have to respond to Weber's argument that empirical and ethical arguments have a different logical structure, which most have not done in any direct manner. Indeed, the jury is still out on whether Habermas himself has done so; see, inter alia, Rorty 2001.

17. Section title borrowed from Laffey and Weldes 1997.

porary IR theorists. Thomas Risse, for example, seeks to delineate a "logic of argumentation" that rests squarely on persuasive power, such that participants "are prepared to change their views of the world or even their interests in light of the better argument" (2000: 7). He discusses the "2+4" talks on the reunification of Germany in these terms, suggesting that Gorbachev was persuaded by "a liberal argument emphasizing democracy and self-determination" to drop his opposition to a reunified Germany's membership in NATO; the argument worked by, in effect, penetrating Gorbachev's head and changing his preferences (27). Michael Barnett seeks to explain the power and influence of norms of Arabism in Middle Eastern politics not by arguing that elites necessarily believed in these notions, but by arguing that their *populations* believed in them; this placed constraints on what politicians could reasonably do (1998: 46–48, 59–61). And Jeffrey Checkel emphasizes processes of "social learning" whereby numerous social actors come to "acquire new values and interests from norms," a procedure characterized by a fair amount of subjective internalization of publicly promulgated ideas (1999: 89–90).

All of these arguments rest on the presumption that it is possible to find evidence about the "real motives" driving particular individuals to make particular choices (Crawford 2002: 49–52, 101–4). But this is a far trickier proposition than most researchers argue; individuals might easily be lying about their motives or claiming to be persuaded by some line of argument in order to garner favor with some audience. In the case of Gorbachev, for example, it remains entirely possible that he was actually calculating the possible benefits to himself and his government of quickly reaching agreement with the United States on the issue, and *we have no way of knowing* whether or not this was the case. Sincerity is difficult enough to evaluate in private life; trying to determine the sincerity of a public pronouncement seems nigh upon impossible.[18] Relying on private sources where it is more unlikely that individuals are distorting their views (Moravcsik 1998: 81–82) does not solve the problem either, inasmuch as even "private" settings are never removed from the effects of power, and such private articulations can easily be just as strategic as their public counterparts (Scott 1990). Finally, there is something of a circularity in using action (and speaking is certainly an action) as evidence of persuasion, given that action is *also* the source of evidence about the "norm" that supposedly persuaded the individual in question; all we actually (and *empirically*) have here is a consistent pattern of action, or a pattern of action consistent

18. Behavioral consistency does not provide a way to do this either, inasmuch as someone may go along with her or his previous public articulations not out of a sincere commitment, but out of a calculation of possible gains from appearing to believe in the position previously adopted. After all, this is precisely what Machiavelli recommended that princes do with respect to Christian values: appear to uphold them, while secretly rejecting them and manipulating them for one's own greatest possible advantage (1994: 54–55).

with some particular specification of a norm, with the word "persuasion" tacked on and masquerading as an explanation.[19]

Weber neatly sidesteps these thorny evidentiary issues by focusing on patterns of claims made in public; there is no implication in his work that *anyone* necessarily "believes" the kind of legitimating rhetoric that they are deploying as a way of justifying a course of action. His sociological focus is on patterns of claims, not the selection of claims by particular individual officials and speakers. This orientation is even apparent in his definition of "motive" as "a complex of meaning which seems, either to the actor himself or to the observer, a sensible 'ground' for the course of action in question" (Weber 1976: 5). Weber's motives are sociological, not personal or individual, in origin; their causal efficacy is also transpersonal or intersubjective.

Weber's discussion of the origins of capitalism[20] proceeds along a similar line, and he repeatedly tries to prevent his readers from misreading his claims as concerns with "actual belief" or any similar notion. Referring to the conception of diligent work in a calling, Weber comments that "it is surely not the case that the idea of a duty in one's vocational calling could grow *only* on the soil of [modern] capitalism," nor is it the case that "under *today's* capitalism, the subjective acquisition of these ethical maxims by capitalism's particular social carriers (such as businesspersons or workers in modern capitalist companies) constitutes a condition for capitalism's further existence" (2002: 18). Rather, the ethical notions in question contributed to the rationalization of money-making activity into "an end in itself that persons were obligated to pursue . . . in opposition to the moral sensitivities of entire epochs in the past" (33). Because of this transformation, the range of available choices was restricted, regardless of whether a particular individual accepted the justifications on a personal level or not.

> The Puritan *wanted* to be a person with a vocational calling; today we *are forced* to be. For to the extent that asceticism moved out of the monastic cell, was transferred to the life of work in a vocational calling, and then commenced to rule over this-worldly morality, it helped to construct the powerful cosmos of the modern economic order. (123)

There is something decidedly positivistic about Weber's avoidance of subjective motivations in his empirical work;[21] but it is a "positivism" shared by

19. "One is often bewitched by a word" (Wittgenstein 1969: §435).

20. I am setting aside any consideration of the empirical validity of Weber's thesis. What I am interested in here is the way in which Weber's argument proceeds, not whether or not it is a reasonable explanation of the origins of capitalism.

21. As opposed to his pedagogical and political work. Weber has no problem discussing internal psychological dispositions and motivations when trying to imbue students with a particular sense of politics and science as disparate callings, but neither of these celebrated lectures is really an empirical analysis in the sense that *The Protestant Ethic* is.

such perhaps unlikely comrades as Michel Foucault and Ludwig Wittgenstein. Foucault claimed to be a positivist to the extent that he too was interested in "a group of verbal performances at the level of the statements and of the form of positivity that characterizes them" rather than "the interiority of an intention, a thought, or a subject" (1972: 125). And Wittgenstein famously argued against the existence of a "private language" in which such subjective motivations could even be expressed; what matters is not the supposed contents of people's heads, but how people *refer to* them and justify their actions as being *based on* them.

> Suppose everyone had a box with something in it: we call it a "beetle." No one can look into anyone else's box, and everyone says he knows what a beetle is only by looking at *his* beetle. . . . But suppose the word "beetle" has a use in these people's language?—If so it would not be used as the name of a thing. The thing in the box has no place in the language-game at all; not even as a *something:* for the box might even be empty.—No, one can "divide through" by the thing in the box; it cancels out, whatever it is. (1953: §293)

Wittgenstein's argument in this passage[22] seems quite applicable to the concept of "motive": no one has direct access to the motivations of another person but must instead rely on behavioral cues and accepted community standards in order to *attribute* motive. The issue is not that motives do not exist (contra Wendt 1999: 179),[23] but that we have no systematic way of talking about—and, hence, analyzing—them without returning to publicly meaningful notions, whether our own or those of the people under investigation. Further, "diplomatic choice of motive is part of the attempt to motivate acts for other members in a situation" (Mills 1940: 907), so we must be especially careful not to rely on individuals' own accounts of their motives as part of a motivational explanation of anything.[24] With all of these potential pitfalls, it seems safer to avoid the whole issue and focus instead on something that we can empirically grasp: the public pattern of justifications for a course of action. And this, I suggest, is just what Weber would have us do.

Boundaries of Action

Weberian legitimation, therefore, is about the production and reproduction of *boundaries of action*. The central issue is how the limits of acceptability are

22. The passage in question is drawn from an argument about pain and the problem of private sensation.

23. Wittgenstein would probably argue that any such claim would simply be nonsensical, as would its opposite.

24. However, individuals' accounts of their motives can be used in transactional explanations. The ensuing narrative provides several examples of this.

drawn; a legitimation process constructs spheres within which certain actions can be performed, and it cordons off others as falling beyond the pale. Just as a sovereign territorial state limits its exercise of "domestic" powers to its territorial borders, a religious empire limits itself to actions that are granted to it by its gods, and a human being limits itself to actions that it considers itself authorized to perform. In a similar fashion, policymakers enact those policies that they can justify in a manner acceptable to their audience; the configuration of the boundaries of acceptable action, produced and reproduced in the course of ongoing political struggle over policy outcomes, are central to the explanation of those outcomes.

One distinguishing characteristic of these boundaries is that by *limiting* action, they *produce* an actor, demarcating a sphere in which that actor can then legitimately act. The boundary of an actor *"never marks a real exterior. . . . It is a line drawn internally, within the network of institutional mechanisms through which a certain social and political order is maintained"* (Mitchell 1991: 90).[25] 'I' am not "inside" my head, any more than 'Germany' is completely "inside" of its boundaries; both 'I' and 'Germany' are rather the results of boundary-drawing processes that never completely "contain" us. Both 'I' and 'Germany' are empowered to make certain decisions in certain contexts about where our proper boundaries lie, and therefore we somehow *transcend* our boundaries (Heidegger 1984); if our boundaries were completely external to us, we couldn't very well affect them in any way. Our capacities for doing so are never the result of some purely "subjective" determination, but depend on our being embedded in various interactions and networks and stories, upon which we can draw in order to produce and sustain those boundaries. The precise content and form of such boundaries give rise to particular types of actors and patterns of action.

Legitimation is a crucial aspect of boundaries, not only in the sense that an actor is permitted to act legitimately only within its boundaries, but also in that the establishment of those boundaries in the first place is an act of legitimation. An actor performs or considers performing an action and offers reasons to justify the action; these reasons constitute the action as the action it is, and they simultaneously serve to draw and redraw the boundaries of the actor itself. I am sitting in my home when a number of armed men break into my living room and demand my cooperation; it makes a great deal of difference whether these men are acting 'in the name of the state' as evidenced by their possession of a warrant, or whether they have no such authorization. The actions performed by the armed men are differently constituted in each case:

---

25. In this way, an actor is always "in front of" itself, existing somewhere 'between' its environment and those aspects of itself which are yoked together to form a boundary between 'inside' and 'outside' (Heidegger [1927] 1962).

a robbery or an assault if they have no warrant, an investigation or a bust if they do. In each case, boundaries are drawn, an actor is defined, an action is performed.[26]

Note that *there is no theory of motivation involved here.* It does not matter what motive the armed men have for breaking into my house: perhaps a particular police officer has a vendetta against me, or perhaps they have reason to suspect that I am harboring fugitives or that I have a great deal of expensive stereo equipment that they could fence. What matters is that in one case they have proper authorization to act in the name of the state, and in the other case they do not. *"Motive" is completely irrelevant.* In fact, motive is irrelevant not merely in a typological or classificatory sense, but in a causal sense as well. The answer to the question "why did these men break into my house?" can be answered without reference to the supposed contents of their heads at all: by looking back to the discussions preceding the action, we can see how characterizations of particular courses of action squared off and grappled until some such characterization emerged victorious and justified the subsequent course of action.[27] It is easy to imagine such conversations going on before the observed course of action was carried out, but only empirical research can disclose which arguments were actually utilized and which were successful.

To use another example, if a state sends its troops into a neighboring state in pursuit of a suspected drug smuggler and justifies its action on the grounds that it has the right to protect its citizens by eliminating threats to their well-being who happen to reside in neighboring countries, that state has just redrawn its boundaries by altering the scope of its responsibility and the extent of its legitimate action. Part of what used to be the "domestic" space of another state has suddenly become part of the "domestic" space of the first state, subject to the first state's laws and authority. To be more precise, the first state has *advanced a claim* that its boundaries should be so altered; the

26. My use of the passive voice when discussing these matters is quite deliberate, because the active voice is itself part of the process of "yoking" (Abbott 1996) attributes together to produce an actor and to legitimate a course of action. If we want to understand this process, we cannot start with fully formed actors, or with descriptions in the active voice. A desire to "preserve" agency by coding all action into active-voiced, first-person narratives—the kinds of accounts that Charles Tilly (2002) refers to as "standard stories"—is, strictly speaking, incompatible with a desire to analyze or explain the phenomenon of action in ways that preserve agency. See the following discussion.

27. I leave aside the curious temporal reversals implied in the possibility of reinterpreting an action subsequently, so that (for example) what was once a "legitimate" investigation or bust can, at a later time, become an "illegitimate" assault or abuse of police powers. Obviously, these subsequent debates and configurations cannot have a causal impact on the original action but need to be explicated and understood in terms of the situation contemporary to the debate itself (Abbott 2001b: 258). See also Jackson 2006.

practical impact of the claim is in fact the subject of empirical research conducted in this mode.

Obviously, a state can not advance a claim like this on its own, since 'the state' absent the activities of its authorized representatives simply does not exist. In the language of principal-agent theory, a state is a funny kind of principal, because outside of the activities of the agents of the state, there is no principal![28] The fact that we use the convenient shorthand "the state did X" is evidence of (and, indeed, a contribution to) the success of a particular legitimation strategy, which has associated traits and attributes and institutions and actions in such a way as to produce an actor that can act (Ringmar 1996b). When we say that "the state acts," we mean that some action is performed *in the name of* the state, with state authorization accomplished through some pattern of official channels (Jackson and Nexon 1999: 308–12). When a head of state speaks, does anyone seriously doubt that she or he is speaking on behalf of a social actor called 'the state'? Accordingly, it seems much better to empirically trace patterns of justification in order to inductively derive the boundaries of actors and their actions than to wade into a mass of empirical detail with these issues already worked out in advance (Neumann 1999: 33–35).[29]

Rhetorical Commonplaces

Legitimation claims are through and through *rhetorical*, in that they are forms of speech designed to achieve victory in a public discussion (Weldes 1999: 117–18). They participate in a "*social and intersubjective* rather than . . . *collective or shared*" discursive space and do not function as the property of any one particular individual. Instead of "ideas" that must be believed, legitimation claims participate in "symbolic technologies . . . systems of representation—metaphorically, symbolic machineries or apparatuses or implements—that have developed in specific spatio-temporal and cultural circumstances and that make possible the articulation and circulation of more or less coherent sets of meanings" (Laffey and Weldes 1997: 209). I use the phrase "participate in" because in order to determine why particular articulations succeed and others do not, it is necessary to relate those specific articulations to the broader

28. A curious fact first noted, perhaps, by Thomas Hobbes, whose conception of the state as an "artificial person" is a remarkably intricate way to deal with this issue. On this point, see Skinner 2002, especially chapter 5.

29. Although it does seem to be the case that only human beings speak in a way that we can understand, this should not be used as the foundation for a claim that the only "real" social actors are individual humans. Scientific realists disagree, abducing an essential nugget of human agency from this observation (Wight 1999), but I have a very hard time regarding this as anything other than a normative position justified on transcendental grounds. See Jackson 2004a.

social contexts in which they occur and upon which they draw in order to advance their claims. A careful empirical analysis of public debates about a course of action is thus called for.

How does public rhetoric work? Following John Shotter, I suggest that an appropriate metaphor to use in thinking about this issue is that of a "living tradition" which consists not of "fully predetermined, already decided distinctions" but of "a certain set of historically developed . . . 'topological' *resources*" that can be "expressed or formulated in different ways in different, concrete circumstances" (Shotter 1993b: 170–71). These topological resources, or rhetorical commonplaces, provide the raw material out of which actors and their actions are produced in the flow of events (Kratochwil 1989: 40–42; Shotter 1993b: 65–69). Specific articulations in the course of a public debate take these more general notions already in circulation and link them to particular policies, legitimating those policies and attributing them as actions to some particular actor. The analysis of legitimation must take into account both of these levels—the general rhetorical commonplaces present among the target audience and the specific deployment of those commonplaces in such a way as to link them to a particular policy.

Each of these two analytically separable levels addresses different explanatory concerns. The notion of a rhetorical commonplace itself explains how policymakers connect their arguments to their audience: public officials cannot simply say anything that they like in defense of a policy, any more than I can prevail in a discussion about where we should go to lunch by discoursing at length on the creative genius of George Lucas, or any more than Slobodan Milošević could whip up a crowd using nationalist language in Times Square or in downtown St. Louis. This is not because the audience in each case "believes" different things, but because each set of speakers, audience, and issues is characterized by a group of rhetorical commonplaces on which speakers can draw with any hope of having the audience follow their arguments, let alone be moved to action by them. Precisely what these resources consist of is an *empirical* question and can only be decided through systematic research on actual patterns of rhetorical deployment.

At the same time, the availability of a rhetorical commonplace does not necessitate or even unproblematically imply a particular course of action. This is because rhetorical commonplaces are only weakly shared between individuals. That is, a rhetorical commonplace is not a univocal, completely fixed bit of meaning that is *identically* possessed by multiple people; that would be a strong form of shared meaning, and (besides being virtually impossible to ascertain empirically) would also have the logical consequence of making debate and discussion unnecessary: if we already agreed in this strong sense, why would we have to talk about it? Although implicitly maintained by many contemporary scholars of "ideas" (Laffey and Weldes 1997: 199–205), the very

notion of strong sharing "disregards the deeply interactive character of language itself, its location in constantly negotiated conversations rather than
individual minds" (Tilly 1998b: 401). Empirical work on the importance of
rhetorical commonplaces should focus on these intersubjective negotiations, a
task quite at variance with the notion of strongly shared bits of meaning.

I therefore conceptualize rhetorical commonplaces as quite vague and mul-
tifaceted, capable of being elaborated in a number of ways and linked to a
number of courses of action; there is no way to know in advance how far a particular commonplace can be stretched, as this depends on contingent social
negotiations and interactive processes. "We can think of every utterance as
working, in terms of the speaker reacting to what others have said previously,
in relation to whom or what the speaker is trying *to be;* that is, how he or she
is trying to 'place,' 'position,' or 'situate' themselves in relation to the others
around them" (Shotter 1993a: 121–22). Viewed in this manner, "the very terms
or units involved in a transaction derive their meaning, significance, and identity from the (changing) functional roles they play within that transaction"
(Emirbayer 1997: 287). What analysts can and should do is to trace patterns of
deployment and try to provide some explanation of why they play out the way
that they do. No sketch of commonplaces alone can set these limits in
advance, because this would presume both a determinate meaning for a commonplace *and* its being strongly shared by speaker and audience (and analyst
too)—thus rendering its actual use in policy debates unnecessary. Careful
empirical attention to deployment is also required.

In general, a particular legitimation claim participates in a flow of events by
utilizing the available rhetorical commonplaces in order to "make sense" out
of a situation. For instance, representatives of the Soviet Union proclaim the
existence of an East German state, which is characterized the next day in the
West German Bundestag as "Soviet-Prussia," and the city of Berlin within it
is characterized as "the last bulwark against Asia for Europe and the entire
Western World!" (VdDB, 13. Sitzung, 21 October 1949: 313–15). Clearly, these
allusions (or at least their component parts) were not dreamt up on the spot,
but preexisted the concrete situation and were available for deployment at this
moment. These allusions are *metaphorical,* in the technical sense in which a
metaphor is a "carrying across" of meaning from one object or situation to
another, and form the basis for actions based on the situation as thus characterized. "We do this as we tell *stories* about the metaphors which we have come
to embrace. First we see something *as some-thing,* in other words, and then we
construct a narrative about this something" (Ringmar 1996b: 451). In this case,
seeing Berlin as a bulwark of 'the West' against 'the East' leads to a proposal
for increased financial support of the city by the West German government;
this characterization makes the policy proposal possible and helps it to win out
over alternative courses of action.

Public rhetoric thus displays a "prosthetic" character and functions much as a blind person's cane in helping actors to make sense of the world: "blind people do not feel their sticks vibrating in the palms of their hands, they experience the terrain ahead of them directly as rough, as a result of their stick-assisted 'way' of investigating it in their movement through it." As long as "the flow of activity" of daily life continues, "we 'see through' the language we use and are unaware of its prosthetic functioning," and it requires distinct conceptual effort to call attention to this aspect of our being and acting in the world (Shotter 1993b: 21–23). Because of this prosthetic character, it makes little sense to inquire into whether legitimation claims are creating or merely reacting to a world, because they are always doing *both at once*. A rhetorical claim reveals the world in a certain way, even as this revelation gives rise to particular actions to be performed within the world, which now "make sense" as a part of the world that has been revealed.

At the same time, a particular deployment always contains one or more *subject-positions* from which action can be taken, and it thus contributes to the production of the actor at the same time as it reveals a particular world in which that actor can subsequently act (Doty 1997: 384–85). For instance, to say that one is a "student" opens up certain possibilities for action, such as enrolling in classes; the world that presents itself to the individual is modified by the subject-position (student) into which he or she is placed by the deployment. Outside of an academic setting, such a deployment makes no sense and thus does not open up the same possibilities for action. Of course, the "academic setting" is itself continually being produced and reproduced by these patterns of deployment (Shotter 1993a: 35–37). The function of rhetorical deployments, then, is to "naturalize" particular social arrangements and subject-positions from which courses of action appear acceptable (Hopf 2002: 407; Weldes 1999: 104–5).

We must be careful not to overstate the coherence of these public patterns of justification, however, or to fall into the habit of formalizing the deployment of particular allusions and representations as if their use were merely the blind application of an unambiguous rule. Although "an 'action' is something for which it is always appropriate to ask the agent for an intelligible account," something that is accomplished "by hermeneutically 'placing' them [the actions] within a larger whole," we should not expect such accountings to be unambiguous or even free of contradiction (Shotter 1993b: 170). The coherence of daily life is quite messy and chaotic when viewed according to the standards of academic discourse, and if we are interested in *actual* processes of legitimation we will have to resist the temptation to overly systematize or formalize the articulations of the actors being analyzed (51–52, 129–31).

At the same time, some degree of formalization is necessary to the construction of a meaningful explanation. The trick is to formalize the appropriate things and oversimplify in the appropriate way (Weber 1999b: 169–71).[30] When dealing with questions of legitimation, formalizing actors and their beliefs or interests is the wrong way to proceed, as this would constitute an unacceptable reification of social boundaries that are themselves being renegotiated and stabilized throughout the process in question. Instead of this reification, analysts of legitimation should engage in a procedure of tracing the "arrestation"[31] of social process and linguistic ambiguity that is characteristic of actual social action. To map out the pattern of arguments actually deployed in a given policy debate does not constitute reification, inasmuch as no claim is made that these arguments were the *only* arguments that could have been deployed.[32] Instead, what is of interest is how actual arguments produced relatively stable boundaries of acceptable action, by drawing on the common stock of rhetorical commonplaces making up the relevant social environment.[33]

How does public rhetoric affect the outcome of policy debates? It should be apparent that it does not do so by modifying the subjective content of anyone's head; belief, whether the belief of a speaker or the beliefs of the listeners, is not relevant to the causal process I am proposing here. Persuasion may indeed be central, but it is a rather special kind of persuasion that comes "at the end of reasons" and aims to "give our world-picture" to someone else (Wittgenstein 1969: §262, 612). This is not a transcendentally *rational* process of persuasion, and it has less to do with any Habermasian "peculiar compulsion of the better argument" (Geuss 1981: 72) than it does with the creative deployment of arguments in such a way as to shape the public discursive space in favor of one or another course of action. Legitimation is thus more like what William Riker called "heresthetic" (1996: 9–10)[34] or Frank Schimmelfennig calls "rhetorical action" (1997: 227–29), in that words and argu-

30. There are obviously as many ways to do this as there are perspectives on questions presenting themselves to be answered. What I offer is, of course, only one possibility.

31. Thanks to Yosef Lapid for suggesting this term. Giddens (1984) suggests simply redefining reification so that it refers to a habit of taking social processes as stable and thing-like—similar to what I have called arrestation—but I think that the change of term signals an important conceptual displacement.

32. Making such a claim would, in effect, reduce action to an epiphenomenal consequence of structural imperatives and thus eliminate agency from the account.

33. In chapter 3 I lay out the methodology for constructing maps of rhetorical commonplaces—what I call "rhetorical topographies"—in more detail.

34. However, I reject the distinction that Riker draws between "heresthetic (manipulation) and rhetoric (persuasion)" (1996: 9), on the grounds that he overestimates the frequency of strong persuasion (resting on the eventual strong sharing of ideas and beliefs) in political debate.

ments are used as means for the shaping of outcomes.[35] The importance of
arguments is the effect that they have in shaping the public debate; it is this
shaping that the analysis of legitimation seeks to capture through a careful
empirical tracing of public debates and the policy outcomes to which they
gave rise.

What kind of evidence is appropriate to such an investigation? Obviously,
private articulations cannot exercise much impact on public debates, inasmuch as they are not direct participants in that debate. Many analysts give
these private sources considerably greater weight than the public articulations,
arguing that these primary sources are more likely to represent the true beliefs
and motivations of the relevant individuals. But as I have argued, the important action for legitimation processes takes place not inside of individual
heads, but in the intersubjective space *between* individuals. Hence the reversal
of the usual historian's hierarchy of evidence—in which private sources are
weighted more heavily than public ones—is justified by the ontological and
epistemological status of the investigation (Ringmar 1996a: 41–42). Because
the relevant processes take place in public, that is where we should look to find
evidence of their operation.

Agency and Causality

I believe that the transactional social constructionist account centered on
legitimation that I have sketched here can fulfill both tasks of a good social-
scientific account that I identified earlier: causally account for the victory of
the policies empirically enacted and do so while preserving human agency.
My account preserves agency better than existing accounts by leaving more
theoretical space within which actors can operate; by not trying to eliminate
contingency from the causal story, I leave room for unpredictable social
actions to have a meaningful effect on outcomes. Agency is also preserved in
that I avoid reifying either "agents" or "structures," even in the analytical and
somewhat indeterminate way that analysts taken with Giddensian "structuration" do: by focusing on ongoing processes, I eschew "bracketing" and
other such methodological strategies. As for causality, my account is capable
of explaining how a course of action came to be enacted without invoking the
results of this enacting as part of the explanation itself. Legitimation explains

35. Both Riker and Schimmelfennig are more willing to talk about the "interests" served
by various deployments and the "motives" driving people who utilize and are persuaded by
these arguments, and thus remain trapped in the decisionist and reductionist account of
social reality that I criticize in the next section. But their conception is closer to my own
than the more Habermasian notions of "communicative action" advanced by other analysts. For another approach similar to mine, although more indebted to Lyotard than to
Wittgenstein and Weber, see Bially Mattern 2001.

both why certain policies came to be and why others were eliminated from consideration. The kind of causality here is mechanistic rather than nomothetic, and "adequate" (in a Weberian sense) rather than necessary, but it is still identifiably causal.

To conclude the chapter, I will briefly elaborate on these points.

AGENCY

Agency, in Giddens's formulation, "refers not to the intentions people have in doing things but to their capability of doing those things in the first place. . . . Agency concerns events of which the individual is the perpetrator, in the sense that the individual could, at any phase in a given sequence of conduct, have acted differently" (1984: 9). This definition captures much of what analysts intuitively mean by agency, highlighting the importance of a certain radical contingency to the notion: agency means that things could have been different, save for the impact and implications of certain actions. A meaningful concept of agency is thus opposed to notions of determinism and inevitability (Abbott 2001a: 201–2), and retaining or preserving agency necessitates a trade-off in terms of the predictive and explanatory capacity of one's account of some outcome: other things being equal, more contingency means more agency, and vice versa.

This consequence has been obscured by the pervasive tendency in contemporary IR theory—and in much of social theory more generally—to address the issue of contingency-versus-determinism via the "agent-structure problem." This latter debate is a more restricted discussion of the basic issues involved, concentrating in particular on the role of the individual in society. It is, in many ways, trying to grapple with the classical philosophical question of free will in a social setting: individual freedom versus contextual necessity. A variety of positions on the issue are possible, ranging from pure individualism to extreme structuralism; much of social theory has traditionally been about staking out a stance on this continuum (Wendt 1987: 337–40).[36]

The basic problem, as Marx noted many years ago, is that "men make history, but they do not make it just as they please; they do not make it under cir-

---

36. What I mean here is not that the agent-structure problem is identical to the hoary old debate between individual freedom and social determinism, but that the agent-structure problem is perhaps best thought of as the reappearance of that older debate at a later point in the "fractal cycle" that is characteristic of academic disciplines (Abbott 2001a: 25–26). It is therefore possible to cash out the notions of "agent" and "structure" in a variety of ways, with a variety of consequences for issues of freedom and necessity, and hybrid positions like "holistic individualism" (Pettit 1993) remain plausible alternatives. But in any event, the internal complexity of the agent-structure debate does not affect the fact that participants in it tend to downplay the connection between agency and contingency that concerns me here.

cumstances chosen by themselves, but under circumstances directly found, given and transmitted from the past" (Marx and Engels 1978: 595). In other words, individuals and social forces are *always* implicated in every social situation, and neither individuals nor social forces stand in complete autonomy from one another. This may be a fairly obvious point, but it is profound in its implications; inasmuch as we consider social life to be at all distinctive from the natural world, social structures and institutions must be "instantiated only in process" (Wendt 1999: 185). And many contemporary social theorists embrace some form of "structuration" as a way of coping with this problem, largely agreeing with Giddens that "analyzing the structuration of social systems means studying the modes in which such systems, grounded in the knowledgeable activities of situated actors who draw upon rules and resources in the diversity of action contexts, are produced and reproduced in interaction" (Giddens 1984: 25). They thus endeavor to seize a middle ground between individualism and structuralism (Adler 1997: 324–25), at least at the theoretical level.

But at a *methodological* level, analysts who loudly proclaim the mutual codetermination of individual agents and social structures in their abstract discussion revert to some kind of separation between agents and structures in their practical analyses. Giddens himself proposes a "methodological bracketing" that alternately regards systems of social action under the rubrics of "strategic conduct" and "institutional analysis": while the former analyzes "the mode in which actors draw upon structural elements . . . in their social relations," the latter "treat[s] rules and resources as chronically reproduced features of social systems" (1979: 80).[37] Although he takes pains to point out that this bracketing is only methodological and analytical, it is striking that the effect of this bracketing is to reinscribe the agent-structure division in a form only slightly at variance with the earlier version of which he was extremely critical. We still have agent-centered stories in which structure is largely exogenous, and structure-centered stories in which agents and their activities are largely exogenous, and no clear guidelines for combining these stories or even for relating them to one another in practice.[38]

37. Giddens maintains the necessity of this methodological bracketing throughout his work; I quote from this early book only because this is perhaps his clearest articulation of his position on this point.

38. To correctly carry out this research agenda, it would be necessary to regard these two moments as taking place simultaneously; as both moments are analytical oversimplifications of a single concrete situation, it is not as if the two moments alternate in a temporal sequence (Giddens 1979: 180–81). Unfortunately, the temptations of this temporal-sequential resolution of the issue seem to have proven too great for many contemporary IR theorists, who either treat "agent" and "structure" moments as occurring at different points in time (Finnemore 1996: 24–25) or simply choose to focus on one moment rather than the other (Flynn and Farrell 1999: 511–12). For a more elaborate discussion of this point, see Jackson and Nexon 2002: 97–99.

Thus the old debate between freedom and necessity simply recurs in a more subtle form. The "institutional" portion or moment of a structurationist analysis still treats social structure as essentially a constraint[39] on individual action and thus a restriction of freedom, while the "strategic" portion or moment of such an analysis stresses choice and thus an overcoming of necessity. It remains quite unclear how even the most sophisticated "both/and" story involving individual agents acting in a social context, with a social context framing the activity of individual agents, does anything but replicate the problem, preventing the construction of "better stories" about social outcomes that do not suffer from damaging conceptual weaknesses.[40]

There is another surprising implication of recasting the contingency-versus-necessity debate as the agent-structure problem, which is the tendency of analysts to conflate the preservation of *agency* with the preservation of *individual agents* that have conditional autonomy from social processes. This position is clear in Checkel's call for bringing domestic political processes back into constructivist accounts (1998), as well as in the neoutilitarian critique of extant accounts for their failure to adequately incorporate "the demands of individuals and societal groups" (Moravcsik 1997: 517). The argument here seems to be that any discussion of individuals and their preferences is somehow *intrinsically* linked to agency, such that the simple presence of an individual mind in a causal process guarantees adequate preservation of agency.[41] If we are operating within the classical agent-structure problem as an individual freedom versus contextual necessity issue—that is, within the agent-structure problem understood in the way that analysts actually *practice* their analyses, as opposed to how they *talk about* them—then this suggestion makes perfect sense, as emphasizing individual agents *does* mean a focus on agency.

However, there is a pernicious contradiction lurking within this position, to the extent that analysts adopting it do not simultaneously abandon their

39. Giddensian institutional analysis is still in essence an analysis of constraint, because of the retention of the basic situation of an (essential) agent acting in a (determinate) context—even if the status of this distinction is analytical rather than ontological. The addition of "resources" (as well as "rules") to the notion of structure does not seriously modify this position, inasmuch as the pattern of resources facing an agent may be thought of as a kind of restriction on that essential agent's possible activities.

40. See also Heikki Patomäki's (1996) argument that this problem becomes particularly intractable when the two stories are assigned characteristically different modes of empiricism: "interpretive" for the agentic and strategic moment and "explanatory" for the structural and institutional one.

41. As an example of this line of argument, see Russell Hardin's (1995: 82–83) argument that the presence of a "causal feedback loop" passing through individuals is sufficient to make an explanation functional rather than functionalist (where the latter is understood to be a denial of agency). No mention is made in this argument of any possible choices that the agents in question had; they are simply slaves of their preferences and their strategic situations, a situation characteristic of neoutilitarian work generally (Jackson 2002a).

epistemological commitment to covering-law models of explanation.[42] The problem is that a covering law does not, by its very conceptual nature, permit much in the way of contingency; covering laws are designed to capture cross-case systematic regularities, an epistemic project that is constitutively opposed to the appreciation of contingency as anything other than random variation that should be controlled or eliminated to the extent possible. Logical positivists and neopositivists adopting this explanatory model aim "at showing that the event in question was not 'a matter of chance,' but was to be expected in view of certain antecedent or simultaneous conditions," and seek to identify *systematic* connections between factors that hold true across cases (Hempel 1965: 235; see also King, Keohane, and Verba 1994: 55–63, 76–82). Given a certain constellation of initial conditions, an outcome follows more or less inevitably, even when the outcome in question involves the activity of an individual actor. But this means that agency—as the theoretical capacity to have done otherwise—is effectively eliminated from the account: individual actors are involved, but only as throughputs for whatever factors the theory systematically connects with outcomes. Individual *agents* may be preserved, but *agency* is sacrificed.

Ironically, therefore, the turn to individuals rather than contexts ends up eliminating agency in almost any meaningful sense.[43] In a further irony, the way to restore agency to a central position is to rethink the concept of "structure," such that we take the Giddensian codetermination of agent and structure into account *methodologically*, and not just *theoretically*. This codetermination means that "structure" is not the name of a thing; it is an analytical category useful for explaining and interpreting social action.[44] Indeed, Giddens's shift from talking about "structure" to talking about "structuration" already points in this direction: he wants social analysis to move "away from structure towards structuration as an active historical process" (1979: 28), a

42. That they do not says a lot about the way that social science has traditionally been constituted as the search for lawlike regularities, such that an embrace of contingency may easily appear to mean the end of social science. It should be apparent that I do not accept that implication. If agency is inextricably linked with contingency, and if the notion of individuals behaving unpredictably is a difficult place to ground a social theory, then maybe we need to look instead to analytically specifiable elements of the social context surrounding those individuals as a place to begin our accounts.

43. There is a neo-Kantian argument that "agency" really means the use of reason by an individual, so that the individual's actions are only determined by her or his own rational deliberations. But an individual constrained by the dictates of reason seems to me to no longer be exercising agency in the sense that they could have acted differently. This would not be a problem if Kant had succeeded in establishing that individual freedom was actually based on reason alone, but he did not succeed in proving this—a fact that often goes unnoticed by the defenders of this position.

44. Indeed, "agent" is not the name of a thing either, if we take Giddens seriously.

stance that I find difficult to reconcile with methodological bracketing. A similar insight grounds Onuf's recommendation to discard the term "structure" altogether: "Constructivists should seriously consider dropping the word *structure* from their vocabularies. *Social arrangement* is a better choice" (1998: 63).

Whether one adopts either of these semantic shifts or not, the point is clear: we cannot think of the concept of "structure" as having anything like a simple empirical referent and still retain a meaningful concept of human agency in our accounts. What this means is that Parsons's definition of structure is the appropriate starting point for the analysis of social outcomes: "Structure does not refer to any ontological stability in phenomena but only to a relative stability—to sufficiently stable uniformities in the results of underlying processes so that their constancy within certain limits is a workable pragmatic assumption" (1954: 217). A particularly useful way of implementing this definition is to break down "social structure" into smaller component parts and then to examine empirically how combinations and interactions between these parts produce relatively stable outcomes—whether we conceptualize those parts as moments in a circuit of capital knitted together by a hegemonic project (Jessop 1990: 198–99, 208–9), or a set of structural positions and nodal points articulated through discourse (Laclau and Mouffe 1985: 111–14), or networks of ties between actors that combine and interact in complex ways (Abbott 2001b: 255–56; Wellman 1997).

Such weak or loose structural accounts do indeed have more of a space for agency, inasmuch as they embrace more indeterminacy and as such grant more autonomy to contingent social action. In addition, the reproduction of a stable social arrangement should always be somewhat surprising to an analyst taking this line: particular actions had to be performed in particular ways in order to bring these structural elements together in *precisely* the way that they were in fact brought together, but these actions were not themselves predetermined. Social actors in this conception are like the "cognitive *bricoleur*" described by Roy Bhaskar, "the paradigm being that of a sculptor at work, fashioning a product out of the material and with the tools available to him or her" (1989: 78). The work of empirical analysis, then, should involve delineating the resources available and tracing the ways that they are deployed in practice—an agenda that would preserve agency at the level of methodology.

Unfortunately, most analysts back away from this consequence by invoking the specter of relativism and the promises of a "naturalistic" approach to the study of social life. Instead of squarely maintaining a focus on practical discursive activities, they begin to talk about "underlying structures, powers, and tendencies that exist, whether or not detected or known through experience and/or discourse." This leads them to suspect that "the surface appearance of objectivity, although possessing causal power, is typically distinct from its underlying—and potentially hidden, reified, or mystified—essential relations" (Patomäki and Wight 2000: 223–25). As a result, the focus of analytical work changes from a detailed tracing of the patterns of social activity that produce and sustain stable configurations to a transcendental explication of the foundational principles governing or underlying those patterns—in effect, a retreat from contingency toward a more profound essentialist determinism.

The major consequence of this retreat is that analysts take *themselves* out of the picture when delineating the resources available to social actors and the character of those actors themselves, imagining that they are somehow capable of penetrating to the "real" essence of social order and grasping its potentials more "objectively" than the social actors on the scene. These accounts easily become quite as statically essentialist as those advanced by any neopositivist—more, even, to the extent that a putative grasp of more fundamental structural realities provides a secure basis from which to castigate other analysts for having misspecified the *real* character of social life. This gesture is particularly pronounced among Marxists and other critical theorists, whose approach virtually *depends* on the epistemically privileged character of their own analyses (Geuss 1981: 76–77). If Marxist categories do not provide a superior grasp of the "deep structures" of the real world, what recommends them? How could one argue for a logical connection between an "ought" and an "is"—as Bhaskar (1998: 62–65) does—without this epistemic privilege?

But there are non-Marxist justifications for this move as well. Drawing on scientific realist theories of reference, Wendt suggests that any meaningful analysis of social life involves an admission that there is a real world outside of our language and theories, a world to which language and theory merely *refer;* otherwise, we have no reason to prefer one account over another (1999: 48–49, 55–56). When applied to social structure, even social structure conceptualized as only instantiated in social process, this perspective means that we must try to ascertain the *real* properties of those structures, so that we have some basis on which to place an analysis of the limits of possible actions (1987: 362–64). And in order to preserve freedom of maneuver for the actors under analysis, it is also necessary to delineate essential characteristics of those actors that are constitutively separate from the structures in which they are embedded; otherwise, there is no way to preserve either human agency (Bhaskar 1998: 92–93) or the states system as a separate domain of analysis (Wendt 1999: 198).

However, this critical realist move is problematic for at least two reasons.[45] In the first place, it repeats the basic error of trying to specify the essential character of actors and their environment, such that particular decisions made by particular actors located at particular places in a social setting become

45. I set aside for the moment the philosophical objections to and problems raised by a scientific or critical realist position per se. On these problems, see Chernoff 2002.

comprehensible and more or less reasonable given this information. Arguing that an actor had three reasonable choices does provide that actor with more agency—more opportunities to have done otherwise—than arguing that the actor had only one reasonable choice, but it also ignores or downplays the extent to which actors may transform their available options (so to speak) on the fly. Examples abound of the capacity of actors to reconceptualize their options, and the putatively "objective" constraints of the extant social order confronting them, in the course of social interaction; this theoretical possibility of endogenously generated change is denied or at least severely restricted by the essentializing procedure employed by most critical realist accounts.

By the same token, critical realism also makes an unjustified leap from a relatively stable pattern of social interaction to some kind of underlying stable structural configuration supporting it. Just because patterns of interaction come together in a particular way, and continue doing so over time, does *not* mean that this is how they had to come together. And making the abductive leap urged by many critical realists means that we blind ourselves at the level of our very analytical tools to the possibilities of rapid, radical change in social arrangements.

> We have only to read any science fiction novel to know that what is presented and experienced as an account of an actual (but in fact imaginary) reality works, so to speak, to "manufacture" the sense of reality it conveys. What if, because we (wrongly) believe that such texts "represent" the true subject-matter of our science, we (wrongly) accord such representations . . . more prominence *scientifically* than the social activities and practices making their production possible? Then we can become the victims of a corporate or institutional self-deception. (Shotter 1993a: 76)[46]

The central problem with most critical realist accounts is that social stability requires *work*—discursive, practical, active work—to be sustained (164–65). And this work *never ceases to be required* to sustain a particular social arrangement. In other words, *there is no moment in which processes of stabilization and shaping give way to* different *processes of maintenance and reproduction*. Social life is almost never stable enough to simply be taken for granted, and when it is, the scope of the resulting theorization is strictly and sharply limited by factors deliberately and decisively beyond the theory's grasp.

Stabilization—the ongoing production and reproduction of social arrangements—never ceases, never finishes, and in a certain sense never fully succeeds (Abbott 2001b: 256–57; Neumann 1999: 35–37). Yet stabilization is the process

---

46. Recall also the discussion of the West Pole Fallacy in chapter 1. Narrative entrapment of this sort, I suggest, is a pervasive temptation in the social sciences, and we must remain vigilant in order to avoid falling into the trap.

that *should* be of interest to social theorists wishing to preserve human agency in their accounts, precisely because it keeps the focus firmly on ongoing social action rather than presumptively parametric limits of such action. Doing so requires stepping beyond covering-law models of human behavior and building more contingency into our accounts of the way that patterns of social activity come together to produce outcomes. The way to do this is to expand on the structuralist insight that actors have room to maneuver in the gaps and holes that are a part of actual social structures, and to acknowledge that these gaps and holes are not merely *between* relatively coherent pieces of structure, but also *within* those structural components.

In other words, the agency that an actor has at any given point in time comes from the *double failure of social structure to cohere on its own* (Jackson 2003: 14–16; Sewell 1992: 18–19). The resources on which actors draw in producing outcomes are themselves ambiguous, standing in need of further specification; their use is in part an effort to lock down their meaning. At the same time, different resources do not simply fit together but have to be made to fit; this also is part of the process of stabilization. Critical realists are correct to emphasize that action is produced out of a context of resources and possibilities, but they go too far in assuming that they can determine the extent of those possibilities *in advance,* instead of leaving that determination to the actors themselves and trying to analyze what they do and did in practice (Shotter 1993a: 77). Taking this step propels us into the realm of transactional social constructionism, wherein analysts trace actual social practices of social stabilization instead of seeking in vain for deeper or more fundamental sources of social stability.

CAUSALITY

One problem with embracing contingency in this way is that this also means abandoning the conventional, neopositivist definition of causality as a systematic correlation between factors across cases. Some IR constructivists interested in intersubjective discursive factors are perfectly willing to cede the whole notion of causality to the neopositivists and argue that their work is concerned instead with processes of "constitution" (Wendt 1998). If we accept this constitutive/causal split, then the stabilization processes that I have been foregrounding seem more constitutive than causal, and seem to form the social preconditions for the correlative relations studied by neopositivists.

John Ruggie's treatment of this issue is emblematic: "constitutive rules . . . define the set of practices that make up any particular consciously organized social activity [and] provide endogenously the noncausal explanations . . . which are logically prior to the domain in which causal explanations take effect" (1998c: 22–24). But this logical priority also implies a *temporal* priority, in that a particular system of constitutive rules, and hence a particular set of constituted actors and actions, provides the relatively historically "fixed" ground on top of which (neopositivist) causal relations can take place. The "system" is therefore "essentialized," even if only temporarily, and processes of stabilization drop out of view.[47] Such reification seems to be the inevitable consequence of retaining a constitutive/causal split in this fashion; as a consequence, the preservation of agency in the terms discussed earlier requires that the constitutive/causal distinction be altered or suspended in some way.

Indeed, Ruggie himself provides a point of departure in pointing toward the "ordinary language meaning" of causality: "whatever antecedent conditions, events, or actions are 'significant' in producing or influencing an effect, result, or consequence" (1998a: 94). By this reckoning, rhetorical commonplaces and the legitimation processes involving them can certainly be understood as causal, to the extent that the overall "shape" of the discursive environment contributes to the formulation of policy initiatives.[48] "The vocalized expectation of an act, its 'reason,' is not only a mediating condition of the act but it is a proximate and controlling condition for which the term 'cause' is not inappropriate" (Mills 1940: 907). I am indeed arguing that "reasons" can be "causes," but in a way somewhat different than that upheld by others who put forth this claim. Whereas Donald Davidson argues that reasons are *only* causal inasmuch as they reflect the subjective disposition of an agent toward an action and its outcome (1963), I am not arguing that reasons can be causes because the reasons offered have anything to do with any such putatively "internal" processes. Rather, I am arguing that reasons can be causes (of social outcomes, not of individual decisions)[49] because they participate in a socially significant process of negotiating and (re)drawing boundaries, simultaneously giving rise to both actions *and* the actors that carry them out.

In addition, "all metaphors and all stories are not available to us at each and every moment," and this availability makes a difference (Ringmar 1996a: 74). A situation is produced as the situation that it is by the deployment of a particular configuration of rhetorical claims and commonplaces. The deploy-

47. This is linked to the pervasive use of "punctuated equilibrium" models in IR work of this kind, in which a system of static constitutive relations is abruptly destabilized by some kind of exogenous shock so that a new one can form; the system is putatively stable up until this point, and stabilization processes are only taken to operate in the aftermath of such a punctuation and then drop out of sight. For a critique of this kind of reasoning, see Jackson and Nexon 1999: 298–99.

48. Rogers Smith suggests naming this role played by public narratives about identity "generative causality" (2003: 46–48). Although I prefer "adequate causality" for reasons that I discuss later, "generative" certainly participates in the same analytical spirit.

49. Elsewhere (Jackson 2002b) I have argued that these are qualitatively different kinds of questions; the former is "sociological" while the latter is "economic." The gap between them is virtually paradigmatic.

ments in question shape the flow of events much like the shape of a riverbed shapes the flow of a river; shifts may occur over time, but the general relationship of significance is indisputable (Wittgenstein 1969: §93–97). This much is an analytical truism. But precisely *which* commonplaces are implicated, and *how* their deployment and interaction contributed to the policy outcome in question, is a matter for empirical investigation. The perspective adopted here maintains only that *some* such commonplaces are implicated, and that their deployment is causally relevant.[50]

I am not arguing that without 'the West' no one would have moved to defend Berlin from the Soviets, or signed a military alliance that included West Germany as an equal partner, or any of the other things that made up postwar German reconstruction. Instead, I am arguing that *the way in which* these things were done—*if* they were even done at all—would be quite different: different reasons would be tendered for the policies, and the policies themselves would therefore be constituted quite differently. A package for European economic recovery without principles like Western unity would *not* be the Marshall Plan as we know it today; nor would a military alliance (even one involving Germany as an equal partner) without Western unity be NATO. One cannot simply "vary" the legitimation practices associated with these policies and have anything meaningful left over for comparison.

To put this another way, public legitimation claims are (jointly) *sufficient* to bring about an outcome, but we can never determine whether they are strictly *necessary* for a particular outcome—since this would involve the evaluation of a counterfactual condition that is never cotenable.[51] We simply cannot rerun history without the notion of 'Western Civilization' and see

50. This stance does not make my empirical account true by definition, any more than the stance that "policy outcomes depend on the preferences and motivations of individuals" makes an account based on that stance true by definition. In both cases, an analytical position is taken that is not itself susceptible to any sort of empirical proof or disproof; it forms the framework within which other pieces of evidence and information can be evaluated. "Testing" my account against an account based on material interests or individual motives would simply be nonsensical, as the accounts inhabit entirely different analytical traditions. Instead, the relevant standard should be a pragmatic one: does my account generate insights about the empirical situation under investigation that solve the problems associated with other accounts, and does it do so in such a way that it consistently fulfills its declared social-theoretical goals?

51. As Ruggie once commented, "Counterfactual historiography is little better than a parlor game under ideal circumstances" (1983: 207) to which I would add that circumstances are rarely ideal—particularly when one rejects a conception of the world as a closed system and admits the constitutive effects of identity articulations and legitimation claims. Indeed, as Weber points out, this kind of "positive" counterfactual reconstruction of history can lead to "freakish results," to the extent that such reconstructions are thought to be anything other than speculative (1999a: 282).

whether or not something like NATO emerged; nor can we compare the emergence of NATO with the emergence of a roughly similar alliance that did not happen to feature the notion of 'Western Civilization.' Hence we should never make claims about necessary causality.[52] Instead, we can make claims about what Weber called "adequate causality," which means that

> in the given historical constellation certain "conditions" are conceptually isolatable which would have led to that effect in the presence of the preponderantly great majority of further conditions conceivable as *possibly* occurring, while the range of those conceivable causal factors whose presence probably would have led to another result . . . seems very limited. (Weber 1999a: 286)

Adequate causation is sharply different from the necessary-and-sufficient kind of causation advocated by neopositivists, in which the aim is the isolation of systematic correlations of factors across cases (King, Keohane, and Verba 1994: 75–82). By contrast, Weber advocates a more speculative procedure, in which a causal configuration—itself an ideal-typical account of a historical situation[53]—is identified and demonstrated by showing how the configuration in question interacts with a range of possible factors, where possible factors emerge from a historically grounded study of the situation itself. In other words, we know that some configuration of factors is causally adequate if we cannot plausibly conceive of that configuration *not* producing the outcome in question.

Causality in this conception involves the concatenation of *causal mechanisms:* the contingent coming-together of processes and patterns of social action in such a way as to generate outcomes (McAdam, Tarrow, and Tilly 2001: 13). The explanation of outcomes thus naturally divides into two linked but analytically distinct stages: the analytical delineation of a set of causal mechanisms deemed likely to matter in particular cases, and the careful empirical tracing of that case or cases to illustrate the particular way in which these

52. But this does not mean that all situations are somehow sui generis; there may be, and probably are, similarities in the causal processes that produce actors and justifications. "Legitimation" is a process that I suspect may be usefully probed in other instances of actor-creation, and the specific kind of "supranational" legitimation of interest to my empirical account may have useful historical analogues as well. But although the forms and patterns may recur across cases, the content will most likely be very different, as well as the ways in which patterns and forms concatenate. On this manner of explanation, see Tilly 1995.

53. Although Fritz Ringer (1997: 111–16) provides an excellent discussion of Weber's strategy of "singular causal analysis," his presentation does downplay the extent to which Weber's delineation of causal moments is ideal-typical rather than "objective" in a neopositivist sense (70–71) and also misunderstands what Weber's treatment does to the traditional notion of "objectivity" (125–26; cf. Hennis 1988).

mechanisms came together. The two stages are interactively linked, however, inasmuch as a particular delineation of causal mechanisms has to do both with theoretical reflection on the general issues involved and empirical knowledge of specific cases.[54] In fact, this kind of close interrelation between theory and empirics is what Weber had in mind by urging social researchers to formulate ideal-types: ways of organizing information so as to generate insight relevant to a set of cultural values (Weber 1999b: 192–93). My own specification of causal mechanisms is no different, albeit more provisional because it is based only on the in-depth analysis of the single case of postwar German reconstruction.

When dealing with rhetorical commonplaces, the central mechanism is of necessity some form of *specification* of a vague, weakly shared notion. As I have suggested earlier, a rhetorical commonplace on its own does nothing; it is merely a potential resource until it is deployed in the course of some specific policy debate (Sewell 1992: 18–19). The success of any particular specification depends on the specific history of that commonplace: its prior dissemination throughout the relevant audiences, its use in distinct (earlier or contemporaneous) legitimation struggles, and in general the whole pattern of usage that made the commonplace available for deployment in the debate in question. Specification participates in an ongoing process of attempting to "fix" a commonplace's meaning and policy implications, so as to make the commonplace available as a rhetorical resource for use in legitimating a course of action.

The chief analytical difficulty is that any effort to specify a rhetorical commonplace—*including* the efforts made by a relatively detached analyst of the debate in question—involves the arrestation of a fluid and flexible notion; while this is precisely what historical actors are trying to accomplish, analysts of the process run the risk of reifying a particular specification to the extent that they accept it rather than accounting for it. The solution, as I discuss further in chapter 4, is to proceed *genealogically:* the tracing of the history of a commonplace should not be the record of any intrinsic essence that the commonplace is purported to possess, but rather a record of how historical actors have sought to stabilize the commonplace and produce the effect of an intrinsic essence, and in so doing provided (perhaps unintentionally) the commonplace to the present actors as a resource. The interaction of this specific history of deployment with the present deployment clarifies the fortunes of the present attempt at specification of the commonplace for the relevant audience.

Ancillary to the specification of a rhetorical commonplace are a pair of mechanisms catching up the ways in which speakers attempt to combine com-

---

54. An excellent example of this is Charles Tilly's *Durable Inequality* (1998a), in which abstract reflection on mechanisms is deftly entwined with richly detailed empirical narration. See also Janice Bially Mattern's analysis of the Suez Crisis (2004).

monplaces with one another so as to create the relatively stable constellations of commonplaces that appear as "positions" within particular legitimation struggles.[55] I utilize two such mechanisms: *breaking,* in which a speaker attempts to capture a commonplace from her opponent and thus dissolve the claimed connection between that commonplace and others, and *joining,* in which a speaker attempts to link a commonplace to others in such a way as to point in a determinate policy direction. Although both breaking and joining also involve efforts to "fix" the meaning of commonplaces, they differ from specifying in that they involve multiple commonplaces simultaneously. The success or failure of these two mechanisms involves not only the specific histories of the commonplaces involved but also the relationship between the proffered connections among commonplaces and alternative connections proffered by opponents.

Because the kind of causation that I am seeking here is Weberian adequate causation, the success or failure of these causal mechanisms should be evaluated in terms of how they fare in producing a provisional victor out of *actual* historical debates surrounding particular policies. Specification, breaking, and joining deal with the relation between commonplaces and arguments actually in use at some given point in time, and not between those arguments and other arguments that were only possible "in theory" but were not actually advanced. I am not certain why an examination of rhetorical commonplaces and legitimation arguments needs to explain why perspectives that were not even offered as alternatives were not considered, or (contra Weldes 1999: 60) why issues that *the analyst* considers critical were not discussed. Not all possible combinations of commonplaces, and not all commonplaces, occur in practice; those that do appear but are provisionally defeated in the course of debate are the important ones for an argument of the sort that I am advancing here.[56] Sketching those combinations is the subject of the next chapter.

55. In the next chapter I am sharply critical of the analysis of policy debates in terms of these "positions." This should not be surprising, given my expressed skepticism about the solidity and stability of such constructions.

56. This does mean that I cannot completely account for the horizon of the possible at any given point in time, but such is not my aim. As I argued earlier, I am not sure that it makes much sense for analysts to even attempt to completely delineate these horizons, because doing so deprives the actors of the agency involved in reconceptualizing those horizons "on the fly."

3 The Topography of Postwar Debates

*I*N ORDER TO GET A handle on the debates surrounding the enacting of policy during the early postwar period, it is first necessary to delineate what I will call the *topography* of those debates.[1] The term is intended to invoke a map of the underlying terrain of a region, which specifies the location of its major physical features; on top of this terrain are constructed the various buildings and other features of the full landscape.[2] Similarly, the topography of a series of debates specifies the various rhetorical commonplaces that are variously deployed and opposed by the advocates of the concrete positions appearing in the course of that debate. All of the positions taken in the course of the debate have some relation to this underlying topography, which is shared by all participants as the very condition of their participating in a discussion in the first place—opposing positions with nothing whatsoever in common cannot engage one another in any sort of a dialogue.

The focus on the topography of an entire debate rather than simply on the positions articulated by either side (the subject of much conventional analysis of political contestation) follows directly from the commitment to transactional social constructionism that animates this entire study. Instead of simply sketching positions that opposing "sides" of a question take up and reinforce, I aim to disclose the common rhetorical resources on which *all* sides of a question draw in making their specific recommendations; "positions" are then understood as deployments of some subset of those resources in a specific configuration. The emphasis remains on the *process* of claims making, rather than on the finished *product* that often appears in the guise of fully determined opposing sides. As discussed in the previous chapter, such an emphasis on

1. Special thanks to Bud Duvall, Ron Krebs, and the participants in the Minnesota International Relations Colloquium for comments on an earlier draft of this chapter.

2. John Shotter (1993b: 39) prefers to refer to "seascapes" in this context, but I feel that the language of landscape and topography captures the point adequately.

dynamic process rather than supposedly fixed and final product preserves contingency and agency better than the alternatives, thus meeting one of the two criteria for a good social explanation.

Adopting this stance also garners significant *practical* advantages. Descriptively, it allows me to avoid the controversies about how best to encapsulate the positions adopted by advocates and opponents of a policy proposal. It also allows me to take account of the fact that the majority of such oversimplifications fail to capture the ambiguities that remain within whatever camps the analyst identifies. Thus, instead of debating whether "isolationism" or "unilateralism" better captures the essence of the position taken up by opponents of the European Recovery Program and the North Atlantic Treaty, I focus on the rhetorical commonplaces that *both* advocates *and* opponents use to articulate their respective stances. This also prevents me from glossing over the differences among advocates and opponents, and returns analytical attention to the actual political struggles that were under way during such debates.

My focus also highlights the fact that advocates and opponents were struggling not only to control the policy outcome but also to control the rhetorical commonplaces that made up the topography of the debate as a whole. A rhetorical victory on such issues can often lead to a victory in the policy-making process. If advocates are successful in linking the rhetorical commonplaces of the debate as a whole to their preferred outcome in such a way as to delegitimate the arguments of their opponents, then their opponents have little effective rhetorical ground on which to stand and oppose the policy (Crawford 2002: 22–23). Indeed, a former opponent may even be brought to support the policy, because the rhetorical ground has (perhaps literally) shifted under her feet.[3] Clashes and debates are therefore not to be regarded as occurring *between* preformed groups but as part of an ongoing process of forming and reforming positions out of a general rhetorical field, the topography of which I will sketch out in this chapter.

In addition to these descriptive advantages, a focus on the topography of a series of debates provides a key analytical advantage: the prospect of causally explaining the outcome of a debate without having to resort either to motivational analysis or to a theoretically ad hoc appeal to various factors external to the debate. The ordinary way in which the analysis of debates is carried out, which involves the specification of opposing positions so that the analyst can ask how position A triumphed over position B, easily falls prey to both of these explanatory traps. On one hand, the victory of some position—say, internationalism—is often explained with reference to external factors, like

3. Although this does not happen often, there are several striking examples of such public "conversions" taking place during and immediately after the debates about German reconstruction. I discuss these moments in the empirical narrative to follow.

the objective presence of an unambiguous Soviet threat, or the supposed lessons of the period between the First and Second World Wars. This simplistic model of cognition has been roundly criticized by scholars for many years, starting with the work of Robert Jervis (1976); and in any event, "circumstances do not convince unless they are recognized," and a skilled political speaker usually has some degree of flexibility in how she or he chooses to characterize those circumstances (Riker 1996: 240). Explanations of the outcome of debates with reference to external factors producing determinate interests simply beg the question of *why* and *how* those factors became important to the debate in question, as well as reducing the debates *themselves* to epiphenomenal elements of the situation (Bially Mattern 2004: 32–42).

On the other hand, constructivists who prefer to ground broad discursive shifts in the motives of individual people exemplify the other problematic analytical move. For example, Michael Barnett's account of how "dialogues" in Arab politics affect the region, while focusing for the most part on properly intersubjective dynamics, descends at crucial moments into the murky waters of speculation about the motives of political elites in an effort to explain the conditions under which "Arab states were more likely to participate in these dialogues, and were more involved in symbolic accumulation and susceptible to symbolic sanctioning" (1998: 45–46). Barnett argues quite convincingly that Nasser did not really *want* to pursue the unification of Egypt and Syria but was symbolically trapped by his public image as the most vocal proponent of Arab nationalism (129–31). But he roots this entrapment in the private motives of Nasser and the Syrian elites to maintain their domestic political positions, which rather reduces any autonomy that the rhetorical invocation of a transnational Arab community might have. A social theory focused on legitimacy should *not* try to explain the decisions of particular individuals, lest it eliminate agency by transforming actors into throughputs for environmental factors.

Many structural analyses also invoke factors external to the debates in question in order to explain their outcome and thus fall into similar traps. Jeffrey Legro, for example, constructs an ideal-typical account of the "dominant 'episteme'" in American foreign policy and then sets about trying to explain "the shift from one stable set of collective views about managing major power relations to another" (2000: 255, 62). Not surprisingly, he turns to factors outside of those sets of collective views themselves to find an answer: novel collective ideas catch on largely to the extent that they "fit" with the structural conditions that they face (Jackson and Nexon 2001: 10; Legro 2000: 265–66). But this makes the "collective views" themselves quite epiphenomenal to the story. If one is interested in policy change, such a stance is problematic, as admittedly epiphenomenal discursive (or ideational) factors cannot really serve as nonredundant elements in a causal complex bringing about policy change. If they are epiphenomenal, why not simply eliminate them from the explanation in favor of the material conditions that dictate their appeal?

By contrast, concentrating on the general rhetorical topography of a debate holds out the possibility of explaining outcomes *endogenously*, with reference to how patterns of claims-making interact with one another and with the discursive resources available to the participants in the debate. We need not fall into the motivational trap, because no claim about belief in or internalization of a position is made; an opponent may simply be outmaneuvered, unable to meaningfully articulate or defend her or his stance on a policy. In this case, an earlier stance may be abandoned, or it may not be; regardless, the fight is lost and the process proceeds (Jackson and Krebs 2004). Some may argue that a particular individual's shift during the course of a debate may be attributed to self-interested calculations about the likely outcome and the possible (even tangible) benefits of being on the winning side of the discussion, but this is not essential to the explanation. Whether a shift was motivated by a genuine change of heart or by a self-interested calculation (or, for that matter, was entirely random) is *completely irrelevant* to the causal process at work.[4] And even if shifts do not occur—as with the Social Democrats who continued to vote against Adenauer's policies, or the Republicans who ended up voting against the ERP and the North Atlantic Treaty—the key fact is that their opponents' skillful capture of the rhetorical ground has rendered their opposition unsuccessful: they are unable to come to power by convincing enough voters to support them in an election, which is probably not unrelated to the outcome of the debates themselves.[5]

Therefore, I claim, a focus on rhetorical topography rather than on fully formed positions can explain the outcome of a discussion by calling attention to the dynamics and relations *between* and *among* positions that are missed by the more conventional analyses of debates. How does one go about undertaking such an analysis? The first step is almost purely inductive: the analyst has to identify the key sites at which discussion takes place, the key players in those discussions (who are "key players" by their occupation of strategic positions, like "federal chancellor" or "chairman of the Senate Committee on Foreign Relations"), and the key dates of discussions about the proper grounds for justifying a particular policy. It is fortunate for this kind of work that modern states have specific institutional locales in which such debates are carried

4. Indeed, a focus on rhetorical commonplaces is compatible with many different accounts of individual motivation—another of its analytical strengths.

5. In fact, neither the Republican opposition in the United States nor the Social Democratic opposition in West Germany was able to take power in its respective state until it had adopted the main outlines of the positions initially advanced by its opponents: after 1952 the Republicans no longer questioned the American commitment to Europe, and after 1959 the Social Democrats no longer questioned the policy of a close alignment with 'the West.'

out and specific points in time at which the debates take place: for example, when a bill receives a hearing in a legislature, when politicians engage in electoral contests for public office, and when international agreements between heads of state and their representatives are negotiated and signed. Ascertaining these figures, dates, and institutional sites is a narrowly empirical matter, and this provides the foundation on which the rest of the analysis is erected.

The debates that are carried out at these sites then need to be analyzed, not with a view to simply characterizing the opposing sides of the discussion but with an aim to disclosing the rhetorical commonplaces that animate the different positions. In doing this, one always has to keep in mind that key commonplaces may *not* be the commonplaces most often deployed. Frequency is a poor measure of the actual importance of some particular argument, although it can be a good measure of whether some speaker or group of speakers thinks that the argument is important (Riker 1996: 27–28, 101–2) or whether a significant proportion of the population believes that the argument is a good one (Legro 2000: 256–58). But using a frequency measurement like this to produce sketches of a debate subtly shifts the question away from the causal role of rhetoric and toward an explanation of the rhetorical choices made by individuals. Obviously speakers select arguments because they think that they will be effective, but this tells us little about the causal impact that particular arguments have. Only analyzing the discourse surrounding policy rather than merely the frequency of the words used can usefully illuminate the social outcomes of some particular policy-making process (Hopf 2004).

Naturally, an analysis of rhetorical topography needs to oversimplify and abridge just as the more conventional analysis of positions does; the difference is that the topographical analysis identifies key commonplaces of the discussion that can be (and are) drawn upon in *various* ways by the participants, as opposed to more conventional analyses that identify positions that are only deployed in the *same* way.[6] The goal here is to construct what might be called a "minimal spanning set" of commonplaces: a set of commonplaces sufficient to capture the basic outlines of the debates under consideration. This is emphatically *not* a simple description of the debates, but a construction of a Weberian ideal-typical model that highlights significant features of the empirical material in question.[7] A combination of primary and secondary sources is

---

6. Recall from the previous chapter's discussion that rhetorical commonplaces are only weakly shared between individual actors; if they were strongly shared, no debate would be necessary.

7. No claim is made here that my characterization of these debates is the final such characterization, or even that it is unquestionably the best for all analytical purposes. Idealtypes, as Weber points out, are means, not ends; the end that they serve is firmly ensconced within the epistemological purposes of the inquiry at hand (1999b: 193).

helpful to this effort, as the secondary sources provide the broader context into which particular rhetorical acts can be placed, while the primary sources help to concretize and check the claims made in the more general overviews. This is a perfectly ordinary example of a "hermeneutic circle," and the delineation of a rhetorical topography is indeed a kind of analytical hermeneutic. The result of such a procedure will be a set of diagrams and charts detailing rhetorical commonplaces and the empirical connections between them; these form the relatively static portrayal of the debates that the empirical narrative proper will then set into motion.

It should also be noted that the analysis of rhetorical topography is a thoroughgoing empirical endeavor. The goal here is to trace the patterns of argument that factually emerge in the debates in question, not to impose some stability on the debates either by reading the historical outcome backward into the debates themselves or by simply sorting locutions into predefined analytical categories. The relatively stable constellations and patterns of commonplaces depicted in the remainder of this chapter are relative stabilities tossed up in the course of the empirical debates themselves and should not be mistaken for "objective" limitations on what it was possible to say at some point in time.[8] A rhetorical topography is merely an interpretive aid that sets the stage for the causal processes discussed in the following chapters, although such a mapping is required to give the subsequent account any meaningful coherence.

Characterizing the Debates

Debates about the shape of the postwar world, and about the role to be played by a German state within it, took place in a variety of locations. Most obviously, there were debates in the occupied zones of Germany itself about the boundaries and orientation of the country: should "West Germany" be accepted as a political entity, and should this new state pursue a policy of close alliance with Western Europe and the United States? The outcome of these debates was by no means predetermined by the bipolar conflict between the United States and the Soviet Union, inasmuch as the meaning and implications of "bipolarity" were themselves matters of great controversy during the incredibly ambiguous postwar period (Weber and Kowert 2002: 1–3). These debates among German politicians, in particular those between the leadership of the SPD (Sozialdemokratische Partei Deutschlands, or Social Democratic Party of Germany) and the CDU (Christliche-Demokratische Union, or

8. Recall the distinction between "reification" and "arrestation" introduced in previous chapters; rhetorical topographies are empirical tracings of arrestation, not reifications of public debates.

Christian Democratic Union),[9] are central to any discussion of postwar reconstruction. Clearly, "the agency and discourse of those who call themselves Germans" will be central to any analysis of the constitution of any postwar German state. But to focus exclusively on such debates in the postwar period would ignore the extent to which postwar politics in Germany was precisely *not* what Wendt calls "self-organizing" but was instead importantly permeated by numerous other concerns (1999: 74–75).

For example, there were also debates about all of these issues in the countries to the west of Germany, with the French remaining highly skeptical of efforts to reconstruct Germany at all or to incorporate West Germany into an alliance (particularly a military alliance), and the British trying to respect French objections while reducing their own financial and military commitment to the occupation. But the debates outside of Germany that ultimately made the most difference for the question of German reconstruction were those carried out in the United States, where questions about the character of Germany were intimately linked to questions about the postwar role of the United States.

The prominent position of the United States in the process of German reconstruction, and the desire of the British and French governments for American economic and military assistance, ensured that the outcome of the American debates would carry considerable weight; the terms of that American debate were also the terms used by U.S. government officials to justify the American policies to their sometimes reluctant allies. In Geir Lundestad's words: "It is hard to imagine that, so soon after the war, the Europeans would have agreed to the reconstruction and rearming of West Germany, if it had not been for both American insistence that this be done and an American presence which could provide insurance against a renewed German threat" (1990: 68). It is therefore the debates carried on in Bonn (including, of course, the debates in which German political leaders engaged before the creation of the BRD) and Washington, and in the various places where the authorized representatives of these governments traveled, that are of central importance to this part of the study.

9. There are certainly other parties involved in postwar German politics: the first Bundestag, elected in 1949, contained representatives of twelve parties, including the CDU's Bavarian ally the CSU (Christlich-Soziale Union, or Christian Social Union). But most of these parties did not have a great deal to say about foreign affairs and the status of the West German state that was appreciably different from what the two main parties said. The exception here is the Communist Party (Kommunistische Partei Deutschlands, or KPD), who represented less a participant in a debate and more a common target for both CDU and SPD criticism. I discuss their marginalization in chapters 5 and 6.

The United States: Beyond "Isolationism" and "Internationalism"

Many accounts of U.S. policy in the early postwar period are written in terms of an opposition between an "isolationist" position—presumably advocating a complete withdrawal from the world and a retreat behind a Fortress America—and an "internationalist" position, presumably its polar opposite. This is not a particularly helpful way of reading the situation, particularly since the terms themselves participate in the very political debates that they are purporting to analyze. They are polemical labels, not analytical terms; and, in any event, they are not particularly accurate terms. "Isolationists," for example, were perfectly happy advocating a strong U.S. presence in Asia during the late 1940s, while "internationalists" remained quite focused on Europe throughout (Christensen 1996: 69–73; Paterson 1988: 79–80).[10] No one of consequence was seriously advocating a *complete* American withdrawal from world affairs in this period; in this sense, not only were there no "isolationists," but there had *never* been any. Even George Washington's famous Farewell Address only cautioned against *political* ties of alliance, leaving the door open for economic and other forms of American involvement.

In fact, the "isolationism" of "isolationists," as much as the "internationalism" of "internationalists," seems to have had an explicitly *metageographical* focus, in which the connection between the United States and Europe played a central role. *Metageography* refers to "the set of spatial structures through which people order their knowledge of the world"; these conceptual notions are not simply reducible to physical or geographical facts, but "precede" them in a logical sense (Lewis and Wigen 1997: ix). The central metageographical notion of the "isolationists" was the absolute distinction of Europe and America; traditional "isolationists" opposed extensive American participation in European affairs, and in particular opposed American participation in balance-of-power politics. The arguments about foreign affairs found in the works of the country's founders had a "prelapsarian" character, "intent upon

10. Consistent with his theoretical commitments, Christensen maintains that the goal of what he calls "Asialationism" (a blending of traditional "isolationist" concerns about the societal consequences of building up a large federal government and an equally traditional concern with China as a field for American concern) "was not so much to expand American commitments in Asia, but to embarrass the administration and undercut expensive policies toward Europe" (Christensen 1996: 71). Jack Snyder, by contrast, roots the differences between "Europe-first internationalists" and "Asia-first nationalists" in the economic interests of the opposing groups (1991: 281–85). These concerns speak to the motivation of various officials and elites, an analytical stance about which I have great reservations, as I have argued in the previous chapter. Regardless, the point is that other analysts have noted this Europe/Asia division, even if their explanations of the phenomenon and its implications differ from mine.

preventing the original sin of a balance of power from being committed in North America" (Ninkovich 1994: 46). But such appeals to turn away from Europe did not yield "a history of peaceful isolation," as American desires focused on westward expansion: first to the shores of the Pacific Ocean, and then beyond it to the "civilizing" of China (Schulte Nordholt 1995: 166, 79–84). The case of "internationalism" is a bit more complex but also centrally revolves around a set of metageographical notions about U.S.-European relations, as I will illustrate later.[11]

In addition, much of what analysts mean by "isolationist" and "internationalist" policies is better captured by the terms *unilateralism* and *multilateralism,* where the first denotes a policy of doing things on one's own and the second denotes a policy of collaborating with others to achieve the chosen ends (Lake 1999: 16; Ruggie 1993: 26–28). The distinctiveness of American involvement in a number of institutional arrangements after the Second World War is not so much the *fact* of such involvement, but the *character* of the involvement: as part of "an institutional form that coordinates relations among three or more states on the basis of generalized principles of conduct" (Ruggie 1993: 11). By contrast, the traditional "isolationist" position was one in which advocates "asked the American people to place their ultimate reliance on a go-it-alone policy backed by armed might" (Divine 1967: 124). This was the case even for considerations related to possible military involvements: advocates of a traditional "isolationist" position "opposed American [military] involvement in both" Europe and the Far East during the crises of the early 1940s, "but their major fears arose out of the European situation" because a European war would involve compromises with allies in a coalition, whereas in a war with Japan "the United States could function quite independently and ran no risk of having its wartime or postwar policies 'dictated' by powerful allies" (Jonas 1966: 23). So the point is not that "isolationism," had it triumphed, would have prevented *any* American involvement in the world, but that the nature of that involvement would have been quite different. For these reasons, Walter McDougall recommends discarding the term "isolationism" altogether in favor of simply unilateralism, "to be *at Liberty* to make foreign policy independent of the 'toils of European ambition'" (1997: 40, emphasis in original).

At the same time, however, *unilateralism* and *multilateralism* are not sufficiently nuanced terms to capture the debate about the postwar role of the United States, because those debates were rarely *about* 'unilateralism' and 'multilateralism' themselves. Prominent political figures debated the provision of economic aid to Western Europe and the participation of the United States in a defensive military alliance with other states and rarely, if ever, discussed

11. I have done so more directly in an earlier publication (Jackson 2004b).

the desirability of multilateral forms of organization in the abstract. To characterize the situation facing American political elites as a "choice" between "unilateralism" and "multilateralism," as many analysts have, implies some kind of distinct preference for one form *in itself* rather than the other. To their credit, most analysts deny this implication even though they retain the language of "choosing." In David Lake's rationalist account, individuals prefer to realize the gains from joint production economies and reduce their governance costs; "multilateralism" is therefore an *effect* of some other factors and is not chosen on its own account (1999). Similarly, in Jeffrey Legro's constructivist account, the "fit" of more multilateral ideas with the political and military situation facing the United States does the causal work in the argument, and not "multilateralism" *itself* (2000). And John Ruggie roots the existence of multilateral strategies in long-standing discussions about American identity (1993). To identify a strategy as multilateral is not necessarily to explain why it emerged.

Instead, we must examine the patterns of justification that supported unilateral and multilateral approaches to American participation in the postwar world. We should not look for some putative moment of "choice" between clearly defined alternatives but should instead consider a series of debates and discussions about particular concrete policies. By examining these debates and their outcome, the process by which some options were delegitimated and others made acceptable can be delineated. It is not as if there were a "magic moment" at which the die was fatefully cast in one direction or the other; rather, what many retrospectively narrate as "the choice between unilateralism and multilateralism" (or between "isolationism" and "internationalism") arose gradually, over the course of several key debates, with the European Recovery Program and the construction of NATO as perhaps the most prominent. Various arguments, positions, and interpretations came together in these debates in such a way as to make multilateral policies more acceptable than unilateral ones.

But this is *still* not specific enough. If we examine the record of American postwar involvement, we discover the persistence of the metageographical element in the policies that the United States pursued: multilateral policies seem to be the rule in Europe, while in the rest of the world, particularly in Asia and Latin America, multilateralism does not seem to be the rule to anything like the same degree (Hemmer and Katzenstein 2002: 579–82). Japan was associated with the United States via the *bi*lateral U.S.-Japan Security Treaty, and the countries of Central and South America, although joined to the United States through their membership in the (multilateral) Organization of American States, "favored an approach which meant at least an implicit recognition of US supremacy" as embodied in "the Monroe Doctrine, a unilateral proclamation on the part of Washington" (Lundestad 1990: 59). Ruggie notes that the American "desire to restructure the international order along multilateral lines" can be seen "at the global level, and within Western Europe and across the North Atlantic" (1993: 28).[12] This seems a striking circumscription of a broad multilateral strategy and its restriction, by and large, to a particular region. So we need to add a metageographical component to the characterization of the opposing points of view about the postwar role of the United States.

Thus, the positions traditionally identified as "isolationism" and "internationalism" are perhaps better identified as *exemplarism* and *vindicationism*. Exemplarism suggests that "perfecting American institutions and practices at home is a full-time job," while vindicationism suggests that "America must move beyond example and undertake active measures to vindicate the right" (Brands 1998: vii–ix).[13] These terms analytically catch up the content of the policy debates better than the traditional ones. Each of these terms, in turn, should be thought of as pointing to complex amalgamations of rhetorical appeals and linked patterns of justification that make certain policies acceptable while ruling others "out of bounds." Many of these commonplaces have been around for quite some time in American political discourse, while others are of a more recent vintage. To ask why one position became dominant in American political life and foreign policy after the Second World War is to ask what kind of changes in the rhetorical resources available to elites resulted in the large-scale adoption of more multilateral policies, at least in Western Europe. This kind of prospective approach retains the insight that multilateralism and unilateralism were *products* of a complex causal process and not simply the result of a single more or less informed choice, and it holds out the potential to explain the regional variation in policy as well.

Schematically, we can represent these opposing positions in debates about American postwar policy as a network of rhetorical commonplaces. These commonplaces give rise, when mobilized in the course of public debate, to divergent policy options. Traditional American exemplarism, for example, has a rhetorical "core" composed of two commitments: the metageographical (almost *ontological*) distinctiveness of America, particularly its distinctiveness

12. Robert Latham similarly notes that the American officials concerned to preserve liberalism concentrated on Western Europe first of all, but he attributes this simply to the fact that Europe was believed to be a "nodal point of strength" for the construction of a liberal world order (1997: 165–67). This does not seem a sufficient explanation; precisely what needs to be accounted for is the emergence of this "belief" in a socially sustainable manner.

13. Brands defines exemplarism in somewhat stricter terms than I do, regarding any stance advocating American involvement in the internal affairs of other countries to be a vindicationist stance; I prefer to regard those arguments advocating informal, generally private, westward-looking "civilizing" practices as compatible with a basically exemplarist stance, given that the primary audience for the "city on the hill" remained Europe.

from Europe (Boorstin 1960: 19–25), and the notion of 'heliotropism,' the vague notion that history follows the path of the sun and that the destiny of (human) civilization consists in a march to the west (Schulte Nordholt 1995: 1–2; Stephanson 1995: 18–20). These commitments justified the policies traditionally associated with the "isolationist" position: a focus on Asia (because Asia lies to the west of the United States and it is the responsibility of the United States to bring the light of civilization to Asia, particularly to China);[14] "Manifest Destiny" and continental expansion; an opposition to "power politics" (because they are traditional European methods) and an emphasis on private initiatives such as missionary activity; and a preference for working unilaterally, because America represented something so strikingly *different* than the rest of the world. It is important to note that this constellation represented more than simply a "position" in American political discourse; it was, instead, the basic framework for discussion of American identity from the founding of the country until the late nineteenth century (Brands 1998: 12–13, 20–21). Advocates of different policies moved within this rhetorical frame, but the frame itself remained largely intact and unchanged.

After the First World War, a new rhetorical resource made its appearance on the scene: anticommunism. Almost immediately after the Russian revolution in 1917, an ideological clash began, wherein the principles of "Bolshevism" were contrasted to "Americanism" in a quite vitriolic manner. But this American opposition to and fear of Bolshevism and communism was *not* directed primarily at the Soviet Union but at supposed internal subversion by disaffected minority groups: "Most Americans were more concerned with Bolshevism at home than with Bolshevism abroad" (Leffler 1994: 14–15). Opposition to communism was something that almost everyone could agree on, as Republicans and Democrats alike used Red-baiting tactics to smear their political opponents.

As might have been expected, the novel rhetorical commonplace did not pose any fundamental challenge to the earlier discursive framework, but it even served as something of an ally: the proper response to communism was internal purification, a recommendation that harmonized nicely with the notion of remaining somewhat aloof from the (European) world. This was rather graphically illustrated by the mass deportation of suspected Communists rounded up during the Palmer raids in 1919; the overriding imperative

---

14. Indeed, Adenauer was quite worried about this tendency in the thinking of some Americans, particularly that of Robert Taft: "Mr. Taft, as comes through clearly in all of his speeches, believes that the United States should support Europe, but [the original text, crossed out by Adenauer, reads "this is not the only possibility"] Europe is not the only base of our [Adenauer means the United States'] policy. Truman and Eisenhower maintain that Europe is more important than Asia, whereas Taft says, Asia is more important" (Booms 1989: 279, 10 May 1952). I will return to this point in chapter 7.

was to cleanse America of these "foreign" influences (Campbell 1992: 161–64; Leffler 1994: 15–16). Even the name of the House committee eventually established to confront communism internally—the House Un-American Activities Committee—supported this exceptionalist spirit, as it implied that to be "American" was to be anticommunist, and vice versa.[15] So anticommunism, as it was introduced onto the American political scene in the interwar period, was articulated as an ally of the exemplarist stance, in stark contrast to the ways in which it would be used a quarter of a century later to advocate pronounced American involvement in European affairs.

Exemplarism in the early twentieth century consisted of a particular configuration of these three rhetorical commonplaces, pointing toward policies of general disengagement from Europe and a concentration on internal, "private" matters. The opposing vindicationist positions—and there have been several in U.S. history—are not so much *opposed to* these basic rhetorical commonplaces as they are a *reconfiguration of* their relationship. The political problem for vindicationist opponents of exemplarism and the relatively unilateral policies that it supported was to find some way to challenge the rhetorical core of exemplarism in a fundamental way and thus delegitimate the policies underpinned by this rhetorical core. They ordinarily did this by attempting to sever the link between American exceptionalism and heliotropism, turning the latter to their advantage by linking it to an alternative rhetorical commonplace.[16] Different vindicationists did this in different ways, but most sought to demonstrate that the United States was part of a larger community of states and peoples, and thus not completely unique. At first this metageographical alternative was referred to simply as "civilization" by such early twentieth century advocates of an expanded American role in the world as Theodore Roosevelt and Henry Cabot Lodge (Roberts 1997: 337–39; Ruggie 1998b: 207–8). Woodrow Wilson also used such language quite readily, justifying the American entry into the First World War on the grounds that "German submarine warfare against commerce is a warfare against mankind.

15. "Other nations never were able to define Communism as somehow 'un-' the identity of that nation. There was no Committee on 'Un-Chinese Activities' in China or 'Un-French Activities' in France despite powerful Communist movements. . . . In no other country was Communism so marked with the sign of an outsider as" in the United States (Kovel 1994: 5).

16. Some evidence exists to suggest that it is now possible to articulate a kind of "exceptionalist vindicationism" that opposes an exemplarist withdrawal from the world by pressing American ontological exceptionalism to the point where principles like state sovereignty lose their resonance and are replaced by a more explicitly imperial logic of authority. But this does not seem to have happened in earnest until Ronald Reagan's election in 1980 and the consolidation of the "war on terrorism" in the early 2000s. I explore this issue in Jackson 2004b.

It is a war against all nations. . . . any government that had hitherto subscribed to the humane practices of civilized nations" should not be engaging in such actions.[17]

Such language was also featured prominently in Franklin D. Roosevelt's wartime rhetoric. To cite merely one example, on returning from the Yalta Conference in March 1945, Roosevelt declared in a speech to Congress that among the problems discussed with the other Allies were "the problems of occupational control of Germany after victory, the complete destruction of her military power, the assurance that neither the Nazis nor Prussian militarism could again be revived to threaten the peace and the civilization of the world" (Roosevelt, 1 March 1945, reprinted in Podell and Aszorin 1988: 524). It is this threat to 'civilization'[18] that justifies both the U.S. participation in the war effort and continued cooperation with the Soviet Union in the pursuance of this effort.

In the years immediately following the Second World War the language shifted to the more exclusive 'Western Civilization,' for complex reasons that are the subject of subsequent chapters. 'Civilization' rendered cooperation with the Soviet Union possible, at least for the duration of the war; its replacement by the more restricted 'Western Civilization' is an important part of the formation of the postwar world and helps to explain the marginalization of the "One World" position—based on the older notion of 'civilization-in-the-singular'—associated with former vice president Henry Wallace.[19] The novel rhetorical commonplace made it possible to firmly link anticommunism with an active involvement in Europe, so as to save 'Western Civilization' from the threat of communism. America was still considered to be exceptional *within* 'Western Civilization,' and 'Western Civilization' was exceptional when compared to the rest of the world, but (in effect) the firm connection between the physical borders of the United States and the boundaries of America were severed. This made policy initiatives such as the European Recovery Program and the North Atlantic Treaty possible.

Another rhetorical commonplace is also in evidence in the American debates: the notion of "liberty," or "democracy," as a type of social order that must be defended. This means more than simply the promotion of democratic regimes abroad, which is sometimes identified as "America's mission" (Smith 1994), but—and perhaps even more importantly—the preservation of a democratic social order at home. Proponents of the ERP, for example, stressed the extent to which the provision of foreign aid was necessary to keep

17. 65th Congress, 1st session, document 5.
18. Significantly, Roosevelt identifies the threat as emanating from the Nazis, and not from the Germans. This distinction figures prominently in the postwar German debates; see the following discussion.
19. I discuss this marginalization of the Wallace position in chapter 5.

the United States from being the only functioning democratic society on the planet, while opponents argued that the funds required to sustain the ERP, and the expansion of governmental controls on the economy that went along with them, would produce a tyrannical government—a "garrison state"—at home and destroy whatever remained of American democracy (Hogan 1998; Leffler 1992: 13). It was on this basis that Senator Robert Taft, a prominent critic of American policies in the early postwar period, opposed a major military buildup that would permit the United States to send troops abroad to resist Soviet expansion wherever it took place: "no nation can be constantly prepared to undertake a full-scale war at any moment and still hope to maintain any of the other purposes in which people are interested. . . . it requires a complete surrender of liberty and the turning over to the central government of power to control in detail the lives of the people and all of their activities" (1951: 68). Together with anticommunism, the ontological distinctiveness of America from Europe, heliotropism, and 'civilization'/'Western Civilization,' the preservation of liberty formed the "lay of the land" in which the debates about the postwar world took place, the set of basic rhetorical elements— albeit elements standing in need of practical political work to lock down their specific meaning—out of which speakers constructed their arguments.

We can represent the prominent configurations in the form of rhetorical network diagrams. These diagrams illustrate the central commonplaces associated with each position and also reinforce the point that the real differences between proponents and opponents of American-led policies of European and German reconstruction involve questions of sequencing and combination rather than wholesale differences of fundamentally opposed notions. Were this not the case, no debate between the positions would be possible, as they would quite literally be lacking a common language with which to have such a discussion in the first place. The exemplarist position looks something like figure 1.

The rhetorical core of this position is the tight linkage between 'American exceptionalism' and 'heliotropism,' producing the familiar and traditional notion of America as a "city on a hill," aloof from the rest of humanity so that it can display its excellence in isolation (Baritz 1964). 'Anticommunism' and 'the preservation of liberty' occupy secondary places in this rhetorical constellation, indicated by their more peripheral position in the diagram. Opposition to an exemplarist stance like this would involve some kind of severing of the exceptionalism-heliotropism link by means of the interpolation of a novel commonplace; this role is played by 'civilization' during the Second World War, and by 'Western Civilization' immediately thereafter. Vindicationists also tried to recruit deployers of the other two key commonplaces to support an alternative policy, arguing that adherents of these goals (anticommunism and the preservation of liberty) needed to support a more active American

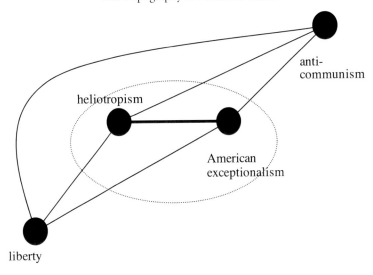

Fig. 1.   The exemplarist position (oval = "city on a hill")

involvement in the world, and in particular in Western Europe. The resulting postwar rhetorical network can be depicted as in figure 2.

The central point of figure 2 is that 'the West' is used in the postwar period to sever the linkage between 'American exceptionalism' and 'heliotropism,' by linking opposition to communism with a policy of vigorous intervention and commitment abroad—particularly in Europe. A striking example of this kind of occidentalist argument can be found in U.S. Secretary of State George Marshall's testimony on the European Recovery Program before Congress in January 1948.[20] Marshall argued that economic aid to Europe was required to prevent "economic distress so intense, social discontents so violent, political confusion so wide-spread, and hopes of the future so shattered that *the historic base of Western civilization, of which we are by belief and inheritance an integral part,* will take on a new form in the image of the tyranny that we fought to destroy in Germany" (*DOSB* 18 January 1948: 71, emphasis added). This argument, presented during the prepared speech portion of Marshall's testimony, represents a deliberate attempt to frame the issue in a specific and occidentalist way.

What we see here is a specific claim advanced by a public official in an institutionalized setting that is designed for policy legitimation struggles.[21] Mar-

---

20. The chapters to follow contain a vast number of such examples; I mention this one at this point only to establish the empirical presence of the argument in the first place.

21. Indeed, what analysts usually term *policy-making* is perhaps best thought of as an extended set of legitimation struggles.

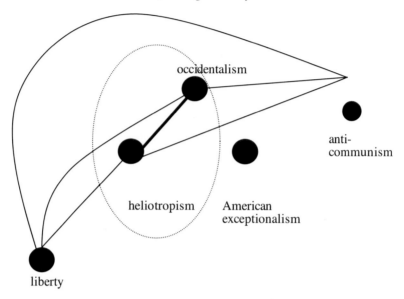

Fig. 2. The vindicationist position in the early postwar period (oval = "leader of the West/free world" [where "free world" means the West and its allies])

shall paints a picture of a Europe on the brink of chaos and concludes that without assistance, Western Civilization will be imperiled by tyranny. This symbolic link between Europe and the United States answers an implicit "so what" question: Why should Americans, and in particular the U.S. government,[22] care what happens in Europe? Marshall's answer is that we are part of a common civilization—in fact, Europe is the "base" and America is something of a later development, according to his formulation—and that therefore "we" have a responsibility to aid European recovery. The occidentalist commonplace helps to "interpellate" the audience (members of Congress, in the first instance, and beyond them the larger audience of the reading/voting public both in the United States and elsewhere) into a particular subject-position (Weldes 1999: 103–7), a position of being in some way *responsible* for what transpires in European affairs. Marshall's argument thus delegitimates a potential exemplarist response that would point in a very different policy direction. The argument would not have this impact were it not for various aspects of the rhetorical power of the novel commonplace of 'Western Civilization' that I will discuss in the next chapter, but the present point is simply

22. The official, governmental involvement is important, inasmuch as exemplarists like Herbert Hoover were perfectly happy to help organize and coordinate private aid to the ailing Europeans but opposed the erection of any formal public institutions to accomplish this. I discuss this point further in chapter 6.

that the commonplace *was* present and *was* used in this fashion throughout the postwar debates.

Germany: The Question of Location

Given the geographical situation of Germany throughout history, it is hardly a surprise that no policy of "German isolationism" exists; the Germans have always been only too aware of the closeness of other populations, and the option of withdrawing from the world has never been a serious policy position.[23] However, one of the roots of American isolationism—a kind of ontological distinctiveness—*has* been a traditional part of debates about German identity and foreign policy. In the German context, this rhetorical commonplace might be called the *Sonderweg* (special, or distinctive, way) tradition, the notion that Germany has its own distinctive course to chart in history and that it should remain as free and independent of other powers as possible (Doering-Manteuffel 1996: 10–11). During the early postwar period, this commonplace made itself felt in the calls for a "third way" in both socioeconomic and foreign policy. Kurt Schumacher, head of the SPD, argued in a 1947 radio address that "the Germans have been asked the question, whether they will work together and learn something positive from the experiences and examples of the world, or simply imitate without opposition, in each occupation zone, the opinions of the respective victorious Power"; his clear preference was for a *German* solution, rather than the simple adoption of any provided by the occupying forces (Schumacher 1985: 523). Drawing different policy conclusions from the same rhetorical commonplace, Alfred Müller-Armack, a neoliberal economic theorist, argued that what was needed in Germany was "a third form of economic system, replacing both *laissez-faire* and economic controls" (Nicholls 1994: 143). Metageographically, according to this commonplace Germany was not so much understood as *separate from* the rest of the world, as it was understood to be *positioned between* opposing options.

A second commonplace might be called 'German national unity.' Given that Germany did not even exist as a country until 1871, this kind of appeal is particularly prominent in German political debate (Greenfeld 1992: 386–87). Especially considering the situation of the country after 1945, when four foreign powers occupied the heart of the country's territory and claimed sovereign authority for themselves, appeals for German unity were often quite pronounced. Schumacher began to argue this line very soon after the end of the war, declaring in a 1945 speech:

23. Interestingly, Adenauer characterized the Social Democratic policy as "isolationist" in a 1952 radio interview and used the manifest absurdity of the notion to criticize the SPD stance. I discuss this interview in chapter 7.

We [Social Democrats] will not abandon our people, who are currently standing on the bottom rung of the international stepladder. We are not Russian
and not English, not French and not American; we are the representatives of
the working people of Germany and thereby representatives of the entire German nation. We will gladly work together with every international factor, but
we refuse to let ourselves be exploited by any one of these factors. (BKS, no. 35:
11.11.1945)[24]

A commitment to German national unity also underpinned Schumacher's
position (and therefore the SPD's official line on the matter until several years
after Schumacher's death) that the West German state should refrain from
making any definitive commitments to the states to its west, as these commitments might prevent the reunification of the country through a definitive settlement (Artner 1985: 17; Schwarz 1966: 512–18). Instead, Schumacher sought
to preserve freedom of action in the hopes of effecting reunification (Artner
1985: 15–16). As Carlo Schmid, a prominent SPD foreign affairs spokesperson,
argued in 1952: "Since the Federal Republic is only a provisional arrangement
covering one section of a country it cannot under any condition enter into
agreements that would presume to determine the definitive status of all Germany. Agreements of such a kind create a double danger: either they handicap
or prevent a reunification of Germany, or it may happen that an all-German
parliament might not feel committed to them" (1952: 534–35).

Of course, appeals to German national unity were by no means the exclusive property of the Social Democrats; indeed, it is hard to imagine any successful German politician at the time who did *not* appeal to German national
unity, which is further evidence that this is a rhetorical commonplace *shared*
by the participants in the debates.[25] Konrad Adenauer, for instance, often
laced his speeches with patriotic appeals and calls for reunification. In a particularly striking example, at the close of a speech delivered in West Berlin in
1950 he invited his audience "to stand and sing the third verse of the national
anthem, the 'Deutschlandlied,'" which had been the German national
anthem during the Imperial and Nazi periods as well as during the Weimar
Republic. "Naturally enough, hardly anybody knew the words. Most of them
sang the traditional and controversial first verse, 'Deutschland, Deutschland
über alles'" (Schwarz 1995: 500–501). But not every speaker drew the same
conclusions about the best *method* of pursuing German reunification as the

24. The last sentence of this quotation is circled in red on Schumacher's transcript,
illustrating the importance that he assigned to the point.

25. Of course, this does not explain why individual politicians chose to appeal to the
commonplace, although the prominence of the commonplace does reflect the fact that successful politicians did empirically incorporate such appeals.

SPD party leaders did. In his first speech before the West German Bundestag, Adenauer argued,

> The division of Germany will one day—this is our firm conviction—vanish again. I fear that if it does not vanish, there will be no peace in Europe. This division of Germany is caused by the tensions that have sprung up between the victorious powers, and these tensions will also vanish. We hope that then nothing will stand in the way of our reunification with our brothers and sisters in the Eastern Zone and Berlin . . . No matter how thick the iron curtain which runs through Germany, it cannot change the spiritual connection [*geistigen Verbundenheit*] between the German people on either side of it. (1975: 168)

As against the SPD position that the Federal Republic was only a temporary construction, Adenauer preferred to bide his time and wait for tensions between the Allies to subside and in the meantime build up the Federal Republic as the core of an eventual all-German state. The appeal to the commonplace of German national unity is as much a part of his articulation as it is a part of Schumacher's, but their conceptions of what this commonplace *means* as a practical matter of policy are quite opposed. As we shall see, the difference between Adenauer and Schumacher has a great deal to do with the position of a further commonplace—'Western Civilization'—in their discourse.

Anticommunism is also present in the German debates, and both of the major German political parties agreed in their rejection of communist (and, as a consequence, Soviet-oriented) solutions and policies. The parties understood anticommunism somewhat differently, however. Adenauer and the CDU held that communism was a violation of natural law that was also sinful because it denied the existence of God. According to the programmatic pamphlet "What Does the CDU Want?" published in 1947, communism was a species of the overriding materialism that had led to "contempt for justice and the worship of power, the denial of the worth of the person and of freedom, the idolizing [*Vergottung*] of the state and uninhibited expansion of its realm." The solution was held to be a "change of world view" and a "moral renewal. . . . In place of the materialist worldview must stand the Christian worldview, in place of principles arising from materialism must stand Christian ethics"— and presumably a party, like the CDU, devoted to such principles (CDU 1947: 3). A standard electoral tactic of the CDU during this period was to equate an SPD electoral victory with the end of German Christianity, a charge against which the SPD was continually on the defensive.

But Schumacher and the SPD were scarcely less adamant than the CDU in their rejection of communism, although they had other grounds for this rejection. The SPD argument was that communism would lead to totalitarianism as it had in the eastern zone of occupation, because the Communists had no sustainable program to support them—only Soviet guns. It was on these grounds that "socialists . . . were the most effective anticommunists," arguing that Marxist thought did not necessarily point in the direction of communism and providing by their own example an alternative path (Mark 1989: 959–60). On the occasion of the forced fusion of the Social Democratic Party and the Communist Party in the Soviet zone of occupation to form a "Socialist Unity Party," Schumacher commented that this represented

> not a unification of the workers, but the conquest of the Social Democratic Party by the Communists. In Germany, Communist policies have collapsed in the same way as the policies of every other dictatorship; this is clearly visible in the eastern zone of occupation. This is why the leadership of the Communist Party are trying to continue their party under another name. . . . Social democrats refuse, however, to be the blood-donors for the weakened corpse of the Communist Party. We will protect our organizational and ideological independence. (1985: 328)

In addition, the SPD as a Marxist party had to be sure to differentiate itself from communism, lest it be accused of acting as the agent of a foreign power—which is what often happened to representatives of the official German Communist Party, the KPD.[26] One way to avoid this characterization, of course, was for the SPD to take the lead in characterizing German communists in this way, which Schumacher often did. For example, in a speech to a regional association of the SPD in 1945, he emphatically[27] declared that "the German politics of the Communist Party is no German politics, but a politics of helping a foreign nation on German soil" (BKS, no. 35, 1.12.1945). Schumacher also made this claim in rejecting a merger with the Communists: "the possibility for a unification of all workers is not present as long as those taking part are not proven to be fully, factually, spiritually, and politically independent from every foreign power" (1985: 327–28). The SPD's strategy for differentiating itself from communism, therefore, partook of a strongly nationalist flavor.

Together with anticommunism, the *Sonderweg* tradition, and the notion of German national unity, one can find in the German debates a very strong commitment to democracy. Schumacher often used a contrast between Euro-

26. See, for example, Adenauer's claim in the Bundestag on 21 October 1949 that "only the 1.5 million Communist votes which were given [in the last election] can be characterized as against the new political situation" of the BRD (VdDB, 21 Oktober 1949). Thus, a Communist vote was figured as a vote against the "staatliche Neuordnung," and the Communists become traitors.

27. The phrase is circled in red in Schumacher's copy.

pean democracy and Soviet totalitarianism or collectivism to emphasize the importance that he and his party placed on democracy: "The theory and practice of Bolshevism is . . . foreign to Europe. . . . *The cultures of Europe and America are not conceivable without democracy.* Today, every form of dictatorship is inimical to Europe and threatens to tear apart the connections to ideas that have been recognized and respected throughout the world. Nazism was depersonalization; the collective, seen in a European light, involves the same danger" (BKS, no. 37: 1.5.1946). Schumacher also maintained that the reeducation of the Germans for democracy was among the most important goals for any sort of German reconstruction, pointing out that "the Weimar Republic did not die of democracy, but rather died of its dearth of democrats" (BKS, no. 43: 6.12.1947).

Adenauer was equally effusive in his praise of democracy, although he and the rest of the CDU seemed to mean something rather different by the term than Schumacher did.

> For us, the concept of "democracy" is not exhausted by a parliamentary form of government. For us, democracy is a worldview, which is likewise rooted in the conceptions of the worth and dignity of the individual person, which has been developed by Christianity. Democracy must respect these inalienable rights in public,[28] economic, and cultural life. (Adenauer 1998: 33)

These differences on the meaning of democracy are in turn related to the different role played by occidentalism in the rhetoric of the two sides. Adenauer deployed 'Western Civilization' in a way similar to the way that the commonplace was used in the United States: occidentalist notions are arranged in opposition to the more "exceptionalist" elements of the rhetorical topography. In this case, 'the West' squared off against the *Sonderweg* tradition, mediating the presumed essential separateness of Germany by introducing an overarching cultural community—Western Civilization—to which it belongs. In his very first speech before the German Bundestag, Adenauer declared: "Cultural affairs are, according to the *Grundgesetz*,[29] are the responsibility of the *Länder*.[30] But I can, in the name of the entire federal government, say this: all of our efforts will be carried out in the spirit of Western Christian culture and with attention to the rights and worth of human beings"

---

28. *Staatlichen Leben,* literally, "state life." "Public life" seems a reasonably close approximation.

29. This "Basic Law" served in place of a constitution for the BRD, helping to underline its provisional character in a legal sense. Carlo Schmid, one of the chief architects of the *Grundgesetz* and later a prominent SPD politician, often used this as part of his argument against the BRD's entering into any binding international agreements.

30. The *Länder* are the individual states of the *Bund,* or federation.

(1975: 169). Germany was therefore figured as a part of a larger whole, and implications for policy are drawn from this fact. This is not substantially different from the way that occidentalist appeals were used in the American context, and the presence of a similar rhetorical commonplace in both sites produced, as events unfold, a kind of trans-state coalition that was united behind the notion of undertaking the common defense of 'Western Civilization.'[31]

Schumacher, significantly, did not disagree with this basic occidentalist commitment; Adenauer and Schumacher agreed on the basic proposition that Germany belonged, *culturally,* to the Western world (Artner 1985: 43–44; Herbst 1989: 7, 110). In 1949 Schumacher argued that

> Indeed, there is for us an absolute necessity for military neutrality, but for us there can never be a political neutrality which considers neither political nor legal and moral aspects, such as the Soviet Russians. This would be no neutrality; it would be a concealed siding with the Russians against the West. (1985: 642)

Thus the general commitment to remaining in and defending 'the West' was important to Schumacher's appeals; the difference was that Schumacher did not conclude that formal accession to 'Western' international institutions and eventual German rearmament were necessary to this endeavor. Instead, Schumacher argued that the preservation of democracy in Europe required the "socialization of the means of production of the large property-holders" and the construction of a socialist Germany (BKS, no. 37, 4.4.1946). But as we shall see, Schumacher's acceptance of and deployment of 'Western Civilization' in his public arguments made him vulnerable to a number of Adenauer's rhetorical tactics, eventually contributing to a delegitimation of the entire SPD *Sonderweg*-based position.

The German debates may be graphically represented in the same way as the American debates were represented. Schumacher's position, which characterized the SPD from shortly after the end of the war until the Bad Godesberg conference in 1959, can be seen in figure 3. The rhetorical center of the SPD position was the idea that a reunified Germany could serve as the foundation for a uniquely European brand of democratic socialism, positioning itself so as to preserve the democratic ideals that are essential for Europeans. Much as the "city on the hill" notion functioned as the rhetorical centerpiece for American exemplarists, this notion of "European socialism" anchored the SPD position and affected how other commonplaces—like anticommunism and democracy—were understood and deployed.

---

31. This "supranational" aspect of the rhetorical commonplace of 'Western Civilization' is a not insignificant component of its power in postwar debates, as I discuss in the next chapter.

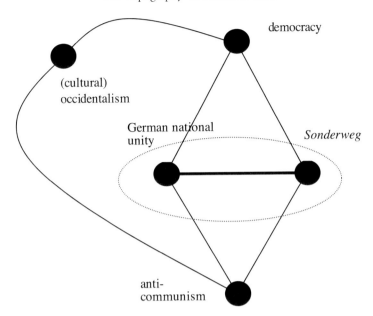

Fig. 3.   The SPD position, 1945–57 (oval = "European socialism")

Opposing the SPD position demanded some kind of severing of the central rhetorical linkage that made the position possible in the first place; Adenauer's way of doing this relied heavily on 'the West,' which formed the centerpiece of the CDU position.[32] Adenauer's "German Catholic condemnation of communism is made not only from a religious and moral basis, but also on the grounds of the supposed excellence of 'Western civilization,' which permits the believer to close his mind to criticism from the other camp with a good conscience" (Grosser 1964: 97). At a speech given in 1946—just after he had been elected president of the Christian Democratic Union in the British Zone—Adenauer defined Christian Democracy in this way.

We name ourselves Christian democrats because we are of the deep conviction that only a democracy which is rooted in a western-Christian worldview, in Christian natural law, and in the basic principles of Christian ethics can

32. Note that I am only discussing positions with respect to foreign policy and overall state identity here; were I focusing on domestic economic organization, the relevant rhetorical core might be a little different. The CDU did, however, rely on a notion of Western Christianity in a number of spheres, deploying the notion to legitimate substantial portions of the *Soziale Markwirtschaft* (Social Market Economy) erected after the CDU electoral victory in 1949 (Gutmann 1990).

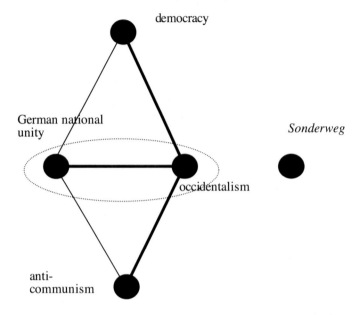

Fig. 4.   The Adenauer/CDU position from 1945 on (oval = *Westbindung*)

accomplish the great task of educating the German people and bringing about
their reascension [*Wiederaufstieg*]. (1975: 87)

Even more striking is Adenauer's analysis of the Nazi period, which diag-
noses the failure of the German social order to prevent a totalitarian dictatorship as a weakness of the spirit. "National Socialism," he argued in his memoirs,[33] "despite its suppression of individual liberty, had found so large a
following because political awareness and responsibility were very poorly
developed in a great many people." This lack of development resulted from a
lack of attention to the "proposition that the dignity of the individual must be
the paramount consideration, even above the power of the state . . . [which]
derives naturally from occidental Christianity" (1966b: 45). Therefore the turn
toward Christian principles represented a solution to the problem of how to
reestablish a legitimate German social order in the wake of the Nazi regime:
the Nazi period was characterized as an aberration, a derogation from the

33. By drawing on Adenauer's memoirs here I am not implying that they are a reliable
source for Adenauer's "true beliefs" about things; recall the discussion of sources of evidence in chapter 2. The quoted statement is exemplary of similar sentiments and arguments expressed by Adenauer in different settings and enjoys no privileged status in revealing his state of mind.

basic principles of the Christian West, and the renewed stress on the dignity of the individual was seen as a return to the proper course.

Figure 4 shows how the CDU position looks in graphical form. The most striking fact that emerges from this rhetorical topography is the centrality of 'Western Civilization' to important elements of *both* the American *and* the German debates, and the presence in each set of debates of a split between a 'Western' position and an opposing position centrally organized around a different metageographical commonplace. This produced a potential transnational coalition around the notion of 'the West,' a transnational coalition on which the reconstruction of Germany was ultimately based. But why did the commonplace of 'Western Civilization' have such power? And how did it get into these political debates in the first place? That will be the subject of the next chapter.

4 The Power of 'Western Civilization'

$\mathcal{B}$EFORE PUBLIC OFFICIALS CAN meaningfully deploy any given rhetorical commonplace as part of an effort to legitimate some particular policy, that commonplace must have been produced and then distributed widely enough so that the use of the commonplace "makes sense" to the target audience (McAdam, Tarrow, and Tilly 2001: 47–50). A justification can only be effective if it draws upon extant elements of the audience's social cosmos; offering justifications for a policy that relied wholly upon articulations that were novel to the audience would be quite ineffective (Jackson and Krebs 2004). In fact, deploying a wholly novel justification would be like reading a claim to a piece of land in a language unknown to that land's inhabitants—the practice might make sense to those performing it but would have no resonance with the inhabitants of that land (Todorov 1984: 28). Unless the aim is *not* to legitimate a policy, or to sidestep the issue by keeping the policy a secret,[1] a public official is constrained in practice to work within the rhetorical resources that are already present. Needless to say, a change in the configuration of those resources will make alternate policies possible, by making available different languages for the legitimation of those alternate policies.

This chapter will address and analyze the discursive shifts that enable the presence in postwar debates of an occidentalist rhetorical commonplace—the notion that the United States and Western Europe are common members of a larger community usually referred to as 'the West' or 'Western Civilization'—on which policymakers interested in German reconstruction could meaningfully draw. This commonplace was prominently featured in debates

1. Indeed, one of the reasons that covert operations are "covert" is precisely the fact that there is no effective way to justify them in public. If such policies and operations come to light in the future, the resulting discussion is usefully considered as the legitimation debate that was postponed at the time when the policy was kept secret. In any event, a policy like "the reconstruction of a defeated enemy" is far too big a thing to accomplish covertly, making the issue somewhat irrelevant to the case under consideration here.

taking place both in the United States and in occupied Germany; its prominence justifies devoting some effort to delineating its history and showing how it came to occupy such a position. Indeed, it is *only* the specific history of the commonplace that can explain the role that it comes to play in the postwar debates; there are no general lawlike reasons why particular commonplaces arise and rise to prominence, but only configurations of mechanisms that come together in specific ways to produce unique outcomes (Tilly 1995; 2002: 69–75).

A Genealogical Account

The kind of analysis that I undertake here might best be characterized as "conceptual history" (Koselleck 1985) or as a *genealogical* tracing of certain discursive mutations that made novel articulations possible. A genealogical account seeks "to maintain passing events in their proper dispersion . . . to identify the accidents, the minute deviations—or conversely, the complete reversals—the errors, the false appraisals, and the faulty calculations that gave birth to those things that continue to exist and have value for us" (Foucault 1977: 146). In this, a genealogical account must be sharply differentiated from an exercise in intellectual history or hermeneutics; a genealogical account "does not ask what could have motivated" a series of articulations, "nor does it seek to rediscover what is expressed in them (the task of hermeneutics)" (Foucault 1972: 162). Instead of intellectual history, in which "a definite discursive totality . . . is treated in such a way that one tries to rediscover beyond the statements themselves the intention of the speaking subject, his conscious activity, what he meant, or, again, the unconscious activity that took place, despite himself, in what he said or in the almost imperceptible fracture of his actual words," genealogy remains, so to speak, on the surface.

> We do not seek below what is manifest the half-silent murmur of another discourse; we must show why it could not be other than it was, in what respect it is exclusive of any other, how it assumes, in the midst of others and in relation to them, a place that no other could occupy. The question proper to such an analysis might be formulated in this way: what is this specific existence that emerges from what is said and nowhere else? (27–28)

Unlike approaches to the history of thought that seek to read the historically developed categories of mature modes of analysis backward into history, and tell a tale about their emergence as a more or less rational process, a genealogical approach remains sensitive to the completely unintended nature of many important discursive shifts. Indeed, 'Western Civilization' is one of the rhetorical commonplaces tossed up by a general mutation in discourse during the nineteenth century that brings an end to the virtually unquestioned dominance of simple progressivist accounts of "civilization" in which all societies would inevitably converge on the series of universal values first disclosed in western Europe. A genealogical account seeks to concretely trace the processes through which alternatives to this progressivist story were made available.

In this chapter, I identify the various streams of thought that came together in an almost wholly unintended manner so as to produce a notion of a civilization as a discrete, essential entity, and how this process was mediated by certain key authors and events. It is this shift from "civiliza*tion*" to "civiliza*tions*" that made possible the prominent role played by 'Western Civilization' in the postwar debates, as this novel occidentalist commonplace was imagined by intellectuals and subsequently disseminated through educational institutions and Oswald Spengler's improbably popular study *The Decline of the West*.

The key feature of the occidentalist commonplace as we know it today is that 'Western Civilization' is considered to be one civilization among others, one of a number of civilizational entities that have existed and according to some analysts continue to exist into the present—and may be of increasing importance in the future. Unlike the older notion of civilization-in-the-singular, the occidentalist conception of 'Western Civilization' admits a measure of civilizational diversity when utilized on a global scale. According to this framework, different civilizations have different paths and different fundamental principles, and it would be wrong for any one civilization—'Western Civilization' in particular—to push its particular values onto other civilizations (Huntington 1996: 310–11, 18). What must therefore be analyzed is the emergence of 'Western Civilization' as a *separate* entity, and a meaningful object of comparison with other similarly constituted objects.

My approach in this chapter thus differs from that of scholars who reject the use of 'Western Civilization' as an analytical term unless it could somehow be made more precise and specific, so that being a part of 'the West' would have consequences—albeit different consequences—as determinate as those that Huntington claims for his version of the concept (Latham 1997: 16–17; Risse-Kappen 1996: 370–71). Anselm Doering-Manteuffel and his collaborators, for example, define a set of "Western values" that can be contrasted with the value systems of other societies—notably with prewar Germany—in order to ascertain how 'Western' a society is or has become (Doering-Manteuffel 1996: 12–14).[2] But any such substantive definition of what "Western values"

2. As it turns out, Doering-Manteuffel is (I would argue) trying to measure the impact of something more like "Americanization," which is a rather different concept. "Americanization" is about the extent to which the socioeconomic relationships within some non-American society become more like those in the United States (Berghahn 1986). In my view the role of a rhetorical commonplace like 'Western Civilization' is less about the promotion

are participates in an essentialist project, in terms of which any ambiguity about what precisely constitutes 'the West' would be damaging, as this would make it impossible to draw definitive conclusions.

For my purposes, debate about the precise boundaries and contents of 'Western Civilization' is not a problem in the slightest; it is less some specific *version* of 'the West' that is important to my argument, and more the *general notion* that there is a civilizational community encompassing the United States and Western Europe. Efforts by historical actors to "lock down" this notion by linking it to specific policies are among the important causal elements of my account. In a sense, it is more the stories told about 'Western Civilization' than any essential 'Western Civilization' in itself that has relevance for my argument; the discursive shifts that I trace in this chapter explain how it became *possible* to tell such stories in the first place. It is not the case that there was always something called 'the West' that people simply began to think about differently in the late nineteenth century. Rather, 'the West' in the form that we know it today did not exist, *could not have existed,* before the discursive shifts that took place during this period.

Discursive Shifts

How does one go about illustrating such discursive shifts? One first identifies the institutional locations where debates about the subject in question—be it sexuality, sovereignty, civilization, or whatever—take place and then scrutinizes those debates in an effort to ferret out the important moments of transition and lines of argumentation. In this, the actions attributed to individual authors are key, inasmuch as they serve as the sites for the reconfiguration of discourse and the vehicles for presenting the altered conceptions (Said 1979: 23). Instances of writing, speaking, and other forms of discursive performance should be scrutinized in order to identify significant shifts and moments of discontinuity, with special attention paid to creative and unpredictable combinations of elements.

Although the aim is always to get at the pathways and potentials characteristic of a whole *series* of articulations, we must be careful to avoid making dis-

---

of specific socioeconomic forms and more about the general framework in which any such agendas might be pursued. "Americanization" versus "Germanization" takes place within a broader discursive context that establishes that there will be some relationship in the first place; that context as it emerges in the postwar period is 'Western Civilization.' Ironically, "Americanization" versus "Germanization" is quite similar in outline to Spengler's vision of what the future of the West would entail: a struggle between an American money-capitalism and a Prussian "socialism" for control of the dying days of the West (Sieferle 1995: 110–11; Spengler 1928: 504–6). What I am interested in is the wider context of this struggle, as framed by occidentalist (and Spenglerian) discourse itself.

cursive formations into a form of deep structural "grammar" that could place some kind of absolute limit on what could be said—and that might be thought of as existing outside of the practical activities of human beings in making sense out of their everyday lives (Shotter 1993b: 98–99). A discourse is a pattern of activity, and not a structural constraint; specific performances and particular arrangements of discursive resources cannot fail to be of great importance. A discourse shapes what can be meaningfully said within it not by imposing some kind of repressive code of silence but simply by containing only a finite number of resources and making possible a finite number of articulations; this is why mutations and recombinations are central to this kind of analysis, as they (often quite unintentionally) make available novel conceptual resources and hence novel articulations.[3] The analysis in this chapter proceeds by identifying certain key discursive formations and how they combine and concatenate in surprising ways throughout the nineteenth and early twentieth century, producing—quite by accident—the conceptual object of 'Western Civilization.'

The result of a genealogical investigation is not quite an explanation of the discursive shifts in question. Foucault himself referred to the genealogical endeavor as a descriptive one.

> To describe a group of statements not as the closed, plethoric totality of a meaning, but as an incomplete, fragmented picture; to describe a group of statements not with reference to the interiority of an intention, a thought, or a subject, but in accordance with the dispersion of an exteriority; to describe a group of statements, in order to rediscover not the moment or the trace of their origin, but the specific forms of an accumulation, is certainly not to uncover an interpretation, to discover a foundation, or to free constituent acts; nor is it to decide on a rationality, or to embrace a teleology. It is to establish what I am quite willing to call a *positivity*. (1972: 125)

The purpose here is not to provide general conditions under which discourses might change, or to account for such changes as realized instances of some covering law. It is sufficient to establish that a change occurred and that the conditions of possibility for articulation were altered.[4] A genealogical analysis *does*, however, seek to portray this shift as the outgrowth of the con-

---

3. While it may be true "in theory" that language is endlessly polysemic and polyvocal, it does not follow that undecidable semantic chaos characterizes the ordinary state of everyday life. "In practice, the dilemmatic themes intrinsic to our ways of talking and knowing are resolved; that is what the practical politics of everyday life is about" (Shotter 1993b: 220). So while in principle any speaker could use any locution, in practice they do not.

4. The decisive evidence that such a shift has occurred is, needless to say, the existence of novel formulations that would have made no sense under the previous arrangement of conceptual and rhetorical resources.

catenations of particular events and articulations: "behind the veil of appearance, a genealogical history does not find reality, but only another interpretation of the difference between appearance and reality. To genealogy, what happens to exist is a matter of how this divide is arranged and rearranged throughout history" (Bartelson 1995: 75). But this is less an explanation (in a neopositivist sense) and more an "account" or an "analysis."[5]

In addition, the genealogical investigation I undertake in this chapter is only one moment of my overall account; the shifts that it seeks to identify constitute only part of the process of postwar German reconstruction. The imagination and dissemination of a commonplace are insufficient to produce subsequent effects; *deployment* of the commonplace in concrete policy debates is also required. Otherwise, the potential articulations made possible by a discursive shift would simply fail to materialize, and thus never present themselves as an object of analysis in the first place. The notion that a discourse could shift without anyone knowing about it is simply a contradiction in terms; it is *because* the rhetorical commonplace of 'Western Civilization' shows up in the debates about postwar German reconstruction that we are able to say that some change has occurred in the first place. But identifying the shift itself through a procedure of genealogical tracing is only one part of a defensible account. To demand of my account in this chapter that it also *explain* the mutation in civilizational discourse would be roughly akin to demanding of a neopositivist study that it account for variations in its independent, *as well as* its dependent, variables, and the same problems of logical regress would be faced. Just as in a neopositivist account the explanation of some phenomenon is the connection between independent and dependent variables, in my account part of the explanation of German reconstruction lies in the connection between discursive shifts and the subsequent deployment of novel rhetorical commonplaces.

Finally, by proceeding genealogically, I avoid the problematic reification characteristic of many other approaches to the study of social life. The patterns that I trace in this chapter are just that: patterns of practical argumentation. They are not successive approximations to some emergent notion of a transatlantic community; nor are they unreflexive applications of a transcendent set of meanings. Noting that the effect of these acts of rhetorical innovation is the production and contingent stabilization of a notion of civilizational community is a far cry from building such an assumption into the analytical apparatus in the first place. While the latter stance would constitute an unac-

---

5. This is why the standard of evaluation for a genealogical account is not its "truth" in the sense of a correspondence with some objectively existing process but its effectiveness at disclosing the conflictual and nonteleological proximate origins of a thing, and denaturalizing entities and concepts that have become taken for granted.

ceptable reification of an ongoing and fluid social process of boundary demarcation, the former is simply an empirical observation about the arrestation of
that fluid process in practice. Taken together with the ideal-typical character
of any particular characterization of a debate in terms of its component
rhetorical commonplaces,[6] this genealogical tracing of a sequence of gestures
and formulations provides an account of the available rhetorical resources
without resorting to an a priori formalization of those resources and their
practical potentials.

Imagining 'Western Civilization'

The first problem that a genealogical analysis of 'the West' and 'Western Civilization' must confront is the fact that people have been talking about 'the
West' in somewhat mythical terms for millennia. "Inherent in the oldest
recoverable meanings of the word *West* were the idea of movement toward or
beyond the (western) horizon and the idea of sunset, evening, the fall of
night" (Gress 1998: 24). But this movement was taken to represent something
mystical, a kind of foreshadowing of human destiny: "In its wisdom the sun
daily searched the western sky in its flight from the east. At that point where
the sun crossed the horizon, there was a happy otherworld hidden from men,
and toward that place earthly glory and power tended" (Baritz 1961: 618).
There was a Babylonian 'West,' a Greek 'West' in which the Elysian plain was
(according to Homer) located, an Egyptian 'West' in which sunset meant
death but "Isis of the west (death) was the goddess of the second life, and the
region of one death was the region of new life," and a Roman imperial 'West'
(Baritz 1961: 619–21; Gress 1998: 25–26). Philosophers and historians as far
back as Herodotus in the fifth century B.C.E. spoke of 'the West' and used the
concept to refer to places and ways of living (Lewis and Wigen 1997: 16). And
there have been multiple 'Wests' in our own century, some pessimistic, others
optimistic and even triumphalist (O'Hagan 2002).

I do not believe that it is necessary to go back to the beginning of recorded
history in order to illustrate the discursive shifts that produce 'Western Civilization' as a conceptual and rhetorical object; nor is it necessary to select a single version of 'the West' as the correct or appropriate one. Although it is certainly the case that these very early notions associating 'the West' with both
decline and rebirth do resurface in the nineteenth-century conceptual object
that is my focus here, they are neither its direct predecessors nor essentially
connected to it in any necessary fashion. 'Western Civilization' as it emerged
in the nineteenth century incorporated and transmuted many of the older

---

6. Recall the discussion in the previous chapter.

notions but did so in a novel context: instead of civilization-in-the-singular, which would indicate a kind of universal goal for all of humanity, what emerged was a notion of one civilization among others. So many of the terms and qualities traditionally attributed to 'the West' remain in the nineteenth-century version, but their meaning and the role that they play within the concept are dramatically different. It is therefore fascinating in a philological or etymological sense to note that the use of the term 'West' to describe a community "may be traced far back to the division between the Western and Eastern parts of the Roman Empire," but this should in no way be taken as implying that the Western Roman Empire or any other 'West' is the same as the 'West' that emerges in the nineteenth century (GoGwilt 1995: 220).

   In what follows I focus on the writings of intellectuals, as discursive shifts for the most part are not the kinds of activities that can be accomplished by people simply living their everyday lives. The creation of a novel commonplace is a somewhat detached pulling-together of notions and concepts that makes room for unfamiliar articulations; this ordinarily requires a certain degree of separation from the push and pull of everyday existence. What I have in mind here is not an essential characteristic of any particular class or group, and more of a function exercised by particular people at a given point in time. "All men are intellectuals," Gramsci points out, "but not all men have in society the function of intellectuals," which is to formulate and sustain conceptions of the world (1971: 8–9). So the persons who are relevant for the imagination of a novel commonplace are those exercising the function of intellectuals, formulating what Mannheim referred to as the "total ideology" or worldview of a group—in effect, the discursive raw materials out of which people "make sense" of their daily lives (Mannheim 1936: 58–59). Anyone who enters into such explicit production is therefore an "intellectual" in the relevant sense, whether or not they are members of the specific social group called "intellectuals."

   In the empirical case at hand, the people responsible for the formulation of the notion of 'Western Civilization' are, for the most part, intellectuals in the narrow sense of professional academics and "men of letters," which makes the selection of materials for discussion somewhat easier. The nineteenth-century German academy looms large in my argument, as it is here that for the first time a number of factors came together in such a way as to make a notion of 'Western Civilization' as a bounded cultural community possible. The shifts in question involve a transition from an explicitly Christian understanding of time according to which every human community had a role to play in one single overall plan of salvation, to a more complex notion of separate communities existing and following autonomous destinies. Needless to say, many of these shifts took place over centuries; they are the backdrop against which the discursive configuration of the nineteenth-century German academy could toss up a notion like 'Western Civilization' in something like its contemporary form.

ESCHATOLOGICAL HISTORY

One of the logical prerequisites for a notion like 'Western Civilization' is a conception of *essential separateness,* an idea that there may be groups of people who are simply different from "us" and who play no essential role in "our" affairs: they may exist, but they might just as well not. Such a notion is completely impossible within the framework of a Christianity perpetually caught between "the constant anticipation of the End of the World on the one hand and the continual deferment of the End on the other" (Koselleck 1985: 6). Human history within this Christian framework was the history of salvation, or the history of God's will unfolding in the world; everything that happened played a role in this overarching story, and the only function of a historian was to figure out what that role was. As St. Augustine, one of the most prolific of such sacred historians, expressed the task, the goal was to disclose the movements of "the pilgrim city of Christ the King" in the mundane events of the world, particularly as it interacted with the city of man (Augustine 1984: 45–46).

In Augustine's work we can see two important aspects of the Christian notion of eschatological history: all things point toward a single and predetermined end, which is salvation; and the purpose of writing history was to fit all things into this predetermined end, which could be known through integrating the evidence of the senses with that of the Bible (431). In this regard, a prophecy from the book of Daniel became quite important, particularly when one of Augustine's pupils wrote an interpretation of that prophecy in which all of human history was divided into four empires. "The decisive element in this pattern was the East-West direction, with history stretching from Babylon to Rome" (Schulte Nordholt 1995: 6). In such a conception, 'the West' could only be a direction or tendency, not a self-contained community or way of life; everything that existed could only be valued inasmuch as it contributed to the overarching scheme, even if within that scheme certain regularities (such as the rise and fall of empires) could be observed (Koselleck 1985: 99–101).

Like all conceptual schemes, this eschatological narrative generated certain anomalies. The difficulties that this scheme presented may be glimpsed in the persistent efforts of Christian scholars to deal with the problem of Islam during the medieval period. "The existence of Islam was the most far-reaching problem in medieval Christendom. It was a problem at every level of experience" (Southern 1962: 22–24). Islam could not simply be ignored, because it stubbornly refused to either disappear or be subsumed into Christianity itself, even though exponents of the doctrine claimed to acknowledge the sovereignty of the same God as the Christians themselves. R. W. Southern has tracked the course of how Christian scholars dealt with this problem: their solutions included placing Islam into the Daniel prophecy as the harbingers of the end of the world (40–41), treating Islam as a Christian heresy (37–39, 56–61), and trying to minimize the differences between Christianity and Islam as part of a strategy of conversion (100–102).

Notably absent from this repertoire is a "civilizational" solution, in which Islam would be recognized as a separate cultural community and left to go its own way; such an option was simply not possible. Although notions like 'Christendom' were around at the time—particularly in the various appeals designed to mobilize Crusades—this did *not* in itself permit the recognition of a non-Christian world that would have equal civilizational status (Hay 1968: 30–34). Part of this is undoubtedly due to the fact that the opposite of 'Christendom' was something like 'heathendom,' which by definition is not the kind of community that can be allowed to go its own way (Bartlett 1993: 253–54; Delanty 1995: 34–35). 'Christendom' was not a *civilization*, at least not in the contemporary sense of that term.

What of 'Europe,' a different and more explicitly territorial notion that might have left room to recognize Islam as simply inhabiting a different parcel of land? Although such a "continental" conceptual architecture (including Asia and Africa along with Europe) had been a part of the available discourse since the time of the early Greek historians, it too had been incorporated into a general eschatological scheme. Each of Noah's three sons had been assigned a continent for his inheritance: Asia to Shem, Africa to Ham, and Europe to Japheth (Hay 1968: 8–14; Lewis and Wigen 1997: 23–24). Accordingly, each continent also played a role in the overall drama of salvation, and between them they encompassed only one world that had only one history. "To be a Christian was . . . to be a member of the universal Christian polity," the City of God on earth, whose destiny it was either to Christianize all of the world or to suffer a world of sorrows in pursuit of eternal life, and sometimes both (Delanty 1995: 28). As long as such a narrative framework existed intact, no notion like 'Western Civilization' would be possible.

THE CONQUEST OF AMERICA

The narrative framework of salvation history, although never perfectly integrated with events, framed the discursive space available[7] to even *conceptualize*

7. I would of course like to say "to Europeans" at this point. But doing so would be anachronistic and also constitute precisely the sort of problematic reification that a genealogical account is designed to avoid. Whether different narratives of self and other were available in other concrete historical settings is a fascinating historical question but does not have any significant bearing on my argument here.

political communities for a number of centuries, until it received a huge shock: the demonstration that there were land masses on the planet that did not seem to appear in the Bible, and that these were inhabited by people who likewise did not appear. "The discovery of America, or of Americans," notes Todorov, "is certainly the most astonishing encounter of our history. We do not have the same sense of radical difference in the 'discovery' of other continents and of other peoples: Europeans have never been altogether ignorant of the existence of Africa, India, or China; some memory of these places was always there already—from the beginning" (1984: 4). Hence the journeys and discoveries of the late fifteenth and early sixteenth centuries provided a blow to the older narrative framework from which it was hard-pressed to recover.

The basic problem is that the salvation narrative could not simply be *rejected,* as it formed the foundation for virtually every political and religious authority that surrounded the "discoverers"; hence efforts were made to integrate the new information (once it was recognized as such)[8] into the narrative. And there were, and remain, only two options for doing so: the first is to regard these new people as a degenerate form of the Christian conquerors themselves, which is a kind of temporal resolution of the problem (Mandalios 2000: 102–4); the second is to acknowledge these new people as some distinct form of social organization that *also* has the right to exist on its own.[9] The first of these responses might be termed the "civilization-in-the-singular" response, as it regards those who do not fit into the traditional narrative to be "uncivilized" and perhaps fitting targets for an active process of 'civilization.' The second might be termed "civilizations-in-the-plural," as it adopts a more relativistic view of social organization and permits other social groupings to go their own way. While the first response represents a transformation of the traditional salvation narrative, the second represents a more radical displacement of that narrative itself, without completely abandoning it.

CIVILIZATION-IN-THE-SINGULAR

One of the key features of the salvation narrative was its sense that, regardless of physical or other conditions of life, being a Christian was certainly prefer-

8. Todorov notes that Columbus, the putative "discoverer of America," never quite accepted that what he had found was something completely outside of the traditional framework; he pursued a "finalist" interpretive strategy in which "the ultimate meaning is given from the start . . . what is sought is the path linking the initial meaning (the apparent signification of the words of the biblical text) with this ultimate meaning" (1984: 17). Hence he could not accept something that did not fit, and it was left to later cartographers to designate the new lands as "America" and radically revise their cartography (Campbell 1992: 109–10; Lewis and Wigen 1997: 26).

9. My thinking on these matters has been decisively influenced by a number of conversations with Naeem Inayatullah. See also Inayatullah and Blaney 2004.

able to not being one. However, there was also awareness that sometime in the past, the ancestors of the present Christians were *not* Christian, but something else, something far less desirable. So there was a discursive place available in which to place people who did not fit as easily into the traditional biblical narrative: by comparing them to other peoples in the past. Hence we find that "in order to describe the Indians, the conquistadors seek comparisons they find immediately either in their own pagan (Greco-Roman) past, or among others geographically closer and already familiar, such as the Muslims" (Todorov 1984: 108–9). This preserved the possibility of salvation by giving the new people a role to play in the traditional narrative. That role was twofold: to serve as an example of what people were like before the coming of reason and Christianity, and to be the focus for missionary efforts designed to convert them to Christianity.[10] Thus, even if the specific place of particular people in the biblical narrative remained a thorny problem, the spirit of that narrative could be retained: the inhabitants of America were just like the past of their conquerors.[11]

It is this discursive constellation that gave rise to the notion of civilization-in-the-singular, which right from the beginning is both a process and a goal. The word itself was coined in France during the eighteenth century, drawing together a number of streams of thought so as to create a term for expressing the distinguishing characteristic of a good society and also the process by which people are made fit for this society (Braudel 1995: 3–4). Jean Starobinski suggests,

> The crucial point is that the use of the same term, *civilization,* to describe both the fundamental process of history and the end result of that process established an antithesis between civilization and a hypothetical primordial state (whether it be called nature, savagery, or barbarism). Minds were spurred to imagine the avenues, the causes, the mechanisms of the journey taken through the ages. (1993: 5)

I would invert the order: the concept 'civilization' combined both a state and a process *precisely because* of the earlier strategy of incorporating people into the traditional narrative as "savages"—living representatives of a past that Europeans had gone beyond. "To civilize" is thus the logical counterpart of

10. It is important to note that "Christianity" here means more than simply a system of doctrinal beliefs, but something more like a social pattern; ever since the colonization of Ireland in the twelfth and thirteenth centuries Christianity had been juxtaposed to the "barbarism" of particular life-styles, and the response of the Christian to barbarism had been defined as evangelism (Bartlett 1993: 21–23).

11. Inayatullah and Blaney point out that such usages are common to the "state of nature" arguments found in Locke, Adam Smith, and Marx, among others (Inayatullah and Blaney 2004: 85–88).

this strategy, a kind of secularized evangelism depending rather more on reason than on God.

At the same time, being "civilized" helps to establish the distance between Europeans and others, placing the Europeans further along in time than those whom they conquered. This rhetorical strategy, suitably elaborated, occurs in a variety of contexts. One of the most (in)famous was the international legal notion of a "standard of civilization" to which the non-European world was obliged to aspire (Gong 1984: 40, 63) and that helped to justify colonial rule as an essentially benevolent effort to spread the blessings of civilization to all (76–80). Edward Said's work on 'Orientalism' (1979) reveals the operation of this strategy in European scholarship on the non-European world,[12] while Johannes Fabian (1983) notes its prominence throughout the discipline of anthropology and Clifford Geertz highlights the ways that it "disarranges" even the observation of non-European societies by Europeans (2000: 43).[13] This discourse remains prominent into the period of the Second World War, and in fact (as we shall see in the next chapter) helps to legitimate such initiatives as the United Nations; its abandonment or transmutation in the early postwar period with respect to transatlantic relations is the crucial turning point in postwar German reconstruction.

CIVILIZATIONS-IN-THE-PLURAL

Although the initial formulations of the temporal opposition between the "civilized" and the "savage" were clearly to the advantage of those who were further along in time, once the term had been coined it could be subjected to quite a different kind of analysis, in which "civilized" could be shown up as a bad thing to be. The usual strategy was to accept the *goals* of 'civilization'—happiness, justice, and the like—and demonstrate that actually existing society did not live up to these goals. The most extreme formulation of this critique was that of Rousseau, who famously equates civilization with inequality and degeneration: far from producing happiness, civilization is a form of

12. In his way of speaking and writing, Said often uses the term *West* to mean the posited, discursively constructed opposite of the Orient, but his use of this concept is somewhat loose; "the essence of Orientalism is the ineradicable distinction between Western superiority and Oriental inferiority," he declares, but he is not particularly interested in how the referent of a term like 'the West' underwent massive shifts over the centuries (1979: 42). This may be due to Said's interest in how the discourse of civilization-in-the-singular tossed up a non-Western Other, whereas I am more interested in how the parallel discourse of civilizations-in-the-plural tossed up a Western Self.

13. Elements of this strategy may also be seen in "development theory," which persistently places "developing" countries at some earlier point on a road to a destination that—presumably—the "developed" countries have already reached (Inayatullah and Blaney 2004: 116–23). Our present theories may not be as far from this "archaic" discourse as we might like to believe.

domestication that makes humans weak (1987: 43). In this, Rousseau picks up some of the connections between 'civilization' and 'politeness' that were a part of the discourse of the time, but he inverts the order so as to make "polite society" an undesirable thing (Starobinski 1993: 11–13).

However, Rousseau did not advocate a return to a presocial existence; although he pointed out that savages were in many ways happier and healthier than civilized man, he also acknowledged that returning to a savage state was not really an option. For all of its drawbacks, civilized society was essential for developing *"perfectibility,* social virtues, and the other faculties that natural man had received in a state of potentiality [but] could never develop by themselves" and for "perfect[ing] human reason" (Rousseau 1987: 59). Rousseau's solution to this problem was a "social compact" that would preserve (natural) individual freedom but also give the benefits of social organization: "each of us places his person and all his power in common under the supreme direction of the general will; and as one we receive each member as an indivisible part of the whole" (148). In many ways, what Rousseau has in mind here is a kind of civilizing of civilization, an attempt to go *beyond* existing forms so as to produce a genuine society: not a return, but an advance.

Scholars have noted the effects of such a formulation on the social order, as it justified all manner of popular resistance to perceived injustices. But for my purposes I want to call attention to another aspect of Rousseau's formulation: the fact that in place of a singular notion of 'civilization' he has explicitly introduced a notion of plurality. This takes place in two ways. Each social compact, Rousseau argues, creates a separate entity; these entities are constitutionally independent and hence cannot be subjected to a single standard or authority. "A town cannot legitimately be in subjection to another town, any more than a nation can be in subjection to another nation, since the essence of the body politic consists in the harmony of obedience and liberty; and the words *subject* and *sovereign* are identical correlatives, whose meaning is combined in the single word 'citizen'" (196). The implication is that each sovereign entity has *its own* "general will," and hence its own way of organizing itself; diversity rather than uniformity is the consequence. Rousseau thus subtly redefines the meaning of 'civilization' to mean less a condition of life and more a formal principle. This is expressed in Rousseau's observation that "the Russians will never be truly civilized, since they have been civilized too early," which plays with the ambiguity of the term.

> Peter [the Great] had a genius for imitation. . . . He saw that his people was barbarous; he did not see that it was not ready for civilization. He wanted to civilize it when all it needed was toughening. First he wanted to make Germans and Englishmen, when he should have made Russians. He prevented his subjects from ever becoming what they could have been by persuading them that they were something they are not. (166)

Therefore, to be *truly* civilized meant to have the kind of laws and institutions appropriate to one's own people, and not merely to imitate the customs of another group; a singular standard of civilization with substantive content was rendered quite a bit more difficult, if not impossible, to articulate. Although Rousseau (like Aristotle and Montesquieu before him) tried to constrain and in a sense discipline this free play of diversity by proposing a set of observations about which climates and which sets of natural resources were appropriate for various kinds of governments, the genie was, as it were, out of the bottle, and discursive space for the articulation of a principle of particularity had been opened. Not surprisingly, given that the most vocal proponents of the language and concept of 'civilization-in-the-singular' were the French (Starobinski 1993: 19–21), it was principally German thinkers who took up the task of producing an alternative notion in this novel discursive space (Bowden 2004: 38–39; Braudel 1995: 5–6). Their alternative to 'civilization' (*Zivilisation*) was 'culture' (*Kultur*), and was decidedly pluralist.

THE NINETEENTH-CENTURY GERMAN ACADEMY: *KULTUR* AND *BILDUNG*

German thinkers accepted the French linkage of civilization and "polite society" but read the opposition in a manner quite reminiscent of Rousseau: *Zivilisation* was shallow, cosmopolitan, and superficial, while *Kultur* was more closely connected to art, morality, and education. For these German thinkers, "'civilization' evoked the tangible amenities of earthly existence; 'culture' suggested spiritual concerns. In short, culture reflected cultivation, whereas civilization was 'merely' a product of man's factual, rational, and technical training" (Ringer 1969: 87–90). Against this conception of civilization, German Romantics stressed a more organic, holistic notion: the *nation*, a singular community that was constituted by its own individual values and principles. While many Romantics "did not dispute the fundamental sameness of human nature" and remained committed to the general Enlightenment notion that history would unfold in a beneficent manner, the central principle of their alternative to 'civilization' was the fundamental difference between national communities, which explained "why generic political prescriptions based on inference from individuals had to be modified for each *Volk*" (Smith 1991: 25–26). It is through the efforts of such Romantic thinkers that the principle of cultural individuality—and hence cultural autonomy—first makes its appearance.[14]

14. Todorov argues that Las Casas was in fact groping toward this kind of position in his later writings (Todorov 1984: 189–92), but even if he was, this does not appear to have had much impact. Indeed, as Todorov notes, it would have been quite difficult for a Church official to have articulated a position that contained such an element of relativism—particularly in an era when heretics were still being literally burned at the stake.

But what about the salvation narrative, the faith in progress, the commitment to universal reason? If nations were culturally distinct, and if political communities could articulate their own set of laws that were appropriate for themselves alone, what was to prevent humanity from fragmenting into mutually isolated associations with nothing in common and no reasonable way to work out their differences? This was a particularly vexing problem for anyone pursuing this strategy, as it held the possibility that universal and transhistorical foundations for political and ethical concerns might not be possible.[15] The effort to reconstitute universality, which might not have been necessary had principles of particularity not been advanced, was therefore a moral, epistemological, and political problem all at the same time. Out of efforts to resolve it would come an important conjuncture in the genealogy of 'Western Civilization': Hegel's philosophical history.

HEGEL'S DIALECTICAL SOLUTION

In this activity of the World Spirit, states, nations, and individuals arise with their *particular determinate principle*. This principle is displayed and actualized in their form of government and in the entire range of their conditions. These states, nations, and individuals are aware of all this, and are deeply committed to the interests involved. Yet at the same time they are the unconscious tools and organs of the World Spirit in its deep activity, wherein these forms pass away, while the Spirit implicitly and explicitly prepares and works out its own transition to its next higher stage. (1988: 100)

This quotation—§344 of the *Philosophy of Right*—sums up Hegel's ingenious solution to the problems raised in the Romantic critique of civilization-in-the-singular. Rather than abandoning either the principle that communities have unique values or the principle that reason can reveal universal truths, Hegel sought to combine these principles dialectically, in a philosophical history that would demonstrate "that Reason rules the world, and that therefore world history has also proceeded rationally" (1986: 20–21). The problem with which Hegel was grappling is directly related to the Romantic notion of individual nations pursuing their own agendas. Were such a conception absolutely accurate, human history as a whole would cease to have any overall meaning, and reason would cease to be a meaningful tool for the articulation of general principles.

15. There were several responses to this problem. Where Scottish Enlightenment thinkers like Hume tried to found a new kind of universal ethics on sentiment and an assumption of a common human nature, Kant found this strategy unsatisfactory inasmuch as it imported merely empirical concerns into a realm that should be based on reason alone. This aspect of the story, although fascinating, is not as directly relevant to my purposes here.

Against this possibility, Hegel argues that the "immense mass of wills, interests, and activities" that appear to make up the history of the world on first approach "are tools and means for the World Spirit to fulfill its end, to raise it to consciousness and actuality" (40). Therefore individuals (by which Hegel means both individual human beings *and* individual nations) retain their individuality, remaining essentially separate entities, but Reason works as it were behind their backs to bring about something greater. Inasmuch as human beings contain the divine in the form of Reason, they are simultaneously tools of the World Spirit *and* ends in themselves, intrinsically related to the goal of World History as the fulfillment of the divine plan (50).

What does this plan entail? According to Hegel, "the essence of Spirit is freedom," which means that Spirit's nature is to emancipate itself from everything external to itself, so that it subsists in itself alone (30). In political terms, this means the liberation of people from natural necessity and the creation of modes of governance that can reconcile the particularity of each individual person with the general imperatives of the group. World History, understood in this sense, is the story of the growth and realization of freedom in this specific sense. As historical, this story unfolds itself in time, beginning with the earliest notions of freedom and proceeding from there. And the direction of this story, for Hegel, is heliotropic: progress follows the path of the sun.

> In the geographical survey the general course of world history is given. The sun, the light, rises in the East [*Morgenlande*].[16] But the light is simple self-relation; that light which is general in itself is at the same time a subject, in the sun . . . World history goes from East to West, for Europe is simply the end of world history, just as Asia is its beginning. For world history there is an East *par excellence*, as opposed to the geographical "East" which is merely relative; although the earth is a sphere, world history does not make a circle around it, but has a much more definite East, and that is Asia. This is where the external physical sun comes up, just as it goes down in the West. (133–34)

From this follows Hegel's division of World History into a succession of four "worlds": an Oriental world in which it is known only that "*one* is free," the despot; a Greek world and a Roman world in which "some are free, but not the human being as such"; and a Germanic world in which all humans are free as such [*der Mensch als Mensch frei ist*], at least in principle (31). It is

---

16. *Morgenland* is also Luther's word for the Orient (Stephanson n.d.: 17). These religious resonances are quite important to Hegel's argument, since the goal of philosophical history is to "recognize the ways of Providence, its means and appearances in history" and "to connect these to that universal principle" so as to determine "what the final goal of the world might be" (Hegel 1986: 26–29). Philosophical history is therefore an appropriation (more precisely, an *Aufhebung*) of the older salvation narrative into a broader set of concerns.

significant that the particularities that Hegel identifies for his stages of the realization of Spirit are *not* nations, but larger collectivities—with the significant exception of ancient Greece (about which more in a moment). These "worlds" play out their destinies in isolation, as the peoples and nations within them "produce themselves" out of their particular concrete spirit. But the kind of spiritual progress that Hegel has in mind does *not* consist of each group eventually coming to consciousness of freedom; each specific group is limited by the potentials of its "world" and its role in World History. Spirit strives to know itself, but as Spirit comes to know itself in one particular world, that world and the people within it experience "decline" [*Untergang*], and World History moves on to another world and other people. The Oriental, Greek, and Roman worlds each played their role, but as Spirit moved on they inevitably declined so as to make room for a more full expression of Spirit in a succeeding world—which unconsciously works out the implications of some problem in the realization of freedom that was posed by the earlier worlds. "The change which is decline is, at the same time, the emergence of a new life; out of life comes death, but out of death a new life emerges." When one world has lived out its destiny, it dies, but Spirit is reborn. But this can only be understood at a certain point in World History.

> This is a great thought, which was grasped by Orientals . . . in relation to natural life in general there is the well-known image of the *Phoenix,* which eternally prepares its funeral pyre and consumes itself upon it, so that a new, rejuvenated, fresh life can emerge out of its ashes. *This image is, however, only Asiatic and Eastern, not Western* [*morgenländisch, nicht abendländisch*]. The Spirit which consumes its outer shell does not simply go over to another shell, and does not simply arise rejuvenated out of the ashes of its corporal form; instead it emerges exalted, transfigured, as a purer Spirit. (97–98, emphasis added)

Although the World Spirit progresses toward its destiny and fulfillment, individual people and nations do not; they serve as the occasions for Spirit to work itself out. And they cannot really understand one another, as they are arranged at different points along the course of Spirit's unfolding; the most that can happen is that thinkers in a later stage—further to the west—can appreciate what was implicitly contained in the images and thoughts of earlier worlds.

Hegel is not specifically deploying the word "civilization," but his solution to the problem of particularity deploys something very much like a number of civilizations in an effort to come to grips with the course of World History. These incommensurable worlds remain linked in an unfolding process of Absolute Reason, but at the same time they remain unique historical totalities—and thus very different from older notions of a single, unitary 'civilization.'

THE *BILDUNG* IDEAL AND ITS CRITICS

Hegel cast a long shadow over German academia in the nineteenth century. The subtlety of Hegel's dialectical formulation, however, was lost on many of his successors in German academia, who took advantage of the elements of civilizational incommensurability in Hegel's account and elaborated a rather more unambiguously exclusive and pluralistic conception of human communities. In particular, Hegel's account of World History served as the framework within which German scholars thought about issues relevant to 'civilization,' as it was self-evident from a Hegelian perspective that the civilization of the contemporary ("Germanic") world formed, in some way, a unity—and that Prussia, and later Germany, had a privileged role as a world-historical nation within that unity. The heart of this world-historical role rested on the widespread idea that the Germans enjoyed a privileged relationship with the Greeks and should pursue an educational ideal that would allow them to emulate the exemplary synthesis of qualities best expressed in Greek examples: *Bildung,* or cultivation (Marchand 1996: 26–28). In this way they could fulfill their destiny and advance the course of history, staying true to the imperatives of *Kultur.*

Upon first glance, the existence of this philhellenism seems to *contradict* the Hegelian notion that successive historical worlds are improved manifestations of Spirit, and hence that earlier worlds have nothing on that score to teach later ones. But Hegel had explicitly left room to appreciate Greek excellence in realms other than the political, suggesting that even though constitutional principles did not transfer from age to age, "things are completely different with science [*Wissenschaft*] and art," including philosophy (1986: 66). The ideal of being educated like a Greek was a cultural ideal, not necessarily a political one (although it had clear political consequences); the desire was for a Greek sense of beauty rather than a Greek constitution (Marchand 1996: 4–6). At the same time, there was a consciousness that the Greeks were not precisely *like* modern Germans, and were not actually their direct spiritual ancestors; the Greeks were instead the highest human ideal. While the German Romantics

> insisted on the infinite variety of societies, and the absence of universals proclaimed by the Enlightenment, they saw a general direction provided by an inner order, supreme force or being. The Greeks were perceived as having transcended mundane chaos and being closer to the ineffable best. . . . It was precisely this . . . that made the Greeks the central concern of *Bildung,* through which the young leaders of Germany were to understand and remake themselves. (Bernal 1987: 288)[17]

17. Note that by my use of a number of Martin Bernal's observations I am not endorsing his conclusions about the reasons for philhellenism in Germany and elsewhere. Bernal attributes much of the impetus for the "cult of Greece" to pure racism, which strikes me as entirely too simplistic an account of the relationship between identity and knowledge.

The notion of *Bildung* had been institutionalized in Prussia during the educational reform measures implemented after Napoleon's victory over Prussia in 1806. Wilhelm von Humboldt, as Prussian minister of education shortly after this catastrophe, put together a curriculum based around the primacy of the study of the Greek language and a hostility to "practical" subjects; the aim was to communicate the ideal of the Greek way of life through an immersion in the Greek world manifested in art and literature (Iggers 1983: 52–53). Humboldt wanted students "to treat classical texts as historical creations" and learn to appreciate the entire world that they represented, rather than simply borrowing flourishes and allusions from them (Gress 1998: 60–62). The overriding lesson was supposed to be one involving balance and nobility, rather than anything more utilitarian (Marchand 1996: 30–31; Ringer 1969: 85–87). The world of the Greeks would thus serve as the model for the world of the Germans.

The line from *Bildung* to a notion of 'the West' is, however, not a simple one. Almost from the moment of the first institutionalization of the *Bildung* system, its advocates were on the defensive, striving to protect their ideal from charges of irrelevancy and from the tendency of lower-level instruction in the Greek language to devolve into rote memorization of grammatical rules (Marchand 1996: 31). But more problematic were the internal critiques, which exploited some of the tensions within the *Bildung* notion itself. One of those tensions lay in the fact that the superiority of the Greeks was supposed to be in the aesthetic field rather than the political, which meant that *physical* objects were available as objects for interpretation as well as textual ones. Hence archaeology, as a field devoted to the recovery and preservation of physical artifacts, had a claim to a role in the study of the Greeks (1996: xx). The problem was that archaeology as a practice was precisely the opposite of the ideal of *Bildung,* as it required technical skills and specializations that went well beyond the general "cultivation" expected of someone educated in the neohumanist mode.

In addition, scholars laboring under the influence of Hegelian idealism generally sought to piece fragments together so as to form "individualities." "An idea, an epoch, a nation: all these may be pictured as 'individualities,' if it is their uniqueness and undivided 'concreteness' which is to be emphasized" (Ringer 1969: 98–99). But archaeology, dealing with particular locations and collections of artifacts, tended to focus "upon full study of the 'physiognomy' of each site, without regard to the artistic value of excavated fragments," and hence to challenge the simpler understanding of "Greek art" or even "the Greeks" as a single unproblematic entity. In addition, the very act of unearthing sculptures from different eras of Greek history—such as the now-famous Pergamum Altar—further fragmented the unity of the ancient world (Marchand 1996: 97–99). The quest for a more accurate picture of the Greeks was calling the traditional ideal image of those Greeks into question.

At the same time, scholars and mavericks alike were increasingly applying archaeological and philological methods to the study of peoples *other than* the Greeks. Heinrich Schliemann undertook expeditions into the Ottoman Empire, where he claimed to have discovered Homer's Troy (a claim that remains controversial today). Others excavated sites in Egypt. Within Germany itself, Jacob Grimm and his brother Wilhelm collected folktales and traced the diffusion of particular words, while local amateurs collected German artifacts for display in local museums (Marchand 1996: 170–72; Mazlish 2001: 295; Smith 1991: 61–62). Wilhelm Riehl, one of the earliest scholars to conduct empirical research on the daily lives of German peasants, articulated a theory of society in which the peasantry formed the true essence of Germany and need to be preserved in their traditional way of life (Smith 1991: 133–35). Such notions tended to support a very different understanding of the proper role for modern Germany to follow: an acceptance and celebration of a "barbarian" past was a far cry from any effort to emulate the Greeks. Indeed, this valorization of the barbarian sometimes linked up with the opposition to *Zivilisation* in regarding the Germans as having traditionally been the brave defenders of *Kultur* against Rome and its supposed decadence (Marchand 1996: 159–62).[18] The application of philological and archaeological methods to non-Greek peoples thus had the potential to tear the *Bildung* ideal completely apart, separating the Germans from the ancient world in a fundamental way.

The philhellenic response to these challenges was twofold. The first defensive move was a reassertion of the exemplary nature of the Greeks, via an explicit discounting of what might have been read as evidence of influence of other peoples on Greek culture (Bernal 1987: 362–64; Marchand 1996: 44–47). But keeping the Greeks essential and pure did not justify their continued centrality to articulations of German national identity. This link was instead made by scholars who stressed the importance of continuing to educate German youth in the classical fashion for the development of such virtues as obedience and "heroic self-sacrifice for the sake of the nation." The use of the Greek ideal as a standard by which to judge the present, which had begun to surface in the writings of people like Nietzsche, also helped to maintain the Greeks as the appropriate goal for Germans to aim for; such thinkers pressed the Greek/German parallel to ever more extreme lengths, until "in effect, the Germans *were* the Greeks; they represented, as it were, the Greeks to modern

18. A debate raged in the middle of the nineteenth century about the significance of "the limes, the series of Roman fortifications on the Empire's German frontier," with historical associations in the east maintaining that "the limes formed the frontier of Germanic civilization against the West, rather than, as more classically inclined Rhinelanders and Bavarians believed, the barricade erected by the civilized Romans against the barbarians of the East" (Marchand 1996: 168).

Europe" (Gress 1998: 65–66).[19] These tactics were moderately successful, but philhellenes remained constantly on the lookout for additional ways to demonstrate and strengthen this connection.

ABENDLAND

Philhellenes would find what they sought in a rather unusual place: an appeal to a unity of Europe that had briefly existed under Charlemagne. This was the conservative Catholic concept of the *Abendland,* literally the "evening country" or the place where the sun goes down; it was quite intimately connected to the older heliotropic tradition.[20] But the *Abendland* notion that gained currency after the French Revolution and began to spread among Catholic intellectuals thereafter differed from the older salvation narrative in one crucial respect: instead of merely a *direction,* this *Abendland* was a *location,* an entity of its own, with a cultural and moral essence distinguishing it from other groupings of human beings. This was not 'civilization-in-the-singular,' as *Abendland* was clearly and essentially limited in its membership; one could not simply "join" the *Abendland,* nor could one leave it—although one could *betray* it by abandoning one's heritage and embracing revolutionary or decadent ideas.

Thus it is no accident that the first articulators of a notion like *Abendland* in the late eighteenth century were those opposed to the French Revolution, chief among them Burke and de Maistre, and those looking for an alternative to the fragmentation of modern life, principally thinkers like Novalis (Delanty 1995: 79–82; Stephanson n.d.: 17–18).[21] The precise *boundaries* of the *Abendland* remained in flux throughout the period of its articulation, although one thing is quite unambiguously clear: the heart of the *Abendland* is Christianity, and often the Catholic Church in particular—but at any rate, Christianity understood as a *whole,* a unit. Burke suggested that "nothing is more certain than that our manners, our civilization, and all the good things which are connected with manners and civilization have, in this European world of ours, depended for ages upon two principles and were, indeed, the result of both combined: I mean the spirit of a gentleman and the spirit of religion," specifically the Christian religion. Burke often refers to this combination as "chivalry" and argues that "it is this which has given its character to modern Europe. It is this which distinguished it under all its forms of government, and

19. Gress dates this equation earlier, finding it in the statements of some scholars at the outset of the nineteenth century; I do not see the matter as quite so unambiguous, as discussions about this continued throughout the nineteenth century.

20. Hegel, as I noted earlier, utilizes the term in opposition to *Morgenland* (the East or the Orient).

21. I choose my words advisedly; none of these thinkers, so far as I know, actually used the word *Abendland* in their construction of a past ideal to serve as a ground on which to

distinguished it to its advantage, from the states of Asia and possibly from those states which flourished in the most brilliant periods of the antique world" (1987: 67–69). Burke's "Europe," although decidedly Christian, is clearly one civilization among others, unlike the older notions of 'Christendom.' It is an *Abendland* notion.

But such an *Abendland* notion could not really solve the problem faced by those German intellectuals seeking to strengthen the connection between Greece and Germany, particularly since the Greeks were not Christian (Gress 1998: 58–59). A solution came from a rather unlikely source: a series of debates within Russia about whether the country was a part of Europe or not, and hence whether it should follow other European countries down the road of industrialization. Needless to say the Russian intellectuals participating in this debate had no intention of solving political and cultural dilemmas faced by German philhellenes; the intersection of the German and Russian debates is quite accidental, but full of argumentative potentials that were eagerly seized upon.

Within Russia, a debate had emerged in the middle of the nineteenth century between Slavophiles and Westerners, who were divided about which future course Russia should pursue: should it remain detached from Europe and true to a "Slavic" essence, or should it take up a position in the circle of European nations? In the period leading up to the Crimean War, the czarist state had seen itself as defending "Holy Russia" separate from Europe, but defeat in the war convinced state officials to begin programs of "Europeanization" in earnest, in an effort to catch up to those European countries that were now demonstrably more powerful than it (Neumann 1996: 47). There was opposition to this from the Slavophiles (rapidly becoming pan-Slavists) who insisted on Russia's essential *difference* from contemporary Europe. In the writings of Nikolay Danilevskiy, this difference took absolute form: Russia and Europe—which Danilevskiy defined as "Germano-Latin civilization"— represented completely separate historical types, with nothing in common. Thus, efforts to "Westernize" Russia were foredoomed to failure, as they represented the importation of essentially foreign institutions and practices (Hughes 1952: 44–48; Neumann 1996: 55–59). Other pan-Slavists took a slightly less extreme path, suggesting that "what is characteristic of contemporary Russia and contemporary Europe is the outcome of historical processes with common roots in ancient Greece. The Russian variant, far from being a poor copy of the European one, is, to the contrary, a morally superior out-

---

critique the present. Novalis preferred *Christendom,* while Burke and de Maistre preferred *Europe.* But what they are articulating is clearly part of the *Abendland* commonplace: a notion of a spiritual or cultural unity that underlay a number of countries and excluded some others.

come of a parallel historical process" (Neumann 1996: 53). But the pan-Slavists generally agreed that Russia represented something quite different from
Europe.

Abendland partisans, particularly German scholars, seized on this notion
quite eagerly. Somewhat at variance with de Maistre's original hopes that a
Catholicized Russia could revitalize a Europe wracked by revolution, late-
nineteenth-century intellectuals argued to the contrary that Russia was,
indeed, essentially separate from Europe and outside of the *Abendland* entirely
(GoGwilt 1995: 227). In adopting portions of the Slavophile position, however, Europeans did not pick up the positive evaluation of the separate Russian essence; Russia was essentially different from 'the West,' but in a *bad* way.
The other consequence of this intersection of debates is that the Slavophile
essentializing of 'the West' was accepted as the heart of the *Abendland,* so that
industrial capitalism, democracy, and freedom were seen as fundamentally
Western notions, instead of being seen as universal values that happened to
have manifested themselves in Europe. Previous discussions of these notions
had not regarded them as fundamentally 'Western' in any real sense but traced
their origin to something other than a cultural and spiritual heritage under-
pinning the European countries: either to an unfolding of universal history or
to some process that could be transplanted and replicated elsewhere (such as
the formation of capital in Marx).[22] This underscores the importance of the
Russian debates, in which outsiders had defined the essence of a community
to which they did not wish to belong (31).

These essential 'Western' values and principles could now quite easily be
linked with the exemplary Greeks, particularly through rather selective readings of concepts like 'democracy' in which "German scholars praised Athen-
ian democracy when it strengthened the state, and reviled democratic rule
when they perceived it to threaten the state's security" (Marchand 1996:
141–42). In a way, the Greeks could be called into service as a way of differentiating Germany from Russia and even provide Germany with a new histori-

---

22. Max Weber also began to work in this field quite early, although his efforts were
considerably more nuanced than those of many of his more conservative contemporaries.
Much of his work after the turn of the century focused on one central question: "What
combination of circumstances called forth the broad range of ideas and cultural forces that
on the one hand arose in the West, and only in the West, and on the other hand stood—
at least as we like to imagine—in a line of historical development endowed in all civilizations with significance and validity?" (Weber 2002: 149). The distinctiveness of the West,
its essential separateness from other world civilizations, becomes Weber's dominant theme
in his researches into the economic ethics of world religions, the origins of capitalism, and
even the character of modern democratic politics (Mommsen 1986). As I discuss later, Talcott Parsons utilizes Weber in precisely this way in advocating fairly extensive programs for
postwar German reconstruction.

cal role of protecting the *Abendland* from Russian barbarism. Thus the contemporary Germans could continue as the spiritual *and civilizational* heirs of the Greeks, united by their common participation in the *Abendland.*

Disseminating the Novel Commonplace

A rhetorical commonplace, once invented, has little impact on the course of events unless it manages to be spread around widely enough that policymakers can draw upon it in their efforts to legitimate a particular policy. A logically ideal formulation for making some course of action acceptable can only be causally relevant if it can be meaningfully deployed; if speakers and their audiences have not been exposed to the commonplaces on which the formulation supervenes beforehand, then the formulation can play no role in producing the outcome. It is therefore necessary to account for the *dissemination* of the notion of 'Western Civilization' that was stabilized during the nineteenth-century debates and to ascertain how the notion traveled from German academic debates into the public at large—into the American and German publics in particular. In this section, I highlight the role played by two overlapping types of social relationships: education and the efforts of public intellectuals. Rhetorical commonplaces, like everything else in social life, travel across concrete social ties, which may however be quite independent of particular formal institutions; it is certainly the case that "ideas do not float freely" and are always bound up with empirical social relations, although they may operate quite independently of particular formal institutions like the state (Risse-Kappen 1994). Tracing those concrete ties is the aim of this section.

THE "IDEAS OF 1914"

The *Kulturpropaganda* (cultural propaganda) of the "ideas of 1914" articulated when the First World War broke out played an important role in disseminating the novel commonplace. The "ideas of 1914" encompassed a variety of documents and manifestos, ranging from purely polemical broadsides to Thomas Mann's *Reflections of a Nonpolitical Man,* all of which "sought to prove Germany's cultural apartness from, and superiority to, the West" (Stern 1961: 207). Part of the way in which this was accomplished was to stress the distinctiveness of German thought and *Kultur* as against the decrepit *Zivilisation* of its enemies. This was a traditional opposition among German intellectuals (196), linked to a sense that modern life was artificial and ungrounded. As Nietzsche expressed it:

> The high points of culture and civilization do not coincide: one should not be deceived about the abysmal antagonism of culture and civilization. The great moments of culture were always, morally speaking, times of corruption; and conversely, the periods when the taming of the human animal ("civilization")

was desired and enforced were times of intolerance against the boldest and most spiritual natures. Civilization has aims different from those of culture—perhaps they are even opposite—(1967: §121)

Such a characterization seemed to call for conscious efforts to overcome the fragmentation of modern life, through the assertion of a fundamentally different approach to social relations.[23] The onset of the war seemed to promise an opportunity to bring this *Kultur*-based approach to fruition, by throwing off the dominance of France and Britain and paving the way for a cultural rebirth. An early and fairly dramatic expression of this hope was the manifesto *Aufruf an die Kulturwelt!* (which might be, and conventionally is, translated "Appeal to the Civilized World," except that this obscures the all-important fact that the German title does *not* speak of *Zivilisation* at all), signed by ninety-three prominent German intellectuals and issued in October 1914 as a response to allegations of German brutality in occupied Belgium (Gruber 1975: 66–67). One of the central goals of the document was to attack the "two Germanies" thesis primarily propounded by a number of French intellectuals, which maintained that German philosophy and German militarism had little to do with one another; there was thus a good Germany and a bad Germany, an intellectual Germany worth preserving and an imperial Germany that needed to be destroyed (Hanna 1996: 9–10). Against this, German intellectuals maintained that "Germany was 'about' *Kultur* . . . or at least about the symbiosis of the ascetic soul and the strong body" (Marchand 1996: 232). The German military was required in order to *preserve* German *Kultur* from those who would subvert or destroy it; this was why the war was being fought in the first place (Hanna 1996: 87–88). Along these lines, Thomas Mann "sought to refute Allied claims that the democratic progressive West was fighting a militaristic, reactionary Germany" by arguing "that the German imperial regime was more representative and democratic than the mechanical vote-counting systems of the Western democracies," and Ernst Troeltsch proposed a "German idea of freedom" somewhat divergent from the liberal individualist notion (Liebersohn 1988: 74–75; Stern 1961: 87). All in all, cultural differences from 'the West' were stressed, and utilized as a justification for the war itself.

The conventional reading of these "ideas of 1914" is that they represent a form of the German *Sonderweg* tradition, which maintained that Germany was following a fundamentally different path than that of its neighbors. But

23. Nietzsche himself is decidedly more ambiguous about this than some of his readers, however; where many of them sought to go back to an earlier and more natural time, the direction of Nietzsche's thought is relentlessly forward, a passage through nihilism to a fundamentally new form of life. Taken as a whole, Nietzsche does not represent a romantic longing for an idealized past, although many of his readers seem to have confused his radicalism with conservatism—a typical problem when dealing with the thought of the "conservative revolutionaries" (Bourdieu 1988: 16–21; Sieferle 1995: 43).

there is a critical ambiguity here that needs to be noted, an ambiguity that is obscured by the fact that in English there is only one word for 'the West' while in German there are *two: West* and *Abendland*. While the former is persistently associated with France and England and *Zivilisation,* the latter is associated with an encompassing community that encompasses all sides of the conflict. I do not want to make too much of this difference of terms, because most people's terminological usage is inconsistent, but keeping the *conceptual* distinction in mind helps to clarify what the "ideas of 1914" were all about: German *Kultur* was arrayed against the "civilized" *West,* but *not,* for the most part, against the *Abendland.*

In fact, there was a strain of *Kulturpropaganda* that upheld Germany as the defender of the West from "Roman-French leveling universalisms" and Asiatic (and later Bolshevik) hordes (Marchand 1996: 235–36). Ernst Troeltsch, after proclaiming a separate German idea of freedom, turned to historical research on the values of Western Civilization in an effort to discover valid principles for action "through a 'critical selection of the cultural possession of a great system of interaction, such as in our case the whole of Western Civilization'" (Iggers 1983: 191, quoting Troeltsch). This is clearly something more than an abandonment of the *Abendland* and looks instead considerably more like a struggle *within* the *Abendland,* a quest for "a stable intellectual order to guide the present" and an effort to steer the *Abendland* in one direction rather than another (Iggers 1983: 193–94; Liebersohn 1988: 76).

I am not claiming that this kind of interpretation of the "ideas of 1914" was the only one floating around academic discourse. Arthur Moeller van den Bruck, coiner of the notion of a "third *Reich*" and later a leading figure in the circle of conservative critics of the Weimar Republic, developed the "ideas of 1914" in a rather different direction immediately after the war, suggesting that Germany could stand between East and West in its own *Sonderweg* in order to develop a unique solution to the problems of modernity (Stern 1961: 219–21). But there was another option, the *Abendland* option, which Mann, Troeltsch, and—as I will argue later—Oswald Spengler advocated, a way of circumscribing a critique of 'the West' (*West*) with a commitment to 'the West' (*Abendland*) itself, even if this commitment was less a choice and more a necessity. The two strategies have very different implications. And (to foreshadow my argument somewhat) it is the *Abendland* strain that survives Germany's defeat in the Second World War and eventually serves as the legitimating rhetoric for Germany's reconstruction as a part of 'the West.'

INTRODUCTION TO CONTEMPORARY CIVILIZATION IN THE WEST

As the "ideas of 1914" helped to propel the notion of 'Western Civilization' into German political debates, they also provoked a reaction from the opposing side, particularly in the United States. As a result of this reaction, the notion of 'Western Civilization' became something *obvious,* something almost unquestionable, because it was knitted into the fabric of everyday life in a fairly comprehensive manner. It is not the case that before this time no one had discussed the ancient Greeks and Romans, or even that no one had noted the connections between elements of modern society and principles articulated millennia previously. It was just that, for most people, ancient history was simply that: ancient history, and certainly of little contemporary relevance. America, after all, was founded upon the notion of making a clean break with history, creating a *novos ordo seclorum,* a new order for the ages (Stephanson 1995: 5–6). And throughout the nineteenth century, most Americans—including many political elites and intellectuals—"remained deeply suspicious of Europe, its institutions, and its culture" (Levine 1996: 60).

The transformation of this view involved a radical reorientation of American higher education, such that young Americans could be taught that they were in fact a part of the larger civilizational community of 'the West.' This was accomplished through what David Gress has termed "the Grand Narrative," which "presented the West as a coherent entity emerging triumphantly through history in a series of stages," telling a tale of relatively simple progress from antiquity to modern times (1998: 39). Eric Wolf is undoubtedly correct that this developmental scheme is "misleading," a judgment with which Gress concurs (Wolf 1982: 5). But regardless of its *validity,* its *impact* is unquestionable. The Grand Narrative is the basic account of 'the West' that one finds in the "culture wars" of the past few decades; no matter which side of those wars a speaker is (or was) on, a shared commitment to a notion of an essential 'Western Civilization' stretching back to the Greeks characterizes almost the entire debate, with the only difference being whether one celebrates or condemns this 'West' (Gress 1998: 468).[24]

Unlike many of the genealogical shifts traced in previous sections, the decision to teach 'Western Civilization' was, in many respects, quite a deliberate one: the occidentalist commonplace was, in this instance, disseminated by design. The central vehicle for this dissemination was a general education course initially established in 1919 at Columbia University called "Contempo-

24. Gress himself tries to present an alternative—but equally substantialist—'West' as a way out of the debate; in doing so, he replicates some of the very problems that he identifies with the Grand Narrative and transforms history into ideology pure and simple (Jackson 1999). This is only a severe problem to the extent that Gress believes his 'West' to be immune to the charges he levels against the Grand Narrative, which he clearly does (1998: 8, 47). His account of the Grand Narrative itself, however, is quite illuminating, even if Gress's purpose in criticizing it is a purpose that is ultimately just as analytically questionable as the Grand Narrative itself.

rary Civilization," popularly known as CC.[25] For decades prior to this time, a debate had been waged within American higher education about the proper function of colleges and universities, a debate that largely concerned a choice between two German models: the notion of *Bildung,* dominant in the German *Gymnasium,* and the notion of specialized technical training, featuring such German innovations as "lectures, seminars, libraries, and laboratories." That Germany should loom so large in these nineteenth-century American educational debates is not surprising; the prestige of a German Ph.D. was high, as German universities were the very model of academic institutions "from the early nineteenth century until the advent of Nazism," far overshadowing French and British institutions (Gruber 1975: 17–19). Proponents of *Bildung* advocated that the four-year college in particular take on a "function . . . analogous to the *Gymnasium*" in Germany (Thomas 1962: 22–24).

In the short term, this educational philosophy lost out to the rise of the elective system and the increasing specialization and professionalization of different "disciplines" of knowledge (Allardyce 1982: 697). But proponents of an American equivalent of *Bildung* tried to reverse this trend, scoring some successes with a general historical survey course instituted at Harvard in 1873 (Allardyce 1982: 700) and Charles Eliot Norton's fine arts survey course, also at Harvard, that began with the Greeks and proceeded through various moments of European art until it came to the present day and America. Norton maintained that "modern students could best apprehend their own civilization by studying the influences that made it, by learning of 'the historic evolution of our civilization'"; his course was designed to do precisely this (Turner 1999: 384–85).

These courses took over and furthered the *Abendland* notion of 'the West' that had emerged in the German academy, modified only by the insertion of the United States into the same historical sequence.[26] When Nicholas Murray

25. In fact, the course had several aims. Another of the contemporary concerns that went into the course was the need for a socialization function, some way that students—particularly the children of recent immigrants—could be imbued with a sense of civic responsibility and sound common values. CC, with its "Western Civ ideal," would serve a "homogenizing and normative" function: to "socialize the young from whatever particularist background traditions to a uniform standard of thinking and behaving that ought to characterize America's expanding educated class" (Lougee 1982: 727). The unity that CC promised would be not merely a curricular unity but a social and cultural one.

26. When Hegel had articulated his scheme of World History, he had termed America "the land of the future, in which world-historical importance will be revealed in the time to come. . . . it is a land of longing for all those who are tired of the historic arsenal of the old Europe." But he wanted little to do with it, declaring instead an intention to deal with "what is and always is—Reason," rather than with what might come to pass in the future: "Let us therefore set the New World and the dreams which may be connected with it aside, and return our attention to the Old World, which is the theatre of World History" (Hegel 1988: 114–15).

Butler, president of Columbia University, became a supporter of general education, his stated reason was that "that common body of knowledge which held educated men together in understanding and in sympathy" had been weakened by specialization and the elective system, and that what was required was "a unifying force of common understanding, common appreciation and common sentiment" (Butler quoted in Levine 1996: 58). As in the German educational system—and directly indebted to the experience of many in American higher education with the German system[27]—the technique for doing this was an emphasis on the unity of the cultural world to which the students belonged, including its ancient origins; the antidote to specialization was occidentalism.[28]

The call for such a course of instruction fused with a more immediate concern in 1917: to provide a context for understanding the First World War. From the beginning of the conflict, even before the United States was directly involved as a belligerent, American academics reacted to the "ideas of 1914" by depicting the conflict as a war of fundamentally opposed conceptions of society, a "fight for civilization and human liberty against barbarism" in which "'the character of civilization itself' was at stake" (Gruber 1975: 57). Accordingly, part of the function of the American university should be to teach people what the stakes were and thus to promote the wider social unity of a shared purpose centered on the defense of civilization.

The American entry into the war raised this possibility in a more concrete way. In April 1918 the War Department established the Students' Army Training Corps, a program whereby students on college campuses would enlist in the army but remain at school until they graduated, whereupon they would be sent to the front (Gruber 1975: 216–18). The students would be required to participate in a "War Issues" course, which would—in the words of the program's director—"enhance the morale of the members of the corps by giving them an understanding of what the war is about and of the supreme impor-

27. For American students in the nineteenth century, graduate education largely meant attending a European university, and German universities above all. "Between 1820 and 1920 almost nine thousand Americans studied in German universities," learning "to apply the methods of science to the accumulation and analysis of data," whether that data was physical or historical (Gruber 1975: 17).

28. The *Report of the Harvard University Committee on the Objectives of a General Education in a Free Society,* although not submitted until 1945 and not published until 1946, introduced its survey of the philosophy of general education in the United States by asserting, "We are all part of an organic process, which is the American, and more broadly, the Western evolution," and that this process had culminated with the concept of the dignity of man: "This concept is essentially that of the western tradition: the view of man as free and not as slave, as an end in himself and not a means" (Harvard Committee 1946: 46). General education, as opposed to specialized instruction, was directly intended to affirm this overarching civilizational unity.

tance to civilization of the cause for which we are fighting." This course, looked at by many faculty members as the only redeeming feature of having soldiers on campus, "had a broad purpose and no uniform syllabus," which meant that particular institutions could draw up their own variant (238–39). The Columbia University faculty used this opportunity to articulate a course that would address overspecialization and serve as the American equivalent of *Bildung.*

What was taught at Columbia was the vast sweep of 'Western Civilization' as a way of explaining present arrangements and why the United States was participating in a war against Germany; ironically, in so doing it had "adopted what had originally been a German invention, the cult of Greece as the origin of the West." The Columbia War Issues course thus specified the conflict as a struggle for the soul of *Western* civilization, a defense of the Greek and Christian legacy from those who would challenge it. The "Grand Narrative" account of 'the West' that was thus promulgated was a replacement for two earlier attempts to situate the United States in a broader sweep of events: the first was the "Teutonic model," a racial account of how American democratic practices derived from the traditional freedoms and biological vigor of Germanic tribes, and Frederick Jackson Turner's "frontier thesis," which accounted for the distinctiveness of American democracy in terms of the existence of a frontier that produced a mobile population committed to securing its own liberties (Gress 1998: 175–79). The Teutonic model was obviously unacceptable during a war with Germany, and the frontier thesis did not serve to justify American participation in the war, as it was more of an exceptionalist argument. But there was another reason for rejecting these alternatives in favor of a Greek-centered *Abendland* account: the conviction by German-trained Columbia historians like James Harvey Robinson that only such a broad sweep would suffice to ground American history in the past and effectively illuminate present events for students (Allardyce 1982: 704–5). All of these streams came together to create a course that was first offered in the fall of 1918—just in time for the end of the war that it had been in part designed to justify.

In January 1919, the Columbia faculty voted to continue the "War Issues" course under a new name: Introduction to Contemporary Civilization (Cross 1995: 12). Justus Buchler, an early advocate of such a course, later recalled:

> Throughout, "Contemporary Civilization" has had to be qualified by the phrase "in the West"; early in the twenties this became explicit.[29] Such a limi-

29. The formal title of the course was altered to Introduction to Contemporary Civilization in the West, although it remained largely known as CC. When I taught the course in 1998–99 and 1999–2000, the official course enrollment sheet from the registrar still listed the course with this title, although the catalog listed the course simply as Contemporary Civilization.

tation was made, not from dim awareness of the Orient—though Orient-con-
sciousness is perforce greater now [1954] than it was after World War I—nor
from perversity and false cultural pride, but because *Western society is the society
of Western students,* and because the number of available men versed in Eastern
culture has always been lamentably small. (1954: 101, emphasis added)

What Buchler claims as obvious in 1954 was, I suggest, a product of the CC
course having been taught continuously since 1919—and not merely at
Columbia. The basic idea behind CC was first exported to the University of
Chicago by Mortimer Adler, who had imbibed the idea of a "general education" based on the reading of original sources and small-group discussion sections during his time at Columbia.[30] Subsequently, many American universities adopted some version of CC as a required introductory course, often
simply copying the CC syllabus and replicating the course quite precisely;
other programs, like that of Stanford University, were largely designed by faculty members who had taught CC at Columbia (Allardyce 1982: 721; Cross
1995: 47–48). Harvard University's version of the course, entitled "Western
Thought and Institutions," was supposed to be "an examination of the institutional and theoretical aspects of the Western heritage" that "would be building upon the experience derived from courses" such as CC (Harvard Committee 1946: 215–17).[31] Samuel Beer, one of the original teachers of this
Harvard course, visited Columbia and sat in on some CC classes while writing up his syllabus (Beer 2002).

The transfer of CC to other institutions was also aided immensely by the
publication of books specifically designed for use with the course, from textbooks like that of Carleton J. H. Hayes (a student of Robinson and his suc-
cessor at Columbia) to the 1946 two-volume *Introduction to Contemporary
Civilization in the West: A Source Book,* containing over two thousand pages of
primary source readings arranged in the by-now-familiar sequence beginning
with the Greeks and ending with modern American democracy (Cross 1995:
58–60; Levine 1996: 62–63). These sourcebooks were adopted by over two
hundred colleges and universities throughout the country, further spreading
the occidentalist commonplace (Buchler 1954: 108). Institutions seeking to
implement the principles of general education had a ready model in the

30. CC as originally designed did not, in fact, utilize primary source materials, but survey textbooks; the 'primary sources' impetus actually came from John Erskine's Great
Books course, which Adler took and subsequently taught in (Cross 1995: 47; Levine 1996:
51–53). But CC was already moving in the direction of primary sources rather than textbooks, although this shift would not be solidified at Columbia until 1946 (Cross 1995: 58).

31. Curiously, the Harvard recommendations for a mandatory general education program were not even implemented at Harvard, where the newly designed courses were made
optional; the older elective system was retained even in the heart of the new general education program (Richter 1970: 3–4).

Columbia course, which further contributed to the course's widespread adoption (Cross 1995: 60–62). Thus the specific vehicle for disseminating the novel commonplace of 'Western Civilization' throughout American higher education was the Columbia CC course, which largely set the form of *how* a general approach to modern society would be taught: with reference to a broad civilizational community in which modern America was embedded.[32]

SPENGLER'S SURPRISING BEST SELLER

'Western Civilization' is not an "idea" in the essentialist sense; there is no single author who articulates it, no single great work that presents the notion to particular individuals so that they can incorporate it into their future thought and action, and no determinate set of policies or actions that flows from it. In a sense there is no "it" to speak of; there is instead a vague and general commitment to working out the implications of a notion in various concrete social settings. But particular individuals may occupy key positions within this process, serving as the occasion for a concatenation of elements to which they give a compelling form, such that their articulation becomes a vehicle by which the commonplace spreads. Oswald Spengler, with his audacious effort at "predetermining history" by "tracing the still untravelled stages in the destiny of a Culture, and specifically the only Culture of our time and on our planet which is actually in the phase of fulfillment—the West-European–American" (1926: 3), performs this role for the occidentalist commonplace.

Spengler's *The Decline of the West*,[33] the first volume of which was published in Germany in 1918, sold fantastically well, especially for a somewhat dense and lengthy piece of prose. "Within eight years after the original pub-

---

32. Admittedly, these courses reached only a small proportion of the population of the United States directly; from 1918 until 1939 an average of only about 0.735 percent of the population of the United States attended college each year (figures computed from Mitchell 1998). But these college-educated individuals constituted the principal interlocutors in the policy debates about postwar reconstruction and thus set the terms for the debates. In addition, these educated individuals served as opinion leaders for their local communities, a pattern that was strikingly apparent in the activities of the Committee for the Marshall Plan that I will discuss in chapter 6.

33. There is of course no ambiguity about the word *Abendland* in Spengler; right from the work's German title—*Der Untergang des Abendlandes*—Spengler's choice of language is clear. Only occasionally does he utilize the alternative formulation "West-European–American" as he does in the beginning of the work. This is a holdover from the first edition of the book, which was somewhat more European in focus; John Farrenkopf plausibly attributes this shift to Spengler's changing assessment of "the prospects of the United States for attaining global hegemony" (Farrenkopf 2001: 159–60). The American edition of the book—published in 1926—utilized the revised version.

lication, total sales had reached a hundred thousand"; the book was translated into "French, Spanish, Italian, Russian, and Arabic," as well as English, where it has never gone completely out of print (Hughes 1952: 65, 89, 97). The book "was the first of the great blockbusters with which we are now familiar" and was disseminated around the world in almost no time (Coker 1998: 147). This is all the more striking because Spengler has largely *vanished* from our contemporary discussions of social theory and politics; who reads or assigns Spengler in college courses these days? Who discusses his theories or his predictions? The situation now is very different from 1919, when the first volume of Spengler's book was published; 1919 was "the 'Spengler year.' Everyone seemed to be reading him; everyone was wondering just who he was" (Hughes 1952: 89). It is different than the interwar period, in which George Kennan "read him and found much that was congenial," and Paul Nitze "steeped himself in Spengler," while prominent theorists from Theodore Adorno to R. G. Collingwood debated Spengler's main themes (Harper 1996: 160, 224; Hughes 1952: 90–96). It is different than the early 1940s, in which Hans Weigert lamented that his students were reading Spengler "without being instructed to do so" (1942: 121). Until the end of the Second World War, Spengler's work was widely discussed; these discussions were critically important to the dissemination of the occidentalist commonplace.

What did Spengler say that was so striking? In one way, he said nothing original; "in modern Germany there were a great many Spenglers before the master-metahistorian had his day" (Stern 1961: 188). Others had predicted decline according to a cyclical model of history, including Heraclitus and Vico (Fischer 1989: 81–89). Many others had insisted on the uniqueness of historical phenomena and the incommensurability of cultures (Farrenkopf 2001: 83–85). And the cultural and spiritual poverty of the modern age was an old Romantic theme, which had been continued by Ernst von Lasalux and Jakob Burckhardt before Nietzsche pronounced the nineteenth century the age of nihilism (Iggers 1983: 129; Schoeps 1955). It is not Spengler's originality that is important. Indeed, "most of Spengler's new theory of history was already in the air" when he began to write his famous book (Hughes 1952: 13). Spengler's importance, rather, lies in his gathering together of a number of strands and working out their implications on a much broader canvas than had previously been accomplished, and in expressing those implications in a way that many readers found fascinating.

Spengler took all of human history as his field and tried to organize *all* of it into a relatively simple pattern of the birth, growth, maturity, and decline of the "higher Cultures," of which he identified eight "all of the same build, the same development, and the same duration": the Egyptian, the Babylonian, the

Chinese, the Indian, the Mexican, the Classical, the Magian,[34] and the Western, also referred to as the "Faustian" Culture (1928: 36). It was these Cultures that were the real subjects of world history, and not continental notions like "Europe": "The word 'Europe' ought to be struck out of history. There is historically no 'European' type . . . 'East' and 'West' are notions that contain real history, whereas 'Europe' is an empty sound" (1926: 16). Spengler was equally critical of the division of history into ancient, medieval, and modern eras, as it "circumscribes the area of history" and "rigs the stage."

> The ground of West Europe is treated as a steady pole, a unique patch chosen on the surface of the sphere for no better reason, it seems, than because we live on it—and great histories of millennial duration and mighty far-away Cultures are made to revolve around this pole in all modesty. It is a quaintly conceived system of sun and planets! We select a single bit of ground as the natural center of the historical system, and make it the central sun. (17)

Against this traditional point of view, Spengler advocated a comparative approach to Cultures that would proceed by drawing analogies between them at various stages of their life-course and interpreting events in diverse Cultures in terms of their significance for that life-course. Every Culture begins as a vital organism, developing its great works of art and distinctive religion, but eventually passes from the country to the city, from a vital connection with the land to the rootless inhabiting of an artificial environment: "all art, all religion and science, become slowly intellectualized, alien to the land, incomprehensible to the peasant of the soil. . . . The immemorially old roots of Being are dried up in the stone-masses of its cities. And the free intellect—fateful word!—appears like a flame, mounts splendid into the air, and pitiably dies" (1928: 90–92).

This final phase of a Culture Spengler called "Civilization," drawing on but subtly transforming the opposition between *Kultur* and *Zivilisation* characteristic of much German thought about these issues. For Spengler, a Civilization phase is inevitable, but it is also specific to each Culture: "every Culture has *its own* Civilization. In this work, for the first time the two words, hitherto used to express an indefinite, more or less ethical, distinction, are used in a *periodic* sense, to express a strict and necessary *organic succession*. The Civilization is the inevitable *destiny* of the Culture . . . a conclusion, the thing-become succeeding the thing-becoming, death following life, rigidity following expansion." It

---

34. The Magian Culture, according to Spengler, encompassed the early Christians, the Muslims, and Byzantium; this culture never came into its own fully because it was forced to grow and develop under the dominion of the later Roman empire, a condition he refers to as "pseudomorphosis." For the Magian Culture, Spengler suggests, "the pseudomorphosis began with Actium; there it should have been Antony who won," which would have permitted the development of a state-form more suited to the Magian soul (1926: 191).

is in this sense that Spengler understands the relationship between the Greeks
and the Romans: "Greek *soul*—Roman *intellect;* and this antithesis is the dif-
ferentia between Culture and Civilization" (31–32). The transition from one
mode to the other, from "the living body of a soul" to "the mummy of it,"
happened for the West in the early nineteenth century, *and there is no going
back* (353). "Every high Culture *is* a tragedy. The history of mankind *as a whole*
is tragic. But the sacrilege and the catastrophe of the Faustian [Western] are
greater than all others, greater than anything Æschylus or Shakespeare ever
imagined," because the West has developed machine technology to an extent
previously unknown and spread it over the entire planet (1932: 90). The
decline of the West is inevitable, and cannot be avoided.

This decline has very specific implications for the policies that states should
follow in the dying days of their Culture. In Spengler's view, "the Germany of
1914 is a completely 'modern' and 'civilized' country; it represents not the past
of the Faustian Culture, but a specific facet within its late phase." The First
World War, therefore, did *not* represent a struggle of *Kultur* versus *Zivilisation.*

> The World War would simply decide which Civilizational power would dom-
> inate the coming world imperium: loot-seeking anglo-saxon capitalism, or
> Prussian-organized socialism. Therefore, it represented a conflict *within* mod-
> ern civilization, not an antimodern defensive battle *against* civilization. A
> return to a pre-civilized situation in the sense of a normatively superior *Kultur*
> was, historically, no longer on the agenda. (Sieferle 1995: 110–11)

In this sense, Spengler's "position was diametrically opposed to the advocates of the 'Ideas of 1914,'" inasmuch as they sought a radical renewal. Spengler felt that such a thing was impossible (Farrenkopf 1994: 66). Neither Germany nor America could escape the embrace of their common Culture; they
could also not avoid the inevitable clash to determine which power would
dominate the last days of Faustian man. Nor could they stave off its inevitable
decline.

During the interwar period, most readers of Spengler either disagreed with
this conclusion or simply failed to understand it. Conservative circles in interwar Germany approvingly cited his indictment of the Weimar Republic and
its culture, which "must rank among one of the most negative. Where others
saw an outpouring of liberated artistic impulses, Spengler only perceived anarchy and decadence; where others saw democratic freedom, he saw nihilism
and the dissolution of all higher values" (Fischer 1989: 211). Establishing a parliamentary democracy in Germany seemed to him a step backward, a flawed
attempt to return to a stage of Culture that had passed by, instead of going
forward to create "Prussian socialism." Spengler understood Germany's defeat
in the war to provide an opportunity for the German people to rearticulate

their principles and learn from their mistakes, and he understood his own job as helping in that process of rearticulation (Sieferle 1995: 112). But many other conservatives clung to the "ideas of 1914" with their promise of a great cultural renewal. Moeller van den Bruck, for instance, "accepted the morphology of the *Decline*" but argued that "the outcome of the war has separated" Germany and Russia "with finality from the decaying West" and "restored the promise of life and growth" (Stern 1961: 238–39).[35] Conservative intellectuals during the Weimar period were not particularly interested in figuring out whether Germany was a part of some larger cultural community or not, but were more focused on subverting democracy; nonetheless, they kept Spengler's name and works in the forefront of public debate.

American commentators, although equally concerned with Spengler's gloomy forecast, disagreed with their conservative German colleagues in understanding liberal democracy as the salvation of 'the West.' Although Spengler had argued in a 1921 essay that the notion of "decline"[36] was not to be confused with the sinking of an ocean liner (1938: 63), American interpreters persisted in regarding decline as something very much like this.[37] Thus they kept looking for ways to stave it off, either by recovering spiritual resources left out of Spengler's characterization of the West[38] or by simply accusing him of having misunderstood America. I will limit my discussion here to two brief examples.

The German émigré Hans Weigert was deeply troubled in 1942 by the fact that "the young people in our colleges and universities are turning to Spengler in search of light on the questions which everyone asks but no one seems able to answer." The problem, as he saw it, was that an uncritical acceptance of Spengler by American students could destroy "the spiritual forces outside of

35. Spengler, of course, disagreed quite fundamentally with this conclusion but agreed to debate Moeller van den Bruck in front of the "June Club," a group of conservative intellectuals assembled and guided by Moeller (Fischer 1989: 60; Stern 1961: 226–28). The debate, which Otto Strasser described as a "fruitful discussion" between "the Pessimist and the Optimist of the West," took place in 1920; the club members "swore to devote [their] lives to the realization of these visions," a somewhat paradoxical oath given the differences of vision between the two men (Stern 1961: 239, quoting Strasser). The subtleties of Spengler's alternative were lost on the members of the June Club.

36. *Untergang.* Recall that this is also the word that Hegel uses to describe what happens to a self-contained "world" after it has run its course, as well as the ordinary word for the setting of the sun—which, not coincidentally, takes place in the west.

37. This misleading image remains in contemporary interpretations of Spengler as well (e.g., Stephanson, n.d.: 25).

38. David Gress makes this criticism of Spengler as well (Gress 1998: 572–73). Indeed, his entire project can be read as this kind of response to Spengler: accepting the basic presuppositions of the *Abendland* discourse, Gress seeks hope in the West reinventing itself.

Germany" that provide the best chance of proving Spengler's prophecies incorrect.

> The final judgment, therefore, has not yet been passed . . . And the decision will not be made by abstract "destiny." It depends on the choice of free men in the lands where free men still exist and guide the fate of their respective nations. . . . Our duty is to read him [Spengler] as Goethe wanted "The Sufferings of [Young] Werther" to be read when he found that the decadent weakness of its hero so infected and disturbed the minds of youth: "Be a man and do not follow him." (1942: 124)

The basic problem is that "Spengler was blinded by what he believed to be the decadence of the Anglo-American world. His basic mistake was to fail to realize that the infected bodies of nations may develop antitoxins strong enough to save their lives" (129). So, contrary to Spengler's predictions, the United States could revitalize the West by marshaling its resources to defeat Germany. But Weigert did credit Spengler with accurately foreseeing the major challenge that Weigert felt would present itself after the defeat of Germany: the challenge of the non-Western Russian soul, which Spengler "makes us aware of . . . even though he does not solve it for us" (130–31). So the basic *outlines* of the *Abendland* notion are accepted, even if Spengler's specific predictions are held to be unwarranted because of his failure to understand America.

The sociologist Talcott Parsons struck a similar tone in a 1942 radio broadcast, in which he sought to deploy Weberian categories as a kind of antidote to Spenglerian pessimism.[39] Parsons diagnosed Nazism as resulting from the incomplete rationalization of "a society and a culture which more than those of Western Europe was bound up with the patterns and values of the pre-

---

39. In a more academic treatment of the same subject published the same year, Parsons drew on Weber in order to make two specific arguments. First, "modern Western society provides particularly fruitful soil" for the rise of large-scale charismatic movements, because "it is a society in which there are important social stresses and strains, and which shows a great deal of relatively diffuse 'social disorganization'" due to the process of rationalization not having gone far enough yet (1993: 170–71). Second, Parsons effectively transmuted Nazi Germany into a bump on the road of rationalization, a roadblock to the future progress of the West. He argued that this barrier needed to be overcome, citing Weber's discussion of the Persians almost taking over Greece. The struggle against Nazi Germany is of equal importance, Parsons reasoned, because the fundamental issues are the same: rationalization versus a resistance to rationalization in "traditionalist" terms, with the United States playing the role of Greece (champion of rationalization) and Nazi Germany playing the role of Persia (exploiting the strains of rationalization to implement a traditionalist mode of authority) (180–81). Of course, this downplays Weber's decided ambivalence about the likely outcome of such a process of rationalization; I have addressed this issue in more detail in Jackson 2002b.

industrial era" (1993: 220). The solution, therefore, was to break up the Junker class after the war and permit rationalization to take its course unimpeded—and to channel German romanticism away from the pursuit of German national power, either by diverting it into "non-political channels of expression" or by having "the German people as such . . . cease to be" a state unit "but be incorporated into a larger one such as a central European Federation" (224). In this way, what he elsewhere called "the potentialities of human development which our Western 'great society' holds" might be tapped and put to use in creating a stable and peaceful world (184).

This refrain became quite common during the years of the Second World War (Farrenkopf 2001: 272). American policymakers were, in the main, familiar with Spengler and his prophecies; George Kennan had restored his German reading ability by spending the summer of 1926 in Heidelberg with books by Spengler and Goethe (Kennan 1967: 19), while Stuart Hughes, author of one of the more sophisticated treatments of Spengler in English, had been a State Department official with responsibility for research on Europe before he entered academia (Hughes 1952). It would not be too much of an exaggeration to interpret a good deal of postwar American foreign policy as an effort to reply to Spengler, to prove that the West had resources and vitality yet to tap.[40] That said, no one read Spengler and *immediately* decided to reconstruct Germany as a part of 'the West'; postwar German reconstruction is not in this sense "Spenglerian," and Spengler should not be praised for having accurately predicted either the Cold War or its aftermath.[41] But postwar German reconstruction *is* shot through with Spenglerian overtones and prob-

---

40. Indeed, John F. Kennedy's briefing papers for the Vienna summit with Khrushchev included a suggestion to "repeat the theme of confidence of the West—anti-Spenglerism. The West on the rise. All we have to do is hold together" (Ninkovich 1994: 244–45).

41. Here I part company with the most insightful of contemporary Spengler commentators—John Farrenkopf—over the issue of the social-scientific worth of Spengler's early studies. (Farrenkopf focuses more of his attention on Spengler's later, less-well-known work on prehistory and the global impact of technical development; but since very few people read this work—which was only published in fragmentary form—and therefore could not have garnered commonplaces from it, I am largely ignoring it here.) Farrenkopf argues that Spengler should be regarded as "a major prophet of the Cold War" and praised for his contention that "the antagonism between Russia and the West was deep and enduring" (Farrenkopf 2001: 275). But this argument fails to appreciate the connection between Spenglerian discourse and the actual policies pursued that helped to concretize and implement the Cold War. Spengler, like Dean Acheson, is important to my account not because he was correct, but because the commonplaces that he deployed had practical effects in policy debates. Spengler might be very useful as "mythistory" (McNeill 1986) but I seriously doubt that his work represents a good place to begin a sustained empirical analysis of the contemporary world.

lematics, illustrating that Spengler's surprise blockbuster was a critical pathway through which the occidentalist commonplace was disseminated.

'Western Civilization' as Supranational Community

The processes that I have traced in this chapter resulted in a novel commonplace—the occidentalist notion of 'Western Civilization' as one entity among others—being made available for use in discussions during the interwar period and afterward. The availability of a commonplace in no way guarantees its use, particularly since what was imagined and disseminated during the century and a half preceding the Second World War was a vague commonplace and not a concrete argument. Interlocutors still disagreed on precisely what it meant to be a part of 'the West,' and subsequent deployments of the commonplace in policy debates would therefore be characterized by a fair amount of specification by particular speakers toward particular ends. But absent the processes that I have sketched here, no speaker would have had the rhetorical raw materials out of which to construct occidentalist arguments in favor of or opposed to particular policies. Imagination and dissemination provide only possibilities, they do not determine outcomes; they are nonetheless *crucial* to an overall account.

It is also important to note that, although 'the West' is a vague commonplace, its meaning is not *completely* indeterminate. To be somewhat schematic, and to draw together aspects that have been implicit in the preceding discussion, the processes outlined in this chapter produced a commonplace with three basic characteristics that would be tapped in subsequent policy debates. First, 'the West' is a supranational entity, in which other states and nations are "nested" (Ferguson and Mansbach 1996: 47–51). Larger and older than its component states, it is also somewhat superior to them; "civilizational" concerns trump merely national ones.[42] Second, 'the West' is an exclusive, essential community: not everyone is 'Western,' and not everyone can or should be 'Western.' There is thus a modicum of recognition of other civilizations, and some kind of civilizational coexistence is possible—unlike in the rival civilization-in-the-singular discourse. Third, 'the West' is already linked to a series of other commonplaces, such as the defense of liberty and an opposition to Russia; hence it is no great trick to draw out those connections in the ensuing debates. These aspects of the commonplace are quite prevalent in the policy debates about postwar German reconstruction to which I now turn.

42. This is very similar to the role played by national identity articulations in somewhat different organizational contexts (Anderson 1991: 9–11). In this way, I am suggesting that 'the West' is an "imagined community" in much the same way as particular "nations" are.

5 Conflicts of Interpretation, 1944–46

THE SHAPE OF THE postwar world was by no means clear to anyone during the closing days of the Second World War (Eisenberg 1996: 6–7; McAllister 2002: 1–4). Faced with an unclear and ambiguous political situation, people naturally tried to "make sense" of their situations through the deployment of rhetorical commonplaces that had become, so to speak, part of their mental furniture, including 'anticommunism,' 'American exceptionalism,' 'German national unity'—and 'Western Civilization.' Not all possible combinations of these commonplaces made their appearance during the period preceding and following the German surrender in May 1945, as I argued in chapter 3, and in practice there were only four major contenders: exemplarism and occidentalist vindicationism in the United States, and the SPD and CDU positions in the occupied zones of Germany.[1] Each of these combinations of commonplaces pointed in different policy directions, rendering particular options acceptable and ruling others out of bounds.

The success of the two occidentalist strategies is a critical part of the explanation of postwar German reconstruction. Whereas traditional American exemplarism afforded a withdrawal from European affairs and an emphasis on purity and continental defense, vindicationism with an occidentalist flavor afforded and justified some form of ongoing involvement in European affairs on the grounds of deep cultural commonality. Where the SPD strategy afforded a trade-off between demilitarization and unification, the CDU's strategy of *Westbindung* pointed in a very different direction: toward closer ties with France, Britain, and especially with the United States, even at the expense of German unity in the short term. How these occidentalist strategies came to enframe and dominate postwar discussions forms the central subject matter of this chapter and the two that follow it.

---

1. Other alternatives, such as a continuation of the "civilization-in-the-singular" wartime alliance or an explicit turn to communism, were rapidly marginalized in the postwar period—as I discuss at appropriate points in the narrative to follow.

Part of the explanation of this dominance lies in the specific history of the occidentalist commonplace itself. Chapter 4 detailed the intellectual and historical processes that placed 'Western Civilization' on the agenda, so to speak, as a socially sustainable way of conceptualizing the relations between the United States and Western Europe, and it also delineated some of the ties between this commonplace and others prevalent in postwar debates. Of particular importance for the American side of the story is the longtime historical connection between 'the West' and 'civilization' (in the sense of "civilization-in-the-singular"), both because particular speakers sometimes exploited the ambiguity between the two as a way of garnering support for particular policies, and because a crucial shift in American public conceptualizations of the postwar world revolved around the deployment of 'the West' in place of 'civilization'—a shift enabled in part by the historical association between the commonplaces. The conservative, anticommunist character of 'Western Civilization' is also important in both debates, as it enables a deft rhetorical tactic combining the breaking of 'anticommunism' from its connection to exceptional or national notions and its joining to a more proactive, transnational set of institutions and organizations.

This outcome was by no means inevitable. A detailed examination of the particular deployment of occidentalist language is required because the previous chapter has only established the availability of 'Western Civilization' for debates about the postwar world: a tool has been added to the toolbox, but this in itself does not necessitate anything. It was (logically) possible to adhere to the notion that the United States is a part of some larger cultural community called 'Western Civilization' and to remain committed to a policy of continental isolation, or to argue that Germany is a 'Western' country but simultaneously remain opposed to the European Recovery Program or to German membership in such a program. We know this because people actually did. It was also (logically) possible to ignore notions like 'Western Civilization' and seek to ground policy on a quite different basis; again, we know this because people actually did so at the time. But these logically possible alternatives were rendered *practically* and *politically* impossible by the creative and contingent ways that commonplaces were deployed during debates.

To anticipate my argument over the next three chapters, the western zones of occupied Germany that became the BRD were included in the ERP and its various component institutions, and eventually incorporated into NATO, because of the conjunction of two sets of rhetorical deployments. On one hand, the ERP itself was characterized by its supporters as a program to defend 'Western Civilization' from the 'Eastern' (sometimes "Asiatic" or "Oriental") communist menace. This way of framing the issue of European recovery, common to American and European officials and other interlocutors, was an important part of the production of the policy in the first place.

But in order to answer the specific question concerning Germany we need to pay attention to a second set of deployments: those that sought to characterize the emerging BRD as a 'Western' country. The conjunction of these two deployments was critical: Germany was incorporated into the ERP because the ERP was constituted and framed by a desire to save 'Western Civilization,' and Germany as a 'Western' country had a claim to be included on an equal basis. A similar logic subsequently governed rearmament, as the now-established 'Western' BRD could rearm under the auspices of NATO—the "Western Alliance"—and hence contribute to the defense of 'the West' as a more or less equal partner.

I am not claiming that this argument is the *only* argument pointing in the direction of reconstructing West Germany within the framework of the ERP or for including the Federal Republic in the organizational beginnings of European integration, but I am claiming that this portrayal of the issue by policymakers and commentators is an important part of the process. The deployment of 'Western Civilization' served as a unifying principle for many of the other arguments, particularly the more technical arguments about how to raise German productivity, solve the transatlantic balance-of-payments crisis and close the dollar gap, and ensure that an economically powerful Germany would not pose a threat to other countries, particularly France. The publicly acceptable answer to these particular puzzles, as evidenced in the deployments of policymakers and commentators, was an occidentalist answer.

We can best see how occidentalist rhetoric was crucial to the construction of a set of socially plausible options for a settlement of the German question through a closer look at specific moments of contention. In this chapter, I address a number of such moments. First, I discuss plans for the U.S. occupation and the early days of its operation, during which two possible policy directions—the punitive "Morgenthau Plan" and a more active rebuilding of German industrial capacity—squared off. I then discuss events in the occupied zones of Germany in particular and trace the formation of the two major political parties (CDU and SPD) with their characteristic positions and rhetorical strategies, emphasizing how these strategies combined to render a potential alternative position—a united, but communist, Germany—quite illegitimate. Finally, I discuss two important events of 1946: the shift in American policy that culminated in Secretary of State James F. Byrnes's "Stuttgart speech" in September 1946 and the formal commitment to rebuild the western zones of Germany; and the effective marginalization within the CDU of Jakob Kaiser's alternative position based on a neutral, but united, Germany. Central to both of these shifts was the decline of the wartime "civilization-in-the-singular" commonplace and a move toward a more particularistic understanding of the roles that the United States and Germany could and should play in the world.

The Initial Situation: Not "Stunde Null"

There was once a fairly prominent way of reading postwar German history that began with the assumption that Germany in 1945 was something of a blank slate: the complete collapse of the Third Reich meant that whatever postwar government and society was erected could essentially start over from scratch. That year thus represented a fundamental break in German history, a moment when everything changed (Ermarth 1993: 3–4). To the credit of this view, in many ways it did seem as if the end of the war in Europe brought a "moment of hiatus when the people of a nation that had ceased to exist touched rock-bottom, when the hands of the stopwatch were reset to zero and began to tick toward an unthinkable future" (Botting 1985: 122–25). Faced with widespread devastation, the "zero hour" (Stunde Null) argument maintains, anything constructed in postwar Germany would be the result of a deliberate choice either to construct a new social order or to restore the older one. As such, the Stunde Null notion has informed and structured many debates about the character of postwar Germany: was it simply an imposed creation of the occupying powers, or the reassertion of indigenous German traditions?

More recent researchers into this question have largely adopted a more nuanced view, agreeing with John Gimbel's suggestion that postwar Germany "arose from a combination of occupation policies on the one hand, and German tradition on the other" (1986: 150). In a recent volume on the question of "Americanization" in Germany, one scholar argues that "American reforms could only be realized successfully if they were agreed to by the Germans, if they fell on fertile ground, or if they were at least tolerated" (Woller 1993: 33). Even in a situation of such collapse, a legitimation problem remains; policy initiatives must be rendered acceptable, and in order to do this a discursive context must be drawn on. And this context predates the events of 1945, both in the United States and in Germany. The initial situation in the immediate postwar period, then, must be thought of as merely one moment in an ongoing discussion and debate about the character of Germany, and the nature of the role that the United States should play in relating to it. It does no good to take a static snapshot of 1945 without providing some of the immediate historical and discursive context.

THE MORGENTHAU PLAN

During the Second World War, American planning for the occupation of Germany was characterized by a profound disagreement about the German character and the possibility of reforming it. This disagreement was reflected in an institutional split between the postwar policies advocated by the State Department and its allies in the private sector and those advocated by the

Department of the Treasury and its outspoken secretary, Henry Morgenthau Jr. Although the State Department decided early on that "Germany must play a vital role in the postwar European economy," the first semiofficial U.S. policy on postwar Germany bore Morgenthau's name (Eisenberg 1996: 15–19). Both positions derived much of their impetus from a diagnosis of the German character, and a disagreement about how best to deal with Germany to preserve the peace.

The policy known as the "Morgenthau Plan," initialed by President Franklin D. Roosevelt and Prime Minister Winston Churchill at the Quebec Conference in September of 1943, provided that Germany should be partitioned into "two autonomous, independent states," and the Ruhr industrial area "should not only be stripped of all presently existing industries but so weakened and controlled that it cannot in the foreseeable future become an industrial area" (Senate 1950: 503).[2] The justification for these harsh measures involved an essentialist diagnosis of the German character: "For the traditional German," Morgenthau argued, "the will to war goes back as far as our own traditional will to freedom" (1945: 105). Hence the only solution to the "German problem" was to remove Germany's ability to ever make war again, particularly through the elimination of "all heavy industries" because "without them, no matter how savage her aggressive aims might be, she cannot make war" (16). The Morgenthau Plan proposal also fit nicely into the rhetorical strategy that Roosevelt had been pursuing throughout the war: Nazism was a crime against 'civilization,' and it could not be bargained with—hence "unconditional surrender," as part of the plan to utterly extirpate Nazism (Ninkovich 1988: 20–21; Harper 1996: 91–93).

Curiously, Roosevelt took pains in discussions with members of his cabinet a few days after the Quebec Conference to distance himself from the plan that he had just made official U.S. policy (Backer 1971: 15–17). This apparent ambivalence has generated an ongoing historical puzzle about Roosevelt's true motives and plans with respect to Germany. A recent treatment points out that the Morgenthau Plan was quite consistent with things that Roosevelt said in numerous private conversations that revealed a "predisposition to treat postwar Germany harshly" (McAllister 2002: 54). Also, Roosevelt personally intervened in the publication of the War Department's first attempt at an

---

2. In his 1945 book, Morgenthau changed his mind about the Ruhr, noting that "the coal cannot be taken away from the Ruhr . . . so the Ruhr should be taken away from Germany" and "placed under the control of a governing body established by the United Nations . . . Of course, no German should sit on the Ruhr's governing commission" (Morgenthau 1945: 20–23). But the basic outlines of his recommendations remained unchanged.

occupation handbook in 1944, on the grounds that the policies proposed were too soft on the Germans, and forced every copy to carry a notification that the handbook was only valid for the predefeat period and that in any event "no steps toward economic rehabilitation for Germany will be undertaken" (Backer 1971: 7–10; Eisenberg 1996: 35–37). But at the same time, Roosevelt encouraged those in the War and State Departments committed to less punitive measures (Eisenberg 1996: 45–46). He suggested to General Lucius Clay—the future military governor of Germany—that "a huge hydroelectric power development serving several of the European countries—a sort of international TVA—was essential to economic rehabilitation," and Germany would presumably be included in any such development (Clay 1950: 5)

What are we to make of this vacillation? Although the balance of opinion among historians seems to be swinging toward a characterization of Roosevelt as a "Morgenthau man" (Fromkin 1995: 481; Eisenberg 1996: 46), committed to a punitive policy, it remains the case that Roosevelt was a "juggler," capable of keeping many different specific conceptions in the air at once, while remaining true to some general principles (Kimball 1991). Those general principles, which involved some kind of concert of great powers managing regional affairs as allies in the interests of world peace (Fromkin 1995: 321–22; Harper 1996: 79), were capable of being concretized in many different directions, as was the rhetorical commonplace of 'civilization' that Roosevelt used to sustain and legitimate them. The punitive Morgenthau Plan was certainly one possible reaction to the 'uncivilized' Nazi regime, but it was by no means the only one.

Indeed, the State and War Departments used similar language in enframing and advancing their own, rather different visions of postwar Germany. The State Department had decided by 1943 that German coal and industrial production were going to be necessary for the reconstruction of Europe and had articulated a plan to "minimize economic controls and to integrate Germany with the capitalist economies of Europe" (Eisenberg 1996: 20–21). But the State Department ran into conflicts with the War Department over the issue of precisely how German productive capacities should be utilized: where State wanted to use German production to restore France "as a bulwark of democracy on the continent of Europe" (FRUS 1945, III: 1434), the War Department's first priority was to ensure that it was not left paying for the support of occupied Germany on its own, and so it wanted to use German resources principally to support the occupation. The army did not particularly *want* occupation responsibilities and tried to get the State Department to assume them but was unsuccessful in this attempt (Gimbel 1976: 25–29). So while the State Department wanted to use Germany to rebuild Europe and particularly France, the army wanted to make Germany self-supporting in order to reduce its own expenses.

These differences, as Melvyn Leffler has suggested, are more "tactical" than "strategic," and the existence of differences should not be allowed to conceal "the similarity of goals" informing both departments' positions (1992: 69–70). In particular, the positions of both departments rested on a desire to allow Germany to rejoin the 'civilized' countries of the world after being denazified and reconstructed. Arguments in favor of this goal were ordinarily advanced in economic terms, as Morgenthau Plan opponents in the administration such as Secretary of War Henry L. Stimson pointed out that "the destruction of Germany's industrial capacity, and particularly of the Ruhr and the Saar . . . would deprive Europe of what had been one of its most important sources of raw materials during the previous eighty years" (Dallek 1995: 473). But also operative was the notion that underneath or behind the present face that Germany presented to the world there was another Germany, an "Old Germany," which could be restored through careful application of American power (Harper 1996: 105–6). The decidedly hostile reaction that the Morgenthau Plan had met with upon being leaked to the press (Ninkovich 1988: 22; McAllister 2002: 55) indicated that there was also support for this position in the wider public.

JCS-1067

The interdepartmental controversy about precisely what to do with postwar Germany resulted in the formulation of a somewhat ambiguous occupation directive in early 1945: JCS-1067 (Eisenberg 1996: 47–48). At first glance, the document looked to be largely a concession to the Morgenthau position, as it declared that "Germany will not be occupied for the purpose of liberation but as a defeated enemy nation" and explicitly instructed the military governor to "take no steps (a) looking toward the economic rehabilitation of Germany, or (b) designed to maintain or strengthen the German economy." German resources should be "fully utilized and consumption held to the minimum in order that imports may be strictly limited and that surpluses may be made available for the occupying forces and United Nations prisoners of war, and for reparation" (State 1950: 22–33). These passages from the document envisioned a hard peace indeed.

But JCS-1067 did not stand alone, and its drafters in the War Department (including John J. McCloy, who would eventually become U.S. high commissioner in Germany after the end of military government) had built in a few "safety valve" clauses that could be used to promote and justify their aims.[3]

---

3. In an interview some years later, McCloy argued that he had in fact placed these clauses into the document, and informed the military government of their possible utility, quite deliberately (Eisenberg 1996: 80–81). Whether or not one accepts McCloy's claims, the fact that he remained a consistent advocate of this use of the relevant clauses certainly indicates that he was trying to circumvent the Morgenthau-esque aspects of the document from the very beginning.

The important clause came in paragraph 5 of the document, which permitted the military governor to utilize economic controls "as they may be essential to protect the safety and meet the needs of the occupying forces and assure the production and maintenance of goods and services required to prevent starvation or such disease and unrest as would endanger these forces" (State 1950: 23). This "disease and unrest" formula served as "the key to a whole series of future actions" and allowed Clay, appointed as deputy military governor in 1945, to begin a program of subtly reconstructing the German economy—or, at any rate, refusing to demolish it any further— almost at once, under the guise of preventing disorder (Backer 1971: 37–38; Eisenberg 1996: 80–82).

With JCS-1067, as with any policy document, the kind of policy that would be concretely enacted depended to a large extent on how the document was interpreted; the mere presence of permissive language cannot explain the implementation of reconstruction policies in Germany. "Much would depend on who was implementing American policy" (Eisenberg 1996: 69). According to his own account,[4] Clay was dissatisfied with JCS-1067 from the first time he saw a draft of the directive and was particularly disturbed by the "Carthaginian peace" that the document as a whole seemed to contemplate. Upon arriving in Germany to assume his duties, he and his staff promptly decided "that Germany would starve unless it could produce for export and that immediate steps would have to be taken to revise industrial production. . . . Fortunately the provisions of JCS-1067 were in some respects general in nature, so that the degree of application was left to the judgment of the military governor" (Clay 1950: 18–19).

But in terms of legitimation, such questions of interpretation are not reducible to the idiosyncratic characteristics of individuals but depend quite significantly on the broader constellation of rhetorical commonplaces on which those individuals can draw to justify their policies. Clay and the State Department might have *wanted* to reconstruct the German economy for a whole variety of reasons, but in the absence of any justification that would resonate with the populace—particularly the American populace, including both houses of Congress—this interpretation could not be advanced and reconstruction could not go very far forward. Resonance would have to be constructed by a creative arrangement of rhetorical commonplaces, and this had not yet been done in the immediate aftermath of the war.

---

4. Of course, memoirs are inherently a problematic source of information for inferences about subjective states of mind, and Clay's memoirs in particular are deeply affected by the mature Cold War tensions present at the time that they were written (McAllister 2002: 113). As I have argued in previous chapters, however, the epistemological problems of using memoirs in this way are no more or no less severe than those associated with any other sources of evidence about motivations.

POTSDAM

After JCS-1067, the second major policy statement on postwar Germany articulated in 1945 was the Potsdam Agreement between the United States, the Soviet Union, and Great Britain, signed in August 1945. The Potsdam Agreement provided for the administration of Germany as an economic whole, foresaw the construction of unified German institutions that would eventually take over the governance of Germany and sign a peace treaty, and expressed support for an international war crimes tribunal. It also implemented a compromise formula on reparations that allowed the military governor of each zone of occupation to remove material from his own zone, provided that a complete centralized accounting be kept and that the Soviet Union be given access to 10 percent of the "usable and complete industrial capital equipment . . . as is unnecessary for the German peace economy" for free, and an additional 15 percent in exchange for the provision of foodstuffs from the Soviet zone.[5]

These provisions were complemented by the "first-charge" principle of paragraph II.B.19, which established that "proceeds of exports from current production and stocks shall be available in the first place . . . to pay for imports approved by the Control Council in Germany" (Senate 1950: 34–50). Advocates of a reconstructed German economy immediately recognized the significance of this first-charge principle, as it allowed Clay to expand the German economy so as to pay for the occupation; "this was a policy change of major import," Clay later noted, and represented "an early appreciation that until Germany was able to produce again it not only would require assistance from the occupying powers but also would be a drag on recovery in Europe" (Clay 1950: 41–42; Backer 1971: 77).

The tension between these two principles was apparent to contemporaries and has not gone unnoticed by later historians. Where the first-charge principle pointed toward a four-power administration of Germany as a single economic unit, the notion that each zonal commander could remove material from his own zone as reparations pointed in precisely the opposite direction. Confusion prevailed among almost everyone who tried to interpret the Potsdam bargain after the agreement was made public, and the tension between these two reparations principles would prove a source of conflict between the Allies over the subsequent months (Eisenberg 1996: 115–18; McAllister 2002: 96–97). The question therefore arises: why did the Potsdam Agreement contain such contradictory provisions?

Some historians have argued that the ambiguity of the document can be resolved by determining which of the two principles was the *real* aim of the

---

5. The Soviets insisted on this provision so that they might have access to the industrial zone of the Ruhr, which lay in the British zone of occupation (Eisenberg 1996: 99–100).

American negotiators. For instance, Marc Trachtenberg argues that the zonal reparations formula indicates that Potsdam was really a blueprint for a spheres-of-influence peace. He argues that in addition to the official stance represented in the documents, which envisioned a unified Germany administered by all four occupying powers collectively, there were "real Potsdam understandings" accepted by the principals that contradicted this official line, permitting each occupying power to do basically whatever it wanted to in its zone and admitting that Germany could not be administered on a four-power basis (1999: 33, 41). James McAllister concurs, suggesting that Byrnes in particular "was well aware of the likely outcome of Potsdam and that his goal was to establish the basis for a friendly division of Germany" (2002: 95).

Other historians prefer to simply interpret the Potsdam Agreements as an incoherent mess and then try to explain how the mess occurred. Carolyn Eisenberg, while disagreeing with Trachtenberg and McAllister on the sources of the split between the public language and the private plans of U.S. officials (she cites psychological and bureaucratic factors rather than a deliberate calculation to win over public opinion), also notes the "disjointed, contradictory, and dangerously misleading" character of the final documents (1996: 113–20). In her reading, U.S. officials had already decided to prioritize European reconstruction over German unity and were prepared to implement this policy regardless of official understandings. Likewise, Deborah Larson suggests that the inexperience of the chief American negotiators in foreign affairs may have also contributed to the confusion (1985).

All of these criticisms imply that the formulas in the Potsdam documents can be criticized inasmuch as they neither completely solved the problems that they addressed nor unproblematically reflected any deep desires on the part of those negotiating the agreements. But from a transactional perspective focusing on legitimation, neither of these features of the documents should be surprising: the whole point of negotiating such agreements is to introduce language that can be later used to justify particular courses of action and forbid others, while relating the new formulations to previous versions in what are often fairly creative ways.[6] Particular linguistic formulations may be used to solve bureaucratic impasses or rally public support for a position; in the absence of these formulations, "policy-making"—largely revolving around debates about what some particular formulation actually means in practice—

6. Whether the future use of this language corresponds to the subjective motivations of the people who negotiated the initial agreement is somewhat beside the point here. What matters is simply that language formulated at one point in time is utilized at a subsequent point in time to justify particular courses of action; "the intent of the framers" is nothing but a rhetorical move deployed in an effort to prevail during a later contentious episode and provides no incontestable basis on which to definitively lock down the meaning of the original agreement (Leyh 1992).

cannot proceed. This is particularly the case for public justifications of positions, which require the deployment of reasons that resonate with the wider
audience by virtue of their deployment of rhetorical commonplaces.

Seen in this way, the most striking thing about the Potsdam Agreements is
the extent to which they *preserved* some semblance of Allied unity; even with
the disagreements about the administration of Germany, the Allies still agreed
to work together. This made sense to the American public largely because of
the ways in which Roosevelt had talked about the postwar world before his
death, which were generally based on the notion that the United States would
cooperate with other 'civilized' powers to keep the peace. This was the part of
his vision of the postwar world that he derived from his cousin Theodore Roosevelt (Fromkin 1995: 443–44; Harper 1996: 32–35). As Byrnes later argued,[7]
the Potsdam Agreements meant that no single accounting of materials
removed as reparation payments would be required, which was a positive
benefit because "we realized that the effort to establish and maintain such an
accounting would be a source of constant friction, accusations, and ill-will"
(1947: 83). In this light, Potsdam removed an obstacle to Allied cooperation,
even if it left many details to be worked out later.

Was this merely a facade of Allied unity, "designed to foster the illusion
that Potsdam had preserved the unity of Germany" (McAllister 2002: 77)?
Were the public declarations in favor of a united Germany merely appeals to
public opinion both in the United States and in Germany, designed to make
the Soviets appear responsible for the division of Germany and "mobilize support in favor of a policy of continued involvement—especially military
involvement" of the United States in Europe (Trachtenberg 1999: 50)? Perhaps. But if so, why would someone like Lucius Clay have been taken in by
such a propagandistic scheme? Since Clay was quite friendly with Byrnes from
Clay's earlier work as Byrnes's deputy in the Office of War Mobilization and
Reconversion, why wouldn't Clay have simply asked Byrnes for a clarification
before undertaking to follow the language of the official Postdam Agreements?
Trachtenberg is forced to attribute a complex series of motivations to Byrnes,
according to which Byrnes "really knew" that Germany could not be administered on a four-power basis but wanted to prove this to others by permitting
people—including some of his close friends—to try earnestly to do so, knowing that they would fail. And the result of this complex maneuvering was to
cast the Soviets in a bad light, so as to keep the American public committed to
a policy of involvement in Europe (Trachtenberg 1999: 49–50).

7. Note that this account should no more be taken to indicate Byrnes's "true motives"
than any of the various historical accounts do. What is significant is that Byrnes presents
the events of Potsdam in this light and seeks to justify the policies enacted there in these
terms.

Rather than this fascinating speculation about true motives—which attributes a good deal of foresight to politicians like Byrnes[8]—it seems an easier (and more convincing) explanation to simply observe the language of the Potsdam Agreements and identify the commonplaces to which they appeal. Ironically, Trachtenberg's explanation, although informed by immense skepticism about the power of public declarations and justifications, depends quite heavily on public language playing a potent role. If public declarations are so irrelevant when compared to the private, "real" understandings in producing action, why should we assume that there would be *any* public relations advantage in building notions of four-power cooperation into the Potsdam Agreements? In order for such an advantage to obtain, public declarations need to have some kind of substantial impact. One simply cannot have it both ways.

Although it is possible to point to a kind of "blowback" effect wherein elites get caught by their own past articulations and are forced to adhere to them—perhaps contrary to their wishes—in the future (Snyder 1991: 41–42), identifying this pattern does not really *explain* it. In addition, if we want to account for the legitimation effects of public articulations, we cannot simply note a tendency among American officials to "oversell" policies in moralistic terms (Lowi 1979: 139) and make things appear, as Dean Acheson once put it, "clearer than the truth" (1969: 375). Instead, we have to explain why the particular presentation made is *understood* to be "clearer than the truth" by the relevant public, and not simply dismissed as a thin covering for other goals.

The missing piece of the puzzle is provided by an appreciation of the extent to which cooperation among the 'civilized' powers was the cornerstone of

8. Indeed, in Trachtenberg's account Byrnes would have had to have known: (1) that the Soviet Union would never participate in a four-power administration of Germany; (2) that an effort by the United States to cooperate with the Soviets would result in failure that could be plausibly blamed on the Soviet Union; (3) that this was so certain that no other American officials need be told about this plan; (4) that the American public would reject the Soviet Union's later account of the negotiations; (5) that the whole panoply of the Cold War was just around the corner, and probably unavoidable. Knowing how events turned out, one can do as Trachtenberg does and reconstruct such a (virtually omniscient) Byrnes, but only at the cost of reading the Cold War back into the unsettled situation of the early postwar period. It is not necessary to claim that under certain circumstances the Soviet Union might have cooperated with the other powers in administering Germany—that would be a revisionist claim that the United States always meant to conduct a Cold War with the Soviet Union—in order to critique Trachtenberg's explanation, and I am not claiming this. Rather, I am merely calling attention to the incompleteness of Trachtenberg's account, and to the fact that it does not provide a plausible causal account that is theoretically coherent, unless one makes heroic assumptions about Byrnes's foreknowledge— a foreknowledge that, one might have expected, Byrnes would mention in his autobiographical account of the events of Potsdam, if for no other reason than to make himself appear prescient. But Byrnes does not do this.

Roosevelt's rhetorical strategy for involving the United States in the Second World War in the first place. Given this strategy, it is not surprising that policymakers were still appealing to this commonplace only a few months after Roosevelt's death; there simply were no other publicly available options, because no one had yet done the political and rhetorical work needed to make them available for deployment. The Potsdam Agreement fits the general Rooseveltian strategy for the postwar world, but without Roosevelt,[9] and is no more a step toward the clear division of Germany than the designation of separate occupation zones themselves was (Ninkovich 1988: 50–51). It is not necessary to claim that American officials were using the Potsdam discussions to set the Soviet Union up for condemnation in the public eye; it is sufficient to point out that Allied cooperation with respect to Germany—the 'civilized' powers of the world versus those who would disrupt the peace—continued in 1945, at least in the important sphere of public legitimation.

Conceiving of a New Germany

The debate about the character and future of Germany was of course not carried out solely by American policymakers; the Germans themselves were understandably involved in a very similar debate of their own. In broad outline, three positions on the character and orientation of any future German state emerged in the immediate postwar period, associated with the names of Konrad Adenauer, Kurt Schumacher, and Jacob Kaiser (Schwarz 1966).

Schumacher, the head of the SPD until his death in 1952, maintained a notion of Germany as a social-democratic state that would, in alliance with other western and central European social democracies, form a powerful counterweight to the Soviet Union (which he argued had hegemonial tendencies). In accord with the rest of his party, Schumacher took great pains to differentiate the SPD from communism and the German Communist Party (KPD); this was an old split in the German Left, but the fact of Soviet occupation of the eastern zone of Germany and the forced merger in that zone of the SPD and the KPD to form a so-called "Socialist Unity Party" made the differentiation even more pressing.

Less anti-Soviet than Schumacher—perhaps by virtue of his position as the head of the Berlin branch of the CDU—Kaiser advocated a kind of "Mitteleuropa" position for Germany, in which a reunified Germany would play a sort of mediating role between the two superpowers, while standing culturally

---

9. Indeed, the absence of Roosevelt himself explains a good deal about the eventual collapse of this strategy: the other Allies could not trust that "Roosevelt's policies would survive the man" (Harper 1996: 130). It also has the advantage of not reading the future back into the past.

on the Christian heritage of Germany. German unity was Kaiser's primary goal, and he was willing to consider all manner of compromises to retain it; Schumacher was also very committed to German unity but nowhere near as willing to submit to Soviet control. Adenauer, on the other hand, stood more firmly on occidentalist rhetoric. His first goal was a closer association between Germany and the West (*Westbindung*); German unity was still important, of course, but only under certain restricted conditions (Doering-Manteuffel 1983: 36–44).

Although Schumacher and Adenauer differed on many issues of social and economic organization, and although Schumacher would become the most outspoken opponent of Adenauer's policy of *Westbindung* in the early years of the Adenauer government, the two did agree on one fundamental principle: the rejection of communism and the concomitant rejection of a major role for the Soviet Union in Germany. Both Schumacher and Adenauer regarded Kaiser's position as somewhat idealistic and as motivated by an ignorance—willful or otherwise—about the true character of Soviet communism. Yet Kaiser based much of his appeal on an invocation of German unity, which could not be simply ignored. Hence, both Schumacher and Adenauer strove to take possession of this rhetorical commonplace through their deployment of other appeals: occidentalism for Adenauer and the CDU, and a *Sonderweg* notion that shaded off into something close to traditional nationalism for Schumacher and the SPD. Kaiser's position could perhaps have defeated these alternatives if the Soviet Union had proven more overtly cooperative and more amenable to the kind of compromises that Kaiser was prepared to make, but Soviet actions were at the very least deeply ambiguous, lending credence to more negative interpretations.

The positions taken up by Schumacher and Adenauer, and the importance of the details of how each arranged the rhetorical commonplaces available to them, can be most easily seen in a comparison of the speeches each gave to the earliest assemblies of their respective parties in 1946. Each of these speeches set out a vision of the future, based largely on a diagnosis of the past and the agreed goal of avoiding anything like the National Socialist dictatorship in the future.

SOCIAL DEMOCRACY AS GERMANY'S FUTURE

For Schumacher, the key to Germany's future was the adherence to democratic principles, and the SPD was the party best equipped to do this. "Today in Germany," he argued, "democracy is not much stronger than the Social Democratic Party."

All the other parties needed the war potential and the supremacy of anglo-saxon weaponry in order to discover that their hearts were set on democracy.

But we did not need this. We would be democratic even if the English and the Americans were fascists. (1985: 394)

Rejection of democratic principles in the past had allowed Hitler to come to power. While the conservative forces were of course to blame for this, Schumacher singled out the communists for special opprobrium.

> For the communists, "democracy" is a completely meaningless phrase. It is instead that old phrase out of the jargon and milieu of the middle of the last century, the "dictatorship of the proletariat," which is present in the hearts of the German communists. . . . Also, the Leninist call for a forced union of parties shows quite clearly that communist politics in Germany is consciously anti-democratic. (394)

Schumacher always characterized the merger creating the "Socialist Unity Party," and the activities of the KPD in general, as "the ancillary politics of a foreign nation on German soil," and he made a point of discrediting the call for "world revolution" as "the cloak for Russian foreign policy" (BKS, no. 35: 1.12.1945). So Schumacher's anticommunism had a decidedly nationalist tinge, even though he was quite consistently critical of the German communists for blending "the ideas of 'socialism' and 'nationalism,'" calling it "politically amoral."

> It seems to me that this is a dangerous precursor to Nazism, to which these political tactics led in the past: a combination of socialist phraseology and stirred-up nationalism. Whether one calls this "national socialism" or "national communism," the effect is the same. . . . No one who wants to be a good German can be a nationalist. (1985: 409)

Communist methods, he charged, were simply un-German: "whether these methods are customary in Turkestan, I do not know; in any case, these methods find only horror and rejection from us" (410). Schumacher here implicitly deployed an occidentalist commonplace and used it to associate communism and totalitarian tactics with the 'East' rather than the 'West.'

The other side of this notion—that Germany should pursue a policy of closer association with 'the West'—was not entirely lacking in Schumacher's appeal either, as he called for "the internationalization of all of Europe. . . . A new Germany will have its highest task in becoming a part of a United States of Europe." But immediately he offered a caveat: "We don't want to exchange German capitalists for foreign capitalists! We want, rather, an international government of which the international labor movement is a part" (407–8). So Schumacher stood in favor of a certain kind of internationalism, albeit one that confined itself to the economic sphere. German unity and national self-determination remained the primary party goals.

I would also like to say that at this party assembly . . . there has often sounded a tone that comes from a time when many social democrats took their opinions about the role of the nation from the German bourgeoisie. But we have our own conception of the nation: we are for the rights of national self-determination, and therefore for the rights of German national self-determination. We want equality in treatment [*Gleichberechtigung*] for this nation. (421)

Hence a Europe-wide socialism was tempered by the importance of German unity, and by the participation of Germany in any such internationalization as an equal partner. "We know that, after the dreadful experiences which Europe has suffered, this cannot be thrown at us as a gift. We know that we must earn it ourselves" (421).

But how would Europe ever consent to treat the Germans as equals? Only when people

realize that in all the years of the spiritual reshaping of the German people into evil and throughout the period of the Hitler dictatorship there was always another Germany. . . . this other Germany consisted of people in all of their humanity. But this other Germany also counted among its ranks truly courageous men and women who were prepared to sacrifice. And it contained the belief and the desire that this Third Reich should not be allowed to live, and it suffered every sacrifice so that this Third Reich might die. (422)

This "other Germany," represented by the Social Democrats, was therefore the cure for Germany's ills. And this other Germany, having learned from the experiences of history, now had something positive to offer the world: Schumacher publicly hoped that a social democratic Germany would act as a kind of "magnet," drawing the rest of Europe and neighboring countries under Soviet domination toward a social democratic solution to their political and economic problems (Abelshauser 1974). As against unification with the East and communism, Schumacher envisioned a socialist alternative. And although he took pains to reject specific nationalist policies, his argument still appealed quite centrally to such a commonplace, in the form of a special task for the German people and the demand for equality of treatment *before* internationalization could proceed.

CHRISTIAN DEMOCRACY AS GERMANY'S SALVATION

Adenauer disagreed, and did so quite consistently and strongly. In addition, he continually linked the SPD with the Soviet Union through their common adherence to Marxism, directly attacking Schumacher's strategy of differentiating himself and his party from the Communists and the Soviets. His primary rhetorical resource for doing this was occidentalism: Adenauer also maintained that the way for Germany to reenter the world of advanced countries and overcome the experiences of its recent past was to turn to an "other Germany," but it was decidedly not a social democratic Germany that would fulfill this function. Instead, the problem was that Germany had turned away from its 'Western' Christian heritage, and only a return to that heritage would solve its problems.

In one of his earliest public speeches as the head of the CDU in the British zone of occupation, Adenauer drew these connections out quite explicitly. After discussing the present situation of Germany, he declared: "National Socialism is the immediate cause of this catastrophe, that is correct. But National Socialism could not have achieved power in Germany if it had not found fertile ground for its poisonous seed among broad classes of the population." The causes of this receptiveness to National Socialism were twofold. First, "the German people of all classes have suffered for many decades from a false conception of the state, of power, and of the situation of the individual person. This conception has made the state an idol and erected an altar to it; the worth and dignity of the individual person has been sacrificed to this idol." And the root of this "Prussian" conception was "the materialistic world-view," particularly "the materialistic world-view of Marxism . . . which inevitably prepared the way in the thoughts and feelings of its adherents for dictatorship" (1975: 84–85). The way lay open for a rhetorical identification of the Social Democratic Party—particularly as long as they continued to advocate a policy that sounded like that of nationalist conservatives in the Weimar Republic— with the Prussians, the Nazis, and other enemies of freedom and democracy.

> The leaders [*Führer*][10] of the social democrats . . . strike very strong national tones in their speeches, and they proclaim socialism as the cure for all the evils of mankind. If you will permit me a slight digression, I repeat: the military men, in very high military positions, recognized [during the Weimar Republic] the utility of the words "national" and "socialism" for propaganda. They combined them in one word and created a new form of socialism, National Socialism.[11] They said to themselves: if we want to reach the broad masses, we

10. Adenauer uses this word, which was also Hitler's title, quite shrewdly; shortly thereafter, discussing the crucial role of the next elections in determining who will be in charge in Germany, he notes that "I think that we should finally have done with the word '*Führer*' and the notion of '*Führung*' ["leadership," but Adenauer is playing with the obvious etymological connection to *Führer*] and say instead that the next elections will determine which party will take over the highest responsibility [*welche Partei . . . die Hauptverantwortung übernehmen soll*] in the British Zone and in Germany" (Adenauer 1975: 100). So even at the level of particular words, Adenauer is equating the social democrats (who have *Führer*) and the Nazis.

11. Note how Adenauer turns Schumacher's diagnosis of Nazism back on him. This tactic, made possible by the occidentalist identification of socialism, communism, and 'the East,' recurs often in the ensuing debates.

need to put some nameless soldier on the top of this movement. So they came up with Hitler. (99)

The obvious implication is that it does not matter which particular individual was in charge; the materialistic worldview that worships the state as an idol would have the same effects regardless. So the solution is not to change leaders, but to change world-views. "National Socialism found its strongest opponents in those Catholic and Protestant-Evangelical parts of Germany which were minimally bewitched by the teachings of Karl Marx, of socialism! This is absolutely clear!" (86).[12] The solution to Germany's problems, Adenauer argued, lay with the erection of Christian democracy.

> We call ourselves Christian Democrats, because we have the deep conviction that only a democracy rooted in the Christian-Western worldview [*christlich-abendländischen Weltanschauung*], in Christian natural rights, and the basic principles of Christian ethics can fulfill the great responsibility to educate the German people and lead to its reemergence [*Wiederaufstieg*].[13] (87)

In particular, "we want our culture to find its basis again in Western Christian culture, the core of which is the noble concept of the dignity of the person and the worth of each individual" (91). The word "again" is key here, as it implies that Germany was once rooted in the Christian 'West' and was led astray by the nefarious doctrines of Prussian materialism; Germany needed to return, not create anew.[14] And it had to return to the Christian West, which

---

12. Of course, this analysis does not consider the voting record of the Catholic Zentrum Party, which—unlike the SPD—"vote[d] for the historic Enabling Act which gave Adolf Hitler complete dictatorial powers in the spring of 1933" (Wighton 1963: 23). The socially plausible character of a commonplace and the factual accuracy of claims resting on a commonplace are two very different things.

13. *Wiederaufstieg* is etymologically related to *Wiederauferstehen*, which means "resurrection," a point that most likely would not have been lost on Adenauer's audience.

14. This position finds a striking parallel in the intellectual journey of Thomas Mann, who had been an outspoken advocate of the "ideas of 1914" during the First World War but had generally supported "the Weimar combination of parliamentary democracy, the reconstruction of capitalism and the culture of individualism" (Sieferle 1995: 94) and had left Germany for the United States shortly after the Nazi seizure of power in 1933. He became a consultant in Germanic Literature at the Library of Congress, in which capacity he delivered a series of public lectures on problems of the postwar world and the position of Germany. "One must not forget how many humane and, in the best sense, democratic tendencies were active in German life," Mann argued in 1943, "tendencies which it has had in common with the great world of Occidental Christian civilization and which were always opposed to nationalistic barbarism" (1963: 33–34). The problem was that Nazi Germany had abandoned those values; as he argued in an earlier public lecture, "I left Germany because in the Germany of today the traditional values underlying Western culture have been rejected and trodden under foot. I have made many sacrifices in order to save the one thing which was denied me in Germany: freedom of thought and expression" (1938: 64).

was "not a geographic, but a world-historical concept" in Adenauer's strategy (Altmann 1993: 37). Adenauer's preferred term for the West was *Abendland,* and he clearly drew on the concept as articulated during the interwar period; this commonplace made "the elimination of a German 'special position' [*Sonderposition*] . . . easier through the recourse to the historical shape of the Christian West" (Hürten 1985: 154).

Of course this meant that Germany would have to rejoin the 'Western' world as a partner, and not merely as a supplier of raw materials or a deindustrialized land of ruins; *Gleichberechtigung* was as much a prominent term in Adenauer's political lexicon as it was in Schumacher's (Granieri 2003: 83). But the appeal for equality of treatment was accompanied by somewhat different preconditions, in keeping with the different rhetorical commonplaces on which each drew: Schumacher's *Sonderweg* commitments meant that the termination of the occupation regime and the restoration of full sovereignty to a German government would have to come *before* any agreement to join with other powers, whereas Adenauer's occidentalism made early cooperation with fellow 'Western' countries, even on a basis falling somewhat short of complete equality, rather more plausible.

Adenauer and Schumacher agreed on the basic proposition that Germany belonged, *culturally,* to the Western world, and so Adenauer had no prominent opposition in postwar Germany to that implication of occidentalism (Artner 1985: 43–44; Herbst 1989: 7, 110). The open question concerned the political implications of this cultural unity. Schumacher did not support Adenauer's policy of *Westbindung,* suggesting instead that Germany needed independence from all countries—including the other 'Western' countries—in order to pursue reunification. But both clearly and stridently rejected communism as a violation of basic 'Western' principles like democracy, making things difficult for any communist party to exercise much influence over the course of public debate. In postwar German politics the KPD mainly served as a way for the SPD to demonstrate its anti-Soviet credentials and as a way for the CDU to illustrate the dangers of Marxist materialism; indeed, the party was banned as a threat to the democratic state in 1956.[15] Communism never really constituted a viable alternative in postwar Germany, and in practice the political debates about Germany's foreign policy orientation would be between the CDU and SPD.

15. The "outsider" status of the KPD was reinforced even before the founding of the BRD by the refusal of the American, British, and French occupation authorities to allow the KPD to change its name to something less clearly marked by a connection to the Soviet Union. Indeed, they even prevented the KPD from adopting the name "Socialist Unity Party" throughout the western zones of occupation, thereby helping to ensure that the party would always bear a kind of political pariah status (Rogers 1995: 86–93).

To the Stuttgart Speech

After the Potsdam conference, American policy toward Germany proceeded along two tracks: on one hand, there were Clay's efforts to begin some measure of economic reconstruction under the "disease and unrest" clause of JCS-1067; on the other, there were the ongoing demolitions of surplus German industrial plants and a pursuit of denazification. This amounted to a kind of global indecision in American policy and reflected a continuing split within the American policy bureaucracy between the War and State departments (Gimbel 1968: 32–34). In September 1946, however, Byrnes gave a speech at Stuttgart in which he announced that "Germany must be given a chance to export goods in order to import enough to make her economy self-sustaining. . . . the German people throughout Germany, under proper safeguards, should be given the primary responsibility for the running of their own affairs. . . . The United States favors the early establishment of a provisional German government" (State 1950: 3–9). Many who had been in the audience greeted the speech with great relief, observing that "the punitive tone" of much previous American policy "had been replaced with constructive purpose. . . . many, including General Clay, shed tears of relief," and the new tone was widely acclaimed by the representatives of all of the German political parties (Clay 1950: 81; Eisenberg 1996: 247–48).

What explains this shift in U.S. policy? Many "traditional" or "postrevisionist" accounts of this period (Gaddis 1972; Trachtenberg 1999), along with IR "realist" accounts (Mearsheimer 1990; Schweller and Wohlforth 2000), portray the shift in American policy as a result of the deepening Cold War: as U.S.-Soviet tensions increased, the United States sought allies on the European continent, and German industry and a strong German economy was necessary for the support of these allies, even if Germany itself was still to be kept disarmed. On the other hand, many "revisionist" (or, perhaps, "neorevisionist") accounts (Leffler 1992) portray the shift in American policy as a result of a change in American priorities that had less to do with Soviet actions directly, and much more to do with an American preference for a liberal world order (Latham 1997) or an economically unified Europe (Eisenberg 1996). For all of their substantive differences, these lines of explanation are united by their failure to take the legitimation problem seriously enough; they generally reason from the supposed preferences of political leaders, and the supposed character of the situation that they faced or thought that they were facing, directly to the novel policies themselves.

But even if U.S. policymakers *wanted* to reconstruct Germany, and even if German politicians *wanted* U.S. help in rebuilding their country, these desires alone are insufficient to explain the changes in policy. Instead, the

question that should be asked about the policy changes of 1946 is, What
made these changes *politically possible?* Why were a constructive U.S. policy
toward Germany, and collaborative activities by certain German politicians
toward their conquerors, socially plausible and publicly acceptable so soon
after the end of the war? The answer involves the deployment of rhetorical
commonplaces, and in particular the rhetorical operations that were performed as part of an effort to make sense of Soviet actions. As a result of particular deployments, the Soviet Union became a "threat," and Germany
ceased to be quite as "threatening." The condition of "being a threat" exists
only in terms of some specific set of deployments, and the proper responses
to that threat are also given by the way in which the threat is defined and
figured in the first place (Weldes 1999: 117–18). So we cannot jump from
some analyst's *subsequent* characterization of a situation as "threatening"
directly to the responses selected by political authorities *at the time;*
processes of public meaning-making always mediate between situations and
responses.

Sophisticated neorevisionists like Melvyn Leffler have also made this point,
suggesting that it was because U.S. officials "saw themselves locked in a titanic
struggle with a totalitarian nation that was intent on exploiting unrest for its
own self-aggrandizement" that Soviet actions were consistently read in the
worst possible light (1992: 261). Like the neorevisionists, I do not account for
the shift in American policy during the important year of 1946 in terms of the
rise of an "objective" Soviet threat; but unlike neorevisionists, I focus on the
ways in which a Soviet threat was produced in a socially sustainable manner
by the deployment of rhetorical commonplaces and discursive resources.
While it is probably true that the "identification of the Soviet Union as the
enemy eased U.S. policymaking" (121), this is *not* an explanation for such an
identification; nor is it an explanation for the specific policies that flowed from
the identification. Instead, a precise characterization of the terms in which
"the Soviet threat" was publicly portrayed is essential to understanding the
critical shifts during this period and why they had direct consequences for the
situation in Germany.

TERMINATING WARTIME COOPERATION

I will start in a somewhat unusual place. On 4 December 1945, Senator James
C. Eastland of Mississippi rose to make a speech calling for a change in U.S.
policy toward Germany, taking the opportunity to critique Henry Morgen-
thau's recently published call for a renewed commitment to a punitive regime
(Morgenthau 1945). Germany, Eastland declared, lay in ruins: "No nation in
modern history has suffered such catastrophe as Germany endures today."
Punitive measures were no longer appropriate, and therefore the Morgenthau
Plan was completely out of date.

In the name of decency, in the name of civilization, for the sake of our own future welfare, and for the future of world peace there must be a complete review and revision of our policies for the reconstruction of the German Nation and the rehabilitation of the German people. (CR, 4 December 1945: 11372)

Note the use of 'civilization,' as Eastland attempted to yoke the earlier civilized/barbarian distinction to a policy of reconstruction, in much the same way that State Department officials had done during the earlier bureaucratic debates: civilized people do not perpetrate atrocities or allow other people to languish in ruins, which is what American policy was doing at the moment. But Eastland did not stop there, and went on to introduce a classic occidentalist line of reasoning in favor of reconstruction.

> It is not to the interest of America that oriental, atheistic philosophies prevail in the heart of Europe, the cradle of western civilization; and yet, if these policies are pursued this will be the result, to the grave detriment of America.

Abruptly the battle lines were drawn quite differently. The Soviet Union was no longer an ally, but the representative of a completely different civilization, and as such stood essentially opposed to the United States. And if the United States wished to defend the civilization of which it was a part, it needed to stop carrying out policies that corresponded to those of the oriental atheists and to take up its "responsibility as a civilized, Christian people in the face of profound misery, suffering, and impending starvation abroad."

But it was not only that the United States had a duty to oppose ruinous conditions in general; it had a duty to the German people in particular. If the United States pursued the Morgenthau proposals for Germany, Eastland warned,

> We are abandoning the principles of Christian civilization, for not since the days of Nero have Christians been treated so cruelly. This plan promises a prolonged era of pitiless hunger, a program of central European chaos and disorder, to be ultimately presided over by the ghouls of revolution, starvation, and atheism, and resulting in the cremation of Christianity in Europe. (11375)

Eastland's objections to U.S. policy were not so much universal as particularist; the real crime was not just that people were starving and the United States was not helping, but that *European Christians* were starving and the United States was abandoning its fellow civilizationists to chaos and atheism. Suddenly, the German people ceased to be complete foreigners and became instead members of a broader community in which the United States also participated: 'Western Civilization,' here appearing in its specifically Christian variant. Therefore, actively reconstructing Germany made sense, whereas it did not before.

Eastland made a further elaboration of his position, which is so striking in its bluntness that I will quote it in full.

> There is involved in the present predicament of Germany the whole question of the relation between the eastern and the western civilizations. Germany has served both as a neutralizing agent and as a barrier between the Oriental hordes and a western civilization 2,000 years old, and for the first time in history we find in Czechoslovakia savage, barbarian Mongolian hordes stalking the streets of western civilization as its conquerors, and threatening not to stop at Vienna and Berlin but to push on to engulf the very civilization from which we ourselves have stemmed. Our treatment of Germany will decide this question of whether Germany is going to clamor for an anschluss[16] to Moscow, or is to be reincorporated into our own civilization and culture, and the time has come for the American people to be told what it would mean if Germany, the most highly industrialized country in Europe, were to be incorporated into a totalitarian tyranny, masked under the guise of a modern democracy but manipulated by a vicious and sadistic minority of totalitarian Communists who have preached openly throughout the world the doctrine that there is nothing left in western civilization worth preserving, and who have been and are the greatest persecutors of the Christian church since the Mohammedan invasion of Spain. (11376)

This is one of the purest articulations of occidentalism as justification for German reconstruction that we might imagine. All of the key elements—'East' versus 'West,' 'Western Civilization' as 2,000 years old and encompassing the United States and much of Europe, Christianity as the foremost expression of 'the West'—are present, making an active reconstruction policy very hard to oppose unless one wishes to be branded a traitor to 'Western Civilization.' This is not to say that every defender of German reconstruction would necessarily agree wholeheartedly with Eastland's rather extreme formulation of the issue; indeed, Eastland's language is quite unrepresentative in its rather colorful presentation, as political figures discussing this issue were normally much more restrained. But it is not much of a leap from Eastland's ravings to the more restrained formulations of others, as we shall see.

For the moment, it is enough to note that Eastland's speech was not without its immediate practical effect; thirty-five senators from both parties put a petition before President Harry Truman on 15 December, in which they asked for an improvement in the food situation in Germany and Austria and requested that private relief organizations be permitted to assist (Kraus 1971: 25). Even before this petition was presented, the State Department (on 12

---

16. A German word meaning "annexation," the term had been most often applied to the Nazi takeover of Austria in 1938. Eastland uses it without special emphasis, but the historical echoes of the term would not have been lost on his Senate audience.

December 1945) released a clarification as to its aims in Germany, which suggested that by no means was the military governor directed to reduce the German people to poverty and ruin and permit them to languish in such a condition, but that the German people were to be permitted to work toward a higher standard of living as long as the dismantling of warmaking facilities continued (Gimbel 1968: 32–34; Backer 1971: 77). While the link between Eastland's speech and the State Department's clarification of policy is not explicit, there is certainly a commonality of design about them, and it would not be long before State Department proclamations took up language very similar to Eastland's as their own.

KENNAN AND CHURCHILL

An early harbinger of this new language was George Kennan's "long telegram," a nominally secret but in fact widely distributed document written in February 1946. Along with Winston Churchill's "iron curtain" speech, delivered at Fulton, Missouri, two weeks later, Kennan's missive was an important moment in the public articulation of a new occidentalist strategy for U.S.-European relations. In many respects, "Churchill said publicly what the professional diplomat wrote privately" (Leffler 1992: 108–9). This much is well-established already; what is less well remarked on is the decidedly occidentalist tone of both deployments. By presenting their analyses of the "Soviet threat" in occidentalist terms, they opened up rhetorical space for a less punitive policy toward Germany, as the significant boundary-lines in the world were redrawn so as to place Germany—at least its western, non-Prussian, part—inside of a 'Western' grouping. Neither Kennan nor Churchill makes this link as explicitly in 1946 as later articulations do, but their deployments are key moments in the overall process.[17]

George Kennan's interpretation of the Soviet Union "as a non-Western Other, essentially outside the legitimate range of actors in international relations" stemmed from before the time when he composed his "long telegram" (Stephanson 1989: 13). Oswald Spengler was not unimportant to Kennan's thinking about these matters; Edward Gibbon also figured quite prominently (Harper 1996: 168–69). Indeed, Kennan's opposition to and caution about the Soviet Union arose not from any particular event or action but from a more fundamental diagnosis of the Soviet Union as the chief opponent of 'Western Civilization.' In his "long telegram" Kennan argued that this civilizational divide and the policies that it produced were much older than the Soviet

17. Indeed, the fact that they do not draw out that implication at this point serves to reinforce my argument that occidentalist language was not simply a way for political elites to justify a policy that they had already decided on (although it was sometimes used in this manner); instead, the unforeseen combination of discursive commonplaces makes possible the reconstruction of Germany, which actively begins at a later time.

Union itself and sprang from a "traditional and instinctive Russian sense of insecurity."

> Originally, this was insecurity of a peaceful agricultural people trying to live on vast exposed plain[18] in a neighborhood of fierce nomadic peoples. To this was added, as Russia came into contact with economically advanced West, fear of more competent, more powerful, more highly organized societies in that area. (Kennan 1967: 550)

This sense of "insecurity . . . afflicted rather Russian rulers than Russian people" and explains why these rulers "have always feared foreign penetration, feared direct contact between Western world and their own, feared what would happen if Russians learned truth about world without or if foreigners learned truth about world within." Kennan thus explained current Soviet actions with reference to a 'non-Western' Russian essence; these essential differences must be recognized by "Western statesmen" who wish to deal with the Soviets (551).

The threat represented by the Soviet Union was therefore something far greater than a simple military matter, but represents a cultural challenge to 'the West' as a whole. Because the "Soviets are still by far the weaker force . . . Gauged against Western world as a whole . . . their success will depend on degree of cohesion, firmness, and vigor which Western world can muster" (558). And the Soviet strategy would take account of this.

> Everything possible will be done to set major Western powers against each other. Anti-British talk will be plugged among Americans, anti-American talk among British. Continentals, *including Germans,* will be taught to abhor both Anglo-Saxon powers. Where suspicions exist, they will be fanned; where not, ignited. No effort will be spared to discredit and combat all efforts which threaten to lead to any sort of unity or cohesion among others from which Russia might be excluded. (556, emphasis added)

Kennan's specific reference to the Germans in this context is illuminating, as in the passage he refers to three "major Western powers" by name: the United States, Britain, and Germany. Unity among these powers is his recommendation for resisting the Soviet threat, as 'the West' must hold together against this onslaught from outside of itself. And Germany must be a part of this grouping. The notion of a natural, 'Western' community was a crucial

---

18. Note the Spenglerian echoes in this characterization of Russia; "the prime symbol of Russia," Spengler had argued, is "the plane without limit" (1926: 201). The characterization of Russia as essentially a vast plane was of course not original to Spengler, but the metaphysical implications that he drew from the interpretation were somewhat more extreme than those drawn by others.

part of the formulation, defining the Soviet threat as something that could not be met simply by American military force or by any kind of isolated policy. When Kennan suggested that "much depends on the health and vigor of our own society" and called for America to provide "guidance" to European societies, he was—in effect—suggesting that the United States assume the active leadership of 'the West' (559).

Kennan's answer to the Soviet threat was to abandon American ontological exceptionalism in favor of an explicit awareness of the wider civilizational community to which the United States belonged. Winston Churchill's speech at Westminster College echoed many of these occidentalist themes, drawing on similar rhetorical commonplaces to advocate more explicit Anglo-American security cooperation in the interests of preserving the peace. The speech is well remembered for the famous declaration that "an iron curtain has descended across the Continent" (Churchill 1949: 100) and its robust, even alarmist, anticommunism; this reading is certainly justifiable, because both of these elements of the speech are in fact quite pronounced. But on closer reading, the occidentalism of Churchill's argument becomes unmistakable. The picture of the world that he presented was divided between "the Soviets and the Western Democracies"; each of these divisions formed an essentially separate cultural community. At the heart of this division sat Germany, and Churchill worried publicly that Soviet activities in their zone of occupation "will give the defeated Germans the power of putting themselves up to auction" between the two communities (101). So Germany has the option of serving as the eastern boundary of 'Western Civilization' against the Soviets, an outcome that Churchill clearly advocates.

Occidentalism is also apparent in Churchill's characterization of the threat posed by the Soviet Union. "I do not believe that Soviet Russia desires war," he declared; "What they desire is the fruits of war and the indefinite expansion of their power and doctrines" (103). The means for accomplishing this aim was not military aggression, but internal subversion.

> In a great number of countries, far from the Russian frontiers and throughout the world, Communist fifth columns are established and work in complete unity and absolute obedience to the directions they receive from the Communist center. Except in the British Commonwealth and in the United States where Communism is in its infancy, the Communist parties or fifth columns constitute a growing challenge and peril to Christian civilization. (102)

Communist gains in any country are losses to every member of "Christian civilization," and no country can simply think about defending itself while abandoning the rest of its civilizational community. "If the Western Democracies stand together," Churchill argued, they will be able to defend themselves and their heritage. "If however they become divided or falter in their duty and if these all-important years are allowed to slip away then indeed catastrophe may overwhelm us all" (103). Churchill thus tied a rhetorical commonplace dealing with the preservation of democratic liberty to an activist foreign policy; occidentalism provided the means for doing so.

Is it not the case, however, that these interpretations of the Soviet threat and the potential for communist infiltration were simply *more accurate* readings of the situation than those readings advanced by dissenters? And doesn't the outcome of events demonstrate that individuals like Churchill and Kennan were simply prescient in their warnings about the Soviet Union? Such an interpretation suffers from its reliance on a questionable premise. To say that occidentalist analyses of the Soviet Union led to the "correct" policies to pursue ignores the role of such analyses in *producing* the very situations that they predicted. The interpretations in question were tendered *during* the ongoing process of making sense out of events on the ground and were not so much pure reactions to the course of events as much as they were techniques for shaping that course.[19] It therefore makes little sense to ask whether occidentalist arguments were more or less "accurate."

'Western Civilization' provided a way of reading and understanding—and when deployed in conjunction with other rhetorical commonplaces, it pointed toward and justified—particular policies. This explicitly occidentalist language, and the interpretation of the Soviet Union that it supported, reconfigured the intersubjective understanding of the situation on the ground in Germany in such a way that it *became* an 'East-West' split, as opposed to a continuation of the wartime alliance. As we shall see, even defenders of some form of continued four-power administration of Germany (and, thus, continued cooperation with the Soviets) utilized the new language in their arguments. The occidentalist tone of the debate about Germany in 1946 made possible later arguments tying the western zones of occupied Germany more firmly to the other 'Western' powers, *even if this was not what those deploying the language in 1946 wanted to accomplish.* Hence we can leave to one side the question of whether U.S. elites "really" wanted a spheres-of-influence peace underpinned by a divided Germany and focus instead on the interaction of discursive articulations.

19. "Those who have reached the right conclusion may be less reasonable and may be treating the information in less justifiable ways than those who are wrong," Robert Jervis observes; "those who disagree, far from being blind to the facts, are often truer to them" (1976: 178). One can readily discern in all of the strongly anti-Soviet voices of the early postwar period a tendency to have made such arguments long before there was sufficient evidence to support them unambiguously, which suggests that their readings of the world situation were rooted in something other than a detached apprehension of Soviet actions—even if "events" might later seem to "prove them right."

PUBLIC INTELLECTUALS

Kennan and Churchill were not alone in making these occidentalist arguments; nor were they alone in drawing conclusions about Germany's future from them. A wide spectrum of public intellectual figures also advanced similar recommendations, becoming in effect spokesmen for a common 'Western' culture that must be conserved and defended against the threat of a Nazi resurgence. Like Adenauer and Eastland, they regarded Germany *itself* as a part of 'the West' but regarded the National Socialist movement to be a deviation from those 'Western' ideals and principles. Hence, they advocated a restoration of those traditional values and a renewed awareness of the *unity* of 'the West' in the face of threats to it—threats that are both internal and external. These public intellectuals were instrumental in articulating a position that would render an active reconstruction of Germany socially plausible. In the interest of space, I will display only two exemplars: Talcott Parsons and T. S. Eliot.

In April 1944, the eminent American sociologist Talcott Parsons was one of the featured speakers at a conference entitled "Germany after the War," for which he prepared a brief memorandum on institutional change and its likely consequences. After the promulgation of the Morgenthau Plan later that year, Parsons revised his memorandum into a more extensive essay, which was published in February 1945 and subsequently distributed to "a large number of those responsible for postwar reconstruction policy on both sides of the Atlantic" (Gerhardt 1993: 54).[20] In that essay, Parsons stressed that the entire conference of academics had been in agreement that "a reintegration of Germany into the community of Western nations" should be the goal of any occupation policy; "ruthlessness" should be avoided (1993: 307). Parsons's reasoning was explicitly occidentalist, particularly when considering how one should solve the problem of German aggression.

> Acceptance of . . . deposition from all immediate hopes of worldly glory as a judgment of God would solve the immediate problem of German aggression. But it would not ensure against its eventual revival, and it would preserve a basis for it because it would consolidate the separateness of the German people instead of assimilating them into the larger community of Western civilization. (320)

Parsons also cautioned that the values of "Western civilization as a whole . . . are by no means dead in Germany" and emphasized that the only long-

20. Parsons was also a part-time adviser to the Foreign Economic Administration Agency between March and October 1945, in which capacity he was a participant in the discussions about reparations policies and deindustrialization practices before and after the Potsdam Conference (Gerhardt 1993: 57).

term solution to the German problem was the integration of Germany into this "moral community . . . based on the values of Christianity and certain derived or closely related secular values" (320–21). Although this language is somewhat more restrained than that deployed by Senator Eastland, the logic of the argument is virtually identical.

The poet and critic T. S. Eliot, as a transplanted American living in London, was another powerful articulator of positions based on the common cultural heritage shared by Europe and America. Eliot thought of himself, and by extension the whole United States, as essentially European[21] and worked to promulgate this notion in his lectures, his poetry, and his work as a publisher (Cooper 1995: 28–29). In his analysis of that common heritage, he always stressed the importance of Christianity, specifically Roman Catholicism—even for Protestantism, which "depends on the survival of that against which it protests" (Eliot 1948: 148–49). In a 1944 lecture, Eliot inveighed against the "provincialism" that led intellectuals to ignore this deeper unity of Europe.

> European literature is a whole, the several members of which cannot flourish, if the same blood-stream does not circulate throughout the whole body. The blood-stream of European literature is Latin and Greek—not as two systems of circulation, but one, for it is through Rome that our parentage in Greece must be traced. . . . What mutual intelligibility can we hope to preserve, except in our common heritage of thought and feeling in those two languages, for the understanding of which, no European people is in any position of advantage over any other? (1944: 30–31)

The critique of the German philhellenic claim to a unique understanding of the Greeks is apparent here; Eliot appropriates what German intellectuals invented and subsequently claimed as a *German* heritage for *Europe as a whole*—including himself as a transplanted American. Eliot repeated this argument in a series of three radio addresses that he gave at the request of the military government in Germany in 1946, suggesting that "Germany would be able to find its way back into the West . . . from which it had separated itself" (Cooper 1995: 42–43). The heart of Eliot's argument was that different European languages and literatures were united by "the sources which we share in

---

21. Compare, intriguingly, Adenauer's comment in a speech of 3 June 1947: "America is a creation of Europe . . . and will therefore not behave indifferently towards Germany, for Russia has encroached far into Europe" (BPA, Bestand Konrad Adenauer, DENA report of a speech in Wiesbaden). Given the skepticism about the strength of this civilizational bond that Adenauer expressed in other speeches, we should be especially careful to regard this more optimistic formulation as a strategic deployment of a commonplace in an effort to "hail" the United States and its representatives into a position of aiding Europe and Germany, and not to think of it as a falsifiable factual claim.

common: that is, the literature of Rome, of Greece, and of Israel" (Eliot 1948: 190). This is the tradition of the *Abendland* as articulated by German intellectuals during the nineteenth and early twentieth centuries, although Eliot does not explicitly acknowledge the conceptual debt—or comment on the historical irony of having to bring this message to the German people.

THE CDU PARALLEL

At the same time as these public rhetorical movements were taking place among U.S. elites, a parallel process was taking place in occupied Germany, inside of the newly forming structures of the CDU. After his dismissal as mayor of Cologne by the British occupation authorities, which seems to have been the result of British opposition to having any conservative Catholic politicians in positions of authority in the first place (Schwarz 1995: 323–24), Adenauer quickly became quite interested in taking over the newly forming nondenominational Christian party. Even before being dismissed, he had written to various politicians in an effort to convince them to join the new party. The terms in which he did so are quite striking, especially in light of the rhetorical strategies that I have discussed here; Adenauer's interpretation of the Soviet threat is almost identical to that advanced by the figures just discussed. "I believe," he wrote in a letter to the mayor of Munich,

> that our people can only be made healthy again when Christian principles rule within them once again. Further, I believe that this is the only way to secure strong resistance to the form of state [*Staatsform*] and the ideological world [*Ideenwelt*] of the east—Russia—and to provide a connection with Western Europe in thought and culture, and also in foreign policy. (Adenauer 1983: 78)

Adenauer urged the mayor and his colleagues to keep this situation in mind when discussing what party to affiliate with in the future, as "only the projected association of all the forces which are based on Christian and democratic principles can protect us from the danger which threatens us from the east" (79). Similarly, he wrote to the mayor of Hamburg that the new party stood for "guiding the state according to Christian principles, that is, according to the principles which have developed in the West [*Abendland*] in the course of the centuries on Christian and humanist foundations" (86).

It is highly significant that Adenauer was utilizing this combination of rhetorical resources, because his next move was to consolidate his control of the emerging party through a combination of careful coalition-building among old political allies and sheer bravado, such as when he strode into the first meeting of local party leaders to set up some administrative machinery for the British zone of occupation (in January 1946) and announced that, as the oldest person present, he was assuming the position of temporary chairman of the meeting. "Once Adenauer was in the chair it was difficult for" even the

most prominent of his opponents "to attempt to dislodge him" (Heidenheimer 1960: 66). Adenauer's organizational position, and the resources that it
included, thus became important vehicles for the promulgation of occidentalist appeals.

At a meeting in Neheim-Hüsten two months later, the assembled delegates
approved Adenauer's position formally and also accepted (with a few minor
modifications) as the working program of the party a document that Adenauer had written virtually by himself. Among the points of this program was
the declaration that among the foremost goals of a CDU government would
be a "return to the foundations of Western-Christian [*christlich-abendländis-
cher*] culture, whose core is the noble view of the dignity of the person and the
worth of each individual human being." The document also maintained that
"the victors, who have the power of the occupation, also have, according to
both human and divine law, duties to the vanquished," which subtly delin-
eates the party's opposition to the (officially atheist) Soviet Union even while
declaring an intent to live in peace with all nations (Konrad-Adenauer-
Stiftung 1975: 131–35).

Shortly after becoming party leader, Adenauer gave a number of major
speeches outlining the new Christian Democratic position, which continued
the deployment of occidentalist language to outline a vision for the future of
Germany in Europe. "The unity of Europe was for Adenauer a bulwark of the
Christian West against Bolshevism," without which 'the West' would not survive the threat from Asia (Altmann 1993: 49).[22] Indeed, Adenauer's early advocacy of some kind of European unification—as early as October 1945, and
even earlier during his tenure as mayor of Cologne before the First World War
(Schwarz 1995: 160–61, 318–20)—was linked to a tradition of "European internationalism" that was intimately bound up with "Christian and secular
humanist notions of natural rights. Federalism, the return to consciousness of

---

22. Adenauer gave an interview the day before he was dismissed as mayor of Cologne in
which he propounded many of these views; the clearest statement of them is in a contemporaneous letter that he wrote to the mayor of Duisburg: "The part of Germany not occupied by Russia is an integral part of Western Europe. If it stays sick, there will be severe
consequences for all of Western Europe, including for France and for Britain. It therefore
lies in the interests of Britain and France, and not only in the interests of that part of Germany not occupied by the Russians, to draw together all of Western Europe under their
leadership, which will reassure the part of Germany not occupied by the Russians both
politically and economically, and also make it healthy again" (Adenauer 1983: 130). Adenauer's phrase "the part of Germany not occupied by the Russians" [*der nicht von Rußland
besetzte Teil Deutschlands*], combined with his diagnosis of the division of Europe as stem-
ming from Russian actions, leaves little doubt as to the "severe consequences" that Adenauer envisions: a Communist takeover.

Western Christian values [*Wiederbesinnung auf die christlich-abendländischen Werte*], humanism and internationalism were closely bound together in the 'European idea' of these years" (Schwarz 1979: 497–98).[23]

A striking example of Adenauer's articulations on this score can be found in a speech delivered before a CDU rally on 5 May 1946, during the lead-up to the British zone elections scheduled for that September. Adenauer began, as might have been expected, with an analysis of the present situation in which Germany found itself. "We must be clear about the reasons for this catastrophe," he argued.

> Let me briefly mention the essential reasons: in the first place, I will mention the exaggeration and excessiveness [*Überspitzung und Übertreibung*] of the Prussian conception of the state, its militarism and its nationalism. Let me repeat: the exaggeration and the excessiveness. In the second place, I will mention Marxism of all shades and colors, and in the third place, National Socialism. (KAS, 5 May 1946: 4)

This is a rather interesting order in which to attribute blame for Germany's postwar situation, and a rhetorically useful one, since it makes possible the claim that "without Marxism and without the exaggerated conception of the state, the development of national socialism would not have been possible" (5). This position also points toward a "United States of Europe": going into Europe would necessarily mean a rejection of the "exaggerated" and "Prussian" conception of the state in favor of a larger political and cultural community. Such a community could even include some of the Soviet republics, provided that they were able to loosen their ties to Moscow.

> Russia has an Asiatic part and a European part, but Russia consists of a number of republics, and a portion of these republics are, alongside Soviet Russia, members of the United Nations Organization.[24] Why shouldn't those Russian republics which stand on European ground also become members of a United

---

23. Winston Churchill also deployed a similar notion of Europe on many occasions, such as in his famous speech at Zurich University in which he called for a United States of Europe. On that occasion, he characterized Europe: "This noble continent, comprising on the whole the fairest and the most cultivated regions of the earth, enjoying a temperate and equable climate, is the home of all the great parent races of the western world. It is the fountain of Christian faith and Christian ethics. It is the origin of most of the culture, arts, and philosophy and science both of ancient and modern times." Because of this cultural commonality, he suggested, "we must build a kind of United States of Europe," so that recovery could be advanced and peace and freedom be secured (1949: 198–202).

24. Adenauer refers here to the famous compromise at the Yalta conference whereby Ukraine and Byelorussia were admitted to the UN as separate voting members (Divine 1967: 265–67).

States of Europe? Why should that not be possible? To the contrary, peace and freedom should be finally established in this anguished corner of Europe! (20)

In this way, Europe could "fulfill the world-historical role" of preserving peace and freedom. "Europe, the West, and the Western spirit [*abendländische Geist*] are indispensable for the entire world!" (20). According to the typescript, this conclusion was greeted with enthusiastic applause.

Whether Adenauer was deploying these ideas cynically, as a way of concealing his *real* goals of regaining some sovereign autonomy for Germany, is quite beside the point. Much recent work on Adenauer has sought to demonstrate that Adenauer was no starry-eyed idealist who let ideas like "Western unity" trump considerations of power and influence (Herbst 1989: 85–86; Bührer 1997: 6–7), a point with which I have few disagreements (although the fact that Adenauer used similar language during cabinet meetings and in other "private" settings does raise a few questions about this interpretation). There is, however, *no incompatibility* between Adenauer as cynical manipulator and Adenauer as true believer, if the intent of the account is to explain the efficacy of his activities; what is important in either case is that, in his speeches, he connected rhetorical commonplaces in a particular way so as to legitimate certain actions while delegitimating others. His specification of 'the West' to include European integration and an opposition to Marxism and materialism was to play a significant role in legitimating policies after the CDU became the ruling party in the area; a first step toward this was taken in the British zonal elections of 1946, in which the CDU won 49.1 percent of the votes cast, as opposed to the SPD's 30.2 percent (Schwarz 1995: 367). Whether Adenauer's language was solely responsible for this electoral victory is beside the point; what matters is that the electoral victory put him and his party in a position to promulgate and elaborate their occidentalist-tinged account.

BYRNES'S COMPROMISE

The occidentalist reading of Soviet actions gained prominence throughout 1946, as numerous public figures utilized it to criticize the Truman administration's handling of the occupation of Germany. But Byrnes's Stuttgart speech does not represent a simple victory of this new interpretation of Soviet actions; instead, it represents an attempt to blend the occidentalist critique with the older, 'civilization-in-the-singular' language of four-power cooperation. Although the speech does represent a shift in U.S. policy, the continuity between Potsdam and Stuttgart should not be overlooked (Ninkovich 1988: 57). This much is apparent from the very language of the speech itself, in which Byrnes explicitly denied that the purpose of the new U.S. policy was to recruit German resources for an anti-Soviet crusade.

It is not in the interest of the German people or in the interest of world peace that Germany should become a pawn or a partner in a military struggle for power between the East and the West. . . . The American people want to help the German people to win their way back to an honorable place among the free and peace-loving nations of the world. (State 1950: 3, 8)

Throughout the speech, in fact, emphasis was placed on continued four-power cooperation in the administration of occupied Germany as a single economic unit. Occidentalist language was deployed, but the policy implications that Byrnes drew from this language were not the same as those drawn by others. The important thing about Byrnes's speech is that the occidentalist language and the reference to civilizational totalities coexists, albeit uneasily, with the remnants of the older Rooseveltian strategy, making for a very complex articulation of policy. The speech was directed at several audiences simultaneously, and the final product was quite capable of being interpreted in several different directions.

For one thing, Byrnes's speech needs to be understood in the context of the difficulties with four-power administration of occupied Germany that stretched back at least to the Potsdam Agreement itself. As required by that document, representatives of the four occupying powers had been meeting regularly in Berlin as the Allied Control Council (ACC) but had been unable to set up effective institutions for governing the entire country. The primary obstacle to such cooperation was not the Soviet Union, but France: as early as September 1945, the French representative to the ACC was vetoing proposals for integrated transportation agencies among the four zones of occupation (Eisenberg 1996: 170–71). French objections also blocked proposals to permit German unions to organize cross-zonally, to establish a central German patent office, and even to establish a central German statistical agency "because it would be a useful tool for German mobilization" (Gimbel 1976: 84–86). The central French goal in the ACC seemed to be the prevention of a unified Germany and the defeat of all proposals that seemed to promote such a goal.[25] Faced with such resistance, the ACC was unable to engage in any serious reconstruction policies for the entirety of occupied Germany.

25. There is quite a bit of controversy about this in recent scholarship, with some historians promulgating a very different view of French actions as opposing all-German institutions as a way to prevent the USSR from gaining a foothold in western Europe (Creswell and Trachtenberg 2003a: 11–13). Setting aside for the moment the methodological issues involved in making and sustaining such a claim (for a discussion of these, see Sheetz 2003 and Creswell and Trachtenberg 2003b), the fact remains that it was French opposition in the ACC that led, proximately, to the paralysis of the four-power institutions, and that the publicly stated reasons for this opposition involved a German, not a Soviet, threat.

Adding to these difficulties was a major dispute about reparations. As discussed earlier, the Potsdam formula allowed each occupying power to take reparations from its own zone, but at the same time anything removed from current production was to be counted as a first charge against imports. Hence the level of reparations was linked to the productivity of the German economy, since a more productive Germany would have more ability to produce a surplus beyond this first charge; increased German production would finance reparations payments. And this increased production, in the view of the American military government, was tied to the question of central administrative agencies for all of occupied Germany. The Soviet Union had agreed to many proposals for such agencies, which held out the possibility of their receiving increased reparations payments (Eisenberg 1996: 209–10), but the French remained obstinate.

The deadlock in the ACC prompted two U.S. actions: Clay's decision to stop all reparations transfers to the other zones in May 1946 and Byrnes's proposal to unify the occupation zones at the meeting of foreign ministers in July 1946. In both of these cases, the proffered justification was an adherence to the principles of Potsdam; Byrnes's offer for zonal unification was open-ended, as he declared the United States willing to unite its zone with any of the other zones. Although only the British accepted the invitation, Clay and other officials in the military government continued trying to bring the other zones in as well (Gimbel 1976: 108–9).

What was the purpose of these maneuvers? The disputes among historians parallel the disputes among the principals involved in their initial articulation. State Department officials like Dean Acheson saw the reparations stop and the bizonal merger with the British zone as, if not explicitly anti-Soviet moves, then as tests of Soviet intentions: if the Soviet Union agreed to centralized institutions, complete with reciprocal monitoring of the events in each zone (which had been the principal Soviet objection to some elements of the proposed central German administrations), then the United States would get its way; otherwise, the United States would go it alone. Different officials seem to have viewed the initiatives differently (Gimbel 1976: 106–9; Eisenberg 1996: 234–36; Trachtenberg 1999: 47–48). Clay pressed for *any* measure of zonal unification, as it would make his job much easier,[26] and Byrnes held out the offer for any other power to join the British and American arrangements at any time, which could just as easily have been an effort "to get the Soviets to adhere to the Potsdam Protocol" as a definitive break with it (McAllister 2002: 116). Thus, what seems to be going on here is a clash about the possibility of future cooperation with the Soviet Union, in which State Department

26. In fact, Clay seems to have "expected . . . that a bizonal merger would force the Soviets' pace and encourage them to participate" (Eisenberg 1996: 236).

officials seemed considerably less optimistic than military government officials. And part of the reason for their pessimism was the introduction of occidentalist arguments during the early part of 1946, in terms of which they read Soviet actions in a worse light than the military government officials did.[27]

This is not to suggest that Clay and others in the military government believed that working with the Soviets had been or would be easy, or that such efforts were necessarily about earnest cooperation. In fact, Clay was quite explicit that his advocacy of four-power central institutions for Germany was part of a strategy of engagement intended to win all of Germany for 'the West.' Clay's plan was to consent to some of the Soviet demands on reparations from current production in exchange for open, monitored elections in the various zones; he argued that in a fair election the German communist parties would likely be defeated. The elections held in the Soviet zone in October 1946 seemed to offer a confirmation of Clay's strategy, as the communist-dominated SED "suffered major losses, with its overall total dipping below the fifty percent mark. . . . In many locations, the Party held only a plurality of votes." Since the SED was the Soviet Union's "chief source of internal influence" and was heavily supported by the Soviets, its loss represented a setback for the Soviet Union (Eisenberg 1996: 252–53).

Heartened by this success, Clay presented an ambitious proposal for increased measures along these lines through a settlement of the reparations question, arguing that such a "full political unification of Germany" would extend "Western liberalism to the borders of countries now under Communist influence . . . the gain for Western democracy is the right to contest its philosophy throughout Germany and to extend its frontier to the borders of Poland and Czechoslovakia" (Eisenberg 1996: 255, quoting Clay). If this is read alongside the occidentalist arguments of Kennan and Churchill, it becomes clear that there was a fundamental agreement on the parties to the geopolitical conflict and the goals of that conflict: the Soviet Union was faced by a 'West' that opposed communism, and a 'Western civilization' to which Germany belongs. Even Clay's relatively optimistic reading of the situation, it seems, was importantly constituted by occidentalist premises.

Thus we can see that the shift in American policy toward Germany throughout 1946 is integrally tied up with the increasing prominence of occi-

27. Indeed, historians following the State Department's line on these events have stressed the anti-Soviet aspects of Byrnes's Stuttgart speech (by promising that American troops would remain in Germany, Soviet expansionism could be deterred), but "the French government and the French public reacted most immediately, sharply, and critically" to the suggestion that German power be in any way enhanced (Gimbel 1976: 124). How one interprets these matters depends on what one feels the "real" goal of the United States officials was—unless one focuses simply on the blending of rhetorical appeals.

dentalist language in official policy declarations—even the pronouncements of those, like Byrnes, who seemed to be trying to preserve as much of the "FDR legacy at Potsdam" as they could (McAllister 2002: 119). Whether or not one believed that cooperation with the Soviets in some limited way was possible, such arguments were increasingly phrased in occidentalist terms.

The existence of this language, and its deployment in critiques of U.S. occupation policy, made it imperative to respond in kind. Byrnes's acknowledgment of the occidentalist metageography in his Stuttgart speech, combined with a denial that these civilizational differences pointed toward implacable hostility in and competition over Germany, illustrates the only viable alternative for defenders of the original FDR vision.

Truman's dismissal of Henry Wallace for his anti–hard line speech in September 1946 exemplified the closing of ranks within the U.S. administration. Unlike Clay, Wallace was not advocating cooperation with the Soviet Union for the ultimate purpose of extending and defending the domain of 'Western Civilization.' Rather, his recommendations were decidedly softer on the Soviet Union, and Truman asked for his resignation so as to preserve the new line of policy—which was not yet open conflict but a decidedly harder line in negotiations (Leffler 1992: 139–40). Although it is probably going too far to declare, as Leffler does, that the firing of Wallace and the consolidation of a harder line in the administration represents the beginning of the Cold War, it is certainly the case that the new consensus behind the existence of a fundamental East-West divide was to prove portentous for the future: in a Foreign Policy Association pamphlet entitled *Russia: Menace or Promise?* published in the summer of 1946, Vera Michaels Dean argued that "Because of her geographic isolation, Russia remained outside the main streams of civilization that shaped Western Europe and the New World. That is why Russia, at first glance, seems so backward" (Dean 1946: 9). This was rapidly becoming the new public common sense about the Soviet Union; what remained was a debate about precisely how to deal with this civilizational divide, and in particular how to deal with it on the ground in occupied Germany.

6 The Turning Point, 1947–48

THE END OF 1946 DID NOT provide a clear trajectory for the future course
of postwar German reconstruction. Although "Bizonia," the organizational
merger of the American and British occupation zones, came into being on 1
January 1947, the door had not yet been definitively closed on four-power
cooperation. The 1949 creation of the Bundesrepublik Deutschland, encompassing both Bizonia and most of the French zone of occupation, did signal
that this door was closed, and provided a tangible manifestation that the era
of four-power cooperation had effectively ended. But it was not the organizational reality of the BRD that made four-power cooperation impossible;
rather, it was the legitimation of the BRD in decisively occidentalist terms and
its firm nesting within a transnational 'Western' community led by the
United States, which ruled the policy of wartime cooperation out of bounds.
Between the beginning of 1947 and the end of 1948, occidentalist language
came to dominate policy-making among the Allies and in the western zones of
occupied Germany, thus making the new trajectory possible.

It seems appropriate to refer to the course of events during this two-year
period as a "turning point," albeit one with a fairly long duration. It would be
a mistake to look for a single, precise instant at which trajectories of social
action changed; *all* social action involves the instantaneous deployment of
social resources that produce outcomes, and the important thing about a turning point is not that it takes place at some precise instant but that it marks a
transition between different conditions of possibility (Abbott 2001b: 247–49).
Before 1947, several trajectories were socially plausible; after 1948, that number had been reduced, and alternatives to the occidentalist trajectory were on
the defensive. Although the locking in of this new trajectory was not completed until the BRD joined NATO in 1955, the trajectory itself emerged during 1947 and 1948 in the context of debates about the European Recovery Program (ERP), popularly known as the Marshall Plan, and the organizational
requirements of making it work. In retrospect—which is the way that turning
points always appear (257–58)—these years are the decisive ones.

This chapter proceeds chronologically. I begin with an analysis of the debates in the United States about whether the United States should adopt a more proactive stance in world politics, actively seeking to prop up certain regimes and economies against a perceived threat of social collapse and opportunistic communist infiltration. Partisans of such a transformed role deployed occidentalist language as a way of breaking the exemplarist connection between 'anticommunism' and 'American exceptionalism' that had supported American foreign policy during the interwar period and that had reemerged shortly after the conclusion of the Second World War. Their occidentalist stance also enabled them to join 'anticommunism' to the defense of the whole of 'Western Civilization,' which they specified in such a way as to require economic assistance. I then shift to debates within the western occupied zones of Germany about how German political parties should respond to the aid package, and to its emphasis on integrating Germany into western Europe more tightly. In these debates too we see an occidentalist position rise to dominance by breaking 'German nationalism' from the *Sonderweg* tradition and thus ruling out the neutralism that this combination supported; 'German nationalism' was also joined to a notion of 'Western Civilization' made manifest in organizations like the Organization of European Economic Cooperation, which administered and coordinated important aspects of the ERP.

It is the conjunction of these two local victories of occidentalist-flavored positions that constitutes the major turning point in postwar German reconstruction. After this point, political debate is largely about securing this novel trajectory. This chapter details how the new policy trajectory came to pass.

Occidentalism and the Marshall Plan

> The proposal [for a European Recovery Program] is now under close scrutiny in Congress and the resulting publicity should keep the nation well informed as to the issues. This is especially desirable because we are dealing with a matter which may largely determine the course of history—certainly the character of Western Civilization—in our time and for many years to come. (Marshall in *DOSB* 25 January 1948: 109)

Historians have long emphasized that there was no "Marshall Plan" in the sense of a coherent, fully articulated program for the reconstruction of Europe. The historian John Gimbel has argued that "the Marshall Plan was a series of decisions that grew out of a continuing bureaucratic struggle between the Army and the State Department over the costs of the German occupation, over reparations, over German exports and imports, over contrasting conceptions of the roles of the American presence in Germany and Europe, and over the contrasting conceptions of the roles being played by Russia and France."

There was no "grand plan" or "historical system" (Gimbel 1976: 4). Perhaps there was no grand plan in the sense often sought by diplomatic historians, but there *was* a plan that emerged from the justifications for an American-led program of European recovery that would include Germany: a pattern of occidentalist justifications, which united diverse bureaucratic initiatives directed at European recovery and made them into "the Marshall Plan."

This pattern of justifications was not created out of whole cloth during the actual debates surrounding the establishment of the European Recovery Program in 1947. Rather, it emerged through a series of exchanges and discussions, and supervened on the rhetorical maneuvers sketched in the previous chapter. The establishment of the European Recovery Program in 1947 is only one moment of this process, although it was decisive for subsequent events. Once occidentalist vindicationism became the controlling strategy for U.S. policy through its use in these debates, it enframed subsequent discussions in a profound way.

PRELUDE: THE TRUMAN DOCTRINE

The formulations deployed in the ERP debates were, in a sense, first tested during the debates surrounding the operational meaning of the "Truman Doctrine" proclaimed on 12 March 1947. The speech itself, a result of President Truman's feeling that "the administration faced the greatest selling job in U.S. history" in getting the necessity of an aid package for Greece and Turkey across to the general public, was designed to silence the arguments of those who doubted that the United States had a crucial role to play in world affairs (Leffler 1992: 145). The speech portrayed the global situation in extremely stark terms, utilizing an opposition between "freedom" and "totalitarianism." This tactic linked communism and National Socialism to form an analogy such that people expected "that the 1940s and 1950s would simply be a replay of the 1930s," marked by implacable hostility between partisans of democratic liberty and extreme governmental control of society (Mark 1989: 958–59; Paterson 1988: 4).

Shades of the wartime civilization-in-the-singular language, now combined with a fierce anticommunism, appeared in the speech's grandiloquent declaration that "at the present moment in world history every nation must choose between alternative ways of life," between a way based on "guarantees of individual liberty" and a way based on "terror and oppression." From the enormity of the stakes, Truman drew the famous policy conclusion.

I believe that it must be the policy of the United States to support free peoples who are resisting attempted subjugation by armed minorities or outside pressures. I believe that we must assist free peoples to work out their own destinies in their own way. . . . Should we fail to aid Greece and Turkey in this fateful hour, the effect will be far-reaching to the West as well as to the East. (Senate 1950: 1256)

Truman's use of an East/West dichotomy near the end of the speech recalls Byrnes's usage of the terms a few months before; 'West' and 'East' were not the primary referents for policy-making, but the existence of discrete cultural and civilizational communities was not unimportant to the policies being pursued. A communist triumph in Greece and Turkey would be an issue for the whole of something called 'the West,' rather than a foreign incident against which the United States could somehow insulate itself, and the importance of these two countries in particular lay in their strategic location on the border where the two civilizations met.

The stage seemed set for a global clash between freedom and totalitarianism, and the open-ended nature of the commitment implied in Truman's speech became the focus of the public debate that followed. Critics of the policy sought to demonstrate to a variety of audiences that U.S. foreign policy should proceed in a more restrained manner than Truman's hyperbolical speech seemed to imply, while defenders of the policy—Dean Acheson chief among them—sought to demonstrate that, in fact, U.S. foreign policy would proceed in a less universalist manner than that envisioned by the speech. In making these arguments, analysts reached for some way to differentiate between areas where the United States would provide aid and areas in which it would not. What they utilized, in hearings before Congress as well as in publications and speeches, was 'Western Civilization.' Occidentalism served as the rhetorical commonplace that limited the Truman Doctrine, differentiating between a center and a periphery, between a domain of vital U.S. interests in preserving the larger civilization of which it was a member and a domain in which there were no vital U.S. interests to pursue.

George Kennan, serving as a lecturer and analyst at the National War College at the time of the Truman Doctrine speech, objected quite strongly to the fact that the speech "placed our aid to Greece in the framework of a universal policy rather than in that of a specific decision addressed to a specific set of circumstances." He had objected to this aspect of the speech during the drafting of the address.[1] It thus seemed to offer a blank check, whereby "all another country had to do, in order to qualify for American aid, was to demonstrate the existence of a Communist threat" (Kennan 1967: 320–22). Kennan preferred a somewhat different approach, which is only implied in his categorical

---

1. Kennan reports this in his memoirs, but he takes pains to verify that he relates the impressions that he had at the time rather than reading backward with the benefit of hindsight. His principal reactions to the Truman Doctrine speech were recorded in presentations that he gave at the War College on 14 and 28 March 1947.

statement of "containment" that appeared in *Foreign Affairs* in July 1947. "It will be clearly seen," Kennan argued in that article, "that the Soviet pressure against the free institutions *of the western world* is something that can be contained by the adroit and vigilant application of counter-force at a series of constantly shifting geographical and political points, corresponding to the shifts and maneuvers of Soviet policy, but which cannot be charmed or talked out of existence" ("X" 1947: 576, emphasis added).

Kennan's analysis is quite complex, more so than is usually discussed (Harper 1996: 198–99). A part of this complexity is suggested by Kennan's deployment of the notion of "the western world." Occidentalism served in Kennan's argument as a way to combat American ontological exceptionalism without adopting the universalism of Truman's formulation. Kennan still supported aid to Greece; his objection was to the basis on which this aid was justified. Indeed, Kennan's principal goal with the containment policy was the preservation of Europe on *civilizational* grounds, as can be seen quite clearly in a presentation which he gave to the War College in March 1947.

> Remember that in abandoning Europe we would be abandoning not only the fountainheads of most of our own culture and tradition; we would also be abandoning almost all the other areas in the world where progressive representative government is a working proposition. (Kennan 1967: 318–19)

Ironically, the journalist and public intellectual Walter Lippmann, who was Kennan's great antagonist during the public discussions about the Truman Doctrine (Steel 1980: 443–45), used very similar arguments as a way of *attacking* the policy of containment. In a series of articles published during September 1947,[2] Lippmann seized on the ambiguities of Kennan's article—and Kennan's failure to spell out the precise means through which a policy of containment could be implemented—in order to argue that such a policy would be ultimately unworkable (1947: 21–22). But Lippmann foresaw another, more tragic consequence of containment: the fact that the pursuit of containment "must alienate the natural allies of the United States . . . the nations of the Atlantic community: that is to say, the nations of western Europe and of the Americas."

> The boundaries of the Atlantic community are not sharp and distinct, particularly in the case of the Germans and the western Slavs and the dependencies and colonies of western Europe. But the nucleus of the Atlantic community is distinct and unmistakable, and among the nations that are indisputably mem-

2. These articles, eventually published in book form as *The Cold War* (Lippmann 1947), were the proximate source for the term *cold war* in its contemporary sense—even though Lippmann only used the term in the book's title, and nowhere in the text (Stephanson 1996: §2).

bers of the Atlantic community there exists a vital connection founded upon their military and political geography, the common traditions of western Christendom, and their economic, political, legal, and moral institutions which, with all their variations and differences, have a common origin and have been shaped by much the same historic experience. (24–25)

Lippmann's "Atlantic community," although it covered a bit more territory than other articulations, was clearly an occidentalist notion: in effect, the Atlantic community was 'Western Civilization' together with the regions it had settled and colonized. Seen in this way, Lippmann's objection to Kennan's article and the Truman Doctrine that he felt it supported (10) was quite similar to Kennan's own objection to the Truman Doctrine, both in their focus (universalism) and in their solution (occidentalism).³ Their rhetorical solutions were, in essential respects, the same.

This rhetorical strategy also made a strong showing in the congressional hearings and floor debate that followed Truman's speech. Here it was put to two uses: the justification of the aid package in the first place (particularly the question of why Turkey should be included along with Greece) and a limitation of the universalism implied in Truman's initial pronouncement.⁴ Dean Acheson, as acting secretary of state while Marshall was away in Moscow at a meeting of the Council of Foreign Ministers, served as the administration's primary spokesman for the aid package and did not hesitate to utilize the symbolic value of Greece in his testimony before various congressional committees. When questioned about the goal of the aid package during the hearings in the House of Representatives, Acheson replied:

3. At the same time, it is important to note that Lippmann seems to have seen earlier than Kennan did that containment, even Kennan's antiuniversalist form, meant the end of "diplomatic dialog, normal relations, probing negotiation and resolution of issues of mutual interest" (Stephanson 1996: §13). What I am interested in here is less the question of what containment implies, and more the fact that both Kennan and Lippmann deployed occidentalist language against the universalism of the Truman Doctrine.

4. Even before the speech, Arthur Vandenberg, chair of the Senate Committee on Foreign Relations, wrote to a fellow congressman that even though he did not know all of the facts, "I sense enough of the facts to realize that the problem in Greece probably cannot be isolated by itself. On the contrary, it is probably symbolic of the worldwide ideological clash between Eastern Communism and Western Democracy; and it may easily be the thing which requires us to make some very fateful and far-reaching decisions" (1952: 340). Vandenberg repeated almost the same phrase during the floor debates surrounding ratification of the bill to provide the aid: "The problem involved in this bill—like the problem involved in every other phase of languishing peace—is the persistent controversy between what we loosely call eastern communism and western democracy. From it inevitably stem persistent difficulties—difficulties between the Soviet Union and its satellites upon the one hand, and the United States and like-minded non-communist states upon the other" (348).

The Greek Nation is one of the oldest in the world. The very principles of democracy originated in Greece. For two and a half thousand years the Greeks have been struggling. Sometimes they lost their independence and the possibility of democracy; then they would rise and get it back again and struggle on further to develop the principles of individual freedom and democracy. . . . We want to give the Greek people the help they so earnestly desire, to get back on their feet and remain a free people, struggling toward a more and more perfect democracy. (House Committee, *Assistance to Greece and Turkey* 1947: 35)

During this hearing, Acheson also argued that "the collapse of the two countries which are almost the links between the East and the West would have a very profound effect" on the question of whether the countries of Europe would be able to sustain a democratic way of life (14). The crucial importance of these two countries, therefore, was intimately linked to their position on a civilizational boundary, making them what Representative Charles Merrow called "the outposts against the westward march of Communism" (15). Other countries, not positioned in such a civilizationally strategic location, would have to be evaluated differently.

One persistent problem that came up repeatedly in the hearings and debates was the inclusion of Turkey in the aid bill in the first place. The grounds offered to justify Turkey's inclusion were more explicitly geostrategic than those introduced into arguments about Greece, but occidentalism played a role in defining precisely *what* was being protected. Representative Frances Bolton pressed Rear Admiral Frank Wooldridge on this point, asking him whether aid should be extended to Cyprus and Crete to aid in "the general protection of the west"; the admiral demurred, declaring, "As long as you have control of Greece and Turkish west ports and the Dardanelles, the sea area can be controlled" (128). So the argument that the United States could afford to let Turkey succumb to communist pressure was met with a civilizational response: Turkey was strategically important for the defense of 'the West.' Here we see occidentalism being specified in such a way as to produce "interests" for the United States, as Turkey became part of the United States' sphere of concern by virtue of its position on the fringes of 'the West' itself.

Of course, the Truman Doctrine was also, and quite obviously, animated by anticommunism, and the urgency of Truman's request to Congress depended quite heavily on the contention that Greece was in imminent danger of being taken over by communist guerrillas. Many of the other scholarly accounts of the Truman Doctrine, whether they hold that the Truman administration's use of anticommunist appeals was ultimately rational (Christensen 1996) or unfortunate and irrational (Freeland 1972), emphasize this anticommunism as though a simple reference to "the communist menace" would have sufficed to command support for a policy of foreign entanglements and the provision of aid. But this is not the case. As I have argued in chapter 3, 'anticommunism' was traditionally directed, not outward, but inward; a "Red Scare" was about self-purification and insulation from foreign influences, not about extending economic and military aid to foreign places. The first "Red Scare" in the United States, which reached its heights in the Palmer raids of late 1919, culminated in the deportation of many radical activists, a kind of effort to purify the body politic against foreign invasion; anticommunism and nativism ran together (Campbell 1992: 161–64; Kovel 1994: 17–21).

So 'anticommunism' was certainly important, but it is not the whole story; the gap between 'anticommunism' and the proffering of aid remains. Those opposed to foreign commitments could have argued that the proper response to communism was the traditional "isolationist" response: seal the borders, hunt down domestic traitors, and invest in continental defense. It is the joining of 'anticommunism' to occidentalism that provided the rhetorical justification for policies involving foreign commitments as principles of American foreign policy. Certain regions of the world were defined as essential because they shared in the civilizational community in which the United States participated, or they were essential to its defense. Hence they had to be defended from the communist menace, which was understood to be *a threat to 'Western Civilization' as a whole, and not merely to the United States of America.* What was important was not merely the 'anticommunist' commonplace, but the occidentalism deployed by defenders and critics of the Truman Doctrine alike in an effort to break down any seemingly universal and open-ended commitments.[5]

SQUARING THE CIRCLE: SELLING THE
EUROPEAN RECOVERY PROGRAM

One of Walter Lippmann's objections to the policy of containment was the implication of such a policy for the future disposition of Germany. He feared the consequences of enlisting German assistance for the execution of a containment policy, because bringing the Germans into an anti-Soviet coalition would require a cultivation of "the national patriotism of the Germans." In this case the United States would be encouraging "the Germans to want something—namely national unity—which we cannot give them except by going to war with Russia" (1947: 47). This would be disastrous, since the Soviet Union had it within its power to reunify the country in a way that the United States and its allies did not; alternatively, a rearmed Germany would probably seek to take back its lost territories by force. But the policy of containment

---

5. It is the case, however, that Congress inserted amendments dealing with China into many of the bills funding the Marshall Plan, which shows that the administration was not entirely successful in getting an occidentalist limitation of the Truman Doctrine accepted by everyone involved. See the following discussion.

would not work without the Germans to serve as part of the boundary against Soviet expansion. Hence:

> The idea that we can foster the sentiment of German unity, and make a trun-
> cated Germany economically strong, can keep her disarmed, and can use her in
> the anti-Soviet coalition is like trying to square the circle. Applied to Germany,
> the policy of containment is a booby trap. (Lippmann 1947: 48)

Lippmann's solution to this insoluble problem was what he called "the Marshall line," according to which the United States would fund the reconstruction efforts of a number of independent states without seeking to fuse them into a coalition and would work toward European integration as a counterweight to Soviet influence in Europe: "Not German unity but European unity, not German self-sufficiency but European self-sufficiency, not a Germany to contain Russia but a Germany neutralized as between Russia and the west, not the Truman Doctrine but the Marshall Plan" (50).

But occidentalism squared this circle.[6] Germany—at least, the part of Germany covered by the western zones of occupation—was determined to be essentially part of 'the West.' On this basis, Germany could be closely integrated into Europe as one part of 'Western Civilization' and form part of an anti-Soviet civilizational bloc. The civilizational logic initially used to circumscribe the Truman Doctrine also shaped the ERP debates, belying Lippmann's effort to oppose the two policies.

CRAFTING THE POLICY

There is a great deal of debate among historians about the origins of the ERP: whose memoranda were most important to the initial proposal, what the real purpose of the proposal was, and so forth. What seems clear is that many U.S. State Department officials, including George Kennan and Will Clayton, were considering some form of reconstruction program that would permit the countries of Western Europe to get back on their feet after the severe winter of 1946–47. The proposed remedy called for more than a simple transfer of resources but involved a close formal cooperation between the recipient countries so that they could reap the benefits of economic integration. And central to all of the various memoranda and preliminary studies was the notion that the western zones of occupied Germany had to be an integral part of any such coordination for Europe as a whole (Hardach 1994: 41–45; Hogan 1987: 26–53). The ERP was thus largely about the utilization of German resources

---

6. Technically, occidentalism reconstituted the problem rather than solving it as originally posed, which is the only way that a circle can be squared; the transcendental character of pi ensures that there is no way to square a circle using only a straight edge and a compass. So "squaring a circle" really means altering the framework such that a solution to the altered problem-situation becomes possible. See Sander 1993.

to rebuild the economy of Europe; legitimating the ERP would have to simultaneously legitimate the new importance placed on Germany.

The arguments used to do this were predominantly economic arguments, featuring references to the necessity of German resources to Europe's economic health;[7] but these arguments in turn rested on the occidentalist consideration that Germany belonged to a larger cultural community and could therefore be *trusted* to use its enhanced economic strength for the right purposes. After all, in the early postwar period "it was by no means clear whether the German economy would be restored in its capacity as one of the biggest industrial 'workshops' in Europe or would instead become a supplier of raw materials such as coal" (Bührer 1995: 89). It was by virtue of its belonging to 'Western Civilization' that Germany was rhetorically permitted to play a producer's role; otherwise, it could have been transformed into a supplier and market for French production.

These considerations played a role in the failure of the Moscow Council of Foreign Ministers meeting in March 1947—the first that George Marshall attended as secretary of state—to reach agreement on Germany. The Soviets seemed willing to make a deal on the economic unification of the zones of occupation in return for sharing in the control of the Ruhr industrial region, but the United States selected another path, one that necessitated the exclusion of the Soviets from Western Europe (Eisenberg 1996: 312–17). This policy outcome had a great deal to do with the occidentalist-flavored policy of promoting Western European integration, advocated by John Foster Dulles (who served as an influential adviser to Marshall at the Moscow conference) and his brother Allen (who had chaired a Council on Foreign Relations study group drafting some briefing papers for the conference). European integration had been a policy goal before this time, but the Dulles brothers lent the policy a civilizational impetus besides.

In January 1947, the Council on Foreign Relations' newly formed Study Group on the Problem of Germany was asked to draft background statements and proposals that could be given to Marshall for the upcoming Moscow meeting. The membership of this group included a number of high-powered individuals, among them the future American High Commissioner of Germany, John McCloy; "the members' assumptions generally paralleled those of the Washington incumbents" responsible for policy formulation, but the environment of the study group allowed them to express some of these assumptions more explicitly (Eisenberg 1996: 281–84). Allen Dulles, president of the council and chair of the study group, opened the group's first meeting

7. Often, these arguments made reference to the Hoover Commission report of 18 March 1947, which explicitly argued that German economic recovery was a prerequisite for the rehabilitation of Western Europe (Hogan 1987: 34–35).

on 10 January with an introductory statement that began with the premise that "American policy should not be guided by feelings of revenge" but should concentrate on harnessing German resources for the good of Western Europe—"Germany belongs predominantly to the culture of the West and not to the area of Slav civilization"—and policy should acknowledge this fact (Dulles quoted in Wala 1994: 101).

This introductory statement served as the basis for an article by Dulles that appeared in *Foreign Affairs* in April 1947 (102). In that article he argued that "the German economy should be organized so as to enable the German people to earn their own way in the world and to contribute to the restoration of European economy" (1947: 421). This goal was to take precedence over the maintenance of four-power unity and joint occupation control; if the Soviet Union would not go along with the revitalization of Germany, the United States should take the lead to "build up the economic life of western Germany as best we can, and integrate it into western Europe. . . . We should view Germany first of all in its European setting" (429–31). But how could such a revitalized Germany be constrained from launching another aggressive war? European integration was itself part of the solution, as was a federal constitutional structure for any future German state. Dulles's comments on this point are striking.

> Historically the German people made their best contribution to western civilization in a decentralized confederation. This was a time for them of relative contentment, of peace and cultural progress. When Germany was a unitary Prussianized state, she repeatedly brought war and catastrophe to herself and Europe. (429)

Dulles even went so far as to propose that the capital of a new German state "be moved westward," away from "the old Prussian capital of Berlin," as if the physical location of the capital in the eastern part of the country would have an independent effect on the political disposition of the German state (429).[8] The overarching point, however, was that Germany could be trusted to the extent that it was firmly anchored in 'the West,' reclaimed for 'Western Civilization' as opposed to being turned over to 'the East.' German reconstruction was therefore firmly linked to occidentalist goals.

Allen Dulles's older brother John Foster Dulles, for his part, was equally

---

8. The concerns to which Dulles gives voice are echoed in debates about the location of the federal capital among the German parties in 1949; see chapter 7. Indeed, several German foreign office officials commented to me (in 1998) that they felt that moving the capital of the Federal Republic to Berlin was a mistake, because Berlin was an 'eastern' city and a capital there would be at odds with—and perhaps even threaten—the 'western' orientation of the country. This is of course only anecdotal, but it does suggest that the concerns that Dulles was addressing in 1947 retained some currency in later years.

occidentalist in his advocacy of European integration. In support of this end, he advised Marshall not to permit the Soviet Union to have a say in the distribution of resources from the Ruhr region of Bizonia but to preserve those resources for the exclusive use of Western Europe: "the economy of central Europe, including Scandinavia, was being integrated into and drained into that of the Soviet Union . . . if this tendency extended on into Western Europe, western civilization and personal freedom, as we had known it, would be impossible" (Dulles briefing memo, quoted in Leffler 1992: 152). After the collapse of the Moscow conference in April 1947, this advice would have freer rein. Indeed, Dulles later wrote:

> The Moscow Conference was, to those who were there, like a streak of lightning that suddenly illuminated a dark and stormy scene. We saw as never before the magnitude of the task of saving Europe for Western civilization. We saw the need of economic and moral support and the need of a program that would be both comprehensive and creative. (Dulles 1950: 105)

Whether this was the sentiment in Dulles's mind in 1947 is quite irrelevant (although his testimony before Congress on the ERP echoed this language). What is relevant is that this language was the language that he selected for expressing the importance of the ERP: the importance of the program was civilizational rather than simply economic or geostrategic.

Marshall made the suggestion for what became the ERP during a commencement speech at Harvard University.[9] According to the speech, "our policy is directed not against any country or doctrine but against hunger, poverty, desperation, and chaos. Its purpose should be the revival of a working economy in the world so as to permit the emergence of political and social conditions in which free institutions can exist." The appeal was thus phrased in rather universalist terms, but there was also an implicit geographical and civilizational focus: Marshall moved directly from observations about how "the division of labor is the basis of modern civilization" to a discussion of Europe's import requirements without pausing to justify this restriction of focus (Senate 1950: 1268–70). Perhaps this was, as John Foster Dulles put it, because it was simply "good sense" for the United States to dedicate its resources "primarily to strengthening the West. . . . It is a vital area of which we are in many ways a part, and it is in great peril" (1950: 211). Or, as Marshall himself put in introducing a proposal for aid to Congress a few months later:

> There is convincing evidence that the peoples of western Europe want to preserve their free society and the heritage that we share with them. To make that

9. By coincidence, T. S. Eliot was also receiving an honorary degree that day (Pogue 1991: 54), thus pairing a key disseminator of occidentalism with a key deployer of the commonplace.

choice conclusive they need our assistance. It is in the American tradition to help. In helping them we will be helping ourselves—because in the larger sense our national interests coincide with those of a free and prosperous Europe. . . . We must not permit the free community of Europe to be extinguished. (Senate 1950: 1277)

Occidentalism was therefore a part of the legitimating narrative of the ERP from the time of its earliest consideration. This was a continuation of the strategy of limiting the universal scope of the Truman Doctrine to only those areas of the world that were "critical"—a judgment made, as argued earlier, in civilizational terms.

The occidentalism of these formulations also indicates a weakness in those academic accounts of postwar reconstruction based on the notion of "liberalism." Robert Latham, for example, rejects an attempt to analyze postwar reconstruction as 'Western' because "the West . . . cannot be reduced to a single mode of organizing social existence" and seems to contain legacies of both liberalism and Nazism (1997: 16–17). Thomas Risse similarly suggests that 'the West' is too broad and diverse a notion, and that it represents "a specific enculturation of a broader liberal worldview" which is itself precise enough to explain specific outcomes (Risse-Kappen 1996: 370–71). But even a quick glance at the language used to legitimate the ERP indicates that this language is civilizational through and through; liberalism, to the extent that it is even mentioned, is listed as a 'Western' civilizational characteristic.

Although the ERP was certainly organized around broadly liberal economic principles, and although realizing this does help to illuminate certain aspects of the program, such an analytic does not get at the fundamental causal question of how the program was made acceptable to the broader public audience. To answer that question, it is necessary to see how the concrete policy debates played out. The ambiguity of 'Western Civilization' is an asset in these debates, inasmuch as the notion can be specified in ways extremely germane to the specific discussion at hand. Latham is correct to argue that the 'Soviet threat' as a conceptual object emerges only from within a particular arrangement of U.S. commitments (1997: 117–19), but he misspecifies the character of these commitments by focusing on their "liberalism." The 'Soviet threat,' at least as it was publicly produced and deployed, was a *civilizational* threat.

SELLING THE POLICY

Throughout the remainder of 1947, a vigorous campaign in favor of the ERP was launched, which consisted of two formally separate but intimately related parts: a pronounced speaking schedule by State Department officials and efforts by a "Citizen's Committee for the Marshall Plan," nominally headed by former Secretary of War Henry L. Stimson, the executive committee of which included such foreign policy establishment figures as Dean Acheson and Alan Dulles (Wala 1994: 190–93). Both parts of this campaign sought to educate the American public about the need for the ERP and did so in pointedly occidentalist terms. At the same time, a series of high-profile committees had been named to study the feasibility of the ERP; the most important of these was the President's Committee on Foreign Aid, chaired by Secretary of Commerce Averill Harriman; the committee's report was presented to the public on 8 November 1947. This report joined with the official and unofficial parts of the campaign for the ERP in placing European recovery on occidentalist grounds.

The official State Department speaking schedule featured numerous addresses setting out the rationale for the ERP. Several of these speeches, such as Marshall's address to the Congress of Industrial Organizations on 15 October 1947, proposed that the solution to Europe's problems was to raise productivity for the long term: "we must be assured that the participating countries will make every possible effort to reach the production rates they have set for themselves and that they will make the necessary reforms. . . . the present situation requires more than stoical, even heroic endurance." But why should the United States, and the CIO in particular, concern itself with European productivity?

> Because the economic stability of Europe is essential to the political stability of Europe, it is of tremendous importance to us, to our peace and security, and it is equally important to the entire world. We are faced with the danger of the actual disappearance of the characteristics of western civilization on which our Government and our manner of living are based. (DOSB 26 October 1947: 827–28)

So the danger, while certainly involving narrow American economic interests, was explicitly framed by an occidentalist context: economic stability was needed for political stability, which in turn was required for civilizational stability. Absent this last step, Marshall would have had to demonstrate that a political collapse of European countries posed a direct threat to the United States; otherwise a response of "why should *we* care?" might intrude and make his entire argument irrelevant. Occidentalism here plays its usual role in breaking down the notion that the United States can simply go it alone in the world, referencing instead a larger cultural community toward which U.S. actions should be oriented.

The public articulations of other members of the State Department further expanded on the occidentalist character of the Marshall Plan.[10] The real tri-

10. See, for example, assistant secretary of state for political affairs Norman Armour before the Boston Conference on Distribution (DOSB 2 November 1947); Francis Russell, director of the State Department's Office of Public Affairs, before the National Cooperative Milk Producers Federation (DOSB 16 November 1947); and Armour at the American Academy of Political Science (DOSB 23 November 1947).

umph of occidentalism, however, came with Marshall's speech in Chicago on 18 November 1947. Reconstructing Europe, he declared, would necessarily involve "the restoration of Germany. Without a revival of German production there can be no revival of Europe's economy" (DOSB 30 November 1947: 1027). Safeguards had to be erected in order to prevent Germany from using its renewed strength to threaten the peace of Europe, safeguards that would involve the use of German resources for the good of Europe as a whole. Contrary to Soviet declarations, Marshall argued, this was not a preference for Germany over the rest of Europe, but a plan to restore Europe's economic viability.

> We are aware of the seriousness and extent of the campaign which is being directed against us as one of the bulwarks of Western civilization. We are not blind to any of the forms which this attack assumes. And we do not propose to stand by and watch the disintegration of the international community to which we belong. . . . We can afford to discount the alarms and excursions intended to distract us, and to proceed with calm determination along the path which our traditions have defined. (1028)

According to Marshall's argument, the United States and Europe belonged to a common cultural community, which the Soviet Union threatened; Germany was a part of this community too, and as such could be reconstructed within the framework of an integrated Europe and a free 'West'; and the traditions of this community gave U.S. policy its direction. The Marshall Plan was thus a program to save 'Western Civilization,' including Germany, and should be implemented on this basis.

Complementing this official campaign were the efforts of the Citizens' Committee for the Marshall Plan. Among the committee's efforts on behalf of the ERP were a number of high-profile newspaper ads and inserts, a series of pamphlets and booklets, and many speaking engagements across the country (Wala 1994: 194–200). Almost all of the committee's efforts involved an article written by Henry Stimson entitled "The Challenge to Americans" that had appeared in the October 1947 issue of *Foreign Affairs*. The committee's publicity materials either featured reprints or excerpts of the piece, or "merely repeated the basic arguments Stimson had made" (202). In effect, the committee's function was to deploy the arguments of Stimson's article more widely and more forcefully. Those arguments were directed against the possibility that the United States would turn its back on the world as it had after World War I.

> The troubles of Europe and Asia are not "other people's troubles"; they are ours. The world is full of friends and enemies; it is full of warring ideas; but there are no more "foreigners," no merely "foreign" ideologies, no merely "foreign" dangers, any more. (Stimson 1947: 6–7)

The central challenge, he continued, was posed by communism, but Stimson's understanding of this challenge was quite subtle. "We must no longer let the tide of Soviet expansion cheaply roll into the empty places left by war, and yet we must make it perfectly clear that we are not ourselves expansionist," he argued. "Our task is to help threatened people help themselves." The proper way to do this was not, however, through any kind of aggressive stance, but rather through a kind of inward focus.

> Soviet intransigence is based in very large part on the belief that all non-Communist systems are doomed. Soviet policy aims to help them die. We must hope that time and the success of freedom and democracy in the western world will convince both the Soviet leaders and the Russian people now behind them that our system is here to stay. (9)

The inward focus was thus a *civilizational* inward focus, a concentration on restoring the functionality of and faith in the basic principles of 'the West': "The problem of Russia is thus reduced to a question of our own fitness to survive" (10). And saving the democratic 'West' would be the best way to demonstrate this fitness.

> The immediate and pressing challenge to our belief in freedom and prosperity is in western Europe. Here are people who have traditionally shared our faith in human dignity. These are the nations by whose citizens our land was settled and in whose tradition our civilization is rooted. They are threatened by Communism—but only because of the dark shadows cast by the hopelessness, hunger, and fear that have been the aftermath of the Nazi war. . . . The reconstruction of western Europe is a task from which Americans can decide to stand apart only if they wish to desert every principle by which they claim to live. And, as a decision of policy, it would be the most tragic mistake in our history. (10–11)

Stimson's argument was thus an occidentalist deployment against 'American exceptionalism' and the policies that it traditionally supported. His concern with breaking down the notion of the "foreign" illustrates one of the central rhetorical capacities of the occidentalist commonplace: its ability to serve as the larger community within which particular nations and states can be effectively "nested." By this logic, the ERP is the logical outgrowth of a civilizational commonality—provoked, perhaps, by Soviet power, but rooted in something other than short-term interests. Spread by the nationwide efforts of the Committee on the Marshall Plan, this framing of the issues soon became readily available to advocates.

The report *European Recovery and American Aid,* released by the Harriman Committee on 7 November 1947, made a very similar appeal, pointing out that whereas "in 1940, it seemed inevitable that a large part of what we call

Western civilization was irreparably lost," the following years proved that "American arms" could retake most of this ground. Even though the wartime alliances had ended, the report argued, "it is safe to say that at no time in history has there been more need for Western Europe and the United States to stand firmly together. And who will say that, if we apply to the making of the peace the same spirit which triumphed in war," which is the spirit of 'Western Civilization,' "we may not see an equally dramatic vindication of the ideals and principles of free men everywhere?" (DOSB 16 November 1947: 948). Whether the plan was thought to be directed against communism or against the breakdown of the European economy—and these were linked inasmuch as communism was usually diagnosed as a response to chaotic economic conditions—the proposed solution was an occidentalist one.

A final, broader component of the public campaign was provided by the extraordinary success of the abridged edition of Arnold Toynbee's *A Study of History* in the United States during 1947. Toynbee, a British historian who had been decisively influenced by Spengler, conceptualized his twelve-volume work as a response to Spengler's account of civilizations (Toynbee 1958: 20–21). The essential difference was that for Toynbee, every civilization had the possibility for renewal, and the trick to staving off decline was simply figuring out how to accomplish this (Schischkoff 1965: 72). Toynbee's more optimistic tone undoubtedly contributed to his success in the United States. But what really helped Toynbee's popularity was the fact that he was the director of the research institute responsible for the formulation of British postwar aims and in this capacity had been interacting with high-level American officials throughout the war. In 1942 he had been sent to the United States for a consultation and remained there for two months, speaking to groups all over the country and delivering a message "that a durable peace would require the United States to take an active part in world affairs." Toynbee's argument was derived from his civilizational analysis and addressed what he regarded as the possible courses of action available to a power in a late stage of a civilization. He urged the Americans to whom he spoke—including John Foster Dulles—to pursue the course of renewal (McNeill 1989: 182–85).

During that same 1942 visit, Toynbee had attended a dinner party with Henry Luce, publisher of a number of American magazines including *Life* and *Time;* Luce was very taken with Toynbee, and when the abridgment of Toynbee's book was published in 1947 Luce publicized it in a number of his magazines and used his influence to have reviews publicized elsewhere as well. "The rise and fall of Toynbee's reputation in the United States hinged, very much, on what Henry Luce thought of him and how his magazines chose to present Toynbee's writings and other pronouncements to their readers" (McNeill 1989: 211–13). And the light in which Toynbee was presented was quite favorable indeed.

To mention only one example, on the cover of *Time* for 17 March 1947[11] stood a picture of Arnold Toynbee, against a background of human figures struggling up a mountain—a frequent image for the dynamics of civilizations in Toynbee's work—over the caption "our civilization is not inexorably doomed." The article itself proclaimed that the contemporary "crisis in Western civilization" demanded that the United States become "the champion of the remnant of Christian civilization against the forces that threatened it." The moral that the author drew from his presentation of Toynbee's theory was that "not materialist but psychic factors are the decisive forces of history . . . the real drama unfolds within the mind of man. It is determined by his responses to the challenges of life; and since his capacity for response is infinitely varied, no civilization, including our own, is inexorably doomed. Under God, man, being the equal of his fate, is the measure of his own aspirations." This was, as William McNeill has pointed out, no more of a distortion than one normally expects from popular reviews of scholarly work; but it did emphasize those elements of Toynbee's approach most congruent with Luce's own vision of an "American Century" (McNeill 1989: 217–18).

"The American reading public . . . manifested for Toynbee's work an enthusiasm that [Spengler's] *Decline* in its best days had never enjoyed" (Hughes 1952: 146). This enthusiasm converted Toynbee into something of a "professional wise man, whose pronouncements on foreign affairs, on the historical past, and on religious and metaphysical questions were all accorded serious attention by a broad spectrum of earnest souls seeking guidance in a tumultuous postwar world" (McNeill 1989: 206). Toynbee gave many public lectures pressing the same themes addressed throughout his writings, further interpreting events in a civilizational framework. Happy being an advocate, he declined to accept the prophet's mantle—although Luce kept after him to do so. But Toynbee was certainly willing to publicly associate himself with the ERP, thus constituting yet another component of the public campaign using occidentalist language to support the program.

CONGRESSIONAL HEARINGS

The next step in implementing the ERP was to get the program approved by Congress. The strategy for all of the aid bills[12] continued the strategy of the broader public campaign: use occidentalist language to join 'anticommunism' to the specific policy of committing American resources abroad and to exclude the ontological exceptionalism that lay at the center of the arguments of exem-

11. This is contemporaneous with the pronouncement of the Truman Doctrine, which is most likely not an accident.

12. Because of the time required for the legislative process, the Truman administration decided to send an interim aid bill through in early November 1947, followed by a long-range bill that would be discussed the following January.

plarist opposition. This rhetorical strategy was in evidence throughout the hearings on the bills before the House Committee on Foreign Affairs and the Senate Committee on Foreign Relations—both the carefully managed hearings in the Senate, where the proceedings were "in the hands of a powerful and expert champion, Arthur Vandenberg," who chaired the committee, and the somewhat more fragmented affair in the House where Chairman Charles Eaton was unable to control his fellow committee members to the same degree (Freeland 1972: 264–67). But the argumentative strategies pursued by the critics and the defenders of the ERP are in evidence in both locations, as well as in the subsequent debate on the floor of Congress.

However, I should be clear about the fact that committee hearings and floor debates in Congress concerning the ERP were *not* primarily concerned with 'Western Civilization.' The vast bulk of the testimony and discussion concerned minutiae and details: quibbles about exactly how much money was required by a particular country, quarrels about how certain figures and estimates were calculated, and concerns about how the program should be administered. This last matter is quite significant to the history of the ERP itself, as the debate turns on the issue of whether the program should be a government-run project or a businesslike quasi-private effort that would be funded by government money.[13] And a considerable amount of time was also spent on the matter of whether specific commodities should be included in the program.[14] But in order for all of this discussion to go on, there was a prior question that needed to be settled: whether the United States should devote *any* resources to a program like this. Occidentalism, along with the other components of the strategy pursued by advocates of the ERP, was not primarily directed at these detail questions but was concerned to frame the issue in such a way as to legitimate the entire program itself. Thus occidentalist allusions appear only sporadically in the documents, but their location is highly significant.

In his initial statement on the Interim Aid bill to a joint session of both Committees, Marshall argued,

> There is convincing evidence that the peoples of western Europe want to preserve their free society *and the heritage we share with them.* To make that choice conclusive they need our assistance. . . . In helping them we will be helping ourselves—because, in the larger sense, our national interests coincide with

13. Details of this aspect of the debate can be found in Arkes 1972 and Hogan 1987.

14. For instance: on 4 February 1948, J. A. Smith of the Northwest Horticultural Council appeared before the House Committee to discuss the benefits of including fresh fruit in the ERP; on 18 February 1948, A. G Bryant, president of the National Machine Tool Builder's association, appeared for a similar purpose but—no surprise—in favor of the inclusion of machine tools. And there are many other instances.

those of a free and prosperous Europe. (House Committee, *Hearings on Emergency Foreign Aid* 1947: 9, emphasis added)

I have added emphasis to the significant section of the argument, which grounds Marshall's evaluation of "our national interests" and serves as the basis for the policy as a whole. It is true that this is only one part of one sentence, but its role in framing the issue is crucial: it implies that if the European countries were no longer willing or able to preserve this heritage, aid would not be forthcoming. The program is cast not merely as an initiative for *economic* recovery, but for *civilizational* recovery as well.[15]

Advocates of ERP also endeavored to join occidentalism with 'anticommunism,' so as to justify an outward-looking foreign policy. A particularly striking example of this tactic came in an exchange between Undersecretary of State Robert Lovett and Representative Chester Merrow (NH) before the House Committee, concerning "national security."

> *Merrow:* Mr. Secretary, I have a feeling that all proposals for assistance to any foreign country could be considered in terms of our own national interest and in terms of the security of the United States. Can it not be correctly said that France and Italy constitute the western front against the spread of communism and Russian aggression?
> *Lovett:* I think it can be said that the countries of western Europe represent an area of free states as compared with the police state group . . .
> *Merrow:* It seems to me that they constitute the western front. (House Committee, *Hearings on Emergency Foreign Aid* 1947: 66)

What is unusual about this formulation is that France and Italy, and the other countries of western Europe, constitute a "western front" only if viewed from the perspective of *the USSR,* and not from the perspective of the United States (from which they would constitute an *eastern* front). Merrow's formulation seems more metageographical than geographical: western Europe constitutes a front *for* 'the West,' rather than being located *in* a westerly direction. Along these lines, Representative Elliott Dirksen (IL), recently returned from a trip to Europe, suggested that aid should certainly be given to Italy because of the situation of Trieste: "Trieste is the contact point between western culture and the Oriental ideology of the Soviet Union, and so millions of people will be glowering across that little contact point, and that is why Italy is so important" (271). When a question about the inclusion of some particular

---

15. Undersecretary of State Robert Lovett was quite explicit about this during the committee's next session: "The purpose of the interim aid bill is stated in the preamble here, but to paraphrase it, we feel that security and economic stability are important considerations in our search for peace. We are trying to help make it possible for western Europe to maintain a form of civilization to which they have been accustomed through the years" (House Committee, *Hearings on Emergency Foreign Aid* 1947b: 58).

country was raised, the answers tend to stem from a blend of 'anticommunism' and 'Western Civilization.'

Nowhere was this more apparent than in the discussion of German participation in the ERP. Vandenberg's first question to Marshall during the Senate
hearings was a request for a clarification of Germany's status, to which Marshall replied that "it is essential that western Germany be considered as an
integral part of the program" (Senate Committee, *European Recovery Program
Hearings* 1948: 11). There was therefore a strong argument on economic
grounds for the inclusion of German resources, but this did not reach a policy
of rehabilitating some part of Germany and permitting it to participate in the
program as a relative equal. When Ambassador Lewis Douglas, the Truman
administration's point man for the legislative campaign, launched into his
elaborate presentation about the importance of western Europe as an object of
U.S. policy, the gap between needing German resources and encouraging
German reconstruction was more explicitly bridged by occidentalist logic.
Douglas introduced a variety of graphs and statistics illustrating western
Europe's importance to world trade, but there was some ambiguity about pre-
cisely which parts of western Europe were included in these figures.

> *Vandenberg:* Mr. Ambassador, your figures do not include western Germany?
> *Douglas:* They do.
> *Vandenberg:* They do include western Germany?
> *Douglas:* They do. All of these figures include western Germany. . . . Those
>   requirements of western Germany were not based upon mere relief for
>   western Germany, but they were calculated upon the assumption that west-
>   ern Germany must recover, for it is generally accepted that barring, of
>   course, the assurances that Germany does not again become a menace to the
>   peace of the world, European recovery in large measure depends upon a
>   recovery of Germany.

But Douglas kept referring to "the 16 countries" of western Europe,
prompting Vandenberg to intervene again.

> *Vandenberg:* Mr. Ambassador, let me again get this straight. You keep men-
>   tioning the 16 countries, and western Germany is not one of the 16 coun-
>   tries.
> *Douglas:* I am sorry. I am probably not defining the matter properly. The 16
>   participating countries plus western Germany. And that applies to all of
>   these groups [of numbers]. If I again lapse into that error I hope everybody
>   will understand that I mean the 16 participating countries plus western Ger-
>   many. (Senate Committee, *European Recovery Program Hearings* 1948: 77)

Throughout the ensuing discussion, there was no further comment raised
about the inclusion of western Germany, suggesting that it was simply
assumed that European recovery meant German recovery and vice versa. This

consensus was surrounded and underpinned by an occidentalist appreciation of the importance of western Europe; Douglas supplemented his economic figures with the observation that "there is another feature about this area of which we are speaking. It was the traditional and historic seat of western culture from which we have derived many of our political institutions, and a large part of our basic philosophy of the freedom of the individual" (79). The purpose of ERP was to preserve this heritage.

> This European program is aimed not at the relief of these countries, not to provide merely the means by which human beings can subsist, and no more, but it is aimed at achieving a true, solid, firm, economic recovery, and reconstruction of this devastated part of the world, and as a consequence, of restoring, or of aiding in restoring, the traditional political institutions which are, with modifications and variations, so intimately related to the basic philosophic conceptions of our own. (81)

Four days later, in his presentation before the House committee, Douglas—apparently having learned from his questioning before the Senate that western Germany's importance needed to be stressed even more forcefully—began his statement with a clearer portrayal of where the boundaries of 'Western Civilization' lay.

> I think that perhaps I can silhouette the character and the quality, the nature and the importance of the area of which we are speaking, by referring to certain facts which disclose its industrial power and its cultural background. They are important, for these 16 nations, the recovery of which we are determined to support, constitute a community of nations of western civilization, of which we are an inescapable member. . . . I should add that when I speak of the participating countries I include western Germany. (House Committee, *European Recovery Program Hearings* 1948: 112)

No one questioned this particular bounding of 'Western Civilization' during the ensuing discussion, and Douglas subsequently used this blending of economic and civilizational factors to advocate and support the promotion of European integration through the aid package.

But the rehabilitation of western Germany, although Germany was accepted by all sides of the discussion to belong to the civilization that was to be preserved by the ERP, still raised a few questions, particularly the question of whether a rehabilitated Germany might pose a renewed threat to peace. The Harriman Committee's report, as noted earlier, had stressed the necessity of German recovery to preserving this region of the world, and Harriman was quite aware of the way in which this proposal might be misunderstood as a prioritizing of German recovery over the recovery of other countries.[16] The

---

16. Harriman stressed this point in his testimony before the committee (Senate Committee, *European Recovery Program Hearings* 1948: 269–70).

way to avoid this misunderstanding was to make it clear to all concerned that Germany was a part of 'Western Civilization' by virtue of something more powerful than simple economic self-interest; integrating western Germany into Europe was an expression of this position. Indeed, the fact that only the *western* zones of occupied Germany were available for such integration was sometimes used as a benefit, as when Allen Dulles argued:

> We stand a real possibility of bringing out the better side of the Germans and knitting them into western culture. . . . We have a chance of doing that because the part of Germany that was most closely associated with the east has been lopped off. . . . that area, where there were great affinity between the Germans and the Russians—the Bavarian and the Rhinelander did not have those affiliations with the east, and therefore the fact that this area is lopped off may be for the moment, at least, a blessing in disguise, and help us in knitting the western states in Germany into a European federation. (House Committee, *European Recovery Program Hearings* 1948: 1640–41)

One of the implications drawn by many observers from this inclusion of western Germany in the ERP regarded the U.S. policy of continuing the demolition of industrial plants for use as reparations payments. Demolition had been provided for in the Potsdam Agreement, as a measure of preventing renewed German aggression by removing plants designed for war production; the delivery of reparations had been restarted in 1947 as part of the joint American-British proclamation of a new (and higher) level of industry in the Bizone (Gimbel 1968: 176–77). This had been a controversial policy for many years; Representative Francis Case of South Dakota had introduced a pair of resolutions intended to stop the dismantling program in occupied Germany on the grounds that it was incompatible with the ERP. Case deployed occidentalist reasoning in advancing his proposal.

> I hope that out of this situation there can come the development of the free states of Europe, which will include Bavaria, Hesse, Wurttemberg-Baden, Westphalia, and the other old states of Germany, along with Belgium, Luxemburg, the Netherlands, and France, and thereby build a bulwark for western civilization to hold the line until mankind, some way, with more wisdom than now seems apparent, finds a way for all the peoples of the world to live together in peace. (CR, 16 December 1947: 11481)

During the committee hearings, similar objections were raised by a variety of speakers. Supporters of continuing the policy argued that the United States was obligated under a variety of international agreements to continue dismantling, and they pointed out that the plants being dismantled were sitting idle and would probably continue to do so for years until the German economy had grown substantially stronger. Confronted with the accusation that these arguments were simply incompatible with a policy of economic recov-

ery, supporters had no good answer and had to admit, in essence, that ERP
would lead to the halting of demolition.[17] Were Germany's importance simply limited to serving as a storehouse of resources, it would have been easy to
respond to these arguments against dismantling: removing equipment from
Germany would strengthen other European allies. But since the incorporation
of Germany had been proposed on terms that accorded it a relatively equal
standing as part of the 'Western Civilization' that was to be preserved through
the ERP, advocates of continued dismantling were somewhat constrained by
the broader contours of their position. As a result, a clause was added to the
ERP appropriations bill mandating that the administrators of the aid program
review the dismantling program to see whether any of the plants designated
for removal might be able to contribute to German—and thus European—
recovery by remaining where they were (Gimbel 1968: 181–84). Such a proposal was made possible by the notion that the Germans could be trusted to
use the plants that were not dismantled for the good of 'the West' as a whole.

THE CHINA QUESTION

Another issue that often arose during the congressional ERP debates was the
question of whether other parts of the world deserved U.S. support as they
also resisted communism. It is a short rhetorical leap from the proposition
that the United States has a vital interest in maintaining the noncommunist
character of western Europe to the proposition that the United States has a
vital interest in maintaining the noncommunist character of *every* point on the
globe simultaneously. Against administration wishes, the House committee[18]
quickly began to contemplate including China in the ERP legislation, partially on the grounds that what applied to Greece certainly applied to China
as well: Communists were threatening to take over, so the United States
should step in and render assistance.

It was difficult to avoid the appearance that the administration's anticommunism extended to Europe but not to other regions of the world, particularly since the administration had been placing pressure on the Chinese government to form a coalition with the Chinese communists. This objection
makes a great deal of sense if one reads the Truman administration as arguing
that the purpose of foreign aid programs such as the ERP was to fight communism and overlooks the occidentalist tone of the justification deployed by

17. See, for example, Marshall's testimony of 12 January 1948 (House Committee, *European Recovery Program Hearings* 1948: 77–78), and Secretary of the Army Kenneth Royall's
testimony of 14 January 1948 (462–63).
18. The Senate committee did not, both because of a general and oft-repeated expectation that China would be dealt with in another bill and because Vandenberg exercised
much firmer control over his committee than Eaton did over his.

the advocates of ERP. When questioned, ERP advocates were generally quite blunt about the status of communism in their justifications.

> *Lodge:* In other words, Mr. Secretary, the economic aid is directed to combating the growth of the popularity of communism?
>
> *Marshall:* It is directed, as I construe it, to preventing a desperate situation regarding human life to develop to a point where people will turn to desperate remedies which are no remedies at all. (House Committee, *Hearings on Emergency Foreign Aid* 1947b: 35)

The argument was that American aid should be directed at improving economic conditions and enhancing "productivity," as this would both restore economic health and make communism an unsustainable alternative (Maier 1987: 125–30). Occidentalism's role in these deliberations was to provide a geographical location for such policies, by establishing western Europe as the kind of place that—with a little help—could effectively mount such resistance, because it was of a piece culturally and civilizationally with the United States, communism's opposite.

So why was this appeal not sufficient to rule out aid to China as a matter of course? Several reasons suggest themselves, including the fact that no one ever explicitly *made* such an argument in support of denying aid to China and the fact that the criticism of the Truman administration for being soft on communism in China was useful for those wishing to score political points. But a more salient reason is the fact that a commitment to preserving 'the West' easily spilled over into a commitment to preserve other areas of the world *inasmuch as they were thought necessary to preserve 'the West.'* This "domino" logic had made its first appearance during the hearings concerning aid to Greece and Turkey, when Turkey's inclusion was justified as necessary to a defensive perimeter for 'the West'; it was repeated during the congressional hearings, not least by Representative Frances Bolton, who had made the argument about Turkey during the earlier hearings (House Committee, *European Recovery Program Hearings* 1948: 198–99). Suddenly the effective borders of the West, or at least the borders needed to defend it, seemed to be spilling out into other parts of the world. One witness made a similar point during his testimony.

> You cannot really deal with Europe without keeping Asia in mind, because so much of the normal trade of Europe is with the East . . . If the Orient falls a [*sic*] prey to chaos and anarchy or if it falls into the hands of the Communists, our efforts to restore economic order in Europe may well prove completely useless. (328)

It is important to note that this logic, while not confining itself to support for the administration's preferred policy, was no less occidentalist, as it *presumed* an American commitment to care for Europe and to devote resources to that end. Thus the entire China argument, far from being a refutation of the importance of occidentalism, is in fact an indication of just how *central* the occidentalist commonplace had become.[19] Even critics of the specific ERP proposal drew on occidentalism, accepting that the United States had a responsibility to shore up 'Western Civilization'—but then disagreeing on the best way to accomplish this goal. In the end, the money allotted for China was much smaller than that allotted for Europe, and the basic principle that the defense of Europe should be the United States' top priority was established—which is not surprising if one examines the structure of the China argument closely.

In fact, the argument about support for China is not different in kind from the argument presented by a number of representatives from tobacco-producing areas of the United States in favor of including explicit language in the aid bills that would permit some of the money granted in aid to be used to purchase tobacco. The argument was that tobacco fit under "the proposition that goods should be made available for incentive purposes" as a way of improving productivity. This "would be a great morale builder" (351–53).[20] The form of the argument is similar to that of the China argument: accepting the basic principle that the point of the proposed foreign aid was to increase productivity, the representatives made a case that tobacco should be utilized to this end. Were they motivated by the fact that, as representatives of tobacco-producing regions, their constituents stood to benefit from such inclusion, and such benefits might translate into reelection for themselves? Quite possibly, even quite probably. But absent the larger pattern of justification for the notion of a massive aid package for Europe in the first place, the claims advanced by these representatives would have made no sense.

One might, following Theodore Lowi, argue that the very fact that China (along with tobacco and numerous other commodities) was being discussed at all stemmed from the necessity to "oversell" foreign policy in a liberal society: because of the continual presence of interest groups that have to be brought, so to speak, on board with any given course of action, political elites need to provoke a crisis in order to get anything done. Hence, the apocalyptic lan-

19. It is in this sense that Thomas Christensen suggests that adversaries like Communist China can be "useful" to leaders facing domestic mobilization barriers: "In the context of the mobilization drive for Europe, domestic politics played a decisive role in the creation of the China Aid Bill" (1996: 64). Of course, the usefulness of such appeals explains neither their existence nor their efficacy, although it might explain the desire of particular individuals to utilize them—if the explanation of such desires was thought to be the goal of the analysis.

20. The language that the representatives wanted—from the Herter Committee report on the foreign aid, which referred to "incentive commodities, such as tobacco and cigarettes, shoes, clothing, and other consumers' goods"—does not seem to have made it into the final text of the Interim Aid bill.

guage that framed these debates; hence also the logrolling compromises characteristic of the aid bills' legislative histories (Lowi 1979: 128–29, 39–41). But while this account might be able to explain the *form* of the ERP debates, it cannot explain its *content*. Not all apocalyptic languages are created equal, and not all patterns of justification point in the same direction. Lowi's analytic provides some leverage over the debate's tone, but it is not a sufficient account of how the ERP came to pass.

Outflanking Opponents

Were these arguments at all effective in convincing *opponents* of the ERP to support the program? Recall that a focus on rhetorical commonplaces and discursive deployments does not allow us to ascertain whether a particular speaker "really believes" what he or she is saying, so the issue here is only whether an argument is effective at silencing the opposition—or at "outflanking" the opposition in such a way that the case of an ERP opponent is appropriated into a position supporting the program. 'The West,' as a widely spread commonplace, often served this purpose, since opponents of the ERP were ordinarily not opponents of 'Western Civilization'[21] and sometimes even utilized occidentalist language in their efforts to defeat the ERP. This opened them up to possible rhetorical counterattacks from ERP defenders and rendered enough erstwhile opponents of the ERP unable to keep up their opposition that the aid package was able to pass through the Congress. I will illustrate these dynamics with a few instances in which critics are directly engaged by defenders.[22]

One particularly striking example of a former opponent of aid to Europe

21. Indeed, sometimes the only response to the occidentalist flavor of the program's defenders was sarcasm. Henry Taylor, an economist, appeared before the House committee to oppose the ERP legislation even while supporting the basic idea of aiding Western Europe; he questioned the basis on which specific dollar allocations had been made.

> England, $5,348,000,000, 32 percent of the entire 17 billion dollars to be paid for by every man and woman who works in America, on top of the latest grant of $3,750,000,000 consumed there since 1945.
> Now, England may need this money, and it may be a good thing to send it to them. I do not think in any such scale, however. They do not need it to keep the people from voting Communist, and they do not need it to keep western civilization from crumbling in England. . . . [mentions and mocks some other figures] . . . Next we have Iceland, and you can imagine how much western civilization is crumbling in Iceland; they get $38,000,000. (House Committee 1948: 775–76)
> The strategy seems to be to argue that Western Civilization is stronger than the advocates of the ERP believe; in this way it is like the position articulated by Ernest Weir. See the following discussion.

22. The format of committee hearings and legislative floor debate prevents these exchanges from occurring as often as they could. I have focused on these moments, even though they are by no means the major component of the congressional debates.

claiming to have been convinced—and expressing his grounds in decidedly occidentalist terms—is the testimony of Hamilton Fish, former representative from New York, former member of the House Committee on Foreign Affairs, and prewar "isolationist" who had been specifically targeted by FDR during the 1944 campaign season as an obstacle to internationalist commitments (Divine 1967: 233–41). Four years after his defeat, he appeared before his former committee espousing a very different philosophy.

> I favor the fundamental principles of the Marshall plan for European economic recovery, subject to the willingness of the recipient nations to establish a defensive union against Soviet aggression. . . . The creation of a union of democratic nations to defend European freedom against Asiatic irony [*sic,* probably supposed to be *tyranny*] is the best way to preserve world peace. (House Committee, *European Recovery Program Hearings* 1948: 1322)

Fish also expressed severe opposition to the dismantling program, arguing that "to dismantle plants, producing useful goods, is a blunder worse than a crime. It is driving the Germans into communism. . . . Congress must insist on a complete readjustment of our policies in Germany." 'Anticommunism' is of course greatly in evidence here, but it is filtered through occidentalism: "I would like to see western Germany built up as a bulwark against Asiatic communism. . . . Germany is a battleground between freedom and democracy, against slavery and communism" (1325–26). Fish proceeded to give what amounted to a testimonial or a confession in which he renounced many of his former positions.

> I was a noninterventionist, and I am proud of it. I was a noninterventionist before this war, and I am very proud of it, because I think the things we said would happen at the time have happened. . . . Everything we said has been verified by time, events, and history. However, as a noninterventionist, the early part—before the last war—I say we have a certain responsibility and we have a certain blame. According to our side, we were maneuvered into war, but we assumed a responsibility. . . . We helped wreck and destroy parts of Europe. Therefore, we have a responsibility now to try to save the free nations of the world. You say I have seen the light, but I accuse others of forcing that issue upon me against my own better judgment.

Fish's logic is striking: it would have been better for the United States to have kept out of the war in the first place, but because that is no longer an option, the United States must take responsibility for protecting and sustaining certain parts of the world. But *only* certain parts:

> I am willing now, because of the security of my own country and trying to keep what the democratic nations have before it is too late, I am willing to say "All right, I am willing for the United States to join a union of free democratic

nations of western Europe." . . . I limit it to that. I am not interested so much in Turkey, Greece, or Asia Minor. Certainly those who know me or knew me in the past know I am not interested in getting into any war about oil in Asia Minor. (1328)

Here we see what amounts to a textbook use of occidentalism to erode the support for the exemplarist position: 'American exceptionalism' is replaced by American membership in a wider civilizational community, and policy implications are drawn from this altered rhetorical configuration. While Fish may differ from administration representatives and other ERP advocates on the specific eastward boundary of 'Western Civilization,' the commitment to the general notion—and the firm inclusion of Germany in the community—by a formerly outspoken "isolationist" is as close to a smoking gun piece of evidence as one is likely to find.

However, not every speaker deploying occidentalism was a supporter of the ERP legislation. Some opponents of ERP linked the civilizational nature of the issues involved in the question of foreign aid with a recommendation that the United States not become involved in aiding European governments to as great an extent as that envisioned in the legislation. For example, Ernest Weir, chairman of the National Steel Corporation, offered his opinion that "the nations of western Europe will not go communistic."

> The nations of Europe fall into two rough divisions—those which have been a genuine part of Western Civilization and those which have not. Or to put it another way, those which have developed the traits of individualism and those which have not. The individualistic nations are not going to jump from a bad condition into a far worse condition just to spite us or themselves. (1697)

Weir was exploiting one of the key ambiguities in the occidentalist position: if 'the West' was such a deep-rooted cultural community, how could it be threatened by communism confronting it from the outside? In an appeal that echoes one of Stimson's central arguments in his *Foreign Affairs* article, Weir suggested that the real issues were *internal* issues, not external ones.

> If the nations of western Europe were actually in danger of going communistic, then I believe that condition would be its own most powerful argument against giving any aid at all. . . . If these peoples are to resist communism it will not be because of billions from America but because of their own inner conviction that there is a better way of life and their own inner determination to have that better way of life. (1697)

Expanding on this line of criticism was Henry Hazlitt, a conservative economist whose book *Will Dollars Save the World?* questioned the efficacy of American aid overall. "Hazlitt denounced the trend in Europe toward nationalization of industry, government control of trade, and social-welfare programs, all of which would restrain production, generate inflation, and worsen Europe's payment deficit with the dollar area" (Hogan 1987: 96). He feared that the ERP would simply strengthen these tendencies.

> We need a collapse in the faith in planned economies. . . . I am not sure that the Marshall plan, by holding up, by propping up, these governments—the governments of planned economy and so forth—might not prolong these planned economies and thereby retard European economy and recovery. (653)

The focus remained on adhering to an orthodox, pro-market kind of economic organization and a concomitant preservation of a relatively small state sector. Robert Taft, the outspoken leader of the anti-Vandenberg wing of the majority Republican Party in the Senate, followed Hazlitt in his criticism of ERP and "approached the whole question of aid to Europe from the perspective of the domestic economy," arguing that the American economy had to be kept "as free from state controls as possible" (Patterson 1972: 385). These arguments illustrated the basic logic of the exemplarist position, combining 'heliotropism' (the American way is the best) with 'American exceptionalism' (America should remain pure and separate from the world, especially the Old World) to advocate a reduced involvement with European affairs.

One response to the conservative opposition to the ERP was a reassertion of the civilizational goals of the program. Robert Patterson, former secretary of war and chairman of the Committee for the Marshall Plan, used part of his testimony before the Senate committee to make precisely such an argument. The proper criterion for evaluating whether aid was being used effectively, Patterson suggested, was whether or not the recipient of the aid had remained true to its "heritage of freedom," broadly understood—and Patterson did not venture to define what he had in mind any more precisely (Senate Committee, *European Recovery Program Hearings* 1948: 764–65). Here we can see an implicit use of what would eventually become the preferred concept for gathering all of the noncommunist states of the world under one designation: the "free world." It is important not to lose sight of the occidentalist elements of this notion: the European countries participating in the ERP should be evaluated as to whether they remain "free," but it is the "freedom" of members of 'Western Civilization' that remains the object of U.S. aid and policy. For countries occupying this core, only free democratic regimes will do, whereas outside of this core a specific commitment to a particular form of liberal democracy is not quite as necessary, because the role of such countries and regions is to *support* the freedom of 'the West' rather than to *belong to* it in a substantive sense.[23] In this sense, the "free world" is a kind of 'West-plus': the

23. U.S. policy in Southeast Asia fits this interpretation, as American officials did not often press for reforms that might weaken the contribution of colonial possessions to the economic health of their colonizers (Leffler 1992: 92–94).

West narrowly understood (western Europe and the United States) as its core, together with its associates and allies (and client regimes).[24]

The other response to the conservative critics depended on the striking fact that even these critics often built occidentalist notions into their arguments. Thus, if it could be demonstrated that 'the West' actually *were* under imminent threat of an assault, it would become incumbent on any serious advocate of even these arguments critical of the ERP to support measures that would defend 'the West' against the common enemy. It is in this respect that the Communist takeover in Czechoslovakia on 25 February 1948 was so useful to the ERP's advocates—here was dramatic evidence that could be used to indicate a threat to the entire 'West' (Kirby 2000: 407–8). Truman and Marshall were not particularly subtle about incorporating this event into their appeals; Truman gave a speech on 17 March in which he explicitly linked the coup and the pending ERP legislation, calling for prompt passage of ERP (along with Universal Military Training) as a response to this communist threat (Freeland 1972: 269–72; Pollard 1985: 151–53).

Because of the occidentalist-flavored 'anticommunism' that ERP opponents drew upon, they were unable to make a compelling reply: such an explicit threat to 'the West' deserved a response, and that response was ERP. In fact, after Taft's proposed amendment reducing the appropriation for the ERP by approximately a billion dollars was defeated (with all of the Democrats and half of the Republicans in the Senate voting to reject the amendment), he announced his support for the program "on the grounds that some aid was necessary in the fight against communism" (Freeland 1972: 266; Patterson 1972: 388). So Taft, at least, seemed to have accepted the occidentalist linkage between 'anticommunism' and some degree of American involvement

---

24. Theodore Achilles, director of the State Department's Office of European Affairs, captured something of this notion in a talk he gave before an American Political Science Association meeting in December 1949: "It is certainly not accidental that all of the radical experiments of the last 5 years in closer international association along regional lines . . . have taken place in Western Europe and the Americas which, taken together, comprise what may, for want of a better term, be called the Atlantic community. It is a community of interest, a community more in the ideological than in the geographic sense, for the close ties which bind many of its members together are imponderable rather than geographic and they extend outside Europe or the Americas to far parts of the world. Its essential characteristics are fundamental belief in the dignity and worth of the individual, and in the importance of the rule of law to safeguard individual freedom. . . . The direction in which we must work is that of progressively closer association, by limited and practicable steps, of more and more of the free world. It is natural that this process should proceed fastest with those countries which have the closest ties of common heritage, tradition, and interest" (DOSB 9 January 1950: 52–53). So the "free world" spreads outward from 'the West' that remains at its core.

in Europe.[25] The rhetorical environment had shifted in a decidedly occidentalist direction.

Occidentalism and the German Reaction

With the exception of the KPD, every German party in the western zones of occupation greeted the ERP positively, although they maintained different views of precisely what the new program meant (Noh 1995: 13–15). Their reactions in the Wirtschaftsrat—the "economic parliament" that had been established to provide a measure of German representation throughout the Bizone—provide an excellent indication of the contours of this support. "The bourgeois parties, which had taken the initiative in the Wirtschaftsrat in June 1947, saw in the European Recovery Program . . . support for their economic policies" (Hardach 1994: 87). The emphasis on the free market and the restoration of economic health was very appealing to these parties, including to the CDU—whose representatives promptly called for an increase in German coal production, as well as a general expansion of the German economy (Bührer 1997: 47). This support was to be expected from the bourgeois parties, as they had been advocating a restoration of some kind of functioning market economy for quite some time, reasoning that only such an economic system could preserve individual freedom and liberty.

More ambiguous was the SPD's response to the ERP; the Social Democrats found themselves "in a real dilemma" concerning the ERP, because supporting the program would make their desires for a centrally planned economy impossible to implement, but opposing the program would cost them popular support, particularly if the ERP succeeded (Ehni 1986: 218). In addition, after the KPD announced its opposition to the program, staunch anticommunists could not very well announce *their* opposition without opening themselves up to being lumped together with the communists. The SPD thus remained cautiously positive but somewhat ambivalent about the ERP, with many segments of the party leadership expecting that the program's market-driven aspects would lead to its failure—after which time the SPD could step in and pick up the pieces (Hardach 1994: 88).

What role did occidentalism, or any rhetorical commonplace, play in these

---

25. The conservative opposition did, however, succeed in leaving its mark on the administrative apparatus erected to administer the ERP: the Economic Cooperation Administration was set up as an independent, "businesslike" organization, headed by an ex-CEO rather than a career civil servant and directed to put itself out of a job by promoting development such that it could be dissolved at the conclusion of the aid program in 1952 (Arkes 1972; Hogan 1991: 101–8). But these decisions, while important to the overall history and structure of the ERP, are not as central to the question of how aid was legitimated in the first place.

decisions? Were there other courses of action open to German political leaders at this point in time? Given the occupation of the country and the fact that
such bizonal German institutions of self-government as there were in 1947
and 1948 depended on the largesse of the occupying authorities in order to
accomplish anything, it may seem that there was little room to maneuver
(Küsters 1995: 76–77). A German rejection of the ERP would have been quite
difficult to coordinate, as the country was not producing enough goods to
feed its own people. "The range of effective choice Germans had . . . was
indeed limited. They could stay with the status quo, with its economic frus-
trations and insecurities, or throw in with the West, which offered them some
hope for the future" (Gimbel 1968: 224). At least the American recovery proposal offered the possibility of movement and also the opportunity for the various political parties to try to control the future economic shape of Germany
(Schwabe 1991: 252). In this sense, there were really no other options open,
and *some* measure of German acceptance of the ERP was rather overdeter-
mined.

But perhaps equally important was the lack of a socially sustainable *basis* on
which to articulate opposition to ERP. What kinds of reasons could have been
given for rejecting an American offer of aid that promised both a growth of
the Bizonal economy and the inclusion of those zones in a larger 'Western'
and European community? The KPD articulated their resistance on the
grounds that capitalism was deeply flawed (and responsible for Hitler's rise),
and also on the grounds that it could not be the responsibility of the bizonal
institutions to make decisions on economic matters that would affect the
whole of Germany: the ERP, it charged, would intensify the splitting of the
country (Ehni 1986: 217–18). But the KPD held out no alternative except
another call for a four-power conference on Germany. Such a conference was
actually held in London in late 1947 but failed to produce any agreement, in
part because the American representatives were unwilling to give up their
plans to utilize German resources as a means of promoting European recovery
(Eisenberg 1996: 353–55). Hence rejecting the ERP meant continuing stagna-
tion and stalemate, which was desirable to nobody.

In addition, it would have been very difficult for either Adenauer or Schumacher to have strongly rejected a plan justified in such openly occidentalist
terms; doing so would have meant a decision not to align oneself with 'the
West.' For Adenauer, who regularly deployed explicitly occidentalist language
in his public statements, this would have been quite unthinkable: as he had
been advocating a policy of closely integrating Germany into 'Western Civilization' since immediately after the Second World War (Schwarz 1995:
307–9), a favorable response to an initiative that would accomplish just this
end was probably quite inevitable. The issue was a little more complicated
with Schumacher, whose only regular use of occidentalist language came in

the context of differentiating socialism from Soviet-style communism; his position was not so clear-cut. Yet their positions were not so far apart: "no one—with the exception of the communists and the neo-Nazis—questioned the domestic-political, societal, and economic Western orientation" of any future German state. "Only political and military integration into the West was in question" (Herbst 1989: 110). Both Adenauer and Schumacher agreed that Germany was in some sense a 'Western' country, but they drew different conclusions from this: Adenauer utilized occidentalism to defuse notions of a separate German path (a *Sonderweg*) while Schumacher continued to advance the notion that Germany had to help other European countries find their way to a socialist "third way" between capitalism and communism. The debate was not over *whether* to accept ERP but over what this acceptance *meant*. The language deployed in these debates would have a significant impact on the course of future events.

"EUROPEAN SOCIALISM"

Schumacher articulated what would become the SPD's public line on the ERP at the party's Nürnberg Conference on 29 June 1947—only a few weeks after Marshall's Harvard speech. Social Democrats should respond to the proposal earnestly, taking seriously the call for "European self-help" and Marshall's declaration that he did not want "to finance each country individually, using the orthodox and missionary methods of specifically American capitalism"[26] (Schumacher 1985: 489). Instead, Schumacher suggested, the ERP presented an opportunity to articulate a socioeconomic "third way" between the "national communism" of the KPD and the "capitalism" of the CDU. "The CDU and the communists want to be the solid, heavy millstones between which the Social Democratic Party will be crushed." The alternative to this strategy of excluding the middle, Schumacher suggests, was to cling to the notion of democracy.

> The communists are the implicit representatives of totalitarianism and anti-democracy. Capitalism uses democracy only as camouflage . . . Only the policies of the SPD are bound to democracy through thick and thin. (516–17)

Schumacher thus seized the ERP as a means of fulfilling Germany's democratic destiny and preserving true democratic freedom against both the forces of a rampant capitalism and totalitarian communism. Schumacher's reference

26. Here Schumacher interprets what Marshall actually said in his Harvard speech somewhat freely. "It would be neither fitting nor efficacious," Marshall had said, "for this Government to undertake to draw up unilaterally a program designed to place Europe on its feet economically. This is the business of Europeans. The initiative, I think, must come from Europe. . . . The program should be a joint one, agreed to by a number, if not all, European nations" (Senate 1950: 1269). Missionary capitalism is nowhere in evidence.

point throughout was 'Europe,' but a Europe of a very particular—social democratic—variety: "*The way of life, the culture, and the economy of this continent is a democratic socialism that affirms the rights of the free person.* We recognize democratic socialism as one of the greatest political methods in the world. And to use this method in world affairs is the duty of all Europeans, the duty of all European socialists" (488, emphasis in original). Schumacher's language here differentiates the SPD's program from that of the Communists by affirming a commitment to democracy, and it roots the SPD's democratic socialism in a wider European tradition. In this way, "European self-help" could be interpreted as a call to socialism, and the SPD could accept the ERP as a means of furthering this end. The German "third way" could serve as the heart of a European "third way."

Schumacher even deployed some occidentalist language in pursuit of his goal. "Europe has not spoken the last word in the development of this continent as an important and indispensable constituent part [*Bestandteil*] of humanity," he declared. "*The West [Abendland] is not dead, for socialism and democracy live*" (488, emphasis in original). And he quotes no less an authority than Stalin himself to affirm the essential difference between 'Eastern' and 'Western' methods of achieving socialism: "Russia does not know the tradition of freedom of the West. Russia's way to socialism is different than that of the West. The western European workers' movement can achieve its goals quite well by means of achieving a parliamentary majority." The fact that "the majority of the German people and the majority of the German working class has declared itself unambiguously for democracy and for the methods of a parliamentary majority" thus shows them to be a part of this 'Western' way to socialism (514).

Schumacher's reading of the ERP illustrates the tensions in his position: on one hand, American aid for Europe was welcomed, but on the other hand, Europe—led by German Social Democrats—needed to keep its distance from American-style capitalism. At the same time, the SPD's anticommunist credentials had to be sustained. On several occasions, particularly when speaking to Americans, Schumacher sounded almost like Adenauer in deploying 'Western Civilization' to address these issues. In November 1947, Schumacher became the first German politician to visit the United States after the war, albeit as a "private" guest of the American Federation of Labor. While in New York, he gave a speech to the Social Democratic Federation in which he characterized the ERP as an "attempt to overcome isolationism" and attributed Soviet resistance to the program to their understanding of the fact that communism couldn't triumph in western Europe in the face of American aid—especially if this were channeled into a social democratic European system: "We have seen that the only wall that protects the whole of Western Civilization from the grasp of a dictatorial regime consists of the *social democratic par-*

ties of western Europe" (BKS, no. 37: 26.10.1947, emphasis in original). Pre-serving 'the West' would solve all of these problems simultaneously.

However, on his return to Germany, Schumacher was confronted with the accusation that his embrace of 'the West' and the ERP meant an abandonment of German unity. The *New York Times* reported that Schumacher was maneuvering to become the first chancellor of a western German state, and that the real purpose of his trip to the United States had been to coordinate with American officials about the details; in response, Schumacher issued a statement emphasizing the SPD's commitment to a united Germany, albeit one that did not rely on "the quislings of a foreign power" to "find a common German standpoint" (BKS, no. 43: 10.11.1947).[27] This was a particularly ironic charge to level at Schumacher, who was generally rather nationalist in his criticisms of various aspects of the occupation regime, causing headaches for all of the occupation powers (Rogers 1995: 112–14). Indeed, Schumacher was the most strident critic of the western Allies' refusal to raise the permitted level of German industry and their unwillingness to definitively settle the question of Germany's territorial integrity as it related to the Ruhr region and the Saar-land.[28] Embracing the ERP came with some political risks—risks that Schumacher dealt with by moving in a more nationalist direction.

THE CHRISTIAN WEST VERSUS THE "THIRD WAY"

Adenauer, as might be expected, took a rather different rhetorical tack, one that placed occidentalist language in a more consistently central location. And by the time that Marshall delivered his speech at Harvard, Adenauer's way of characterizing the ERP was virtually assured of dominance within the CDU: Jakob Kaiser, Adenauer's only serious rival for the leadership of the party, had effectively been eliminated from contention. Kaiser, as previously noted, was advocating some kind of an agreement with the USSR in order to preserve German unity; he utilized his position as the head of the CDU in the Soviet zone of occupation to call for a trans-zonal party organization that could advance such a goal. While Adenauer "pursued the consolidation of the west-

27. According to several of the newspapers that carried this statement, Schumacher's use of *quisling* as a common noun (generalizing the last name of the Norwegian politician installed by the Nazis as prime minister in 1942 and executed as a traitor in 1945) was the first such use of the term.

28. On the Saar issue, see chapter 7. Schumacher's strident nationalist rhetoric gave him a reputation that sometimes led to foreign papers misattributing nationalist quotations to him, as when the American military paper *Stars and Stripes* reported on 20 August 1947 that Schumacher had accused the western Allies of having violated the Atlantic Charter by effectively permitting the annexation of parts of Germany. In fact, according to the transcript in BKS no. 42, this charge was made by the person who introduced Schumacher and not by Schumacher himself.

ern zones in freedom and advocated dependence on the free West, for Kaiser national unity remained the decisive point of departure" (Kleinmann 1993: 59). At the heart of these differences was a disagreement about Germany's place in the world; Adenauer remained a firm occidentalist, while Kaiser continued to champion "a synthesis between East and West on German soil" together with a kind of "Christian Socialism" that incorporated far more elements of state intervention in the economy than other CDU officials were prepared to accept (Schwarz 1995: 365). In an address to the first party assembly of the CDU in the Soviet zone, Kaiser argued that

> Germany today feels the influence of the West [*Westens*] and the East. It struggles to characterize its own essence, and it will discover how to find this characterization. The Union [Kaiser's preferred term for the CDU] will participate in this process. The life of our people depends, not least, on an understanding between East and West. To contribute to this understanding is our most solemn task. (Kaiser quoted in Kleinmann 1993: 59–60)

In 1945 and 1946, such a role of "bridging" the differences between the major powers might have seemed more feasible, but by 1947—with the collapse of the Moscow Conference and the solidification of the American plan to utilize German resources for the development of Europe—such appeals looked increasingly utopian. In addition, Soviet actions in their zone of occupation, from their blunt interventions in local politics to their widespread removal of industrial plants as reparations, had not made a positive impression on the German public; these too made bridging 'East' and 'West' seem unlikely (Ninkovich 1988: 114). When set together with the fact that the United States was proposing a reconstruction plan premised *precisely* on the rhetorical grounds that Adenauer had publicly advocated, the ascendance of his point of view rather than Kaiser's within the party seems rather natural.

But this is not simply a case of one view being correct and the other having misread the political situation. In February 1947, *before* the collapse of the Moscow Conference, Adenauer had utilized his mastery of bureaucratic political strategy to prevent Kaiser from becoming the chief foreign policy spokesman for the CDU. Adenauer managed to cast doubt on Kaiser's fitness to serve in *any* supra-zonal party capacity because of the precariousness of his position in the Soviet zone and his consequent vulnerability to Soviet pressure. Kaiser, whose "evangelistic zeal and feeling of personal mission exposed him to his rival's parries" during debate, did not help his cause by advancing language that sounded uncomfortably close to Nazi language about the unique destiny of the German people. After a particularly colorful outburst, Adenauer declared "that further discussion was superfluous" and left the room; the meeting collapsed, no supra-zonal foreign policy committee was created, and Kaiser's position was weakened (Heidenheimer 1960: 97–100;

Schwarz 1995: 367–69). After Kaiser was removed from his official post in the Soviet zone by the USSR in late 1947, he became almost completely dependent on Adenauer, who kept Kaiser around as something of a symbol of Soviet misdeeds—without, however, accepting any of Kaiser's substantive recommendations for promoting German unity at the expense of more solid ties to 'the West.'

At the first CDU party rally in the British zone in August 1947, Adenauer proclaimed the new line: Germany's task was to help save the West through an alignment with other Western powers and a "return" to the fundamental principles of western Christianity "in private life, in politics, in public life, in economics" so that a viable future could be secured (Konrad-Adenauer-Stiftung 1975: 331). Instead of a Germany that could bridge 'East' and 'West,' or a coalition of parties that could present an all-German front, what was required was a clear choice for one side or the other: the atheistic materialism of the SPD or the return to 'Western' Christian values of the CDU (343–44). Adenauer expressed himself in the language of "destiny," but this was a decidedly occidentalist destiny.

> The destiny of Germany is also the destiny of Europe . . . That Germany is and remains the core of Europe, that it is inhabited by many millions of people whose diligence and capacity are indispensable for Europe, that it contains within it resources which must be raised in the interest of all of Europe—these facts lay a sacred duty upon us: never to slack off in our work, never to exhaust our patience, and always to remain true to the task which God has given to us. That applies to us, to the CDU and CSU in Germany, above all, because we see ourselves also as the guardians of the Christian-western spirit [*christlich-abendländischen Geistes*].

Much as Schumacher argued that Germany had a special role to play in promoting a certain kind of Europe, Adenauer suggested that only a certain kind of Europe would do: a Christian-western one. But Adenauer did not stop merely with Europe.

> The West [*Abendland*], the Christian West, is no geographical concept: it is a spiritual and historical concept [*geistes-geschichtlicher Begriff*] that also encompasses America [*der auch Amerika mit unfaßt*]. It is this Christian West that we want to try to save. We will do everything in our power, in the hope and with the conviction that God will not abandon the German people. (Konrad-Adenauer-Stiftung 1975: 351)

Several things are notable about this formulation: the prominent use of the term *Abendland* instead of the more neutral *West* (which had been Kaiser's preferred usage); the definition of 'the West' as something out of the history of the spirit (invoking Hegel and Spengler); the explicit inclusion of America as a part of a larger *Abendland* community of which Germany is also a part, a formulation not too different from many of those used to justify the ERP in the first place; and the portrayal of the stakes as the very survival of 'the West,' which was also not too different from appeals surrounding the ERP. Whether these parallels to the American debates were deliberate or accidental, they are certainly unmistakable.

Adenauer's Europe was a means for promoting the survival of 'the West,' and the ERP fits into this overall strategy. During that speech, he appealed to French political leaders—who were understandably somewhat reluctant to see Germany restored to strength[29]—using this logic. "The war industry of Germany is destroyed. It is completely unthinkable that we would again achieve sole control of the Ruhr coal production and the entire Ruhr region. How could Germany ever—as far as one can generally see into the future—be characterized as a threat to France under these circumstances?" But Adenauer acknowledged that these material conditions were insufficient for a real reassurance of French leaders and the French public.

> But the most important thing is, on the contrary, *never* material power; the decisive factor is instead spirit [*Geist*]. If France believes that it must secure itself against Germany, it must in the first place seek to win the Germans spiritually for itself. France has every opportunity in its hands to come to a lasting spiritual and economic understanding with Germany. Wouldn't it be clever, wouldn't it be extremely great and magnanimous, if France didn't push the helping hand presently extended to it by America away from a Germany which has been brought quite low? (Konrad-Adenauer-Stiftung 1975: 350)

The common participation of America, France, and Germany in a wider cultural and civilizational community underpinned Adenauer's suggestion that France drop its objections to German participation in the ERP as an equal partner. In addition, these cultural and spiritual bonds served as a resource for future reconciliation between the two countries in defense of their common 'Western' ideals. Inasmuch as ERP contributes to this aim, it is strongly welcomed.

Others in the CDU leadership echoed and expanded on Adenauer's occidentalist themes. Hans-Erich Stier, a professor from Münster, argued that task of the CDU was to reestablish the "time-honored fundamental values on

---

29. Whether this was purely a public position adopted for domestic political reasons (Creswell and Trachtenberg 2003a) or whether the traditional historical account of French fears captures what political elites were actually thinking (Sheetz 2003) is beside the point. Whether Germany was to be restored to a position of strength depended on finding a publicly acceptable formula, regardless of what political elites might or might not have been thinking at the time. I take up this point in chapter 7.

which Western culture [*die abendländische Kultur*] rests—truth, freedom, humanity, Christianity" as the cornerstone of the new Germany (399). Christine Teusch applied this logic to the schools, arguing that the CDU needed to put these values at the center of public education in order to "save Germany, the heart of Europe, for Christian-western culture—perhaps for the last time—and then in spite of defeat and powerlessness to leave to our children's children a better future as an inheritance" (418). This was the discursive context in which the celebration of the ERP was carried out by the CDU—as another means of preserving 'the West' and of solidifying Germany's membership in it.

Adenauer's position was largely free from the tensions and dilemmas with which Schumacher had to grapple. By wholeheartedly selecting 'the West' over 'the East,' Adenauer was not placed in the position of simultaneously accepting and fundamentally disagreeing with the policies of the western Allies; his criticisms came from a position "inside" of a set of significant social boundaries and thus appeared to be details of implementation rather than categorical differences of principle. Besides making his position more acceptable to the American administrators of the ERP, this combination of commonplaces also permitted a number of attacks on Schumacher for his attempt to preserve a German *Sonderweg.* As we shall see, those attacks had highly significant consequences.

Toward the BRD

For all of their differences, there were significant points of rhetorical agreement between Adenauer and Schumacher. The most significant of these was their opposition to the continued policy of *Demontage,* or dismantling, which reached its most intense phase in 1947 before the ERP was instituted. "The opportunity concealed in Marshall's offer was . . . recognized, or at any rate suspected, in the relevant political and economic circles of western Germany:[30] lingering restrictive elements of the Allied occupation policies could be attacked more easily, and dismantling and industrial decartelization could be denounced as irreconcilable with the ERP" (Bührer 1997: 49). In particular, the occidentalist language used to justify the ERP made the unequal treatment of one of the participants in the program quite a bit more difficult to justify. Regardless of the contribution of the ERP to the narrowly defined economic recovery of the German zones of occupation, the rhetorical terms on which the aid was extended constituted a "psychological breakthrough" in terms of the place of a future German state in the world: "If the western allies

---

30. Note that the term used in the German original is quite anachronistic when referring to the situation in 1947; *Westdeutschland* had not yet come into being and would not for another two years.

were clearly successful in rebuilding the German economy, it would only be a matter of time until all controls, decrees, and regulations [imposed by the occupying Allies] were repealed" (Herbst 1989: 47). Then the "equality of treatment," or *Gleichberechtigung,* called for by every prominent German politician in the western zones would be achieved.

Halting the dismantling of industrial plants was the first step in this process. By 1947 "dismantling had become a *Kampfbegriff*," a political rallying point and hot-button issue that signified a vast number of criticisms of the Allied occupation; "the fight against dismantling was considered to be a superior moral and patriotic act" (Foschepoth 1986: 161). The ERP provided German politicians with a basis on which to argue "against dismantling and reparations in the name of European recovery, European stability, and insurance against Communism with such conviction that—had they not been Germans—they might have testified with great success before the United States congressional committees in favor of the Marshall Plan" (Gimbel 1968: 244). For instance, Schumacher argued that a continuation of the policy would inflict "psychological damage," and he advanced the veiled threat that "we have no idea whether it can ever be repaired"—and whether a lasting reconciliation between Germany and other European countries could be achieved if this policy continued (1985: 501). The SPD remained openly confrontational on this point—and on the related issue of the levels of imports and exports permitted to the Bizone—through 1948; Schumacher's Hannover office even sent out a confidential memo to local SPD offices recommending a "completely public" discussion of the extent to which Allied policy "makes every success of the Marshall Plan impossible and sooner or later leads to political consequences for the western world which it is the goal of the Marshall Plan to avoid" (BKS, D10 no. 35: 5).[31] Other parties, although not quite so confrontational, advanced similar arguments.

BIZONAL ORGANIZATION: THE WIRTSCHAFTSRAT

These arguments became even easier to articulate with the 1948 decision of the western Allies to permit the Bizone to have its own representation in the Organization for European Economic Cooperation (OEEC), the institution set up to coordinate the European use of resources provided under the ERP. Although the Bizone would be initially represented by members of the occupation authority, the explicit promise that these responsibilities would be turned over to a future German government gave critics of the demolition policy even more rhetorical ammunition (Bührer 1997: 63–64, 80). The bilat-

---

31. Schumacher's name is not directly mentioned on the document, which lists Fritz Heine as the person responsible for it. Heine was a full-time board member of the SPD and would not have issued such a document without Schumacher's at least tacit approval.

eral agreement between the United States and the Bizone, which was required by the ERP legislation, added further support by explicitly including the Bizone in the most-favored-nation system of trade arrangements erected among the ERP participants (Hardach 1994: 112–14). The overall logic of ERP—the reincorporation of the western portions of Germany in some larger community—was celebrated and seized upon by German politicians, particularly those whose rhetoric was already as occidentalist as the justifications for ERP itself.

As it happened, the politicians in the best position to take advantage of this were CDU politicians and their allies, because the SPD had decided in July 1947 to withdraw from the executive arm of the Bizone's Wirtschaftsrat, or Economic Council. The roots of this action are complex and reflect another moment in the ongoing controversy between the SPD and the CDU about the best way to manage the relationship between occupiers and occupied. Even before the creation of the Bizone, the American occupying authorities had been pushing to turn more administrative and governmental capacity over to Germans, as a preparation for withdrawing their forces and establishing some kind of German government that would function under Allied supervision (Gimbel 1968: 47–48). The "parallel structure" that General Clay had erected as early as 1946, in which every Allied agency was paired with a German agency to implement its policies, was in part designed to make such a transition easier (Clay 1950: 65–66). But initially these efforts were understood to be preparation for an eventual *all-German* government, something that no longer looked likely by the time the ERP was announced. Thus there was some resistance to building up bizonal institutions like the Wirtschaftsrat too much, lest they appear to be an embryonic West German government— and therefore an explicit abandonment of German unity. Politically, "if the initiative for a break" from the principle of German unity "seemed to come from the west . . . politicians [Adenauer and Schumacher in particular] would publicly denounce it" (Eisenberg 1996: 356). The commonplace of German unity was too prominent for such an explicit refutation to be possible.

So what was to be done about the more and more explicit steps toward a West German government that the Allies were undertaking by establishing the Bizone and by permitting parties to operate bizonally? Led by Schumacher, the SPD adopted a two-pronged strategy that was quite similar to his later stance on the institutions of the BRD: the SPD maintained that institutions that had not been freely erected by all-German elections did not and could not constitute a "state," but only a temporary arrangement, and hence could make no decisions binding for the (projected) postreunification period, particularly on fundamental matters like the joining of any international organizations (Schwarz 1966: 512–18). Accordingly, Schumacher was more hesitant about any formal ties between the Bizone and the OEEC.

At the same time, however, the SPD strove mightily to control the bizonal institutions, fully cognizant of the fact that decisions made within them *would*—whether appropriately or not—have an impact on the future. But the SPD would not accept coalitional or partial control, insisting on total control or sitting in opposition (Drummond 1982: 31). Part of this stance was premised on the notion that the policies enacted by the bourgeois parties were destined to fail eventually, and that it would be better for the SPD to emerge from such a crisis untainted. Schumacher's advocacy of such a position was so strong that it led to a rather unusual situation when the directors of the various departments of the Bizonal administration were first selected; although the SPD controlled the executive committee, and thus the power to nominate the directors, the SPD went into opposition when it became apparent that the SPD could not get a slate in which SPD members held the posts of both Economics and Finance (Gimbel 1968: 186–87).

Once again, Adenauer's position was less conflicted than Schumacher's. Adenauer emphasized the extent to which any West German institutions needed to be submerged within a larger Western grouping. While he often referred to 'Europe' in this context, he emphasized that this was only one portion of a larger civilizational entity: "The unity of Europe meant, for Adenauer, a bulwark of the Christian West against Bolshevism" (Altmann 1993: 49). The general notion was that an emphasis on integrating Europe (under the general auspices of Western Civilization) would solve several problems simultaneously: it would promote reconciliation with France, improve stability, make it possible for Germany to regain some status as a participant in international politics, *and* it would allow Adenauer to deal with the objections that he was abandoning German unity. According to this line, a West German state might be acceptable if it were to be incorporated into some larger Western grouping.

In fact, Adenauer's position was remarkably close to that advanced by American representatives as a way of allaying French fears about a resurgent Germany. One sure way of ensuring that a German state would not be a threat to France was to restrict the autonomy of such a state, constituting it in such a way as to deny it the ability to prepare for and launch a military invasion. But what guarantee would the French have that such a policy would be effective? As with Adenauer, the answer was a civilizational one: because of the threat to 'the West' by outside powers, Germany as a Western country would not pose a threat to its fellow 'Western' countries. The real danger, the Americans argued, was that the Russians would manage to co-opt Germany and turn the entire country—all four zones of occupation—to the east (Eisenberg 1996: 366). Forestalling this possibility was a key element of the American strategy, even to the point of agreeing, in principle, to construct some kind of 'Western' security system that might address French insecurities (Leffler 1992:

202–3; Trachtenberg 1999: 77–78). Occidentalism here provided a notion on which both occupiers and occupied could find common ground.

THE LONDON AGREEMENTS

Given these similarities, one might have expected Adenauer to greet the London Agreements formally paving the way for a West German state somewhat favorably, or at any rate more favorably than Schumacher and the SPD. The German reaction to the decisions was important, as it would be quite difficult, perhaps impossible, to force a West German state on a populace that fundamentally rejected such a construction and refused to regard it as legitimate. Schumacher could be expected to remain wary of any move that looked to be institutionalizing the division of the country into two halves. But Adenauer also reacted quite negatively to the decisions and was so "appalled" and "alarmed that he took the highly uncharacteristic step of visiting the Social Democrat headquarters in the hope of forging a united front among the German political parties." The SPD was not prepared to issue a joint declaration condemning the decisions, even though Schumacher had been making statements against a *Weststaat* for some time (Schumacher 1985: 575–79; Schwarz 1995: 400–401). Apparently the SPD's policy about remaining in opposition extended even to the making of such declarations.

Adenauer's opposition, perhaps puzzling at first glance, makes sense when one examines the terms in which that opposition was couched: Adenauer's chief complaint was that the proposed new state would be not so much a part of a Western grouping as it would be an inferior partner of other European states. He particularly objected to the continued provisions for control of German resources and decisions, noting that "this is not an agreement which has been conceived of in its design and nature as a temporary one," and that therefore it would be quite difficult to overcome its more restrictive precepts (1975: 111). Of particular concern were the provisions involving the control of the Ruhr; the entire region was to be placed under the control of an international authority in which each of the western zones of occupied Germany would get one representative, but these three German votes would be more than counterbalanced by three votes apiece for the United States, France, and Britain, and one vote for each of the Benelux countries. This, Adenauer observed in a speech, amounted to "nothing other than an economic annexation of Germany . . . Economic annexation—which Spengler already predicted would occur[32]—is infinitely more dangerous and more serious than political annexa-

---

32. Adenauer referred here to Spengler's contention that in the latter stages of a Culture political control will be replaced by a more efficient form of purely economic control (Spengler 1928: chap. 13). Adenauer's entire argument on this point was vintage Spengler, except that Adenauer condemned this phenomenon while Spengler was (as usual) more resigned to it.

tion for those affected by it . . . those who are annexed economically have nothing to proclaim; no one speaks of them, they have no voice" (113).

This was fairly strong language for a politician largely in sympathy with the notion of a separate West German state as part of a larger 'Western' grouping. The heart of Adenauer's position was his demand for a German "voice" in the disposition of the Ruhr's resources; it is striking that he utilized a metaphor of citizenship to express this demand, as the implication is that the proposed West German state will not be an equal citizen of 'the West'—as if 'the West' were something like a country, only larger. Hence Adenauer *accepted* the basic notion advanced by the Allies—that the Ruhr should be used to strengthen the entire 'West'—but demands that a West German state be a full member of this larger community. At the CDU's second party rally in August 1948, Adenauer was even sharper in his criticisms, noting that "in large part, an anti-Christian spirit rules" in the world, and that this spirit "is in essence responsible for the present situation." He referenced the communist drive to eliminate religion but promptly made reference to American occupation policies besides.

> National Socialism committed dreadful crimes, crimes of which historians in future times will still write with trepidation [*schaudern*]. But the *Morgenthau Plan*—which, thank God, was not completely carried out, but which was prepared for and thought through in great detail—represents an offense against humanity which, at a minimum, stands worthily on the side of National Socialist crimes.[33] . . . This Morgenthau Plan is a thing of the past. There will come a time when anyone involved in formulating it will be ashamed to speak about it. But I have the feeling that definite preliminary elements [*gewisse Ausläufer*] of this Morgenthau Plan are still being implemented among us. It is time that these be done away with. I am referring, in the first place, to this *insane dismantling policy.* (Konrad-Adenauer-Stiftung 1975: 585–86, emphasis in original)

Adenauer linked the continued dismantling of industrial plants with the unequal treatment for Germany proposed in the London Agreements, as both served to reinforce the second-class status of whatever German state would be produced by the proposed process. "The London Agreement," he declared, "is in its present form simply intolerable and impossible for we Germans . . . We hope that this London Agreement can, on the contrary, be altered so that we Germans can be included in European reconstruction equally and with equal responsibility [*gleichberechtigt und gleichverpflichtet*]" (591). Thus far Ade-

---

33. Note that this condemnation of the Morgenthau Plan is not too different from that advanced by conservative critics in the United States, such as Senator Eastland. See chapter 5.

nauer's objections sounded quite like Schumacher's: first equality of status, then a use of German resources for the good of the whole.

But Adenauer's occidentalist commitments allowed him to portray the situation as rather more dire than Schumacher held that it was, and thus leave the door open for some cooperation even *before* equal status had been restored. The world was divided in two, between "the enormous power of Asia, represented by Russia and its satellite states, and strengthened by the vanguard of the communist parties in the various countries of the world; an enormous power which is of a completely different spirit and a completely different way of thinking than we Western Europeans [*abendländischen Europäer*]." This spirit could and should be the basis of a new and better way of relating.

> North and South America belong also to this "European," Western spirit,[34] so that in truth two great fronts have been built or are in the process of being built. Europe plays, despite its smallness and despite its military weakness, a very large role in this struggle, because it is precisely in Europe that the source and the refuge of the Christian-Western spirit may be found. (587–88)

And the only way to save Europe was to include Germany on an equal basis: "an integration of Europe without Germany, in any case without the three western zones of Germany, would mean nothing. Without Germany, such integration is worthless." Hence "the future of Europe . . . is dependent on this relationship [between the European countries] being normalized [*beruhigt*] and ordered" (590). This pointed in the direction of equal treatment for Germany, but also toward Germany's subsumption into a broader civilizational community; the latter remains the basis for the former. Where Schumacher wanted to wait, Adenauer was willing to begin work immediately—as long as the right basis for further discussions could be established. And that basis was an occidentalist one.

The Berlin Airlift

The British and American military governors, for their part, proceeded quickly with their plans to strengthen Bizonia. In early June 1948 they had implemented a currency reform, replacing the old Nazi currency with the new Deutschmark. This had been done even though no agreement had been reached with the Soviet Union on how such a currency reform should be carried out, and as a result the new currency effectively terminated any possibility of administering the German economy on a unified basis, since the two halves of the country (the currency reform had taken effect both in Bizonia

---

34. Note the parallels to Lippmann's notion of the "Atlantic Community."

and in the French zone, excluding only the Soviet zone) were now being explicitly constituted as separate economic units (Eisenberg 1996: 409–10). At this point the Soviets moved to block Allied access to Berlin, and the Allies responded with an airlift, inaugurating a "test of wills" with the potential to lead to war (Leffler 1992: 217). During the course of this airlift, as the Allies, and particularly the United States, demonstrated themselves to be committed to remaining in Berlin and not abandoning the former German capital to the Russians, the notion that the Germans in the western zones of occupation and their occupiers were participants in a common endeavor began to grow (Ermarth 1993: 13–14). Defending Berlin was a visible sign of some kind of common enterprise, including the Germans but excluding the Russians. It underscored the basic principle of 'Western' unity on which both the ERP and the proposed West German state rested.

But why did the Allies remain in Berlin in the first place? If they were simply committed to the creation of a West German state, could this not have been accomplished without defying the Russians and risking an all-out war? Berlin, as most scholars and contemporary analysts argued, had no strategic value; as a completely surrounded enclave in the midst of the Soviet zone of occupation, it provided no military advantage to the Allies (Trachtenberg 1999: 81–82). Truman's top military advisers recommended that the United States withdraw, as Berlin "had no intrinsic strategic importance," and that remaining there "diverted assets from more essential military undertakings" (Leffler 1992: 220). Instead, Berlin's importance was almost wholly symbolic; remaining in Berlin was a symbol of the American willingness to resist the Soviet Union in Europe, and a reinforcement of the occidentalist commitment embodied in the ERP (Ninkovich 1994: 176–77).

In fact, the Berlin airlift reinforced this commitment in a rhetorical sense as well; at the time, Clay argued of the airlift that "morally and spiritually, it was the reply of Western civilization to the challenge of totalitarianism which was willing to destroy through starvation thousands of men, women, and children in the effort to control their souls and minds" (1950: 386). This formulation was not uncommon. The American efforts on behalf of 'the West' to defend and sustain a number of Germans provided a visible confirmation of an American commitment to include Germany as part of that 'West.' The airlift thus presented an opportunity for German politicians comfortable with occidentalist appeals; if the Allies were willing to include Germany this far, perhaps they might be willing to do so even further.

7 Securing the New Trajectory, 1949–55

$\mathcal{A}$LTHOUGH THE EVENTS OF 1947–48 had defined a new occidentalist trajectory for postwar German reconstruction, they had not guaranteed its future survival. A "turning point" only appears as such in retrospect; viewed prospectively, all that appears are instantaneous moments of contingency (Abbott 2001b: 248).[1] Even after the turning point, there were still moments during which the trajectory could have been derailed; if it had been derailed, we would probably not speak of the events of 1947 and 1948 as a turning point in the first place. Like the notion of a "rhetorical commonplace," the concept of a "turning point" is ideal-typical, serving as a way to organize information and make sense out of a series of events.

That a turning point appears in retrospect is a result of the success of the various occidentalist-tinged efforts in securing the new trajectory after the Berlin Airlift. This was far from inevitable; there is nothing about the Berlin Airlift *itself* that dictated one or another course of action. There were other socially plausible ways that the Berlin Airlift, and the Soviet Union's actions in the eastern zone of occupation, could have been understood; the continued presence of opponents to the occidentalist legitimation strategy illustrates the point. What remains to be shown is how the occidentalist strategy achieved a position of dominance in public debate—a dominance so profound that it became quite commonsensical for future political actors (Katzenstein 1997b: 9).

This dominance should not be seen as a shift in the "political culture" of

---

1. This is much like a "streak" in a professional sport like baseball: viewed retrospectively, a streak is a sequence of events forming a clear pattern (such as reaching first base successfully in many consecutive games), while if viewed prospectively, the same events result from a number of contingent circumstances (such as a ball glancing off of a fielder's glove, or someone failing to pitch as effectively as they ordinarily would). Seidel 1988 provides an excellent discussion of Joe DiMaggio's record fifty-six-game hitting streak in 1941 that highlights this peculiar aspect of social trajectories.

196

either the BRD or the United States. Political culture explanations focus on the subjective internalization of justifications over time, such that politicians at a future point in time are constrained by the beliefs that they have inherited from the resolution of previous episodes (Berger 1996: 327; Duffield 1998: 26–27, 34). The process is cumulative, so that the resolution of successive episodes produces a "gradual emergence of a robust . . . foreign policy consensus" (Banchoff 1999: 174) driven by "the weight of past political choices" (Katzenstein 1997a: 254). The problem with political culture explanations is not so much that they are wrong as that they are not really *explanations*. Noting that a particular course of action is consistent with a particular set of beliefs is a useful contribution, but this is not the same thing as explaining why a set of beliefs persist over time—or even why a particular set triumphed over others at a given moment. Political culture explanations, in common with other types of identity explanations that treat identities as settled ideational commitments (Bially Mattern 2004: 52), rely on a stable background of shared meanings in order to explain the resolution of contemporary debates, and as such are not particularly helpful for explaining the emergence of that consensus in the first place.

In addition, political culture accounts tend to rely on a kind of punctuated equilibrium model of social change in which moments of flux are succeeded by more settled times of relative calm. Thus we have pluralistic security communities generated by shared ideas about belonging together that were presumably worked out at some point in the past (Adler and Barnett 1998); similarly, we have postreunification Germany behaving in ways that are at variance with the predictions of realist and liberal IR theory and refraining from asserting itself in various contexts, and doing so because of the political culture previously institutionalized within it (Duffield 1999; Katzenstein 1997b). It remains unclear in such accounts precisely *how* this transition from contestation to working within a stable cultural framework takes place. The problem is compounded when the "cultural framework" in question is conceptualized as being composed of subjectively internalized beliefs, since *measuring* the consensus presumed to characterize settled times becomes practically impossible.[2]

It is better, therefore, to stop looking for those mythical moments during which a trajectory becomes inevitable, and to focus instead on the ongoing processes through which a course of action is *made to appear* inevitable (Hopf

---

2. Analysts interested in political culture have developed some ingenious proxies for subjective beliefs, often involving careful readings of public performances and documents (Duffield 1998: 36–38; Legro 2000: 256–58). The difficulty with such proxies is that they convert public rhetoric into a static indicator rather than appreciating its role as an intervention into an ongoing process of debate, and thus they cause "legitimation" in the sense that I have been using it throughout this book to vanish from view.

2002: 406–7; Weldes 1999: 103–5, 240–42). No trajectory is *actually* inevitable, although it can come to seem that way in retrospect. Trajectories, like the structural elements of social life more generally, are "continuously enacted by actors doing things with others. . . . the social process is *always* instantaneous," and the outcome of a moment of contestation can never be taken for granted in virtue of what has preceded it (Abbott 2001b: 255–57). What is significant about the years from 1949 through 1955 is not simply that different perspectives on policy squared off and one emerged victorious; what is significant is that occidentalist approaches to the constitution of the postwar world defeated opposing approaches through the specification, breaking, and joining of key rhetorical commonplaces in such a way that the available field of rhetorical resources was reconfigured for the short-term future. *Subjective* internalization plays little role here; what matters instead is the *intersubjective* availability of the raw materials on which to successfully legitimate policy options such as an American withdrawal from Europe or a neutralization of the BRD. This is not to say that after 1955 these policy alternatives were definitively ruled out for all time, but only to note that producing such policies in a socially sustainable way would necessitate a kind of practical discursive work that would only have effects in the medium to long term. After all, even the most long-standing set of policies can be made to seem unacceptable if the right circumstances produce commonplaces that can be drawn on to legitimate such an endeavor.[3]

Moments of Actual Contingency

That having been said, not *every* event after the Berlin Airlift represents an equally significant moment in terms of the occidentalist trajectory. In particular, there are three moments during which the new trajectory might easily have been derailed; I will discuss these three moments in subsequent sections of the chapter. The first moment is a series of debates about the *status* of the BRD itself, and in particular about its relationship to early organized efforts at European integration such as the Council of Europe and the European Coal and Steel Community. The second moment involves the American presidential election (and in particular the Republican primary contest) of 1952, during which Robert Taft—the only candidate explicitly standing for an alternative to the occidentalist policy framework—was defeated. The third key moment involves the settlement of the question of German rearmament under the aus-

---

3. See, for example, Crawford's (2002) discussion of how "colonialism" came to be regarded as normatively unacceptable. See also the discussion of reshaping cultural resources in McAdam, Tarrow, and Tilly 2001: 47–50.

pices of NATO, a settlement that passed through the Bundestag elections of 1953 in which Adenauer's position was ratified by the electorate.

Each of these moments could have worked out differently, leading to very different outcomes. We know this because each moment involves the concrete proposal of an alternate, socially plausible course of action—a course of action that was ruled out during the moment in question. As such, these three moments represent the actual points of contingency in the process of postwar German reconstruction. And in all three moments, occidentalism—and the transatlantic coalition that it sustained—played a key role in shaping the outcome actually enacted, as I will discuss in detail.

But there are also several moments cited in the historical literature about postwar reconstruction that do *not,* in my view, constitute significant moments for the trajectory of postwar German reconstruction. Chief among these is the 1952 "Stalin Note," wherein Stalin proposed an end to the four-power occupation of Germany, instead establishing an all-German government and a German national army, in return for a halting of efforts to bring the BRD into the emerging Western political and military system (Steininger 1990). Advocates of reunification at any price were quite enthused by this offer, but Adenauer, in common with American officials like Acheson and McCloy, opposed treating the note as a serious offer and instead wanted to press ahead with the existing trajectory. It does appear that "the Western powers, principally the United States, insisted that German leaders make a choice between pressing for negotiations for reunification and following the path of European integration and tight association with the United States," and that "Adenauer made that choice" and had to present the consequences to the rest of his government and his country (Schwartz 1991: 268). But by 1952 there was really no serious chance that the western Allies would do anything else (McAllister 2002: 220–22), and Adenauer himself was quite opposed to taking Stalin's proposal seriously (Schwarz 1995: 652–56; Granieri 2003: 52–54). Without a plausible counterfactual trajectory, this event should not be counted as a significant moment when things might well have turned out differently.[4]

Something similar can be said of two other moments often cited as significant branch points in the history of postwar German reconstruction: Truman's narrow election victory in 1948, which kept Acheson and McCloy serving as the central U.S. policymakers with responsibility for Germany; and the difficulties raised by France's veto of the organization first proposed to

4. Adenauer's presence as chancellor, and his occidentalism-based working relationship with the representatives of the western Allies (particularly with American officials), were the significant factors making alternative trajectories infeasible. See the following discussion.

house German rearmament, the Europäische Verteidungsgemeinschaft (EVG, or European Defense Community). For the first moment, it is important to remember that Truman's opponent Thomas E. Dewey "hesitated to play politics with foreign policy issues" and generally followed John Foster Dulles's advice to propose the continuation of the broad contours of Truman's policies with respect to Europe (Leffler 1992: 221). Especially when one considers that Dulles—a committed and outspoken occidentalist—would most likely have become secretary of state in a Dewey administration, Truman's electoral victory recedes in importance for the trajectory of postwar German reconstruction.

As for EVG, recent scholarship has focused overmuch on the collapse of the specific organizational arrangements involved and has not adequately appreciated the significance of the fact that the reaction to the demise of EVG was to rearm the BRD under the auspices of NATO—precisely what Adenauer had been pressing for throughout the treaty negotiations (Schwarz 1995: 650). Indeed, the demise of the EVG only appears to be a significant branch point if one focuses on putative U.S. desires to withdraw from western Europe altogether, as the EVG seemed to promise and support such a course of action (Sheetz 1999). Otherwise, what is striking about the demise of the EVG is precisely how *little* it mattered to the actual, occidentalist, trajectory of postwar German reconstruction; the response on all sides was to reach for the paradigmatic occidentalist organization—NATO, the "Western Alliance"—to break the impasse, not to fundamentally reconceptualize the relationship between the United States and Western Europe.[5] The important rhetorical contours of the postwar world had already been established, and the collapse of the EVG did little to alter them.

In the remainder of this chapter, I will discuss the three *significant* moments of contingency during which the occidentalist trajectory was secured. Each of these three moments features a socially plausible alternate trajectory. In each of these three moments the alternate trajectory was defeated through a sequence of events that depended, at least in part, on the deployment of occidentalist commonplaces so as to render that alternate course of action unacceptable. In all three moments, other factors (such as the vagaries of electoral processes and the impact of idiosyncratic biographical and psychological elements) are also implicated in the selection of a trajectory, but occidentalism provides the common thread linking all of these factors together. Schumacher and Taft were both very stubborn individuals, and this

---

5. Indeed, part of the reason that the EVG failed was precisely that it was not occidentalist enough of an organization to contain French public fears of being abandoned on the Continent to face a rearmed Germany; see the following discussion.

stubbornness certainly hurt their chances of influencing social and political outcomes, but this alone is insufficient to explain how events turned out.

The Character of the Bundesrepublik Deutschland

Historians generally agree that the formation of a West German government in 1949 was an initiative underwritten and most strongly advocated by representatives of the United States, and that in doing so the U.S. representatives had to face opposition from the French, the British, and the SPD, all of whom objected to the American proposals to various degrees and on various grounds. And most historians agree that some of the strongest supporters of the U.S. effort were the group of German politicians around Konrad Adenauer, both in the CDU and in other associated political parties. But here the consensus ends. Scholars disagree on the explanation for this somewhat peculiar political alignment, which pitted the representatives of the leader of an alliance *against* their closest allies and grouped them *with* a substantial portion of the enemy that the alliance had initially been formed to defeat. This alignment cannot be adequately explained by accounts that focus on the Soviet threat, as such a threat should (according to most theories) have generated a systemic incentive for *all* of the Allies to create a West German state as quickly as possible so that it could aid in the struggle. Accounts that focus on the fact that the United States twisted the arms of its allies in order to get its proposals enacted fail to explain *why* the United States wanted a separate West German state in the first place. They also fail to explain the U.S. success: U.S. pressure was not quite a dictating of terms to its allies, but something more subtle.

A concentration on rhetorical commonplaces and legitimation processes clears up these ambiguities. U.S. representatives and their German allies successfully deployed occidentalist arguments in support of an independent West German state, noting—as they had during the ERP debates—that such a state would be a trustworthy partner inasmuch as it shared the basic cultural and civilizational presuppositions of its neighbors to the west. *As a part of 'Western Civilization,'* a separate West German state could be legitimately constructed; as a wayward power returning to its proper civilizational fold, a separate West German state could be accepted (if grudgingly) by its neighbors; as a member of a larger community, the new state's westward orientation could be solidified and institutionalized. Occidentalism served as the condition of possibility for the creation of a West German state, and for its acceptance by its opponents both within and without.

However, such a strategy could only work if the new West German government was, in fact, closely aligned with its former occupiers and pursued a course that strengthened that alignment. In a sense, occidentalism had to be built into the foundations of the new state. Adenauer's policy of *West-bindung*—the policy of pursuing ties with other 'Western' countries as the highest priority, even taking temporary precedence over reunification—fit the bill.[6] But it first had to square off against Schumacher's neutralist alternative. This contest initially occurred in two important public discussions: first, the debates during the founding of the BRD, which revolved around the legal status of the new governmental entity; and second, the debates immediately afterward that dealt with the best way to resolve the ongoing dismantling of industrial plants and the restrictions on the productivity of the Ruhr industrial region. The resolution of these debates provided the raw materials on which Adenauer would successfully draw during debates about the relationship of the BRD to such organizations as the Council of Europe. A critical issue during these debates concerned the status of the Saar territory (a part of the former German Reich) occupied by France and whether it should be permitted to join the Council of Europe as an independent country alongside the BRD. In all of these debates, the occidentalist position prevailed; had it not, the results might well have been very different.

THE STATUS OF THE BRD

The SPD position on *any* kind of governing organizations limited to the western zones of occupied Germany was that such arrangements were unable to authoritatively claim to represent "Germany" as a whole, as we have seen in the previous chapter. Hence the organizations should endeavor to refrain from entering into any definitive commitments with other states and also refrain from making major alterations to German society that might be overridden when a truly representative all-German government could be elected. At the same time, SPD representatives from Schumacher on down did acknowledge a need for relatively representative governing organizations in the meantime and thus did participate in the very processes of governing that they were at the same time fundamentally questioning. During the Parliamentary Council called by the occupying Allies in 1949 for the purpose of drafting the basic guidelines[7] for a new West German state, these tensions

6. Ronald Granieri's insightful observation that *Westbindung* as a policy made use of a certain indeterminacy in the notion of 'the West,' such that both Atlanticism and European integration qualified as closer ties with 'the West' (Granieri 2003: 15–19), and that Adenauer himself made use of this ambiguity during his efforts to hold the CDU-led Bundestag coalition together (29–30), simply strengthens the point. The rhetorical commonplace of 'the West' did not function by containing a firm blueprint for precisely what "closer ties with the West" should look like; in this sense, the ambiguity and complexity of *Westbindung* simply reflects the character of the commonplace on which it was founded.

7. The most important concession that the Germans had already won was a change of name for the founding document of the new state. The London Agreements had specified that a meeting of German representatives would draft a constitution for a new state, but the

became apparent. Carlo Schmid, rapidly becoming the SPD's leading authority on questions of international and public law, staked out the SPD position in terms that highlighted the central position of the commonplace of 'German national unity.'

> This emergency construction [*Notbau*] creates no political and autonomous (in the historical sense) state construction. To speak in pictures: it is as though we had made three or four of the rooms of a demolished house somewhat liveable—only three, because a higher power is making it impossible to touch the fourth room, and is compelling its residents to live among the debris. . . . We have as little created a new state as we would have divided that old house by doing what we did. We have only made some structural alterations to our demolished state construction. That is all. (BCS, no. 85: 8.5.1949)

As far as the official SPD position was concerned, Germany had never ceased to exist as a state—and in particular had never ceased to exist within its prewar boundaries. Formal arrangements that would jeopardize this claim, and thus postpone the practical realization of German unity, had to be opposed in the name of defending the nation. In doing so, the SPD appealed to and reproduced a kind of liberal nationalism popular with left-leaning intellectuals—a position that admitted German guilt for war atrocities and rejected Hitler's elevation of the concept of the *Volk* to a position of supreme authority, but which also held the old national state in very high regard and was very quick to call attention to the treatment of Germans in the East, particularly those expelled from Poland shortly after the end of the war (Roth 2001: 618–21).[8] From such a perspective, the defense of the nation and the pursuit of equality with other national sovereign states appeared to be among the highest of priorities.

German representatives of the *Land* governments did not want to create a constitution [*Verfassung*], as this appeared too permanent an acceptance of the division of the country. Instead, they appealed to the military governors for permission to change the name of the document to *Grundgesetz,* or Basic Law, on the grounds that this would accentuate the provisional character of the new state institutions. After some discussion, the military governors agreed (Hahn 1993: 31–32).

   8. For example, Alfred Weber—Max Weber's brother—organized a meeting in Heidelberg on 27–28 June 1947; the meeting was attended by lots of unattached-but-left-leaning intellectuals, and they hammered out a position very much like that of the SPD: no separate peace with any occupying power, no *Weststaat* that would compromise German unity, and a continued pressing of territorial claims both East and West (A. Weber 1947). Marianne Weber, Max Weber's widow, caused a ruckus by urging that considerations regarding the portion of the German Reich that was given to Poland in 1945 needed to be thought of in the light of the contemporary expulsion of Germans from Poland (98–99). The fact that the issue was subsequently debated at great length illustrates the social plausibility of a position combining left-leaning political and social reforms with a defense of the territorial integrity of the nation.

The CDU response to this position drew on the notion of a larger 'Western' community to which a West German state would belong. This occidentalist strategy permitted the articulation of what would later become known as the "policy of strength," the notion that the only way to reunify Germany was for a strong 'West' to confront the Soviets with a demand to abandon its zone of occupation. "I am of the strong conviction," Adenauer declared a few weeks before the Parliamentary Council opened, "that only when we, at a minimum, first strengthen the west politically and economically will we be able to bind the east and the west together in unity."[9] For this reason—and because "Russia has through its policies made it impossible to construct an organization for all of Germany"—Adenauer voiced his support for the Parliamentary Council (Konrad-Adenauer-Stiftung 1975: 592). By casting the blame for the country's division on the Russians, and by outlining a future scenario whereby a West German state could incorporate the eastern zone of occupation, Adenauer constructed a powerful rhetorical stance, from which both the SPD *and* the Allies could be criticized: the SPD for resisting Allied efforts to improve the situation of the western zones, and the Allies if they did not follow through fully on their policy of including Germany in 'the West.'

As president of the Parliamentary Council, Adenauer had several opportunities to test the viability of this position. The CDU's basic goal at the parliamentary conference, as expressed by Dr. Ernst Wilhelm Meyer at the CDU party rally just days before the Parliamentary Council opened its deliberations, was to produce a "return to fundamentals" in matters of constitutional law. These fundamentals "can only be the Greek and the Christian, if the West [*Abendland*] remains dear to us, for Western culture is supported by these." Among the fundamental principles bequeathed to the West from these two traditions, Meyer cited the familiar notions of the worth and dignity of the individual person, the rule of law, and the protection of society from overweening governmental authority. The stakes involved were high.

> The creation of a Western—which means a Greek and Christian—public law [*Staatsrechts*] is no matter of idle talk, but a demand of the heart; it is no tactical ploy, but follows from the fact that today more than ever before we need to fight the Satanic, the evil, within ourselves and within everyone. (Konrad-Adenauer-Stiftung 1975: 639–40)

As a consequence of these principles, Meyer drew out the argument for a *Bundesstaat* (a federal state) rather than a *Staatenbund* (a confederation) as the

9. "East" and "West" in this passage refer to the halves of Germany, not to the larger Western Civilization (for which Adenauer ordinarily uses the term *Abendland,* while in this sentence he uses the more generic *West*).

organizational principle for a new Germany. The federal government should be responsible for setting the broad boundaries of political and social life, but not for an overwhelming level of detailed regulation (645–46). The result of such a design based on Western principles would be that the new German state would be able to join with its natural allies in preserving 'Western Civilization.'

> A future German public law which is erected on Greek and Christian foundations will lead, almost naturally, to tighter cultural bonds with the West. . . . We are, and will remain, the strongest bulwark against communism. (654)

Adenauer's strategy throughout the Parliamentary Council sessions adhered to this program, as he sought to strike a balance between the autonomy of the *Länder* and the authority of the federal government.

One of Adenauer's greatest successes during these debates was on the issue of taxation powers. The SPD understandably wished the federal government to have broad powers in this domain, so that they could implement plans for socialization; the CDU was quite opposed. General Lucius Clay, who was serving his final few months as military governor, was also committed to preventing the federal government from having such powers. This was in accord with his previous decisions and pronouncements on matters ranging from the socialization of industry to worker participation in management decisions (Eisenberg 1996: 343–47). Adenauer was able to use this common commitment to 'Western democracy' during the final days of negotiation over the *Grundgesetz*, using the threat of an Allied veto to force compromises by the SPD representatives (Heidenheimer 1960: 170–71; Schwarz 1995: 416–18). He also utilized such appeals to urge acceptance of compromise proposals by those within his own party, pointing out that when deciding whether to accept any compromise with the SPD the members should ask themselves "whether the price we pay is not really a small price in contrast to the contribution we make in protecting Germany and Europe from Bolshevist Asia" (quoted in Heidenheimer 1960: 172).

Clay, for his part, used a creative interpretation of his instructions to withhold a letter from the Allied governments—which urged an upholding of the principle of decentralization in financial matters but conceded that some procedures for equalizing disparate *Land* financial burdens might be acceptable—until *after* an SPD meeting at which Schumacher attacked the CDU for bowing to Allied pressure; he thus deprived Schumacher of an important propaganda victory, eliminating the impression that the Allies had caved in to Schumacher's pressure tactics (Clay 1950: 431–32; Gimbel 1968: 227–30). Indeed, the final resolution of the dispute involved the incorporation of language that Clay himself had suggested into the final document, further underscoring the basic commonality of aims between Clay and Adenauer—a commonality expressed in and made possible by the language of the defense of 'the West' (Clay 1950: 433–35; Hahn 1993: 40–44).

Did this kind of commonality represent an imposition by the Allies—and specifically by the Americans—of a specific way of doing things on the Germans? Arguments like this are often made in connection with the Parliamentary Council and the *Grundgesetz* that it produced. Many scholars also see the *Soziale Marktwirtschaft,* or Social Market Economy—the CDU alternative to the SPD's planned socialist economy—as deriving from "programs and convictions held by the dominant factions in the American business community and the U.S. Military Government in Germany" (Berghahn 1984: 189). This is often characterized as a form of "hegemonic socialization" in which "foreign elites . . . internalize the norms and value orientations espoused by the hegemon" (Ikenberry and Kupchan 1990: 285). The key to this process is usually understood to be some kind of material incentive provided for willing accomplices, such that the hegemon (the United States, in this case) provides rewards for inhabitants of the subordinate political community (occupied Germany) who choose to go along with its goals and perhaps provides disincentives to those choosing to oppose the hegemon (Doering-Manteuffel 1996: 6–7; Ikenberry and Kupchan 1990: 290–92; Schimmelfennig 2000: 115–16). On this account, rhetorical commonplaces are merely a cover for what is *really* going on: the transformation of Germany into something more acceptable to the Americans.

But such explanations can only succeed at the cost of eliminating legitimation from view. Even if the American occupying forces wanted to impose their views on German political elites, it is unlikely that policies based on those views would have been socially sustainable in the absence of a common language that occupiers and occupied could speak. That there *was* such a language—drawing on the commonplace of 'Western Civilization'—is an important part of the story, providing the context within which particular details about state/market balances and electoral laws could be worked out.

While the notion that Germany belonged to a larger civilizational community called 'Western Civilization' and should therefore be organized in a 'Western' manner was not *dominant* in the period before the Second World War (Doering-Manteuffel 1996: 22), it was clearly present in the cosmos of public rhetoric. The "neoliberal" tradition of thinking about society and the economy was also present, and this tradition rooted itself in a liberal Catholic anthropology that stressed the commonalities between Germany and other Western countries (Friedrich 1955: 513–14; Gutmann 1990). The existence of such discursive resources provided the materials to legitimate the new state and solidify its character as a member of the liberal, market-oriented (but not laissez-faire) 'West.' In fact, "the American reforms could only be realized successfully if they were agreed to by the Germans, if they fell on fertile ground, or if they were at least tolerated" (Woller 1993: 33), which meant that proposals had to find some rhetorical support in the commonplaces already existing on the ground. In the absence of these discursive materials it would have been much more difficult, if not impossible, to effect such a settlement.

At the same time, the mere presence of the occidentalist commonplace was not sufficient to uniquely determine the outcome of the process. The existence of Schumacher's hard-line position demonstrates that there *was* another socially plausible option available: reject Allied initiatives and engage in various forms of resistance. The specific actions undertaken by Clay and Adenauer to deploy occidentalist language and produce a more cooperative stance were also crucial in bringing about the defeat of the SPD proposals. This is true even if it remained the case that the Allies deployed superior material resources in support of their goals. Had the proposals in question been completely unfamiliar, the initiatives might simply have been rejected out of hand.[10] An imported set of notions would have been vulnerable to accusations that those espousing them were betraying their heritage, so the existence of antecedents in a German tradition was essential.

Similar notions were at play in the selection of the federal capital, a matter that the military governors and other apparatuses of the occupation had little to do with. The SPD preferred Frankfurt, an industrial city and Social Democratic stronghold; it was also the location of the Wirtschaftsrat and thus presented a logical choice for a federal capital, as the party representatives were already gathered there. The Parliamentary Council had not met in Frankfurt, however, but in the relatively provincial town of Bonn—which Adenauer proposed as the federal capital during the deliberations. In support of this goal, he emphasized the symbolic value of erecting a capital in the Rhineland "because the ties between the Rhenish west and Germany's western neighbors are stronger than the relations between Frankfurt and the western neighbors" (Schwarz 1995: 409, quoting Adenauer). While it was certainly an exercise of power on Adenauer's part to have the capital located in Bonn—he was the strongest advocate of such a move, perhaps in part because Bonn was only a short ferry-ride away from his home in Rhöndorf—the bases of that power were largely symbolic and rhetorical, including a declaration by Schumacher that the selection of Frankfurt would be a defeat for the CDU (Heidenheimer

10. The question about the importance of American power speaks to the question of "Americanization" rather than to the broader issue of founding a West German state in the first place and incorporating it in a broader civilizational community. On this level, it is clear that significant elements of the West German economy and society were "Americanized," but I would suggest that the condition of possibility for doing so was the more encompassing notion of belonging to 'Western Civilization.' Recall the discussion in chapter 4.

1960: 173–74; Schwarz 1995: 419–20). Selecting Bonn as the capital, and doing so for these civilizational reasons, was thus part of the way in which occidentalist notions were enshrined in the very design of the new state.

The 'westward' orientation of the BRD was very much in evidence during the first debates held in the Bundestag, the new German parliament, after a very close election that resulted in Adenauer becoming federal chancellor by a one-vote margin (Schwarz 1995: 444). Shortly after assembling his cabinet, Adenauer appeared in the Bundestag to deliver his first *Regierungserklärung*, an official statement of the government's policies and plans. In the course of the speech, Adenauer declared:

> According to the Basic Law, cultural affairs are the responsibility of the *Länder*. But in the name of the entire government I can say the following: the entirety of our work will be carried out in the spirit of Christian-Western [*christlich-abendländisch*] culture, and with attention to the rights and worth of human beings. (VdDB 20.9.1949: 30)

Adenauer utilized this occidentalist appeal to frame and ground his other proposals, including a desire to work closely with France and with the other Western Allies, a willingness to take steps toward European integration, and the preservation of the free market. This language was also deployed by representatives of some of the smaller parties that were in alliance with the CDU. Speaking for the Center Party, Helene Wessel argued that

> Europe was created and formed 2000 years ago from the interaction of Greece and Rome. From Greece came the spiritual content and the worth of the individual personality with which the western world rose to its true greatness. From Rome came the orderly power to construct governments. Europe came out of these two powers. . . . For this reason we support the government's intention to work towards European integration. We will fight for such European integration because we believe that the Christian-Western cultural values which Europe still maintains must be preserved for all humankind. (73)

Schumacher, for his part, mocked the allusion to a governmental policy founded on Western cultural values that ignored "the right to a basic material existence," which he characterized as "the first of all rights" (41). It is notable that he did not challenge the occidentalist commonplace but rather sought to turn it to his advantage. Schumacher took a similar approach to the question of European integration, first pointing out that the SPD had made a call for "a United States of Europe a firm component of our foreign policy" ever since 1925, but immediately qualified his support for such initiatives.

However . . . we should also not give a blank check here. That would only encourage hegemonial tendencies in Europe and weaken the good will towards international cooperation enjoyed by broad masses of the German people. Europe means equal treatment, ladies and gentlemen! (42)

Schumacher thus presented an alternative policy approach to the enthusiasm for integration voiced by Adenauer. The differences between their approaches can be traced to this disagreement about the community to which Germany should belong: in Adenauer's case it was an old community that was being restored (and that Germany was already a part of), whereas in Schumacher's case it was a new community that could only be built by a number of parties equal from the outset.

Issues such as dismantling and the situation in Berlin were frequent topics as well. In fact, the very first motion introduced in the Bundestag—introduced a week before a government was even formed—called for an end to the dismantling of German industrial facilities on the grounds that it was incompatible with the principles of the ERP. Günter Henle of the CDU underscored this point during the early debates, arguing that "reconstruction and dismantling at the same time are simply opposites which do not go together." But he also deployed occidentalist reasoning to make the point.

As I said once in the Wirtschaftsrat: the decisive security guarantee for the western world does not lie in dismantling and similar measures, but in the winning of the soul of the German people for the ideals of the West. In the elections an overwhelming majority of the German people stood up for these ideals, and our entire task here is oriented to strengthening these beliefs in them. (VdDB 23.9.1949: 96)

From the context, it is apparent that the "overwhelming majority" to which Henle refers seems to include all of those voters who did not vote for the Communists. By grouping all of the noncommunist parties together in this way, opposition was rendered quite difficult—unless the opponent wanted to abandon the ground of 'Western Civilization' in favor of something else. 'Europe' was not available as an alternate basis for policy articulation, as it had been effectively seized by the occidentalist speakers as a bulwark of 'Western Civilization' against the East; "few considered it necessary to distinguish between European and Atlantic cooperation," and *Westbindung* could quite comfortably refer to both Europe and the broader 'western Civilization' within which Europe was nested (Granieri 2003: 31). This association was strengthened by many of the comments made about the ongoing situation in Berlin, in which the city was characterized as an outpost for both Europe and 'the West,' metonymically standing in for both. This declaration by a delegate of the extremely federalist Bavarian Party, which was greeted by enthusiastic applause from all sides of the chamber, provides a striking example.

> We consider the struggle which Berlin has engaged in over the past weeks and months to be the same as that which Vienna survived at the time of the Turkish invasion . . . Therefore we take the position that Berlin and its inhabitants, who have in these weeks and months taken on the role of the breakwater for Western culture, Christendom, and civilization itself against the East, deserve the full material and ideal support of every German *Land* and the entire German people. (VdDB 30.9.1949: 240)

Language like this, which Adenauer himself echoed on the occasion of the founding of the German Democratic Republic in October 1949—Berlin, he suggested, "stands out in the Soviet Zone as an outpost and bulwark of the democratic western part of Germany, more than this, as a bulwark of democratic western Europe" (VdDB 21.10.1949: 309)—underscored the connections between the BRD and its 'Western' neighbors, making possible a number of common enterprises and agreements.

Among the first of these was the demand by the Allied High Commission—which had replaced the military government with the establishment of the BRD—that Adenauer's government take steps to associate itself with the Ruhr Authority, the international board that was supposed to govern that industrial region. As part of a package deal, Adenauer was offered a curtailment of the dismantling policy, as well as the freedom for the BRD to join international organizations (such as the OEEC and the Council of Europe) on its own behalf. The BRD would thus be well on its way to gaining the equality that both Adenauer and Schumacher always claimed it was entitled to.[11] The occidentalist commonplace made possible the deal that Adenauer was offered; the fact that Adenauer could refer to common European and 'Western' enterprises in which Germany wanted to participate provided the discursive resources needed to legitimate his efforts and to outflank his opponents. The high commissioners were happy to propose and agree to proposals that integrated Germany more fully into western Europe, allayed French skepticism, and made German resources available for the benefit of the larger community; Adenauer was well aware of the opportunities this provided for him to increase the BRD's freedom to maneuver. Occidentalist rhetoric made such maneuvers possible, as Adenauer was able to transform what might otherwise

11. Indeed, Adenauer had begun asserting such equality almost from the beginning, defying an instruction from the high commissioners to remain standing on the ground in front of a carpet on which the commissioners stood when they were presenting him with the final version of the Occupation Statute; instead, Adenauer strode onto the carpet, literally and figuratively placing him on a level with the commissioners (Schwartz 1991: 57).

have looked unduly assertive for a recently defeated power into a common subordination to a larger ('Western') cause.

This technique also worked well in dealing with criticisms of the policy of aligning more closely with the West that were advanced by Schumacher and other SPD representatives. References to 'the West' helped to transform controls on German industry into "a European virtue rather than a one-sided attack on German interests" (Schwarz 1995: 483). Hence anyone opposing them would appear to be an opponent of both Europe and 'the West.' Inasmuch as Schumacher did not want to come across as taking such a position, he and his party remained in a bit of a bind when the time came to begin discussing the "Petersberg Agreements" that Adenauer had negotiated with the High Commission. These agreements granted the BRD more elements of sovereignty in return for a series of formal commitments to 'Western' organizations. On one hand, Schumacher noted,

> We social democrats have always decided unequivocally for the human and cultural style of the West. We could not have chosen anything else, because such a decision is appropriate to our intellectual heritage and our way of thinking and feeling.

But having articulated such a position as a way of avoiding a charge of being an Eastern-oriented communist or a separatist, it was difficult to then oppose policies that seemed in accord with that overwhelming imperative and commitment. Schumacher articulated his opposition to Adenauer's proposal to join the Ruhr Authority by trying to recapture the notion of Europe for a socialist agenda.

> The idea for a United States of Europe is in its inner depths and outward extent an idea drawn from a great tradition. But it is the tradition of freedom and the reconciliation of people, not the tradition of European heavy industry. (VdDB 15.11.1949: 401–2)

But Adenauer responded to Schumacher by reiterating the fact that his policy would bring a halt to dismantling, while Schumacher could offer no alternative. Eventually Schumacher, frustrated, accused Adenauer of being the "Chancellor of the Allies"[12] and simply implementing their dictates—thus betraying the German nation. Schumacher could thus be linked, somewhat ironically, with the extreme nationalism of the Nazis.

Schumacher's position appeared to "refuse European integration" and other aspects of a close alignment with the Western Allies "with accusations,

---

12. Early in the morning of 25 November. I discuss this episode in greater detail in Jackson 2006.

well known from the time of the Weimar Republic, against a selling-off of the nation and a politics of self-satisfaction" (Schwarz 1979: 498–99). Adenauer was also able to point to the existence of this alternative stance as part of a strategy of obtaining concessions from the Allies, reminding them on many occasions that the alternative to himself as chancellor was probably Schumacher, with whom they would find it more difficult to work—in part because of the different configuration of rhetorical commonplaces that Schumacher deployed (Schwartz 1991: 78–80; Trachtenberg 1999: 131–34). Adenauer's support of the policy of subsuming the BRD into a larger community to which the Allies had already pledged their allegiance, combined with Schumacher's hesitation about and opposition to such initiatives, formed the core of his foreign policy.

THE SAAR PROBLEM

When one looks at a map of contemporary Germany, the borders of the country seem unproblematically fixed and stable: the country is bounded in the east by the Oder and Neisse Rivers and extends just over the Rhine River to the west. This stability is misleading, however, if we project it backward into the immediate postwar period. "Germany" occupied a rather different space on the territorial map of Europe during the early part of the twentieth century, and it was far from clear precisely what space it would occupy after the Second World War. The commonplace of 'German national unity' was ordinarily deployed so as to indicate a return to the prewar[13] boundaries of the country, which included significant amounts of territory to the east of the Oder and Neisse rivers—territory that the Soviet Union had placed under Polish jurisdiction when it unilaterally shifted that country to the west. 'German national unity,' then, meant not merely the unification of the four zones of occupation under a functioning central government but was also concerned with the "lost" territory to the east.

There was also a pressing territorial dispute in the west, involving the Saar region that bordered France. Immediately after the war the French government had separated this region—with its coal mines and steelworks—from its zone of occupation and initiated measures designed to entwine the region's economy and politics with those of France (Schwarz 1995: 488–89). The issue provoked strident nationalist language from all German political parties and served as a significant obstacle to a harmonious relationship between the BRD and the 'Western' Allies for many years. Matters came to a head in early 1950 when the French government promulgated a "Saar convention" that almost

---

13. The 1937 boundaries of the country, in fact, which were officially established as the borders of Germany by the four occupying governments on 5 June 1945 (Ruhm von Oppen 1955: 35).

amounted to an economic annexation of the region; the subsequent public debate illustrated both the contrast between Adenauer and Schumacher on these issues of territorial and national integrity and the way that Adenauer's occidentalist-based strategy managed to prevail and encourage the Europeanization of the whole issue. In this instance, as throughout the period, "contrasting historical narratives . . . shaped assessments of the German policy alternatives" (Banchoff 1999: 17). The interaction between these narratives, and the connections between the commonplaces out of which they were constructed, help to explain the victory of one stance over the other.

The SPD stance on the Saar issue was quite explicit in drawing parallels between the situation in the east and the situation in the west. During a speech in January 1950, Schumacher made the connection quite plain.

> What are we experiencing today in the Saar? We are experiencing an effort to dissolve a piece of the German economy and the German nation [*Volk*] and the German soil [*Boden*] before the conclusion of a peace treaty. If we do not fight against this, we ruin the direction of our politics against the Oder-Neisse line! Never forget that the political-moral power of our struggle to win back the territories to the east of the Oder-Neisse line rests on the fact that we Germans have not recognized this line. Therefore the issue should be settled by a peace treaty. But now in the Saar we have a west-Soviet policy, measured in proportion to the Oder and Neisse. (BKS no. 50: 21.1.1950)

Schumacher's language was explicitly nationalist, even down to the use of the words *Volk* and *Boden*. His equation of the French actions in the Saar with the Soviet actions in the eastern territories, a charge that he and other SPD representatives made quite often, was quite an incendiary one and provided Adenauer with a perfect illustration that a Schumacher government would be less inclined to work together with the 'Western' Allies (McAllister 2002: 179–81).[14]

During the first Bundestag debate on the issue, Adenauer presented his opposition to the Saar convention in relatively moderate terms, emphasizing the fact that whatever the situation of the Saar now it was only a provisional

---

14. That Schumacher's stance generated unease can be seen from an editorial in the *Neue Zeitung*—an American paper published under the auspices of the occupation authority—from November 1949 entitled "Borders of Opposition": "Adenauer's words build bridges to countries that Germany needs and which need Germany. Schumacher's words, which are perhaps only designated for private use [*Hausgebrauch*], endanger such bridges. Dr. Schumacher has not only neglected to choose the best words, but he has sought out the worst time to do so" (BPA, Bestand Kurt Schumacher, 11.11.1949). Note also that the editorial writer acknowledges that these sentiments may be widespread in private but bases her or his condemnation of Schumacher on the fact that he has given public voice to these sentiments.

situation pending the conclusion of a formal peace treaty. He also drew on the east-west parallel but refrained from emphasizing the Oder-Neisse line and focused instead on the long-standing demand for free elections in the eastern zone of occupation and called for elections in the Saar before any agreement was concluded (VdDB 10.3.1950: 1557–58). Schumacher was more blunt, accusing the Allies of employing "methods that are not really appropriate to the West" and arguing that the real issue here was not legal formulations so much as "the dissolution of a German territory from Germany" (1562–63). Perhaps realizing how he must have sounded, Schumacher addressed the issue of nationalism head-on: "It is unjust to want to accuse the German nation of a nationalist mortal sin for claiming what every nation claims for itself as a matter of course." He also claimed that to accuse the SPD of nationalist excesses was unjustified, given the party's record of opposing nationalism and Nazism. He also warned of a "new nationalism" that would be provoked by condemning the SPD.

> I must pronounce a warning: in Germany today, every nationalism is anti-democratic and anti-Western, and is untrustworthy with respect to the decisive questions of our age concerning Europe and democracy. I would like to warn that these attacks on false fronts and this politics of cheap shots will weaken those factors in Germany without which there would be no German democracy and no European democracy. (1568–69)

Here we see Schumacher attempting to respecify 'German national unity' in terms more conducive to his project of promoting a European mode of social democracy. As long as the reaction from all corners of the German political scene was simple outrage at the French actions, Schumacher's blending of nationalism and Europe did not raise questions. But when the Allies formally invited the BRD to join the Europarat (Council of Europe) and stipulated that the Saar would join as an independent member at the same time, the tensions in Schumacher's position became apparent and contributed to the defeat of his proposals. The SPD categorically rejected the invitation, noting that to join alongside the Saar would be tantamount to recognizing its independent status; in a press conference Schumacher argued that the Europarat would only represent "a substitute Europe . . . that would be a simple sacrifice to the onrush from the east in virtue of its capitalist structure and its dearth of democracy and socialist potential" (BKS U052 no. 167: 14.6.1950).

Adenauer countered by posing the question in terms of a choice for the 'West.'

> Whoever stands for the refusal of the invitation [to join the Europarat] stands against the West . . . if the BRD does not take part in the Europarat, this will abort the Europarat and finish off the effort to precipitate a European confed-

eration. To the contrary, we must remain clear that a coming-together of the European countries that will duplicate the strength of these individual countries is absolutely necessary in the light of the threat from the east. (VdDB 13.6.1950: 2466)

Schumacher was thus caught on the horns of a rhetorical dilemma. On one hand, rejecting the Europarat cast doubt on his claim to be a good European who was interested in strengthening Europe and 'the West' against the East. Several representatives of the governing parties pointed this out during the Bundestag debate, as did a number of contemporary newspaper editorials. The fact that representatives of the Communist Party criticized the Europarat in very similar terms also made things difficult for Schumacher, as such public agreement threatened to undo the careful demarcation between the SPD and the KPD that was a central component of his public position. On the other hand, accepting the invitation would be tantamount to abandoning the SPD claim to stand for 'German national unity.' Adenauer's position effectively exploited the tensions between Schumacher's anticommunism and his nationalism, endeavoring to solve the national question by "nesting" the German nation in a set of larger communities—Europe and 'the West.'

Faced with such a constellation, the SPD position could make little headway, and the party had to settle for being outvoted in the Bundestag and then consenting to send an SPD delegation to the Europarat in an effort to shore up its European credentials. Schumacher tried to justify this reversal by arguing that "the SPD has never, in the 80 years of its history, renounced a forum or ceded to its political opponents the right to speak in the name of our entire people" (Schumacher 1985: 802). This justification exemplified the political problem generated by a prominent commonplace concerning community membership: the SPD could not credibly refuse to participate in European institutions without thereby opening itself up to accusations of abandoning the community to its opponents.[15] By playing the nationalist card, Schumacher made himself and his party unacceptable to the Allies, especially by contrast to Adenauer's enthusiastic embrace of 'western' integration—and his use of the contrast with Schumacher to discipline his own governing coalition (Schwarz 1979: 498–99) and to extract concessions from the Allies. In this way, the occidentalist trajectory of German reconstruction was partially secured.

15. This pattern—opposition, defeat, and reluctant acceptance—would later characterize the SPD's response to the Schuman Plan and other organizational aspects of European integration. But these later contests drew on the formulas first deployed during the Saar debates and do not represent much novel in terms of legitimation.

The American Presidential Primary of 1952

A second key moment during which the trajectory of postwar reconstruction might have been pushed off onto a quite different path involved the selection of Dwight D. Eisenhower rather than Robert Taft as the Republican nominee for president in 1952. Taft, a leader of the so-called isolationists in the U.S. Congress, had expressed a determination to alter the course of American foreign policy so as to focus more on the territorial defense of the country; this meant, among other things, a withdrawal of American forces from various locations around the world. Had Taft been selected as the Republican nominee—an outcome that seemed entirely plausible before Eisenhower's entry into the race as a Republican—the character of the American commitment to Europe and to postwar Germany would likely have been very different. Eisenhower, although differing from the Truman administration on many of the specifics of alliance politics, presented no fundamental discontinuity with the basic policy of a transatlantic military alliance. Eisenhower's selection as the nominee helped to ensure that the occidentalist trajectory would continue, and that the United States would remain committed to the defense of Europe on 'civilizational' grounds.

The background to the 1952 presidential primary concerns the "Great Debate" about the character of the U.S. military commitment to Europe that took place in the U.S. Senate during the early part of 1951. And the background for this debate involves the commitment embodied in the North Atlantic Treaty, which entered into force in 1949 and which committed the United States to come to the defense of any signatory that was attacked. The negotiations culminating in the North Atlantic Treaty were thoroughly marked by occidentalism; this rhetorical resource subsequently played a key role during the "Great Debate" and the ensuing presidential primary. Taft's opposition to the implications that the Truman administration drew from the notion of 'Western Civilization' allowed him to be portrayed as endangering 'the West' and may well have cost him the nomination.

THE NORTH ATLANTIC TREATY

It is well established among diplomatic historians that the initial impetus for the formation of the North Atlantic Treaty[16] was a British initiative to organize the defense of Western Europe and to include the United States in some capacity (Folly 1980). The British approach proceeded via the Treaty of Dunkirk and subsequently via the Brussels Pact leading up to the formation of the "Western Union"; efforts were made throughout to solidify some sort of formal American commitment to these organizations, but this became

---

16. I have treated the 'Western' origins of NATO more extensively in Jackson 2003.

deeply problematic in that a constitutively European organization was simply not broad enough to contain the United States. The principles on which membership was justified were not comprehensive enough to justify formal American participation (Kaplan 1985: 114–15). The solution to this problem was an Atlantic or civilizational one, in which explicit reference was made to a much more expansive community (Ireland 1981: 72–74). This community, not surprisingly, was 'Western Civilization.'

As early as December 1947 Ernst Bevin, the British foreign secretary, was deploying such language in discussions with Marshall; on 22 December he asked if he could show a record of his recent talks with Marshall to the French foreign minister in an effort to get France on board as well. That record read, in part:

> His [Bevin's] own idea was that we must devise some western democratic system comprising the Americans, ourselves, France, Italy etc., and of course the Dominions. This would not be a formal alliance but an understanding backed by power, money and resolute action. It would be a sort of spiritual federation of the west . . . The Secretary of State [Bevin] said that he now felt that the spiritual consolidation of western civilization was possible. (FRUS 1948/III: 1–2)

A few weeks later Bevin presented Marshall with a more detailed series of reflections on the subject, in which occidentalist language was featured prominently.

> We shall be hard put to it to stem the further encroachment of the Soviet tide. It is not enough to reinforce the physical barriers which still guard our Western civilisation. We must also organize and consolidate the ethical and spiritual forces inherent in this Western civilisation of which we are the chief protagonists. This in my view can only be done by creating some form of Union in Western Europe, whether of a formal or informal character, backed by the Americas and the Dominions . . . Essential though it is, progress in the economic field will not in itself suffice to call a halt to the Russian threat. Political and indeed spiritual forces must be mobilised in our defense. (5)

As for the extent of this association, Bevin felt that it should include, at a minimum, "Scandinavia, the Low Countries, France, Italy, Greece and possibly Portugal." However, he added, "As soon as circumstances permit we should, of course, wish also to include Spain and Germany without whom no Western system can be complete" (5). Bevin did not limit his use of such language to confidential conversations with diplomats but proposed this occidentalist basis for any future alliance in his initial presentation of the proposal to the British House of Commons. He noted that the Soviet Union had imposed an alliance on the countries of eastern Europe and rejected any suggestion that such a thing would happen in the West.

Neither we, the United States nor France is going to approach Western Europe on that basis. It is not in keeping with the spirit of Western civilisation, and if we are to have an organism in the West it must be a spiritual union. While, no doubt, there must be treaties or, at least, understandings, the union must primarily be a fusion derived from the basic freedoms and ethical principles for which we all stand. It must be on terms of equality and it must contain all the elements of freedom for which we all stand.[17] (5)

From the outset, the NAT was constituted as the institutionalization of a 'Western' community (McCalla 1996: 462). This extended to the fact that the Soviet Union was rarely mentioned in the course of the negotiations; rather, the rhetorical focus was on the need to defend the values of 'the West' by providing some degree of explicit support for those values—even if the initial commitments embodied in the treaty were quite modest (Coker 1998: 60–61). Pitching the treaty in this manner permitted advocates of such a drastic departure from the traditional American policy of avoiding peacetime alliances to garner the support of people like George Kennan, who had initially been quite opposed to the notion of a formal treaty (Ireland 1981: 83). But Kennan altered his recommendation in May 1948, arguing that public statements by Bevin and the Canadian foreign minister had altered the rhetorical landscape: "I think we must be very careful not to place ourselves in the position of being the obstacle to further progress toward the political union of the western democracies" (FRUS 1948/III: 128).[18]

Dean Acheson, who had become secretary of state in early 1949 with Marshall's departure, was a great supporter of this initiative, understanding much of his task to involve "prevent[ing] Europe and the United States—the essential components of One World—from being isolated from each other" (Harper 1996: 276–77). Hence it is not surprising to find him continuing to deploy the occidentalist language that he earlier used in justifying the ERP, both during the NAT discussions and afterward. A particularly striking example of this rhetoric is a speech that he delivered in April 1950, in which he sought to define the "most important problem of the security and well-being of our country" in occidentalist terms.

We are faced with a threat—in all sober truth I say this—we are faced with a threat not only to our country but also to the civilization in which we live and to the whole physical environment in which that civilization can exist. . . . To understand this threat to our country and our civilization, we have to go back

17. House of Commons, 22 January 1948, col. 407–8.
18. Occidentalist language also helped to garner the support of powerful senators like Arthur Vandenberg, who had already (during the ERP debates, as discussed in the previous chapter) accepted and helped to advance the occidentalist strategy against its exemplarist rival.

200 years and examine the ideas on which the United States was founded. We could go back more than 2000 years, to the very beginning of Western civilization. For more than 2000 years, the ideas we inherited, and live by today, have been fought over, have been suppressed, and have been reborn in the minds of men. (*DOSB* 1 May 1950: 673)

Because of the enormity of this threat, Acheson suggested, extreme measures—such as the formation and strengthening of a peacetime alliance—had been required. Indeed, what was required was a form of what he called "total diplomacy," a weakening of the divide between international and domestic issues and a consequent focus on the preservation of Western Civilization as a whole. "More than the institution of democratic government is at stake," he argued. "The threat, as I have said, is to our civilization, and each of us is a bearer of that civilization. And, therefore, each of us has a part to play in this total diplomacy" (677). This language provided the basis for the NAT by portraying the world situation as posing a threat to something larger than merely the United States and thus calling for a response beyond national or continental defense.

Both the preamble of the treaty and the specification of obligations under the treaty in article 5 extended the occidentalist strategy first utilized in U.S. policy discussions during the ERP debates. Both clauses drew on the notion of civilizational commonality to justify the treaty and the commitments that it entailed. The preamble declared that the parties to the treaty "are determined to safeguard the freedom, common heritage and civilization of their peoples, founded on the principles of democracy, individual liberty and the rule of law," a locution that constituted the resulting alliance as a civilizational one. Article 5 built on this logic by proposing an indivisible notion of security.

> The Parties agree that an armed attack against one or more of them in Europe or North America shall be considered an attack against them all and consequently they agree that, if such an armed attack occurs, each of them . . . will assist the Party or Parties so attacked by taking forthwith, individual and in concert with other Parties, such action as it deems necessary, including the use of armed force, to restore and maintain the security of the North Atlantic area. (NATO 1989: 376–77)

This indivisible notion of security was a logical consequence of thinking of the alliance members as belonging to a common 'Western Civilization.' Thanks in no small part to the earlier campaigns to legitimate the ERP, the idea was quite commonsensical by this point. Indeed, it would not be an exaggeration to say that the ERP debates unintentionally paved the way for the NAT, even though part of the initial appeal of the ERP was that it promised to serve as a substitute for a military commitment to Europe (Latham 1997: 143–45, 69–70; Pollard 1985). The NAT was an extension of the basic occidentalist logic that had underpinned the ERP; in this light the shift from economic to military means should be seen as a relatively minor innovation.

THE "GREAT DEBATE" AND ITS AFTERMATH

Given this basic continuity between the ERP and the NAT, it is not surprising that those senators most opposed to ERP on exceptionalist grounds—the so-called isolationists—were equally hesitant about the military commitment expressed in the NAT. Led by Robert Taft and Kenneth Wherry, these senators reacted strongly to a Truman administration policy pronouncement in September 1950 that called for the transformation of "American military forces already in Europe . . . from occupation forces designed to contain Germany to combat forces which would help to contain the Soviet Union," the strengthening of those forces via the deployment of four additional divisions, and the appointment of Eisenhower as the supreme commander for Allied Forces in Europe (Williams 1985: 37–38). The ensuing congressional debate was anything but "anticlimactic" (contra Lake 1999: 139). The fact that "it did not alter the fundamental nature of the strategy that had evolved between 1947 and 1949" (139) demonstrates not that the debate was irrelevant, but that it was resolved in such a way as to continue the previous trajectory. Occidentalism is critical to this outcome and thus critical to the continuation of the American military commitment to Europe.

Exemplarist critics of the Truman administration's proposal adopted several lines of attack, including a suggestion that the president lacked the authority to undertake a measure like this, a complaint that the NAT itself did not foresee such a commitment of American ground forces to Europe, and a warning that such a military buildup would spell the end of liberty in the United States (Ireland 1981: 208–10; Leffler 1992: 406–7; Williams 1985: 52–57). The traditional elements of the exemplarist position that were in evidence in these arguments—in particular, the equation of governmental power with an erosion of liberty[19]—were bolstered by what might be considered a rhetorical counterattack attempting to respecify the by this point unavoidable commonplace of 'Western Civilization' in such a way as to avoid the military security implications drawn by Acheson and others in the Truman administration. This move was inaugurated by Herbert Hoover's call for a reorientation of American foreign policy so that it might "preserve for the world this Western Hemisphere Gibraltar of Western Civilization" (1955: 7).

Hoover, although a staunch exemplarist, was no stranger to occidentalist language. In 1942, he had observed that "we are in a gigantic war. Our first

19. This argument was linked to denunciations of large standing armies, traditionally regarded in American political thought as enemies of domestic liberty and as endangering the principles of popular sovereignty and limited government (Hogan 1998).

task is to win it. Having set our hand to the task, we cannot stop until lasting peace has been made. Only from a lasting peace can we hope to save our civilization" (Hoover and Gibson 1942: 6). The disagreements between the anti-German forces after the First World War he chalked up to the fact that "Americans generally failed to realize how far, in our 300 years of separation, our outlook, our political and social ideas and ideals had grown apart from the practical methods and problems of Europe," thus reinscribing the U.S./Europe division within the general notion of 'Western Civilization' (104–5). And in a very Spenglerian mode, he and his coauthor observed:

> We cannot avoid the haunting fear that the decline and fall of the League and other liberal efforts were a part of a decline and fall of civilization on the continent of Europe—a vast compound of impersonal forces driving inexorably to some dreadful fate. (141)

Hoover thus began to articulate an alternative specification of the occidentalist commonplace, one that did *not* point in the direction of American ground forces in Europe or a strong set of transatlantic political and military ties. The cornerstone of this alternative was the idea that the United States should provide a kind of citadel for 'the West,' a position that could be defended autonomously and thus ensure the survival of 'Western Civilization' even if Europe fell to the Soviets. As Hoover argued in a nationally broadcast speech in December 1950:

> We are not blind to the need to preserve Western Civilization on the Continent of Europe or to our cultural and religious ties to it. But the prime obligation of defense of Western Continental Europe rests upon the nations of Europe. The test is whether they have the spiritual force, the will, and acceptance of unity among them by their own volition. America cannot create their spiritual forces; we cannot buy them with money. (Hoover 1955: 8)

Robert Taft took up this argument in a speech on the Senate floor on January 1951, in which he reiterated the need for Europe to provide for its own land defense and urged that the United States shift its emphasis to air and sea power. This shift would permit the United States to deter a Soviet attack on Europe by threatening to bomb the USSR if it made any aggressive moves (CR 5.1.1951: 57–58). This would be, he subsequently argued, "a kind of Monroe Doctrine for Europe" and not necessitate a "depart[ure] from the principle of maintaining a free hand to fight a war which may be forced upon us, in such a manner and in such places as are best suited at the time to meet those conditions which are changing so rapidly in the modern world" (Taft 1951: 19–20). He based much of his opposition to permanently deploying troops to Europe on the fact that such ground forces would not suffice to deter a Soviet attack, but also on the contention that "the control of sea and air can establish a power which can never be challenged by Russia and which can to a great extent protect Europe . . . There is no need for a specific line of defense in every section of the world, but we can exercise a power for peace over a vast area" (79).

The administration response to this critique was twofold. First, a number of experts testified that a reliance on sea and air power alone would not suffice to defend Europe; this was presented as a technical military judgment and was thus very difficult to combat (Williams 1985: 58–59).[20] The other response was more explicitly occidentalist, as Acheson argued before a Senate committee that "under the heel of an aggressor, Western Europe would represent 200,000,000 slaves, compelled to bend their energies and employ their resources for the destruction of the United States and the remainder of Western Civilization" (Leffler 1992: 407, quoting Acheson).

Both responses illustrated a subtle shift in the terms of the debate: the questions being explored were now questions of *what kind* of commitment and *for how long* specific policies should be pursued, rather than *whether* there should be any commitment at all. Occidentalism had become an established part of the topography; the notion of a common 'Western Civilization' was now so prominent that discussions about particular policies effectively had to take it into account.

Note that my argument here is not weakened even if analysts like Trachtenberg and Sheetz are correct in arguing that the U.S. officials discussing these problems contemplated only a *temporary* commitment of American troops to the European continent (Sheetz 1999: 25; Trachtenberg 1999: 147–49). There is nothing in the commonplace of 'Western Civilization' that *necessarily* points in the direction of a permanent commitment of troops, or even to a commitment of troops at all. All that is engendered by 'Western Civilization' is *some* kind of American responsibility for preserving Europe; the specific techniques selected to fulfill this responsibility are a separate question. The point is that a commitment was contemplated and carried out *at all*, which was not a foregone conclusion prior to the discursive deployments that I have traced here.

The rhetorical problem with the Taft-Hoover respecification of 'Western Civilization' was quite simple: If an actual threat to 'Western Civilization' that

20. Interestingly, the desire for such a technically proficient way of deterring the Soviets and keeping the United States safe would resurface several decades later in the drive to produce a space-based missile defense system. Frances FitzGerald has traced the connection between Ronald Reagan, the program's strongest public advocate, and the rhetorical commonplaces deployed by Taft and his allies in the early 1950s. She notes that "SDI was a program in search of technologies for an undesigned system at a price the nation might be willing to pay," thus underscoring the fact that constellations of rhetorical commonplaces, once defeated in one round of contestation, can reemerge at a later date if suitably reconfigured (2000: 372).

could *not* be met by any means other than ground troops could be demonstrated, opponents like Taft were rhetorically trapped, unable to oppose the policy unless they could come up with a technical rebuttal and prove that ground troops were not in fact required. Administration representatives, aware of the situation, paraded distinguished witnesses—including General Eisenhower, who had been recalled from Europe to give testimony precisely on this matter—before the Senate and its committees to establish that ground troops *were,* in fact, required (Williams 1985: 69–71). In the absence of a compelling technical rebuttal, the only remaining option was for opponents of U.S. troops in Europe to renounce their commitment to defending 'Western Civilization,' an unappealing prospect in a time when anticommunism and occidentalism continued to be closely associated. Indeed, Taft himself declined to take this option and explicitly acknowledged that Europe presented "special problems" for American policy.

> Undoubtedly the special problems of Europe and its importance to the cause of freedom throughout the world force us to act there more vigorously and make some exceptions to the general rules of policy. Our cultural background springs from Europe, and many of our basic principles of liberty and justice were derived from European institutions. American language and ideas, American institutions, and American methods of thought are largely derived from Europe. (1951: 82)

On this basis, Europe needed to be treated differently than other regions: less as an outsider and more as a member of the civilizational club. So even if Taft and Hoover *wanted* to withdraw American troops from Europe, they were not able to garner enough support for such a proposal to make it happen; the rhetorical ground on which they had to fight was stacked against them. Indeed, Taft even voted *for* the Senate resolution that officially approved the deployment of divisions to Europe and the naming of Eisenhower as supreme commander (Ireland 1981: 211–12).[21] The defense of the West had become unquestionable; the only remaining issue was how best to accomplish this.

Realists such as Mark Sheetz explain these American policy decisions not as a consequence of rhetorical commitments but as the pressures of bipolarity, suggesting that a basic American desire to withdraw from Europe was foiled by systemic imperatives: "the United States, despite repeated attempts to withdraw from Europe in the early postwar period, was compelled to remain by the structure of the bipolar international system" (1999: 6). What is lacking in this argument is a compelling link between supposed "systemic pressures" and the actions of units; such problems of linkage are endemic to IR theorizing about the activities of states within a closed and analytically autonomous

21. Taft's vote was especially significant, given that he had voted against the initial NAT—and against the ERP legislation.

system, and cannot be solved.[22] It is unclear how something like "bipolarity" could compel action except by being incorporated into concrete debates as a rhetorical commonplace—in which case the pressure in question is no longer "systemic" in the strong sense but simply one among other elements of a discursive field. And as I have argued, the rhetorical topography of these policy debates had less to do with states in anarchy and more to do with *civilizations;* the "Soviet threat" was primarily constituted as a threat to something called 'Western Civilization.' To put this another way: Sheetz's argument provides no compelling account of a *mechanism* whereby a desire for U.S. withdrawal might be translated into policies of explicit commitment to the defense of Europe. I suggest that my focus on rhetorical commonplaces does just this: regardless of what individual politicians might have wanted, they could not, in the end, successfully legitimate a policy that did not involve some kind of commitment to the defense of Europe.

However, the strength of such sentiments in the United States worried Adenauer and his advisers greatly, particularly as Taft began his third race for president in late 1951. Indeed, "the fear of an isolationist U.S. policy became *a constitutive element* of [Adenauer's] picture of America," and he worried continually about how to shore up 'the West' in light of what he saw as an uncertain American commitment to the defense of Europe (Altmann 1993: 40). Adenauer had Herbert Blankenhorn, a close adviser on foreign policy matters, monitor the course of the American elections closely,[23] and the dangers of a renewed American "isolationism" were discussed at a number of cabinet meetings.[24] Heinz Krekeler, the German consul-general in the United States, reported with concern in March 1952,

> The assumption of the leadership of the "free world" is not celebrated throughout the United States with parades as the fulfillment of a great patriotic dream, but is instead regarded in general as an occasion for melancholy considerations of the burden on the American taxpayer. Mixed in with this regret is impa-

22. As I noted in earlier chapters, this is why structural theorists like Waltz maintain that systemic pressures cannot explain the policy decisions of particular units. See also Goddard and Nexon 2005.

23. See, for example, the report from Blankenhorn dated 10 May 1952 on the positions of the various American presidential candidates, in which Blankenhorn notes that the election really came down to a determination as to whether "the present political course of the United States will be continued by the new administration" or a "change in the direction of a stronger isolationism" would take hold (AA 211–00/80-III-6372/52, Band 468).

24. For example, a meeting on 10 May 1952 featured the observation by Adenauer that "Truman and Eisenhower take the position that Europe is more important than Asia, while Taft says that Asia is more important. From these standpoints derive very different considerations of things" (Booms 1989: 279).

tience with the political foolishness—not only of the Russians, but also of the Europeans—which makes the costly American engagement on the other side of the Atlantic and the Pacific necessary.

Although this attitude was not a controlling one in the U.S. government, because "many important men in the State Department and in Congress are . . . well (and sometimes excellently) informed about European things" and have "recognized the leadership role of the United States in the still free 'Western world,'" it was still a cause for concern, as the American commitment could not be completely relied upon (AA 210 B-III-335/52, Abteilung 3 Band 292, 6 März 1952).

Although the defense of Europe had been legitimated, and had been legitimated in occidentalist terms, this does not necessarily translate into enthusiastic acceptance, and it did not seem to the German observers to have done so in this case. But this should not be surprising, as legitimation and subjective acceptance are different phenomena. A police officer may *legitimately* pull me over for speeding or for cutting across a double yellow line to reach a left-turn lane that I have not reached the proper entry point for yet, but this does *not* mean that I necessarily have to be enthused or even happy about it. It *does*, however, deprive me of being able to legitimately refuse to pay the fine. The American commitment to the defense of Europe should be thought of in this way: as a feature of the intersubjective political environment rather than as a subjectively internalized belief or persuasive concept.

As I have argued throughout this account, weakly shared rhetorical commonplaces can have profound causal effects when they are specified and deployed in fortuitous circumstances. The "Great Debate" was just such a circumstance, especially since it laid the groundwork for the subsequent campaign season, which might be seen as an extension of the "Great Debate" itself. Taft's failure to secure a compelling legitimation for his position—and in particular his failure to explain how one could be simultaneously committed to 'the West' and opposed to policies constituted as measures undertaken to defend 'the West'—contributed to his loss of the Republican Party's presidential nomination at the convention in July 1952. The representatives of the "important eastern states that ruled the Republican Party" were dissatisfied with Taft's views on foreign policy and also felt that they did not play well to the public; hence Taft was not electable (Patterson 1972: 558–62). Of course, many other factors, such as a controversy involving slates of delegates from Texas and Taft's own aloof style of public speaking, contributed to this result. Additionally, Taft had the bad luck to be running against the supreme commander of the Allied Forces, who had led the troops over the English Channel into France on D-Day—and who was also firmly and publicly committed to the principle that 'the West' must stand together against the communist threat (Ninkovich 1994: 212–13). In this way, occidentalism provides part of the explanation for Taft's defeat—a defeat that further solidified the trajectory of postwar reconstruction.

German Rearmament

Although appearing obvious in retrospect, the rearmament of the BRD was a complicated and controversial measure when first proposed and undertaken (Ninkovich 1988: 82–83). Several kinds of resistance needed to be overcome: domestic opposition within the BRD; opposition within the United States; and international opposition, particularly by France. Although the actors could not have known it at the time, the discussions and negotiations surrounding the founding of the West German state and the inclusion of that state in 'Western' initiatives such as the ERP laid the foundation for the eventual rearmament of the BRD under the auspices of NATO. The pattern by which this was accomplished was very much the same as during the earlier moments of reconstruction, with the added impetus that the deployment and formalization of the earlier rhetorical appeals provided a basis on which future discussions could build.

The BRD's inclusion in NATO was made possible by the concatenation of the two streams of legitimation discussed earlier in this chapter: one that constituted the BRD as a member of 'Western Civilization' and another that constituted NATO as an alliance dedicated to the defense of 'Western Civilization.' The combination of these two arguments pointed in one ineluctable direction: every member of 'Western Civilization,' *including* the BRD, should contribute to the defense of the whole. Opponents of this conclusion, be they German social democrats, American exemplarists, or French nationalists, attempted to sever these rhetorical links but were ultimately unable to do so.

ENVISIONING A GERMAN MILITARY ROLE

As early as Bevin's initial proposal to Marshall concerning what would become the North Atlantic Treaty, eventual German participation had been envisioned: "As soon as circumstances permit we should, of course, wish also to include Spain and Germany without whom no Western system can be complete" (FRUS 1948/III: 5). During the first confidential discussions between British, American, and Canadian officials about the shape of their alliance, a decision was made that "when circumstances permit, Germany (or the three Western Zones), Austria (or the three Western Zones) and Spain should be invited to adhere" to any such treaty of alliance, although this objective "*should not be publicly disclosed*"—presumably until some suitable formula for legitimating such a course of action could be found (FRUS 1948/III: 75, emphasis in original). That basis would be the self-same occidentalist strategy that had helped to produce the NAT by rhetorically outflanking American exemplarist logic; NATO's constitution as the military arm of 'Western Civilization' would provide the rhetorical resources for legitimating the BRD's association with, and eventual accession to, NATO (Leffler 1992: 280–84, 345–46; Eisenberg 1996: 471–74).

The logic was simple: inasmuch as the BRD was considered to be a 'Western' country, it too had a role to play in the defense of 'the West.' John McCloy, who had become the American high commissioner for Germany with the end of military government in 1949, never lost an opportunity to stress the need to incorporate the BRD into some larger organization of Europe—nested within the West as a whole—as a way of dealing with the German problem (Schwartz 1991: 297–99). In a speech delivered before a British audience in April 1950, he began by characterizing "the Soviet pressure to absorb Berlin and force us out" as "strong proof of the challenge of Western ideals. . . . As an outpost behind the Iron Curtain, Berlin is a constant reminder to the satellite peoples of the possibility of a different way of life" (*DOSB* 17 April 1950: 587). This is almost the same formulation as that deployed by Adenauer and has the same rhetorical effect of nesting the BRD within a larger civilizational community: not merely Germany and not merely Europe, but 'the West' as a whole has a stake in the defense of Berlin. McCloy went on to draw the conclusion that it was necessary to include the BRD in the process of creating "a genuine European community" on this basis, calling for "prompt action."

> Today, the West has the opportunity to unite for its own defense. Tomorrow may be too late. Today, Germany is still in a formative stage and, I believe, wants to join a united Europe. Tomorrow, the situation in Germany and in other European countries may have taken a turn which will make action more difficult. (588)

By "defense" here McCloy meant something more than simply military defense against outside aggression, but something more like the consolidation of a 'Western,' democratic way of life throughout Europe. "The demands of security, of economic, and of spiritual health, all call for the same solution," he argued. "Events press us to this solution and by 'events' I do not mean merely the East-West split, but the deeper moral, political, and economic forces that surge in Europe today" (588). McCloy's deemphasizing of the "East-West split" is rather ironic here, since his entire argument is predicated on such a split in a civilizational, if not merely in a military, sense; on another occasion he referred to "the competition with the Soviets in Germany as the 'struggle for the soul of Faust' and was convinced that 'at this stage in history there is a better chance to influence the German mind than there has been for a century'" (McCloy quoted in Schwartz 1993: 37–38).

The basis on which the BRD could and should be rehabilitated was its membership in a larger 'Western' community; this would solve the German problem and also aid in the consolidation of 'the West' as a whole. Acheson echoed this position in a speech to a British audience[25] a few weeks later, citing "the world's need for German energies, talents, and enthusiasm in the preservation of civilization" as a reason for taking steps to promote the "reestablishment of Germany in the family of Western civilization" via a deepening and strengthening of European and Western political, military, and economic integration. Further, and perhaps more strikingly, Acheson argued that this policy was

> the reflection of an attitude on our part which views the problems of the entire Western community as our own and is not motivated by narrow national purposes. The guaranty of this lies, I think, in our own awareness that such an approach to our mutual problems will call upon us in the United States to make sacrifices no less disagreeable and no less difficult than those which will be called for by any of the countries on this side of the Atlantic. (DOSB 22 May 1950: 790–91)

It does not matter whether what Acheson is saying about the United States' motives is *true* or not. What is important to note is that by deploying the occidentalist commonplace in this manner he is contributing to an active and ongoing constitution of U.S. policy as dealing with the conceptual object of 'the West' rather than with a more parochial or narrow political community. It is also important to note the dates of these speeches, as both of them came *before* the invasion of South Korea by North Korean forces in mid-June 1950. The deployment of occidentalist arguments provides the context in which the invasion of South Korea could later be interpreted as calling for a more explicit effort to defend Europe—and the BRD in particular—from a military invasion. While the Korean situation remains an important part of the explanation for German rearmament and the shift from the relatively minor institutional commitments of the NAT to a more comprehensive alliance organized as NATO, it is the occidentalist rhetoric that provides the context in which the military situation in Southeast Asia could be plausibly used as a reason to press ahead with the reestablishment of a German military contribution under the auspices of an invigorated 'Western' alliance.

25. During the speech, Acheson also took pains to situate the U.S.-U.K. 'special relationship' within the broader notion of the West, arguing that the "strictly bilateral nature of our relationship has been broadened to include the problems of a wider community, of which we are both a part. Our own prospects for the future are deeply entwined in the fortunes of this wider community. . . . this also requires from us, as well as from all members of the larger community to which we belong, a deeper understanding not only of the nature of our common problems but also of the kind of action necessary to meet them" (DOSB 22 May 1950: 789).

The occidentalist framework was not merely used by the American representatives in Allied discussions about Germany but was also utilized in discussions among the Germans themselves about the possibility of a BRD defense contribution. Shortly after the Federal Republic was founded in 1949, Acheson came to Germany—largely at McCloy's urging—and met with both Adenauer and Schumacher. This visit helped to cement the informal coalition between Adenauer and the Americans, a coalition that (as I have argued) was made socially plausible largely on occidentalist grounds. Adenauer used his meeting with Acheson, which came *before* Acheson's meeting with Schumacher, to present a vintage occidentalist argument about Germany's future, linking the Federal Republic with the tradition of Charlemagne in holding the line for 'Western Civilization' against the Eastern barbarians. As Acheson later recalled:

> He [Adenauer] wanted Germans to be citizens of Europe, to cooperate, with France especially, in developing common interests and outlook and in burying the rivalries of the past few centuries. Their common heritage had come to them down the Rhine, as the successors of Charlemagne, who guarded European civilization when human sacrifice was still practiced in eastern Germany. They must lead in the rebirth of Europe. (1969: 341)

Adenauer also prepared Acheson for his meeting with Schumacher by telling him what to expect: a nationalist, *Sonderweg* claim that would reject European integration and close cooperation with the United States. Schumacher did not disappoint, and from that point on Acheson would regard Adenauer as the United States' man in Germany (Harper 1996: 209–11; Schwartz 1991: 78–80; Schwarz 1995: 486). In a way, Adenauer and Acheson found themselves standing back-to-back against domestic political opponents, in favor of a strengthened 'Western' alliance against more parochial points of view. Occidentalist language made this situation possible.

Adenauer's own advocating of a German defense contribution can be traced back to very early in the history of the BRD; as early as January 1949, before the new government was even erected, he had raised the issue of the military defense of Germany with the military government but had been privately reprimanded by the Allies for doing so. There was also great domestic opposition to any talk of rearmament; the Social Democrats were strongly opposed to such suggestions and criticized Adenauer quite strongly whenever the issue came up (Artner 1985: 4–5; Drummond 1982: 7–9). Given this opposition, the question of *why* Adenauer kept raising the issue becomes important; Adenauer's biographer Hans-Peter Schwarz suggests that "Adenauer's preoccupation with the military situation, long before he was encouraged or forced into it by the Western Allies, is one aspect of his character that is not easy to explain" (Schwarz 1995: 521). The solution to this puzzle, I think, is not to treat the issue as one of Adenauer's "character" and instead to keep a focus on the possibilities afforded by the rhetorical commonplaces available to him. Military integration was the logical implication of a policy of *Westbindung,* precisely if 'the West' appeared to be under a military threat.

Adenauer always interpreted the Soviet presence in the eastern zone of occupation as a prelude to an invasion, and the strengthening of the East German *Volkspolizei* (an armed police force that might serve as the advance troops for an invasion) and the invasion of South Korea could be interpreted similarly—much as the coup in Czechoslovakia had been interpreted in a similar way during the debates about ERP two years previously. Military integration should therefore be understood as a continuation of the strategy that led Adenauer to pursue closer integration on all fronts, particularly since the rhetorical grounds for doing so were the same in all cases: as a 'Western' country, the BRD belonged inside 'Western' organizations and should be an equal partner in common 'Western' endeavors.[26]

OUTFLANKING OPPONENTS: OCCIDENTALISM AS SOLUTION TO THE GERMAN QUESTION

The occidentalist project for the construction of a strong 'Western' alliance faced two major opposing positions: the SPD's advocacy of a policy of "forward defense," which rejected the need for German contribution to the defense of Europe (Drummond 1982: 40–41), and the French fears that a rearmed Germany would pose a security threat to France (Trachtenberg 1999: 73).[27] In both instances, advocates of an alliance featuring a commitment of ground troops from all participating countries—including the BRD, whose participation in the first place was opposed by the SPD and (at least initially) by French officials—used occidentalist appeals to make their case and to rhetorically outflank their opponents.

The essence of the SPD argument against any form of German rearmament was the familiar claim that because the BRD was not really a German state, but only a provisional institution pending reunification, it should not take any steps that would tend to entrench itself or restrict the freedom of

26. This logic is apparent in Adenauer's response to the Schuman Plan when it was proposed in May 1950. Adenauer supported the initiative in broadly occidentalist terms, casting the plan as an effort to strengthen 'the West' by constructing a strong Europe. He also used the plan as an argument in favor of the BRD's accession to the Council of Europe; he sometimes had to defend this position against members of his own cabinet, such as Jakob Kaiser, who feared that joining such an organization would make German reunification harder to achieve. Adenauer's response was to stress the impact that a strong 'West' would have on the east (Schwarz 1995: 504–7).

27. I have addressed the third major group of opponents—Taft Republicans in the United States—earlier.

action of any future unified Germany (Drummond 1982: 75–76). Rearmament, as proposed by the Allies, involved both; the initial proposal was for German troops to join a West European army, which would cement the 'westward' orientation of the country and perhaps hinder reunification efforts. From these presuppositions Schumacher articulated a policy of "forward defense," wherein he called for the defense of German territory by a stronger commitment of Allied, and particularly American, troops. "I don't understand," he commented at a press conference, "why the Americans are training their new divisions with the newest weapons in Arizona and Texas. They could also do this in Grafenwörth and on the Lüneberg Heath, and this would have greater utility for democracy" (1985: 833).[28] He argued that this would also serve the cause of reunification, as the option of a demilitarized German state—which might be acceptable to the Soviets—would be kept open.

Adenauer also felt that a commitment by the Allies to defend Germany would be in order, but he wanted to secure a German commitment to any such defense effort; the occidentalist themes undergirding his strategy almost demanded it. In August 1949, shortly before the Federal Republic was established, he delivered a speech in which, according to a contemporary newspaper article,[29] he argued:

> We must expect of the Western world that they will take over the defense of our people in the struggle for the preservation of Europe until we are in a position to defend ourselves. Christian-western [*christlich-abendländische*] Europe cannot survive the threat from the East if foreign statesmen and military leaders, without considering the German situation, publicly debate whether the line of defense [for Europe] should be drawn on the Elbe or on the Rhine. Europe must be defended where the furthest outpost of Christian-western thinking can be found.

28. Schumacher's implication is that training American troops in Germany would demonstrate a commitment to defend Germany from a Soviet attack.

29. I was unable to locate the original version of this speech, and none of the German archivists with whom I spoke were able to do so either. This quotation in the text is drawn from an article in the *Rhenische Post* of 12 August 1949, the day after the speech was delivered; in the original German all of the verbs are in "indirect speech," indicating a paraphrase rather than a literal quotation. The German original reads: "Von der westlichen Welt aber müßten wir erwarten, daß sie in dem Kampf um die Erhaltung Europas so lange den Schutz unseres Volkes übernehme, bis es in der Lage sei, sich selbst zu verteidigen. Das christlich-abendländische Europa könne nicht gegenüber der Gefahr des Ostens bestehen, wenn ausländliche Staatsmänner und Herrführer ohne Befragung deutscher Stellen sich in aller Öffentlichkeit überlegten, ob die Verteidigungslinie an der Elbe oder am Rhein zu ziehen sei. Europa müsse da verteidigt werden, wo die letzten Vorposten christlich-abendländischen Denkens sich befänden." Note that *Stellen* can also mean "contribution," particularly when used in a military sense, although in this context I think that "situation" is a better translation.

The occidentalism of Adenauer's formulation also provided a powerful rhetorical weapon against the Social Democrats, along the lines that were successful in previous controversies. Inasmuch as the SPD wanted to differentiate itself from the Soviet Union by declaring itself *culturally* aligned with the West, the party's refusal of explicit *political* and *military* alignment appeared to be somewhat of a contradiction. This was exacerbated by the SPD's explicit disavowals of "neutralism," by which party spokespersons seemed to mean a kind of isolation from diplomatic activity (Artner 1985: 43–45). In general the SPD's position on these issues was rather complex, but the one consistent point was, as SPD foreign policy spokesman Carlo Schmid argued in 1952, that "a nation cannot be brought into a supranational community through the instrumentality of a third party without risk of becoming a mere object of policy. A free people must have sovereign rights before it can give them up" (535). Unfortunately for the SPD, this looked suspiciously like the older German nationalist position, a parallel that Adenauer and his allies were quick to point out during parliamentary debates on the subject.[30] The SPD's position also looked hypocritical to American observers such as Hamilton Fish Armstrong, who commented in a *Foreign Affairs* editorial:

> The German Social Democrats fix their eyes exclusively on German reunification. That naturally is the objective of all German parties, but the Social Democratic leaders believe, or pretend to believe, that the Soviets will accept it if they are promised that united Germany will be neutral and unarmed. Hence the dogma of the Social Democrats that they must not rearm now. This enables them to dwell on the advantages of not having to pay for a military establishment and ultimately being able to trade freely alike with the West (to which they concede they feel akin spiritually) and the Soviet bloc (where lie the best markets for German heavy industry). This attractive vista ignores the fact that unarmed Germany would be impotent either to defend herself alone or to help defend both herself and the Western civilization to which she claims to want to belong (in all respects, that is, save contributing to its defense). (Armstrong 1953: 180–81)

The CDU also used such attacks during the 1953 election campaign, even putting out campaign posters declaring "With Adenauer and the West, for Peace and Security" (Drummond 1982: 110). Touting the benefits of Adenauer's *Westbindung* policy, the CDU soared to a landslide victory, effectively foreclosing the SPD's alternative and paving the way to German rearmament (Schwarz 1997: 80).[31]

---

30. For example, Franz Joseph Strauß compared the SPD's position to a "Rapallo" position: a desire to play one side off against the other, as German politicians had attempted to do before the First World War (VdDB, 7 February 1952: 8118–19).

31. Obviously the CDU's election victory was not entirely due to their occidentalist rhetoric, but this was certainly a part of the story. Among other things, the SPD's foreign

Adenauer drew two conclusions from this. The first was that there was no significant difference between American isolationist politics and the SPD's demand that the BRD refrain from making any definite commitments to the Allies and retain a free hand—and in particular refrain from making any commitments that might bind a reunified German state. Adenauer even characterized this stance in a radio interview as "German isolationism."

> *Adenauer:* . . . very often there is only the policy of the lesser evil. But since 1945 there has been a policy of the greater evil, a German isolationism.
>
> *Interviewer:*[32] We know this specific word only in American politics. There it means a propensity—which keeps springing up over and over—to hold oneself apart from every interaction with the world [*Welthändeln*], above all to hold oneself apart from Europe, and to defend only the narrowest interests of one's own country. . . . what would the corresponding policy be in Germany?
>
> *Adenauer:* Exactly the same, except with one difference. . . . We are a weak and exceedingly exposed country. We can accomplish nothing on our own, relying only on our own power.[33] We cannot be a no-man's-land between East and West; in that case we would have no friends anywhere and in any case a dangerous neighbor to the East. *It does not matter whether one calls this 'neutrality' or not.* Every refusal of the Federal Republic to pursue common matters with the West, or with Europe, would already be a German isolationism, a dangerous flight into having nothing to do with the world [*Nichthandeln*]. (BPA, Bestand Konrad Adenauer, 5 March 1952: 8–9)

The struggle against a possible return to "isolationist" policies in the United States was thereby constituted as being continuous with Adenauer's struggle against the SPD's more nationalist notion of foreign policy, further cementing the informal alliance between Adenauer and one branch of the American foreign policy establishment.

Adenauer's second conclusion was that the solution to these challenges lay in the same strategy that he had been pursuing: an emphasis on European integration, not so that Europe could play an autonomous role in the world, but so that the defense of 'the West' on the European continent could be carried out *even if* the United States one day decided to withdraw its troops. As this corresponded quite well to the goals of American officials like Acheson and McCloy, and enjoyed considerable popular support in the United States

---

policy alternative, whatever its merits, was more complicated and took longer to explain, whereas the CDU's proposal fit easily into a slogan (Drummond 1982: 110).

32. Ernst Friedländer, a popular journalist and public commentator on foreign affairs who was later elected to numerous leadership positions within the European movement.

33. Elsewhere in this interview Adenauer comments that isolationism is a reasonable policy for the United States (if an unfortunate one for Europeans) because of the United States' "incomparable strength and its almost unassailable geographical situation."

as well,[34] such a policy served to strengthen Adenauer's relations with the Americans.[35]

This emphasis on European integration and 'Western' unity also served to address the French reservations about German rearmament and therefore to dissolve the final barrier to the reemergence of the BRD as a legitimate actor on the world stage, and a legitimate partner in the 'Western Alliance.' The French had been wary of most steps to build up any kind of German power and had insisted on the retention of controls over the BRD. Rearmament was a matter that did not sit well with French politicians, and as soon as Acheson proposed the use of German troops as part of the NATO defense effort, the French responded with the Pleven Plan, which called for German military units of no larger than battalion size to be integrated into a European Army. While this appeared to be a concession, "the plan made German rearmament contingent on the creation of a new set of European institutions. . . . If progress were ever to be made along these lines, it would take years" (Leffler 1992: 398, 390).

Neither the Americans nor the Germans were particularly happy with the French proposal, but they took it as the basis for discussion in the hopes that something better might be made of it (Large 1993: 378–80). Adenauer in particular hoped to use the European Army proposal as a stepping-stone to an eventual accession of the BRD to NATO (386–87). Given NATO's constitutive identity as the 'Western Alliance' and the fact that the United States had committed to defend the territories of all signatory countries on this basis, Adenauer's desire for NATO membership is hardly surprising; the problem was that such a step would mean the elimination of many occupation controls, which made the French uneasy. The trick was to find a formula that would solve both problems simultaneously.

The rhetorical commonplace that would enable such a solution was already at hand, inasmuch as some elements of the French government were already accustomed to speaking of Germany and France as participants in a common 'Western' community. Robert Schuman, sometime French foreign minister and initial proposer of the economic integration of the French and German

34. There were several resolutions in the U.S. Congress in support of European unity, and Krekeler archived numerous newspaper clippings detailing the popularity of the notion of European integration. See also Schwabe 1995: 116–18.

35. This reading accords well with Ronald Granieri's characterization of Adenauer as "a German statesman, and a proud European . . . always looking for the best deal for Germany within Europe and within the West" (Granieri 2003: 230). But the fact that Adenauer was always looking to hedge his bets and enact contingency plans in no way subtracts from the importance of the occidentalist rhetorical commonplaces I have been emphasizing through this account; 'Europe,' at this point in time, was less an alternative to 'the West' than a nested subordinate part of it.

economies, connected his initiatives with the example of the Carolingian Empire (Herbst 1989: 22–23). The French high commissioner André François-Poncet, "a Germanist with a deep knowledge of the country's language and culture," often deployed much more explicitly occidentalist rhetoric in his discussions of Germany (Schwarz 1995: 478). One particularly notable example comes in a speech he delivered to the Association of Foreign Press Correspondents in March 1951 (KAS I-172-009-2: 14 March 1951),[36] in which he declared that "We are going through a period which history may call one day the reawakening of the West. . . . Western Europe now recognizes the solidarity which binds together those of its peoples who remain true to Christian-western civilization in the face of the common danger of communism." But this was more than a defensive reaction by a few European countries, as evidenced by the participation of the United States in the effort of consolidation.

> In the same way, the United States of America has become aware of the solidarity that binds its fate with that of Western Europe. In doing so it has broken with a deeply-rooted tradition. . . . And thus Western solidarity has developed into a comprehensive [*umfassenderen*] organization. Western Europe has become an Atlantic Europe.

François-Poncet was also quite explicit about Germany's role in such a Europe: "Germany obviously has a place in this humanistic and Christian West—a reunified Germany if possible, but in the absence of a complete Germany, at the minimum a Federal Germany." He was even more expansive in his praise of Adenauer, using him as an example of the kind of actions required to vanquish Spengler's prophecies.

> It is only fair of Chancellor Adenauer to say: he was, and remains, one of the best pioneers of the awakening West. And whatever position we may hold, inside or outside of this hall, in life, or on the earth in general, I believe that we can and must shake hands and combine our powers in order to reproach Spengler's lies. It is not true that the West is doomed to decline, as this grouchy philosopher prophesized! It lies with us to prove that it is awakening and, for the good of all humankind, will once again be ready to repulse the onslaught of the barbarians. In this spirit, ladies and gentlemen, I raise my glass to the prosperity of the Association of Foreign Press Correspondents, who are one with us in the fight for the victory of the West![37]

36. English, French, and German texts have been preserved; I have quoted from the German, because the English translation is quite terrible. I am not certain what language François-Poncet actually spoke in; he was fully bilingual and the speech was held in Bad Godesburg, so he could in fact have been speaking in German.

37. The reference to the press being part of the fight for the West refers to the fact that earlier in the speech François-Poncet included freedom of the press in his list of traditional Western values.

So the occidentalist commonplace was also a part of French discourse about Germany; unfortunately, this did not necessarily point to some concrete policy to follow. "The problem for the Western powers was that their individual and collective interest in tying West Germany firmly to the West did not easily translate into an agreement about the particular system into which West Germany should be integrated" (Schmidt 1995: 162). The package that was negotiated—the European Defense Community—contained many of the problems of the original French proposal but seemed at least to promise some measure of military integration; Acheson hit on the idea of linking the EDC with another, more comprehensive set of treaties, which would dissolve the last of the occupation regime and clarify the status of EDC as a subunit of NATO (Leffler 1992: 414–15). In this way the whole package could be presented as the logical consequence of integration and could be characterized as a further elaboration of the civilizational imperative to defend 'the West.'

One consequence of this occidentalist approach was Adenauer's attempt to have a "binding clause" inserted into the general package of treaties. Such a clause would mean that a future all-German government would be bound by the treaty commitments of the BRD and would remain a member of the EDC (Herbst 1989: 117). Adenauer desired such a clause in part because he was unsure about the orientation of his countrymen and also because of "German isolationism"—the SPD was out of power at the time, but this might not always be the case, and there were also those in his own party who would put reunification ahead of a 'Western' alignment. In its original form, the clause would have reciprocally bound a reunified Germany to the Western Allies and the Western Allies to a reunified Germany, but there was opposition to Adenauer's initiative on both sides: the Allies resisted being bound, and even within Adenauer's cabinet there was opposition to the effort to bind a future all-German government.

Adenauer exerted himself mightily, particularly in cabinet meetings,[38] but upon realizing the depth of opposition to the proposal, he agreed to drop it—only to discover that the Allies had decided that because such a big deal had been made of it, dropping the clause would look like a victory for the Soviet Union. So a new version of the clause was drafted, according to which a future all-German government was not bound to accept the obligations incurred by the BRD, but the BRD was obliged to consult with the Allies before entering into any arrangements that would affect those obligations—even by reunifying the country (Schwartz 1991: 275–76; Schwarz 1995: 670–77). Occidentalism may have sufficed to bind the BRD, but it was not as powerful when

---

38. One cabinet meeting in particular, in fact: the meeting of 10 May 1952, in which a binding of the Federal Republic to 'the West' was presented as the only alternative to "the end of Europe in the form and culture it has enjoyed until now" (Booms 1989: 279).

stacked *against* German unity (particularly against the possibility of future German unity)[39] in such an obvious way. But in *alliance* with a call for German unity, 'the West' sufficed to legitimate the sorts of formal arrangements that Schmid and others in the SPD resisted.

Such a rhetorical consensus also underpinned the reaction of the Allies to Stalin's initiative on March 1952, in which Stalin sent a note proposing an end to the four-power occupation of Germany and the establishment of an all-German government and a German national army, in return for a halting of efforts to bring the BRD into the emerging Western political and military system. Advocates of reunification at any price were quite enthused by this offer, but Adenauer, in common with American officials like Acheson and McCloy, opposed treating the note as a serious offer and instead wanted to press ahead with the EDC and the rest of the treaty package. The presence of occidentalist language, which Adenauer utilized to confirm that his strategy was the best way to achieve reunification on acceptable terms, enabled, but did not determine, his decision.

As for EDC itself, despite the support of Eisenhower and John Foster Dulles after they assumed control of American foreign policy in early 1953,[40] the treaty package floundered when submitted to the French Assembly for ratification. The basic problem was that in the years since a French government had proposed the plan for German rearmament, various restrictions on German troops had been downplayed. "This was precisely the problem with the German [negotiating] success: The more attractive the Germans were able to render this scheme from their point of view, the less attractive it became to the French" (Large 1993: 392). In addition, many French politicians doubted that a purely European organization would be capable of containing a

39. The problem with declaring that any future German state would be bound to EDC and 'the West' was that the Soviet Union could sign a similar treaty with East Germany declaring that any future German state would be bound by its commitments to the East. The net effect would be to foreclose the possibility of German unity for the foreseeable future. Regardless of the plausibility of Adenauer's "policy of strength," it at least promised the possibility of eventual reunification in a way that the binding clause did not; hence one policy could survive politically while the other could not.

40. Eisenhower and Dulles generally supported the EDC and European unity more broadly in decidedly occidentalist terms. For instance, Eisenhower declared in 1951 that "with unity achieved, Europe could build adequate security and . . . continue the march of human betterment that has characterized western civilization" (Schwartz 1991: 224). Dulles's views and characteristic articulations have been discussed in previous chapters. It may also be true, however, that Eisenhower and Dulles were interested in EDC because it held out the possibility of withdrawing American troops from Europe after the Europeans were able to provide for their own defense (McAllister 2002: 212–13). But this question of motive is not strictly relevant to my account here, which stands without a strong specification of the motivations of the individual people involved.

rearmed Germany; instead, they wanted a more permanent and formal commitment from the United States to remain militarily involved on the continent. Although realists understand this as a simple calculation of relative military capacities (McAllister 2002: 216–17), the legitimation aspect should not be overlooked—particularly since the United States was not about to commit enough troops to Europe to *physically* resist a potential German invasion of France. Instead, what French politicians sought was an alternate *justification* for German rearmament, one that kept the United States involved instead of abandoning the European countries to their own devices.[41]

Adenauer and Dulles rushed to salvage the situation and quickly centered on a proposal by British foreign secretary Anthony Eden to expand the Western European Union to include the BRD and to associate the new WEU explicitly with NATO (Schwarz 1997: 116–17). The new policy proved acceptable to France because it permitted a French veto over German troop strength; but more importantly, it proved acceptable to all parties because, after all, NATO was the 'Western Alliance'—and thus the proper place for a 'Western' country to be.

The speeches made on the occasion of the BRD's formal accession to NATO on 5 May 1955 confirmed the new social fact: "We stand among the free, linked in true partnership with the former occupying powers. . . . There is only one place for us in the world: on the side of the free peoples of the world, within the Western community" (138–39, quoting Adenauer). The accession of the BRD to NATO, and the completion of the reconstruction process whereby it was recreated as an actor, also marked the triumph of the rhetorical commonplaces that legitimated the BRD's new role.

41. This is often noted by certain realist scholars but is not sufficiently or appropriately appreciated. For example, Creswell and Trachtenberg point out that "policy has to be packaged with an eye to domestic political realities" but conclude—somewhat oddly—that therefore analysts should ignore public rhetoric in favor of a focus on the real motivations of public officials (2003a: 27). This seems a very bizarre conclusion, since by the authors' own admission a precise delineation of individual motives would not tell us much about the formation of public policy! If public rhetoric is important, it should remain important throughout the process and should be taken seriously not as a guide to subjective motivations but as an intersubjective causal factor in its own right.

8 The Fate of "Western Civilization"

> Just as the popular mind separates the lightning from the flash and takes the latter
> for an *action,* for the operation of a subject called lightning, so popular morality also
> separates strength from expressions of strength, as if there were a neutral substratum
> behind the strong man, which was *free* to express strength or not to do so. But there
> is no such substratum; there is no 'being' behind doing, effecting, becoming; 'the
> doer' is merely a fiction added to the deed—the deed is everything.
> —Friedrich Nietzsche, *On the Genealogy of Morals*

*F*OR OSWALD SPENGLER, the study of the rise and fall of civilizations was
far more than a matter of antiquarian interest. Indeed, Spengler's purpose was
an entirely "presentist" one, in that he sought guidance for the future in the
dynamics of the past. Although this in itself is not particularly unusual, Spengler's particular twist on the notion of learning from the past is quite striking.
He saw his task as the explication of "an organic necessity in life, that of Destiny"—a kind of causation deeper than ordinary cause and effect, which "suf-
fuses the whole of mythological religions and artistic thought and constitutes
the essence and kernel of all history" (1926: 7). His researches into the logic of
Destiny led him to the conclusion that every civilization "passes through the
age-phases of the individual man. Each has its childhood, youth, manhood,
and old age" (107), a rigid four-part sequence that Spengler elsewhere refers to
as Spring/Summer/Fall/Winter. At each stage of development, critical events
take place as a result of the civilization's unfolding Destiny—a Destiny with
an inevitable end in the soul-less, rationalized, abstract Cosmopolis inhabited
by people who had lost all organic connection with the natural world (1928:
99–102). And after this, only a steady slide into the ahistorical night, and the
abandonment of the West to history.[1]

Spengler's consistency is admirable: having set out to identify an unbreak-

1. There is some evidence that Spengler changed his mind about this in his later writings, noting that the great technical advances of Western Civilization combined with its
global reach meant that even those struggling against the West would be in important
respects Western—and so in a sense the West would be the last civilization (Farrenkopf
2000: 34–36). But this is a complex question of Spengler scholarship (particularly involving
the interpretation of the rough notes that Spengler left behind at his death) that need not
detain us here.

able pattern characteristic of the life-course of a civilization, he applied that pattern rigorously to the civilization within which he found himself. This dogged persistence makes a certain kind of sense: if civilizations have essences, and if those essences unfold according to an unshakeable logic, then the only logical conclusion is that the West, like every other civilization, will also have its inevitable period of decline. It is thus Spengler's civilizational essentialism that permits him to make such a bold (if perhaps disheartening) prediction: no civilization "is at liberty to *choose* the path and conduct of its thought, but here for the first time a Culture can foresee the way that destiny has chosen for it" (1926: 159, emphasis in original) and meet its end bravely and stoically.

Of course, civilizational essentialism only points in the direction of an inevitable decline if the author in question claims to have identified a pattern of civilizational rise and fall. Samuel Huntington, so much like Spengler in his conception of civilizations as constitutively autonomous communities that exchange nothing of consequence, nonetheless offers different predictions for the future because his civilizations are not marked by anything like an inherent life-course. Instead, civilizational decline for Huntington means not the exhaustion of spiritual energies and a loss of vitality but merely a shift in the relative capabilities of civilizations vis-à-vis one another (1996: 83–84). Civilizations *themselves* remain intact in Huntington's analysis; the boundaries between them seem to have been set centuries ago, and no amount of contemporary political effort can do much to alter them (157–58). Here we see a different, although equally essentialist, prediction: because civilizations are relatively immutable cultural communities, we will *always* have the West with us, although its relative power and influence will diminish.

Essentialism and Prediction

The logical link between essentialism and prediction is a profound one. Prediction ordinarily rests on a claim to have grasped the central features of some entity or phenomenon; this is the basis from which the prediction can be made. Because we know certain things about, say, the constitutive essence of "gold," or of a "client state," we can make contingent predictions about what will happen to the entity in question in the presence of posited environmental conditions (Sylvan and Majeski 1998: 85–89). Similarly, an observation that an association between factors persistently obtains under certain conditions becomes the basis for a prediction if the association is systematic rather than accidental (King, Keohane, and Verba 1994: 56–58), which means that the mechanism producing the association will continue to operate under somewhat different conditions (Bhaskar 1989). It is the claim to have grasped the core of the entity or phenomenon that entails the capacity to accurately depict its likely future state.

Whether or not all predictions involve essentialist assumptions,[2] the fact remains that virtually all predictions by IR theorists operate in an essentialist manner. Because of something essential about democracies, a democratic dyad is less likely to fight a war than a nondemocratic dyad (Russett 1993). Because of something essential about anarchy, states that do not look first to the preservation of their own security are not likely to survive and prosper, so successful states will look to their own interests above all (Sterling-Folker 2002b). Because of something essential about internalized notions of community, states in a security community are less likely to resort to force to resolve their disputes (Adler and Barnett 1998). In all of these cases, the causal logic runs *from* a putatively dispositional property of the thing under investigation *to* an outcome made likely by that dispositional property. It matters little whether the property in question is material, ideational, cultural, institutional, or some combination thereof; the important point is that IR predictions rest on essentialist claims.

A prediction about the future of the West that proceeded along these lines would have to be likewise essentialist and stem from a determinate specification of what Western Civilization *really* was. The approach that I have adopted throughout this book takes a different tack. Instead of treating "Western Civilization" as the name of a discrete thing, I have instead treated 'Western Civilization' as a rhetorical commonplace. This commonplace envisions a cultural community spanning the Atlantic Ocean and binding the United States to Europe in a fundamental way; as such, it has practical implications for policy when deployed as part of a process of legitimation. In combination with other commonplaces, 'Western Civilization' served as an adequate cause for the contours of postwar German reconstruction, including the BRD's inclusion in the Marshall Plan and its eventual accession to NATO. Causal weight does not inhere in 'the West' *itself*, but in the concrete manner in which the commonplace was deployed, and how that deployment shaped the contours of the socially and politically possible.

Over the preceding chapters I have presented an account of postwar German reconstruction that emphasizes the role of 'the West' as a rhetorical commonplace in making specific policies and organizations possible: the European Recovery Program, NATO, and the Bundesrepublik Deutschland itself. 'Western Civilization' was a key part of the rhetorical strategy used to legitimate Adenauer's *Westbindung* and Acheson's vindicationist call for concrete American involvement in Europe. The commonplace enabled Adenauer to break 'German national unity' away from a commitment to a separate German path and thus outflank his Social Democratic opponents. Similarly, the

2. For a sustained argument that a nonessentialist, conventionalist form of predictive social science is both possible and desirable, see Chernoff 2005.

commonplace enabled Acheson and Marshall and their allies to join 'anti-communism' to an activist American foreign policy in such a way that their exemplarist opponents were unable to prevail. I do not want to claim that 'Western Civilization' was *solely* responsible for the course of postwar German reconstruction, or that there was any kind of a determinate straight line from the notion of 'the West' to a rearmed BRD operating under the auspices of NATO, but rather that 'Western Civilization' played a causally important—and previously, largely *overlooked*—role in the process.

'The West' in my account is therefore an element of a causal story that is not specifically *about* civilizations; it is a story about a particular set of policies and organizations, and about the rhetorical strategies that established them as socially and politically plausible during a particular period of time. My account focused on "postwar reconstruction" defined as the reestablishment of "Germany" as an actor in interstate relations partly as a way of keeping the empirical material manageable and partly because the reconstruction of a former enemy poses a puzzle that existing accounts in IR theory and diplomatic history have failed to adequately solve. Because of this focus, I have of necessity left aside many other aspects of the rhetorical commonplace of 'Western Civilization' that are not as strictly relevant to the specific empirical case under discussion. Henry James's comments about the art of the novel seem quite applicable to every scholar undertaking case studies of almost any sort.

> Really, universally, relations stop nowhere, and the exquisite problem of the artist is eternally to draw, by a geometry of his own, the circle within which they shall happily *appear* to do so. (1986: 37)

My empirical narrative's end in 1955 with the accession of the BRD to NATO should by no means be taken as an indication that the process of legitimating postwar Germany somehow *came to an end* in 1955. Social arrangements are almost never stable enough to do without an ongoing process of legitimation that helps to produce and reproduce those arrangements by rendering them socially and politically plausible—and only "total institutions" like prison camps and military training facilities can operate for long in the absence of a process of legitimation rendering them acceptable in the eyes of those over whom they exercise dominion (Sofsky 1997). But the BRD's accession to NATO did reshape the debate, as it foreclosed certain policy options in a formal, organizational way; henceforth, advocates of a Germany positioned between 'East' and 'West' would have to confront not only a powerful rhetorical constellation but also the set of institutionalized practices underpinned by that constellation. The year 1955 is thus the end of "postwar German reconstruction," and the end of my argument about what 'Western Civilization' helped to bring about in the early postwar period.

Decisions, Fit, and Social Arrangements

Of course, 'the West' did not simply disappear after postwar reconstruction was completed. The specification of 'Western Civilization' that emerged during the early postwar debates continued to play a significant role over the next several decades, and the commonplace remains a prominent part of our present rhetorical topography. Questions about the fate of 'the West,' and by implication about the policies and organizations that it supports and supported, are therefore questions about the apparent stability of the occidentalist configuration of commonplaces that I have argued was initially forged over the course of debate about postwar German reconstruction. But the answers to such questions cannot be sought in any putatively dispositional character of Western Civilization, because there is no such dispositional character. Instead, we must seek the sources of stability elsewhere, and avoid the West Pole Fallacy implicit in efforts to explain the stability of 'Western Civilization' by presuming the stable existence of a *real* entity called Western Civilization.

Claims about the essence of a social arrangement should be understood not as descriptive statements that could be evaluated for their empirical accuracy but should instead be seen as performative practices that aim to bring about the situation that they envision (Butler 1999: 22–23, 32–33). "The book is on the table" is a relatively straightforward empirical claim that can be verified or falsified through simple observation; "a colonial past causes persistent underdevelopment" or "democracies do not go to war with one another" present a variety of technical obstacles to their evaluation but still remain within the sphere of statements that can be meaningfully evaluated on empirical grounds. But how would one evaluate a claim about the values and institutions of Western Civilization? Empirical observation of a set of social arrangements would not suffice to establish that those values and institutions were *essentially* Western; still less would public opinion poll data suffice to establish the veracity of the claim, since that would only demonstrate that a random sample of people *claimed* to uphold certain values and institutions. Empirical observation can only tell us what values and institutions a community displays at a given point or points in time, and cannot justify the conceptual leap involved in regarding those attributes as constituting the essence of the community in question.

Instead, a claim about essentially 'Western' values and institutions, or a claim about the boundaries (geographical and/or conceptual) of 'the West,' should be understood in the same way that we understand a promise or an authoritative declaration (Onuf 1998: 67–68; Searle 1995: 54–55, 57). Huntington's statement that "Western civilization" has "a sense of individualism and a tradition of individual rights and liberties unique among civilized soci-

eties" (1996: 71)—that individualism is an essentially "Western" value—
should be seen as roughly akin to a statement like "with this ring, I thee wed."
Neither statement is a strictly empirical claim even though both refer to
empirical features of the world. Rather, both statements *intervene* into an
ongoing flow of social transactions and endeavor to shape and direct it: the
marriage statement seeks to effect a change in the status of the relationship
between the individuals involved, and Huntington's statement seeks to effect
the contours of the boundary between 'Westerners' and 'non-Westerners.'
Both statements are active interventions rather than passive reflections.

Indeed, this is what it means to say that Western Civilization is socially
constructed (Hacking 1999: 12–14): the attributes that the community is
thought to have, the boundaries that it is thought to possess, even the very
existence of a notion of transnational cultural community, arise not from natural necessity but from contingent social action. The deployment of 'the
West' as a rhetorical commonplace in the course of concrete public debates
and political struggles may produce the *effect* or *impression* that there is a thing
called "Western Civilization" out there in the world that exists independently
of social actions oriented toward it, but this is an effect rather than a cause.

In a way, the question about the future of 'the West' can be answered simply, if a bit flippantly, as follows: if 'Western Civilization' disappears as a
rhetorical commonplace with any political and social traction, then the entire
debate about whether the West is declining or prospering also disappears.
Were the commonplace to vanish from the political field, we would of course
still have those institutions and creative works that we now think of as "Western." But absent the commonplace that we presently use to comprehend them
and to gather them together into a civilizational whole, they would be more
like the ruins of Greek and Roman temples and other buildings that dot the
landscape of contemporary Europe: relics of a way of being-in-the-world that
no longer exists. A community is not constituted by its physical resources and
products, but by the political and social practices that gather those resources
up into a whole and define the limits of their acceptable use. Without the
practices of community, there is no effective community.

More precisely formulated, the question then becomes: why have occidentalist practices of community persisted, and are they likely to persist into the
future? A solution to this puzzle would permit us to respond to both Spengler
and Huntington, as well as to every other civilizational essentialist, by "squaring the circle" and shifting the problem from one of civilizational analysis to
one of social identity. The fate of 'Western Civilization' depends on the continued *use* of the rhetorical commonplace. There are three basic ways to
explain such continued use: use arises from individual and collective *decisions;*
use arises from the *fit* between rhetorical strategies and material environmental conditions; or use arises, as it were, from *previous use,* as the reshaping of

the field of possibilities at one point in time gives rise to a range of possibilities characteristic of the next point in time, and so on and so forth. I prefer the third explanation, for reasons that I will make clear through a brief consideration of the other two alternatives.

DECISIONS

The majority of empirical work in IR theory and diplomatic history displays a basic conceptual pattern that emphasizes individual decisions and the motivations behind them. Such empirical work looks for characteristic patterns of decision making or for typical factors motivating those decisions. Expressed another way, mainstream empirical work in IR and diplomatic history looks for the *interests*—whether material or ideal—of individuals in some specific historical context and examines how those interests lead to specific decisions, and ultimately to outcomes. The "individuals" in question may be biologically autonomous members of the species *Homo sapiens,* private social groups, organizations, or even states; regardless, the explanation proceeds by determining interests and showing how those interests led to decisions that sustained or transformed a given set of social arrangements.[3]

Much of the debate between scholars working in this broad tradition involves the appropriate basis from which to derive the interests of individuals. Should we examine the documentary record, as diplomatic historians do, in order to ascertain how actors conceptualized their interests? Or should we use a theoretical model of the international system as either a realm of dangerous anarchy (for realists) or the absence of a hierarchical authority to enforce binding agreements (for liberals)? Should we look to the normative precepts and structures of international society, as IR constructivists do, or look to more "material" factors, such as troop strength and economic productivity? Regardless of their answers to such questions, these accounts proceed in a similar fashion after determining where to look for interests, and set about reconstructing historical situations in such a way as to demonstrate how those interests were translated into decisions and thence into outcomes.

For decisionists, the stability of the occidentalist rhetorical configuration, and the institutional and organizational arrangements to which it was linked, is explained with reference to the factors that motivated individuals to keep on selecting it during the period after 1955. Whether the configuration will remain stable in the future is a function of whether the interests of the individuals involved are shifting in a direction that makes 'the West' less appealing as a means to achieve their ends.

3. In effect, such an approach transforms a social arrangement into a coordinated set of individual choices (Olson 1965). For an application of this analytic to the problem of institutional choice in postwar Germany, see Bernhard 2005.

Many decisionist arguments rest on material interests. Chris Coker (1998), in broad agreement with other IR realists (Harries 1992–93; Kagan 2003; Mearsheimer 1990; O'Brien 1992–93), argues that the stability of the notion of 'the West' was due to the persistence of the bipolar balance between the United States and the Soviet Union; with the collapse of the Soviet Union, there is less of a perceived need to promote unity between the United States and Europe, and so we should expect to see 'Western Civilization' and 'Western' organizations like NATO fade away. On the other hand, liberal rationalists like Celeste Wallander (2000) and David Lake (1999) argue that the instrumental value of organizations like NATO provides an incentive for states and state officials to preserve the arrangements, and perhaps even to preserve the 'Western' rhetoric that legitimates them.[4] Depending on how material interests are defined and specified, different predicted consequences result.

It is critical to decisionist accounts that actor interests provide a relatively clear and unambiguous basis on which individuals can make their decisions about organizational arrangements and policy options. In the absence of such exogenously specified interests, there would be no way to *account for* individual decisions and hence no way to reliably predict whether individuals would go on making those same decisions in the future—which would eliminate the decisionist account's capacity to explain the stability of social arrangements. Focusing on material interests provides a simple solution to this problem, since an individual's interests can be more or less straightforwardly read off from a specification of the strategic situation facing that individual. The material situation of individuals thus becomes the guarantor of social stability, or the motor of social change.

But adopting this strategy would also mean having to regard the vibrant political debates that raged in the early postwar world—debates that were in large part about the character of the postwar world and the proper responses to it—as epiphenomenal. And this, in turn, would demand that we ignore the role played by particular commonplaces, like 'Western Civilization,' in *constituting* the interests of individuals. As I have argued, the character of the postwar world was quite ambiguous, and the deployment of rhetorical commonplaces in legitimation contests helped to reduce this ambiguity by foreclosing some options and rendering others publicly acceptable. A focus on putatively exogenous material interests would have to discount this ambiguity and account for social stability in terms that are ultimately nonsocial—and therefore deny that social action can alter interests.

---

4. Note that decisionists interested in material interests do not tend to pay overmuch attention to public rhetoric; their arguments are much more focused on the institutions and organizations that I have argued are underpinned by the rhetorical commonplace of 'Western Civilization.'

IR constructivists would readily assent to the proposition that interests cannot be treated as exogenous. Indeed, this forms the leading edge of many constructivist critiques of realism and liberalism, as constructivists seek to ground the interests of state and other actors in identity, culture, and forms of social interaction (Barnett 1999; Finnemore 1996; Wendt 1992). But on closer examination, the basic explanatory logic of many constructivist accounts is not all that different from that on offer in realist and liberal accounts, differing only in that the interests in question are *ideal* rather than *material*. Instead of making decisions based on inputs from their physical environment, individuals are held to make decisions based on internalized norms or principled beliefs according to a "logic of appropriateness" rather than a "logic of consequences" (Finnemore and Sikkink 1998). The central role of individual decisions in producing social outcomes, and the relatively unambiguous character of the (ideal) interests on which those decisions are based, remains unquestioned.

The stability of practices of transnational community in such constructivist accounts depends on the existence of norms pointing toward interstate cooperation (Hampton 1995: 612–13; Risse-Kappen 1996: 374–78) or on values shared between two state communities (Schimmelfennig 1998–99: 213–16). These norms and values, in turn, depend on some kind of historical process of socialization, whereby the members of a particular society come to accept these norms and values; the anchor of stability is this commitment on the part of individuals to certain principles and worldviews (Duffield 1998: 23–25, 33–34). The resulting domestic cultural arrangements are *presumptively* slow to change, which permits them to function as an explanation for the persistence of a set of decisions consistent with the values in question but often out of step with expectations based on material interests (Duffield 1999).

The problem with such accounts is that the ideal interests that arise from processes of socialization and from the construction of a domestic cultural consensus, although not exogenous to social relations in the way that *material* interests would be, are nonetheless exogenous to the specific situation being explained. Accounts of postwar reconstruction adopting this perspective maintain that the period immediately following the Second World War was in some way a privileged opportunity to construct social identities, and that once constructed these identities persisted because later historical periods did not provide such opportunities (Banchoff 1999: 57–58, 177–79; Berger 1998: 12–13, 199–200). Lacking a clearer theoretical specification of what makes a particular historical moment ripe for a reconfiguration of a cultural consensus, these accounts end up *describing* stability rather than *explaining* it. Noting that the ideal interests of various actors have remained consistent over a period of time is not the same thing as explaining why they have done so—particularly since theorists adopting this approach have already admitted that social processes can reconfigure interests. How could we reliably predict that the future will bring a continuation of the past, rather than another reconfiguration?

In order to fulfill the requirements of a decisionist account, interests have to be both unambiguous and exogenous to the situation being analyzed. Both of these aspects are quite problematic, given the role played by public rhetoric in shaping conceptions of the world that entail particular policy outcomes. For this reason, "interests" are probably better regarded as a "symbol" around which debate can be organized rather than an unambiguous determination that halts debate (Wolfers [1952] 1962). We require an account of how those "interests" were determined, and how the debates about interests were settled, since it is *these debates themselves* that determine the contours of interest and cause the policy outcomes concretely selected (Weldes 1999: 98–102). Decisionist accounts, with their presumption that interests remain exogenous, are unable to provide such a contribution, so a forecast about the fate of 'the West' must come from another perspective.

FIT

Another way to explain the stability of practices of community is to look not to individual decisions in favor of those practices but to the correspondence between social practices and the surrounding material environment. The important causal factor in such an account is not individual interests, but the "fit" between social practices and some deeper or broader structure of the situation. Structures "explain why different units behave similarly and, despite their variations, produce outcomes that fall within expected ranges" (Waltz 1979: 72); they therefore explain the stability of social practices not because they precisely determine individual outcomes—which would be a form of structural determinism—but instead because structures represent a kind of necessity of the last instance: a set of "objective" factors against which options are tried, such that only one remains at the end. Any social uniformities that are produced need to be accounted for as the interaction of contingent actor choices with the objective possibilities inherent in the essence of the relevant social structure or structures.

In an approach based on fit, 'Western Civilization' would persist as an operative notion of community if it corresponded to the relevant structural conditions better than alternative notions did. Knowing something about the structure of the situation would enable analysts to forecast future trajectories without having to pass through the heads of individuals and determine what their interests were; the causal logic here is *evolutionary* rather than instrumental, as ineffective social practices (and those actors who persist in utilizing them) are selected out of the system and thus vanish from view (Sterling-Folker 2002a: 78–80; Waltz 1979: 74–77).

Whether 'Western Civilization' will persist thus becomes a function of structural conditions. Structural realists focusing on bipolarity would generally agree with Kenneth Waltz's suggestion that "the tightening of the Soviet Union's control over the states of Eastern Europe led to the Marshall Plan and the Atlantic Defense Treaty, and these in turn gave rise to the Cominform and the Warsaw Pact. The plan to form a West German government produced the Berlin Blockade" (1979: 171); they would connect the end of bipolarity with the decline of 'Western Civilization.' A very similar notion underpins Jeffrey Legro's contention that "isolationist" policies were simply not functional in the postwar world, and that the dominant episteme shifted to notions that better corresponded to the structural conditions of the time (Jackson and Nexon 2001: 12, 18; Legro 2000: 265–66); in the absence of bipolarity, it is doubtful that 'the West' will persist, as it is likely to be replaced by a notion that better corresponds to the present condition of the international system.

A somewhat different variant of structural explanation can be found in neo-Gramscian work that prioritizes not the polarity of an anarchical system of states but rather "a picture of a particular configuration of forces" that "does not determine actions in any direct mechanical way but imposes pressures and constraints" (Cox 1996: 97–98). These historical structures exercise their effects indirectly, in such a way that actors always have some room to maneuver more or less strategically (Block 1977; Jessop 1990). But in the last instance what accounts for the stability of social practices is not strategy, but the existence of hegemony "based on a coherent conjunction or fit between a configuration of material power, the prevalent collective image of world order (including certain norms) and a set of institutions which administer the order with a certain semblance of universality (that is, not just as the overt instruments of a particular state's dominance)" (Cox 1996: 103). Once again, the persistence of 'Western Civilization' as a practice of community is a function of external structural conditions that may provide a limited menu of options from which actors may choose but that also provide unshakable limits beyond which social practices cannot be sustained.

The difficulty with any approach based on fit is that it, in effect, transforms *agency* into a theoretical residual; it becomes quite impossible to give a theoretically plausible account of how agency played a role in the processes of producing social arrangements. Successful policy of almost any kind is explained as a kind of fortuitous happenstance, as actors toss up suggestions for ordering the world, and forces quite beyond their control determine whether these plans will come to fruition. We might try to escape this conundrum by following Robert Latham in declaring that certain actors are able "to shape practices and ideas in the international realm, which is an ability that is mostly dependent on the effective presence of institutions, norms, and material resources. This shaping presence is hegemony and the agent that effects it is the hegemon" (1997: 61–62). In this sense, fit would become endogenous to social practices rather than remaining external to them.

But the difficulty with adopting such a position is that by modifying the notion of "fit," the explanation becomes unable to causally account for the stability of social practices. Endogenizing the notion of a correspondence between practices of community like 'Western Civilization' and the social structures that putatively surround and constrain them means that the fit of particular legitimating practices with the structural environment has largely to do with active processes of tying practices together to form relatively coherent wholes (Laffey and Weldes 1997: 202–3). Particular constellations of resources and strategies are thus never automatic but represent *ongoing accomplishments of practice* (Doty 1997: 376–79), including practices of legitimation. If 'Western Civilization' helps to *constitute* the very structural conditions that are subsequently cited as providing the external support for the stability of 'Western Civilization,' we have either a tautology or an abandonment of explanation in favor of analytical description.[5] In either case, the fate of 'Western Civilization' remains a problem to be solved.

ONGOING STABILIZATION

We are thus left with the challenge of accounting for the stability of practices of community based on 'the West' while not mitigating the power of such practices to constitute actors, their interests, and the structural environment in which they find themselves. To move "downward" from this point and try to ground stability on individual decisions, or to move "upward" from this point and try to ground stability on structural conditions, produces either tautology (practices of community are stable because they are stable) or the abandonment of agency and causality in favor of description (practices of community are stable, but we cannot say much about *why* they are stable and whether they will remain so). We confront here another variant of the endemic macro-micro problem of social explanation—whether to lodge our causal mecha-

5. Latham's account of postwar reconstruction opts for the latter, explicitly eschewing causal analysis in favor of an account that contains "an argument about the logic of forces bearing on social or historical outcomes and developments" (1997: 6–7). Thus Latham is able to account for the success of various American initiatives and the construction of postwar hegemony only in retrospect, using the later impact of particular decisions to explain the ultimate meaning that those decisions had for the course of events. Thus he interprets the entire process of postwar order-construction, including the American role in German reconstruction, as an effort to order "liberal modernity . . . in a purposive fashion" (36), and does so even when the decision makers themselves were not aware that their policies contributed to this project, noting that "policymakers were rarely self-reflexive about their role in liberal order-making as they devised policies and made decisions" (80–81). Latham's account remains philosophically consistent, but at the cost of abandoning causation.

nisms within particular actors or in the social space between them (Singer 1961)—but with a twist: *neither* macro *nor* micro explanations for stability appear adequate. This suggests the need for a third option.

The explanation of postwar German reconstruction that I have proposed in this book implicitly contains just such a third option: a "meso" explanation[6] focusing on the creative deployment of social resources and tracing the ways in which particular configurations of such resources generate social outcomes such as policies, institutions, and organizations (Katznelson 1997; Tilly 1995). The object of explanation here is not individual decisions or behaviors; my account is (deliberately) unable to definitively explain why Konrad Adenauer or Dean Acheson *as individuals* oriented their activities toward 'the West' as opposed to adopting some very different social goal. Such a biographical or psychological explanation, although interesting in its own right, is not strictly necessary to an explanation of social arrangements that focuses on concatenations of social practice. Concentrating on the motives of individuals is a very different analytical exercise than concentrating on the social conditions of possibility that make social action possible, as Weber's well-known but often misunderstood comment about the relationship of ideas and interests reminds us:

> Not ideas, but material and ideal interests, directly govern the actions of human beings. Yet very frequently the 'world images' that have been created by 'ideas' have, like switchmen, determined the tracks along which the dynamic of interest has moved such action. (1946: 280)[7]

There are *three* conceptual categories differentiated in Weber's claim, and not merely *two*. Weber's dictum is usually understood as elucidating a relationship between ideas and interests, which it clearly does do; but in addition, it distinguishes between two different kinds of interests and separates "ideas" from both. This is critical: interests, whether material or ideal, are for Weber the "locomotive" (if you will) of the actions of *particular* individuals: people do what they believe it is in their interest to do. But this is not particularly interesting from a sociological perspective. What is far more interesting is how those interests are shaped by the social context into which they are inserted, and how the contours of that context produce and sustain social arrangements. Individual motives and interests, although they certainly exist, are in

6. Dan Nexon and I have been working on fleshing out the implications of such a "meso" perspective for IR for some time; preliminary statements can be found in Jackson and Nexon 1999 and Jackson and Nexon 2000.

7. I have slightly modified the translation, to accentuate the fact that Weber refers to 'human beings' (*Menschen*) rather than 'men' (*Männer*), and the fact that the verb *fortbewegt* is active, not passive as it appears in the Gerth and Mills rendition.

the strictest sense *irrelevant* to such an explanation; what matters is not why some particular individual made a particular decision but the causal impact of the actions that they concretely undertook.

The social context within which actions take place is composed not of more or less determinate structural elements but of ambiguous cultural resources that always stand in need of further specification through concrete acts of deployment and utilization. There is nothing about the 'special relationship' between Britain and the United States (Bially Mattern 2004), or about the notions of 'Europe' (Neumann 1999) or 'the United States' (Weldes 1999) or 'Sweden' (Ringmar 1996a) or any other concept of community that *necessitates* a particular policy outcome or set of institutional and organizational arrangements; rather, it is ongoing social practices of *stabilization and destabilization* that produce these outcomes. Both the delegitimation of existing arrangements (Crawford 2002: 101–3; Hall 1999: 41–43) and the legitimation of alternatives (Campbell 1992: 157–61; Crawford 2002: 72–76; Gusterson 1999) have to be regarded as *endogenous to the situation being analyzed,* instead of being reduced to an epiphenomenal effect of presumptively exogenous structural factors and conditions (Guzzini 2000). In this way, both micro- and macroreductionism are avoided, and social processes and practices remain firmly at the center of the account.

How does this provide an answer to the problem of the stability of social arrangements? The course I am proposing here, which I have adopted throughout this book, deals with questions of stability by suggesting that the terms in which the problem is normally posed are, in fact, the source of the problem. When we ask why some set of community practices and the arrangements that they support are stable, we are (implicitly or explicitly) envisioning a situation in which *social arrangements possess a thinglike, essentialist character.* We ask about the stability of 'Western' arrangements during the period after 1955 as though those arrangements, once produced, become a single object to be explained in total. But this is a profoundly misleading characterization. Social arrangements *are not things* or even *thinglike;* they are instead *relative stabilities in patterns of social action*—relative stabilities that have to be ongoingly and unceasingly reproduced from moment to moment. In a sense, there is no "there" there; there is only the empirical observation of a clustering or concatenation of actions, the fixity or consistency of which is a function of our retrospective analysis rather than inhering in some dispositional character of the arrangements themselves.

There is no such thing as a stable social arrangement, *really.* Instead, there are patterns of social actions that tend to either sustain or to transform a pre-existing pattern, and do so at *every individual moment.* Social life, to use Andrew Abbott's felicitous phrasing, is "*always* instantaneous . . . all structures are continually reenacted . . . all reproduction hinges on continuous action"

(2001b: 257). As such, we should not be asking about the stability of 'Western' practices of community; we should instead be analyzing the ways in which, at some specific moment, social resources are deployed so as to produce a particular outcome. Such deployment also shapes the topography of resources available at the next successive moment, so that at any particular point in time there are only a finite number of possible courses of action available based on the available set of social resources. The possibilities of any given moment are, in this sense, indebted to the actions undertaken in the previous moment; the actualization of one of those possibilities shapes the possibilities characteristic of the next moment. And so on, and so on, and so on, ad infinitum.[8]

We should therefore *abandon* long-term stability as a research problematique and take up the task of ideal-typically delineating generalizable social processes, patterns of social resources, and mechanisms of deployment that combine in historically unique ways to generate historically unique outcomes at particular moments (Jackson 2006; Tilly 1998a: 13–14, 104–7). In this book I have illustrated that 'the West' is usefully treated as an actualization of possibilities through a series of legitimation contests; I suspect that other putatively essential communities would benefit from such an analysis. But legitimation is only one generalizable social process; we should also continue constructing other processual analytics, and applying them to other cases.

---

8. As Charles Tilly once said in response to a question put to him during a roundtable on the book *Dynamics of Contention* (McAdam, Tarrow, and Tilly 2001): "how is why." Searching for something nonprocessual that underlies or surrounds or constrains social processes is futile, and we should simply stop trying: "Philosophy is a battle against the bewitchment of our intelligence by means of language" (Wittgenstein 1953: §109).

References

Documents

AA   Auswärtiges Amt, Bundesrepublik Deutschland, various collections.

BCS   Bestand Carlo Schmid, Archiv der Sozialen Demokratie, Friedrich-Ebert-Stiftung (Mappe number given in the in-text citation).

BKS   Bestand Kurt Schumacher, Archiv der Sozialen Demokratie, Friedrich-Ebert-Stiftung (Mappe number given in the in-text citation).

BPA   Bundespresseamt, Bestände Konrad Adenauer and Kurt Schumacher.

CR   Congressional Record of the United States.

DOSB   Department of State Bulletin.

FRUS   Foreign Relations of the U.S.

KAS   Konrad-Adenauer-Stiftung, Bestand: Reden Konrad Adenauers.

VdDB   *Verhandlungen des Deutschen Bundestags,* Stenographische Bericht (date given in the in-text citation).

House Committee on Foreign Affairs. *Assistance to Greece and Turkey,* 1947a.

House Committee on Foreign Affairs. *Hearings on Emergency Foreign Aid,* 1947b.

House Committee on Foreign Affairs. *European Recovery Program Hearings,* 1948.

ECA. "Report to Congress." Washington, DC: Economic Cooperation Administration, 1948–51.

Federal Government, German. "Twelfth, Final Report." Bonn: Federal Minister for the Marshall Plan, 1953.

Senate Committee on Foreign Relations. *A Decade of American Foreign Policy: Basic Documents, 1941–49.* Washington, DC: U.S. Government Printing Office, 1950.

Senate Committee on Foreign Relations. *European Recovery Program Hearings,* 1948.

State, Department of. *Germany 1947–1949: The Story in Documents.* Washington, DC: U.S. Government Printing Office, 1950.

Secondary Sources

Abbott, Andrew. "Things of Boundaries." *Social Research* 62 (1996): 857–82.

Abbott, Andrew. *Chaos of Disciplines.* Chicago: University of Chicago Press, 2001a.

Abbott, Andrew. *Time Matters: On Theory and Method.* Chicago: University of Chicago Press, 2001b.

Abelshauser, Werner. "Zur Entstehung der 'Magnet-Theorie' in der Deutschlandpolitik." *Vierteljahrshefte für Zeitgeschichte* 27, no. 4 (1974): 661–79.

Acheson, Dean. *Present at the Creation.* New York: W. W. Norton, 1969.

Adenauer, Konrad. *Erinnerungen, 1953–1955.* Stuttgart: Deutsche Verlags-Anstalt, 1966a.

Adenauer, Konrad. *Memoirs 1945–53.* Translated by Beate Ruhm von Oppen. Chicago: Henry Regnery, 1966b.

Adenauer, Konrad. *Reden 1917–1967.* Edited by Hans-Peter Schwarz. Stuttgart: Deutsche Verlags-Anstalt, 1975.

Adenauer, Konrad. *Briefe, 1945–1947.* Edited by Hans-Peter Mensing. Berlin: Wolf Jobst Siedler Verlag, 1983.

Adenauer, Konrad. *Die Demokratie ist für uns eine Weltanschauung: Reden und Gespräche 1946–1967.* Edited by Felix Becker. Cologne: Böhlau Verlag, 1998.

Adler, Emanuel. "Seizing the Middle Ground: Constructivism in World Politics." *European Journal of International Relations* 3, no. 3 (1997): 319–63.

Adler, Emanuel, and Michael Barnett. "A Framework for the Study of Security Communities." In *Security Communities,* edited by Emanuel Adler and Michael Barnett, 29–65. Cambridge: Cambridge University Press, 1998.

Allardyce, Gilbert. "The Rise and Fall of the Western Civilization Course." *American Historical Review* 87 (1982): 695–725.

Altmann, Normen. *Konrad Adenauer im Kalten Krieg: Wahrnehmungen und Politik, 1945–1956.* Mannheim: Palatium Verlag, 1993.

Anderson, Benedict. *Imagined Communities.* Rev. ed. London: Verso, 1991.

Arkes, Hadley. *Bureaucracy, the Marshall Plan, and the National Interest.* Princeton: Princeton University Press, 1972.

Armstrong, Hamilton Fish. "The World Is Round." *Foreign Affairs* 31, no. 2 (1953): 175–99.

Arnason, Johann P. "Civilizational Patterns and Civilizing Processes." *International Sociology* 16, no. 3 (2001): 387–405.

Artner, Stephen J. *A Change of Course: The West German Social Democrats and NATO, 1957–1961.* Westport, CT: Greenwood, 1985.

Augustine. *Concerning the City of God Against the Pagans.* New York: Penguin Classics, 1984.

Backer, John D. *Priming the German Economy.* Durham: Duke University Press, 1971.

Banchoff, Thomas. *The German Problem Transformed: Institutions, Politics, and Foreign Policy, 1945–1995.* Ann Arbor: University of Michigan Press, 1999.

Baritz, Loren. "The Idea of the West." *American Historical Review* 66 (1961): 618–40.

Baritz, Loren. *City on a Hill: A History of Myths and Ideas in America.* New York: Wiley, 1964.

Barnett, Michael. *Dialogues in Arab Politics.* New York: Columbia University Press, 1998.

Barnett, Michael. "Culture, Strategy, and Foreign Policy Change: Israel's Road to Oslo." *European Journal of International Relations* 5, no. 1 (1999): 5–36.

Bartelson, Jens. *A Genealogy of Sovereignty.* Cambridge: Cambridge University Press, 1995.

Bartlett, Robert. *The Making of Europe.* Princeton: Princeton University Press, 1993.

Beer, Samuel H. Personal Communication. 2002.

Berger, Thomas U. "Norms, Identity, and National Security in Germany and Japan." In *The Culture of National Security,* edited by Peter Katzenstein, 317–56. New York: Columbia University Press, 1996.

Berger, Thomas U. *Cultures of Antimilitarism: National Security in Germany and Japan.* Baltimore: Johns Hopkins University Press, 1998.

Berghahn, Volker. "Ideas into Politics: The Case of Ludwig Erhard." In *Ideas into Politics,* edited by R. J. Bullen, H. Pogge von Strandmann, and A. B. Polonsky, 178–92. Totowa, NJ: Barnes and Noble, 1984.

Berghahn, Volker. *The Americanisation of West German Industry, 1945–1973.* Cambridge: Cambridge University Press, 1986.

Bernal, Martin. *Black Athena.* Vol. 1. New Brunswick: Rutgers University Press, 1987.

Bernhard, Michael. *Institutions and the Fate of Democracy: Germany and Poland in the Twentieth Century.* Pittsburgh: University of Pittsburgh Press, 2005.

Bernstein, Richard, and Mark Landler. 2004. "German Leader to Oppose Sending NATO Troops to Iraq." *New York Times Online.* http://www.nytimes.com/archive (accessed 21 May 2004).

Bhaskar, Roy. "On the Possibility of Social Scientific Knowledge and the Limits of Naturalism." In *Reclaiming Reality,* 66–88. London: Verso, 1989.

Bhaskar, Roy. *The Possibility of Naturalism.* 3d ed. London: Routledge, 1998.

Bially Mattern, Janice. "The Power Politics of Identity." *European Journal of International Relations* 7, no. 3 (2001): 349–97.

Bially Mattern, Janice. *Ordering International Politics: Identity, Crisis, and Representational Force.* New York: Routledge, 2004.

Block, Fred. *The Origins of International Economic Disorder.* Berkeley: University of California Press, 1977.

Blyth, Mark. "Structures Do Not Come with an Instruction Sheet: Interests, Ideas, and Progress in Political Science." *Perspectives on Politics* 1, no. 4 (2003): 695–703.

Booms, Hans, ed. *Die Kabinettsprotokolle der Bundesregierung, 1952.* Vol. 5. Boppard am Rhein: Harald Boldt Verlag, 1989.

Boorstin, Daniel. *America and the Image of Europe.* New York: Meridian, 1960.

Botting, Douglas. *From the Ruins of the Reich: Germany, 1945–1949.* New York: Meridian, 1985.

Bourdieu, Pierre. *The Political Ontology of Martin Heidegger.* Stanford: Stanford University Press, 1988.

Bowden, Brett. "The Ideal of Civilisation: Its Origins and Socio-Political Character." *Critical Review of International Social and Political Philosophy* 7, no. 1 (2004): 25–50.

Brands, H. W. *What America Owes the World: The Struggle for the Soul of Foreign Policy.* Cambridge: Cambridge University Press, 1998.

Braudel, Fernand. "History and the Social Sciences: The Longue Durée." In *On History,* 25–54. Chicago: University of Chicago Press, 1958.

Braudel, Fernand. *A History of Civilizations.* New York: Penguin, 1995.

Brubaker, Rogers. *Nationalism Reframed.* Cambridge: Cambridge University Press, 1996.

Buchler, Justus. "Reconstruction in the Liberal Arts." In *A History of Columbia College on Morningside,* edited by Dwight C. Miner, 48–135. New York: Columbia University Press, 1954.

Bührer, Werner. "German Industry and European Integration in the 1950s." In *Western Europe and Germany: The Beginnings of European Integration, 1945–1960,* edited by Clemens Wurm, 87–114. Oxford: Berg, 1995.

Bührer, Werner. *Westdeutschland in der OEEC.* Munich: R. Oldenbourg Verlag, 1997.

Burke, Edmund. *Reflections on the Revolution in France.* 1970. Reprint, Indianapolis: Hackett, [1790] 1987.

Butler, Judith P. *Gender Trouble: Feminism and the Subversion of Identity.* New York: Routledge, 1999.

Byrnes, James F. *Speaking Frankly.* New York: Harper and Brothers, 1947.

Campbell, David. *Writing Security.* Minneapolis: University of Minnesota Press, 1992.

CDU. "Was Will die CDU?" Cologne: CDU des Rheinlandes, 1947.

Chase-Dunn, Christopher, and Thomas Hall. *Rise and Demise.* Boulder, CO: Westview, 1997.

Checkel, Jeffrey T. "The Constructivist Turn in International Relations Theory." *World Politics* 50 (1998): 324–48.

Checkel, Jeffrey T. "Norms, Institutions, and National Identity in Contemporary Europe." *International Studies Quarterly* 43, no. 1 (1999): 83–114.

Chernoff, Fred. "Scientific Realism as a Meta-Theory of International Politics." *International Studies Quarterly* 46, no. 2 (2002): 189–207.

Chernoff, Fred. *The Power of International Theory: Reforging the Link to Foreign Policy-making through Scientific Inquiry.* London: Routledge, 2005.

Christensen, Thomas J. *Useful Adversaries: Grand Strategy, Domestic Mobilization, and Sino-American Conflict, 1947–1958.* Princeton: Princeton University Press, 1996.

Churchill, Winston. *The Sinews of Peace: Post-War Speeches.* Boston: Houghton Mifflin, 1949.

Clay, Lucius D. *Decision in Germany.* New York: Doubleday, 1950.

Coker, Christopher. *Twilight of the West.* Boulder, CO: Westview, 1998.

Collins, Randall. "Civilizations as Zones of Prestige and Social Contact." *International Sociology* 16, no. 3 (2001): 421–37.

Cooper, John Xiros. *T. S. Eliot and the Ideology of Four Quartets.* Cambridge: Cambridge University Press, 1995.

Cox, Robert. "Social Forces, States, and World Orders: Beyond International Relations Theory." In *Approaches to World Order,* 85–123. Cambridge: Cambridge University Press, 1996.

Cox, Robert W. *The Political Economy of a Plural World.* London: Routledge, 2002.

Crawford, Neta C. *Argument and Change in World Politics.* Cambridge: Cambridge University Press, 2002.

Creswell, Michael, and Marc Trachtenberg. "France and the German Question, 1945–1955." *Journal of Cold War Studies* 5, no. 3 (2003a): 5–28.

Creswell, Michael, and Marc Trachtenberg. "New Light on an Old Issue?" *Journal of Cold War Studies* 5, no. 3 (2003b): 46–53.

Cross, Timothy P. *An Oasis of Order: The Core Curriculum at Columbia College.* New York: Columbia University Office of University Publications, 1995.

Dallek, Robert. *Franklin D. Roosevelt and American Foreign Policy, 1932–1945.* New York: Oxford University Press, 1995.

Davidson, Donald. "Actions, Reasons, and Causes." *Journal of Philosophy* 60 (1963): 685–700.

Dean, Vera Micheles. *Russia: Menace or Promise?* New York: Foreign Policy Association, 1946.

Delanty, Gerard. *Inventing Europe.* London: Macmillan, 1995.

Deutsch, Karl Wolfgang. *Political Community at the International Level: Problems of Definition and Measurement.* Garden City, NY: Doubleday, 1954.

Divine, Robert A. *Second Chance: The Triumph of Internationalism in America during World War II.* New York: Atheneum, 1967.

Doering-Manteuffel, Anselm. *Die Bundesrepublik Deutschland in der Ära Adenauer.* Darmstadt: Wissenschaftliche Buchgesellschaft, 1983.

Doering-Manteuffel, Anselm. "Wie westlich sind die Deutschen?" *Historisch-Politische Mitteilungen* 3 (1996): 1–38.

Doty, Roxanne Lynn. "Foreign Policy as Social Construction: A Post-Positivist Analysis of U.S. Counterinsurgency Policy in the Philippines." *International Studies Quarterly* 37, no. 3 (1993): 297–320.

Doty, Roxanne Lynn. "Aporia: A Critical Exploration of the Agent-Structure Problematique in International Relations Theory." *European Journal of International Relations* 3, no. 3 (1997): 365–92.

Drummond, Gordon. *The German Social Democrats in Opposition, 1949–1960.* Norman: University of Oklahoma Press, 1982.

Duffield, John S. *World Power Forsaken: Political Culture, International Institutions, and German Security Policy after Unification.* Stanford: Stanford University Press, 1998.

Duffield, John. "Political Culture and State Behavior: Why Germany Confounds Neorealism." *International Organization* 53, no. 4 (1999): 765–803.

Dulles, Alan. "Alternatives for Germany." *Foreign Affairs* 25, no. 3 (1947): 421–32.

Dulles, John Foster. *War or Peace.* New York: Macmillan, 1950.

Eagle Forum. 2004. The Western Civilization Project. http://www.eagleforum.org/alert/2004/Tancredo.html (accessed 27 May 2004).

Ehni, Hans-Peter. "Die Reaktion der SPD auf den Marshall-Plan." In *Der Marshall-Plan und die Europäische Linke,* edited by Othmar Nikola Haberl and Lutz Niethammer, 217–30. Frankfurt am Main: Athenäum Verlag, 1986.

Eisenberg, Carolyn. *Drawing the Line: The American Decision to Divide Germany, 1944–1949.* Cambridge: Cambridge University Press, 1996.

Elias, Norbert. *What Is Sociology?* New York: Columbia University Press, 1970.

Elias, Norbert. *The Society of Individuals.* Oxford: Basil Blackwell, 1991.

Eliot, T. S. *What Is a Classic?* London: Faber and Faber, 1944.

Eliot, T. S. *Christianity and Culture.* San Diego: Harvest, 1948.

Emirbayer, Mustafa. "Manifesto for a Relational Sociology." *American Journal of Sociology* 103, no. 2 (1997): 281–317.

Ermarth, Michael. "Introduction." In *America and the Shaping of German Society, 1945–1955,* edited by Michael Ermarth, 1–19. Providence: Berg, 1993.

Fabian, Johannes. *Time and the Other: How Anthropology Makes Its Object.* New York: Columbia University Press, 1983.

Farrenkopf, John. "Klio und Cäsar: Spenglers Philosophie der Weltgeschichte im Dienste der Staatkunst." In *Der Fall Spengler: Eine Kritische Bilanz,* edited by Alexander Demandt and John Farrenkopf, 45–73. Cologne: Böhlau Verlag, 1994.

Farrenkopf, John. "Spengler's Theory of Civilization." *Thesis Eleven* 62 (2000): 23–38.

Farrenkopf, John. *Prophet of Decline: Spengler on World History and Politics.* Baton Rouge: Louisiana State University Press, 2001.

Ferguson, Yale, and Richard Mansbach. *Polities: Authority, Identities, and Change.* Columbia: University of South Carolina Press, 1996.

Finnemore, Martha. *National Interests in International Society.* Ithaca: Cornell University Press, 1996.

Finnemore, Martha, and Kathryn Sikkink. "International Norm Dynamics and Political Change." *International Organization* 52, no. 4 (1998): 887–917.

Fischer, Klaus P. *History and Prophecy: Oswald Spengler and the Decline of the West.* New York: Peter Lang, 1989.

FitzGerald, Frances. *Way Out There in the Blue.* New York: Simon and Schuster, 2000.

Flynn, Gregory, and Henry Farrell. "Piecing Together the Democratic Peace: The CSCE, Norms, and the 'Construction' of Security in Post-Cold War Europe." *International Organization* 53, no. 3 (1999): 505–35.

Folly, Martin. "Breaking the Vicious Circle." *Diplomatic History* 12, no. 1 (1980): 59–77.

Foschepoth, Josef. "Zur deutschen Reaktion auf Niederlage und Besatzung." In *Westdeutschland 1945–1955,* edited by Ludolf Herbst, 153–67. Munich: R. Oldenbourg Verlag, 1986.

Foucault, Michel. *The Archaeology of Knowledge.* Translated by A. M. Sheridan Smith. New York: Pantheon, 1972.

Foucault, Michel. "Nietzsche, Genealogy, History." In *Language, Counter-memory, Practice,* edited by Donald F. Bouchard, 139–64. Ithaca: Cornell University Press, 1977.

Freeland, Richard. *The Truman Doctrine and the Origins of McCarthyism.* New York: Alfred A. Knopf, 1972.

Friedrich, Carl J. "The Political Thought of Neo-Liberalism." *American Political Science Review* 49, no. 2 (1955): 509–25.

Fromkin, David. *In the Time of the Americans.* New York: Alfred A. Knopf, 1995.

Gaddis, John Lewis. *The United States and the Origins of the Cold War, 1941–1947.* New York: Columbia University Press, 1972.

Gaddis, John Lewis. "The Long Peace: Elements of Stability in the Postwar International System." *International Security* 10, no. 4 (1986): 99–142.

Geertz, Clifford. *Local Knowledge: Further Essays in Interpretive Anthropology.* 3d ed. New York: Basic Books, 2000.

Gellner, Ernest. *Nations and Nationalism.* Ithaca: Cornell University Press, 1983.

Gerhardt, Uta. "Introduction." In *Talcott Parsons on National Socialism,* edited by Uta Gerhardt, 1–57. New York: Aldine de Gruyter, 1993.

Geuss, Raymond. *The Idea of a Critical Theory.* Cambridge: Cambridge University Press, 1981.

Giddens, Anthony. *Central Problems in Social Theory: Action, Structure, and Contradiction in Social Analysis.* Berkeley: University of California Press, 1979.

Giddens, Anthony. *The Constitution of Society.* Berkeley: University of California Press, 1984.

Gimbel, John. *The American Occupation of Germany: Politics and the Military, 1945–1949.* Stanford: Stanford University Press, 1968.

Gimbel, John. *The Origins of the Marshall Plan.* Stanford: Stanford University Press, 1976.

Gimbel, John. "Amerikanische Besatzungspolitik und Deutsche Tradition." In *Westdeutschland 1945–1955,* edited by Ludolf Herbst, 147–53. Munich: R. Oldenbourg Verlag, 1986.

Goddard, Stacie, and Daniel H. Nexon. "Paradigm Lost? Reassessing *Theory of International Politics.*" *European Journal of International Relations* 11, no. 1 (2005): 9–61.

Goff, Patricia M., and Kevin C. Dunn. "Introduction: In Defense of Identity." In *Identity and Global Politics: Theoretical and Empirical Elaborations,* edited by Patricia M. Goff and Kevin C. Dunn, 1–8. New York: Palgrave Macmillan, 2004.

GoGwilt, Christopher. *The Invention of the West: Joseph Conrad and the Double-Mapping of Europe and Empire.* Stanford: Stanford University Press, 1995.

Gong, Gerritt. *The Standard of 'Civilization' in International Society.* Oxford: Oxford University Press, 1984.

Gramsci, Antonio. *Selections from the Prison Notebooks.* Translated by Quintin Hoare and Geoffrey Nowell Smith. New York: International Publishers, 1971.

Granieri, Ronald J. *The Ambivalent Alliance: Konrad Adenauer, the CDU/CSU, and the West, 1949–1966.* New York: Berghahn, 2003.

Greenfeld, Liah. *Nationalism: Five Roads to Modernity.* Cambridge: Harvard University Press, 1992.

Gress, David. *From Plato to NATO: The Idea of the West and Its Opponents.* New York: Free Press, 1998.

Grosser, Alfred. *The Federal Republic of Germany.* New York: Frederick A. Praeger, 1964.

Gruber, Carol S. *Mars and Minerva.* Baton Rouge: Louisiana State University Press, 1975.

Gusterson, Hugh. "Presenting the Creation: Dean Acheson and the Rhetorical Legitimation of NATO." *Alternatives* 24 (1999): 39–57.

Gutmann, Gernot. "Soziale Marktwirtschaft als Gesellschaftsidee." In *Soziales Denken in Deutschland Zwischen Tradition und Innovation,* edited by Jorg-Dieter Gauger and Klaus Wiegelt, 198–223. Bonn: Bouvier, 1990.

Guzzini, Stefano. "A Reconstruction of Constructivism in International Relations." *European Journal of International Relations* 6, no. 2 (2000): 147–82.

Habermas, Jürgen. *Legitimation Crisis.* Translated by Thomas McCarthy. Boston: Beacon, 1975.

Habermas, Jürgen. *The Theory of Communicative Action: Reason and the Rationaliza-tion of Society*. Translated by Thomas McCarthy. Vol. 1. Boston: Beacon, 1984.

Hacking, Ian. *The Social Construction of What?* Cambridge: Harvard University Press, 1999.

Hahn, Erich. "U.S. Policy on a West German Constitution, 1947–1949." In *American Policy and the Reconstruction of West Germany, 1945–1955*, edited by Jeffry M. Diefendorf, Axel Frohn, and Hermann-Josef Rupieper, 21–44. Cambridge: Cambridge University Press, 1993.

Hall, Rodney Bruce. *National Collective Identity: Social Constructs and International Systems*. New York: Columbia University Press, 1999.

Hampton, Mary N. "NATO at the Creation: U.S. Foreign Policy, West Germany, and the Wilsonian Impulse." *Security Studies* 4, no. 3 (1995): 610–56.

Handler, R. "Is 'Identity' a Useful Cross-Cultural Concept?" In *Commemorations: The Politics of National Identity*, edited by John R. Gillis, 27–40. Princeton: Princeton University Press, 1994.

Hanna, Martha. *The Mobilization of Intellect*. Cambridge: Harvard University Press, 1996.

Hardach, Gerd. *Der Marshall-Plan*. Munich: Deutscher Taschenbuch Verlag, 1994.

Hardin, Russell. *One for All: The Logic of Group Conflict*. Princeton: Princeton University Press, 1995.

Harper, John Lamberton. *American Visions of Europe*. Cambridge: Cambridge University Press, 1996.

Harries, Owen. "The Collapse of 'The West.'" *Foreign Affairs* 72 (1992–93): 41–53.

Harvard Committee on General Education in a Free Society. *General Education in a Free Society: Report of the Harvard Committee*. Cambridge: Harvard University, 1946.

Hay, Denys. *Europe: The Emergence of an Idea*. Edinburgh: Edinburgh University Press, 1968.

Hegel, G. W. F. *Vorlesungen über die Philosophie der Geschichte*. Frankfurt am Main: Suhrkamp Taschenbuch Verlag, 1986.

Hegel, G. W. F. *Introduction to the Philosophy of History, with selections from the Phi-losophy of Right*. Translated by Leo Rauch. Indianapolis: Hackett, 1988.

Heidegger, Martin. *Being and Time*. Translated by John Macquarrie and Edward Robinson. San Francisco: HarperCollins, [1927] 1962.

Heidegger, Martin. *The Metaphysical Foundations of Logic*. Translated by Michael Heim. Bloomington: Indiana University Press, 1984.

Heidenheimer, Arnold. *Adenauer and the CDU*. The Hague: Martinus Nijhoff, 1960.

Hemmer, Christopher, and Peter Katzenstein. "Why Is There No NATO in Asia? Collective Identity, Regionalism, and the Origins of Multilateralism." *Interna-tional Organization* 56, no. 3 (2002): 575–607.

Hempel, Carl. "The Function of General Laws in History." In *Aspects of Scientific Explanation and Other Essays*, 231–44. New York: Free Press, 1965.

Hennis, Wilhelm. *Max Weber: Essays in Reconstruction*. London: Allen and Unwin, 1988.

Herbst, Ludolf. *Option für den Westen*. Munich: Deutscher Taschenbuch, 1989.

Hogan, Michael. *The Marshall Plan: American, Britain, and the Reconstruction of Western Europe, 1947–1952*. Cambridge: Cambridge University Press, 1987.

Hogan, Michael. "European Integration and German Reintegration: Marshall Planners and the Search for Recovery and Security in Western Europe." In *The Marshall Plan and Germany*, edited by Charles Maier and Günter Bischof, 115–70. Providence: Berg, 1991.

Hogan, Michael. *A Cross of Iron*. Cambridge: Cambridge University Press, 1998.

Hoover, Herbert. *Addresses upon the American Road, 1950–1955*. Stanford: Stanford University Press, 1955.

Hoover, Herbert, and Hugh Gibson. *The Problems of Lasting Peace*. Garden City, NY: Doubleday, Doran, 1942.

Hopf, Ted. "Making the Future Inevitable: Legitimizing, Naturalising, and Stabilizing. The Transition in Estonia, Ukraine, and Uzbekistan." *European Journal of International Relations* 8, no. 3 (2002): 403–36.

Hopf, Ted. "Discourse and Content Analysis: Some Fundamental Ambiguities." *Qualitative Methods* 2, no. 1 (2004): 31–33.

Horowitz, David, ed. *Corporations and the Cold War*. New York: Monthly Review Press, 1969.

Hughes, H. Stuart. *Oswald Spengler: A Critical Estimate*. New York: Charles Scribner's Sons, 1952.

Huntington, Samuel P. *The Clash of Civilizations and the Remaking of World Order*. New York: Simon and Schuster, 1996.

Huntington, Samuel P. *Who Are We? The Challenges to America's National Identity*. New York: Simon and Schuster, 2004.

Hurd, Ian. "Legitimacy and Authority in International Politics." *International Organization* 53, no. 2 (1999): 379–408.

Hürten, Heinz. "Der Topos vom Christlichen Abendland in Literatur und Publistik nach den beiden Weltkriegen." In *Katholizimus, nationaler Gedanke und Europa seit 1800*, edited by Albrecht Langner, 131–54. Paderborn: Ferdinand Schöningh, 1985.

Iggers, Georg. *The German Conception of History*. Hanover, NH: Wesleyan University Press, 1983.

Ikenberry, G. John. *After Victory: Institutions, Strategic Restraint, and the Rebuilding of Order after Major Wars*. Princeton: Princeton University Press, 2001.

Ikenberry, G. John, and Charles A. Kupchan. "Socialization and Hegemonic Power." *International Organization* 44, no. 3 (1990): 283–315.

Inayatullah, Naeem, and David Blaney. *International Relations and the Problem of Difference*. London: Routledge, 2004.

Ireland, Timothy P. *Creating the Entangling Alliance*. Westport, CT: Greenwood Press, 1981.

Jackson, Patrick Thaddeus. "'Civilization' on Trial." *Millennium* 28, no. 1 (1999): 141–53.

Jackson, Patrick Thaddeus. "Jeremy Bentham, Foreign Secretary: *or,* the Opportunity Costs of Neo-Utilitarian Analyses of Foreign Policy." *Review of International Political Economy* 9, no. 4 (2002a): 735–53.

Jackson, Patrick Thaddeus. "Rethinking Weber: Toward a Non-Individualist Sociology of World Politics." *International Review of Sociology* 12, no. 3 (2002b): 439–68.

Jackson, Patrick Thaddeus. "Defending the West: Occidentalism and the Formation of NATO." *Journal of Political Philosophy* 11, no. 3 (2003): 223–52.

Jackson, Patrick Thaddeus. "Hegel's House, or, 'People Are States Too.'" *Review of International Studies* 30 (2004a): 281–87.

Jackson, Patrick Thaddeus. "*Whose* Identity? Rhetorical Commonplaces in 'American' Wartime Foreign Policy." In *Identity and Global Politics,* edited by Patricia Goff and Kevin Dunn, 169–89. New York: Palgrave, 2004b.

Jackson, Patrick Thaddeus. "The Present as History." In *The Oxford Handbook of Contextual Political Analysis,* edited by Charles Tilly and Robert Goodin. Oxford: Oxford University Press, 2006.

Jackson, Patrick Thaddeus. "Making Sense of Making Sense: Configurational Analysis and the Double Hermeneutic." In *Interpretation and Method: Empirical Research Methods and the Interpretive Turn,* edited by Dvora Yanow and Peregrine Schwartz-Shea. Armonk, NY: M. E. Sharpe, forthcoming.

Jackson, Patrick Thaddeus, and Ron Krebs. "Twisting Tongues." Manuscript, 2004. Washington DC, American University.

Jackson, Patrick Thaddeus, and Daniel H. Nexon. "Relations Before States: Substance, Process, and the Study of World Politics." *European Journal of International Relations* 5, no. 3 (1999): 291–332.

Jackson, Patrick Thaddeus, and Daniel H. Nexon. "Theorizing Identity: Toward a Relational Constructivism." Manuscript, 2000. Columbia University, New York.

Jackson, Patrick Thaddeus, and Daniel H. Nexon. "Whence Causal Mechanisms? A Comment on Legro." *Dialogue-IO* 55, no. 2 (spring 2001): 1–21. Available at http://mitpress.mit.edu/io (accessed 7 August 2001).

Jackson, Patrick Thaddeus, and Daniel H. Nexon. "Globalization, the Comparative Method, and Comparing Constructions." In *Constructivism and Comparative Politics,* edited by Daniel M. Green, 88–120. Armonk, NY: M. E. Sharpe, 2002.

James, Henry. *Roderick Hudson.* London: Penguin Classics, 1986.

Jervis, Robert. *Perception and Misperception in International Politics.* Princeton: Princeton University Press, 1976.

Jessop, Bob. *State Theory: Putting Capitalist States in Their Place.* University Park: Pennsylvania State University Press, 1990.

Jonas, Manfred. *Isolationism in America, 1935–1941.* Ithaca: Cornell University Press, 1966.

Kagan, Robert. *Of Paradise and Power: America and Europe in the New World Order.* 1st ed. New York: Alfred A. Knopf, 2003.

Kaplan, Lawrence S. "An Unequal Triad: The United States, Western Union, and NATO." In *Western Security: The Formative Years,* edited by Olav Riste, 107–27. Oslo: Universitetsforlaget, 1985.

Katzenstein, Peter. "The Smaller European States, Germany, and Europe." In *Tamed Power: Germany in Europe,* edited by Peter Katzenstein, 251–304. Ithaca: Cornell University Press, 1997a.

Katzenstein, Peter. "United Germany in an Integrating Europe." In *Tamed Power:*

Germany in Europe, edited by Peter Katzenstein, 1–48. Ithaca: Cornell University Press, 1997b.

Katznelson, Ira. "Structure and Configuration in Comparative Politics." In *Comparative Politics: Rationality, Culture, and Structure,* edited by Mark Irving Lichbach and Alan S. Zuckerman, 81–112. Cambridge: Cambridge University Press, 1997.

Keck, Margaret, and Kathryn Sikkink. *Activists Beyond Borders.* Ithaca: Cornell University Press, 1998.

Kelsen, Hans. "The Legal Status of Germany According to the Declaration of Berlin." *American Journal of International Law* 39 (1945): 518–26.

Kennan, George. *Memoirs, 1925–1950.* New York: Pantheon, 1967.

Kimball, Warren F. *The Juggler: Franklin Roosevelt as Wartime Statesman.* Princeton: Princeton University Press, 1991.

Kindleberger, Charles. *The World in Depression, 1929–1939.* Berkeley: University of California Press, 1974.

King, Gary, Robert O. Keohane, and Sidney Verba. *Designing Social Inquiry: Scientific Inference in Qualitative Research.* Princeton: Princeton University Press, 1994.

Kirby, Dianne. "Divinely Sanctioned: The Anglo-American Cold War Alliance and the Defence of Western Civilization and Christianity, 1945–48." *Journal of Contemporary History* 35, no. 3 (2000): 385–412.

Kleinmann, Hans-Otto. *Geschichte der CDU, 1945–1982.* Stuttgart: Deutsche Verlags-Anstalt, 1993.

Klotz, Audie. *Protesting Prejudice: Apartheid and the Politics of Norms in International Relations.* Ithaca: Cornell University Press, 1995.

Konrad-Adenauer-Stiftung. *Konrad Adenauer und die CDU der Britischen Besatzungszone, 1946–1949.* Bonn: Eichholz-Verlag, 1975.

Koselleck, Reinhart. *Futures Past: On the Semantics of Historical Time.* Translated by Keith Tribe. Cambridge: MIT Press, 1985.

Kovel, Joel. *Red Hunting in the Promised Land.* New York: Basic Books, 1994.

Kratochwil, Friedrich. *Rules, Norms, and Decisions.* Cambridge: Cambridge University Press, 1989.

Kraus, Hannelore. "Vorstellungen von Senatoren und Repräsenten des amerikanischen Kongress zur Deutschlandpolitik nach dem Zweiten Weltkriege." Ph.D. dissertation, Department of Philosophischen Fakultät, Ruprecht-Karl-Universität, Heidelberg, 1971.

Küsters, Hans Jürgen. "West Germany's Foreign Policy in Western Europe, 1949–58: The Art of the Possible." In *Western Europe and Germany: The Beginnings of European Integration, 1945–1960,* edited by Clemens Wurm, 55–86. Oxford: Berg, 1995.

Laclau, Ernesto, and Chantal Mouffe. *Hegemony and Socialist Strategy: Towards a Radical Democratic Politics.* Translated by Winston Moore and Paul Cammack. London: Verso, 1985.

Laffey, Mark, and Jutta Weldes. "Beyond Belief: Ideas and Symbolic Technologies in the Study of International Relations." *European Journal of International Relations* 3, no. 2 (1997): 193–237.

Lake, David A. *Entangling Relations: American Foreign Policy in Its Century.* Princeton: Princeton University Press, 1999.

Lapid, Yosef. "Culture's Ship: Returns and Departures in International Relations Theory." In *The Return of Culture and Identity in IR Theory*, edited by Yosef Lapid and Friedrich Kratochwil, 3–20. Boulder, CO: Lynne Rienner, 1996.

Large, David Clay. "Grand Illusions: The United States, the Federal Republic of Germany, and the European Defense Community, 1950–1954." In *American Policy and the Reconstruction of West Germany, 1945–1955*, edited by Jeffry M. Diefendorf, Axel Frohn, and Hermann-Josef Rupieper, 375–94. Cambridge: Cambridge University Press, 1993.

Larson, Deborah Welch. *Origins of Containment: A Psychological Explanation*. Princeton: Princeton University Press, 1985.

Latham, Robert. *The Liberal Moment: Modernity, Security, and the Making of Postwar International Order*. New York: Columbia University Press, 1997.

Leffler, Melvyn P. *A Preponderance of Power*. Stanford: Stanford University Press, 1992.

Leffler, Melvyn P. *The Specter of Communism*. New York: Hill and Wang, 1994.

Legro, Jeffrey. "Whence American Internationalism." *International Organization* 54, no. 2 (2000): 253–89.

Levi, Margaret. *Of Rule and Revenue*. Berkeley: University of California Press, 1988.

Levine, Lawrence W. *The Opening of the American Mind: Canons, Culture, and History*. Boston: Beacon, 1996.

Lewis, Martin W., and Kären E. Wigen. *The Myth of Continents: A Critique of Metageography*. Berkeley: University of California Press, 1997.

Leyh, Gregory, ed. *Legal Hermeneutics: History, Theory, and Practice*. Berkeley: University of California Press, 1992.

Liebersohn, Harry. *Fate and Utopia in German Sociology, 1870–1923*. Cambridge: MIT Press, 1988.

Lippmann, Walter. *The Cold War*. New York: Harper and Brothers, 1947.

Lougee, Carolyn C. "Comment on Gilbert Allardyce." *American Historical Review* 87 (1982): 726–29.

Lowi, Theodore J. *The End of Liberalism*. 2d ed. New York: W. W. Norton, 1979.

Lundestad, Geir. *The American 'Empire.'* Oslo: Universitetsforlaget AS, 1990.

Machiavelli, Niccolò. *Selected Political Writings*. Edited by David Wootton. Indianapolis: Hackett, 1994.

MacIntyre, Alasdair. *After Virtue*. Notre Dame: University of Notre Dame Press, 1984.

Maier, Charles. *In Search of Stability: Explorations in Historical Political Economy*. Cambridge: Cambridge University Press, 1987.

Mandalios, John. "Being and Cultural Difference: (Mis)understanding Otherness in Early Modernity." *Thesis Eleven* 62 (2000): 91–108.

Mann, Thomas. *The Coming Victory of Democracy*. New York: Alfred A. Knopf, 1938.

Mann, Thomas. *Thomas Mann's Addresses delivered at the Library of Congress, 1942–1949*. Washington, DC: Library of Congress, 1963.

Mannheim, Karl. *Ideology and Utopia*. San Diego: Harvest, 1936.

Marchand, Suzanne. *Down from Olympus: Archaeology and Philhellenism in Germany, 1750–1970*. Princeton: Princeton University Press, 1996.

Mark, Eduard. "October or Thermidor? Interpretations of Stalinism and the Perception of Soviet Foreign Policy in the United States, 1927–1947." *American Historical Review* 94, no. 4 (1989): 937–62.

Marx, Karl, and Friedrich Engels. *The Marx/Engels Reader*. Edited by Robert C. Tucker. 2d ed. New York: W. W. Norton, 1978.

Mazlish, Bruce. "Civilization in a Historical and Global Perspective." *International Sociology* 16, no. 3 (2001): 293–300.

McAdam, Doug, Sidney Tarrow, and Charles Tilly. *Dynamics of Contention*. Cambridge: Cambridge University Press, 2001.

McAllister, James. *No Exit: America and the German Problem, 1943–1954*. Ithaca: Cornell University Press, 2002.

McCalla, Robert B. "NATO's Persistence after the Cold War." *International Organization* 50, no. 3 (1996): 445–75.

McDougall, Walter A. *Promised Land, Crusader State*. Boston: Mariner, 1997.

McNeill, William H. *Mythistory and Other Essays*. Chicago: University of Chicago Press, 1986.

McNeill, William H. *Arnold J. Toynbee: A Life*. New York: Oxford University Press, 1989.

McNeill, William H. "Information and Transportation Nets in World History." In *World System History: The Social Science of Long-Term Change*, edited by Robert A. Denemark, Jonathan Friedman, Barry K. Gills, and George Modelski, 201–15. London: Routledge, 2000.

Mearsheimer, John. "Back to the Future: Instability in Europe after the Cold War." *International Security* 15, no. 1 (1990): 5–56.

Melko, Matthew. *The Nature of Civilizations*. Boston: F. Porter Sargent, 1969.

Melleuish, Gregory. "The Clash of Civilizations: A Model of Historical Development?" *Thesis Eleven* 62 (2000): 109–20.

Mills, C. Wright. "Situated Actions and Vocabularies of Motive." *American Sociological Review* 5, no. 6 (1940): 904–13.

Milne, A. A. *The Complete Tales of Winnie-the-Pooh*. New York: Dutton Children's Books, 1994.

Milward, Alan. *The Reconstruction of Western Europe, 1945–51*. London: Methuen, 1984.

Mitchell, B. R. *USA—International Historical Statistics for the Americas, 1750–1993*. 4th ed. New York: Stockton, 1998.

Mitchell, Timothy. "The Limits of the State: Beyond Statist Approaches and Their Critics." *American Political Science Review* 85, no. 1 (1991): 77–96.

Mommsen, Wolfgang J. "Max Webers Begriff der Universalgeschichte." In *Max Weber, der Historiker*, edited by Jürgen Kocka, 50–65. Göttingen: Vandenhoeck und Ruprecht, 1986.

Moravcsik, Andrew. "Taking Preferences Seriously: A Liberal Theory of International Politics." *International Organization* 51, no. 4 (1997): 513–53.

Moravcsik, Andrew. *The Choice for Europe: Social Purpose and State Power from Messina to Maastricht*. Ithaca: Cornell University Press, 1998.

Morgenthau, Henry. *Germany Is Our Problem*. New York: Harper and Brothers, 1945.

NATO. *NATO Facts and Figures*. Brussels: NATO Information Service, 1989.

Neumann, Iver. *Russia and the Idea of Europe.* London: Routledge, 1996.

Neumann, Iver. *Uses of the Other.* Minneapolis: University of Minnesota Press, 1999.

Nicholls, A. J. *Freedom With Responsibility: The Social Market Economy in Germany, 1918–1963.* Oxford: Clarendon, 1994.

Nietzsche, Friedrich. *On the Genealogy of Morals.* Translated by Walter Kaufmann. New York: Random House, 1967.

Ninkovich, Frank. *Germany and the United States: The Transformation of the German Question since 1945.* Boston: Twayne, 1988.

Ninkovich, Frank. *Modernity and Power: A History of the Domino Theory in the Twentieth Century.* Chicago: University of Chicago Press, 1994.

Noh, Meung-Hoan. *Westintegration versus Osthandel: Politik und Wirtschaft in den Ost-West-Beziehungen der Bundesrepublik Deutschland 1949–1958.* Frankfurt am Main: Peter Lang, 1995.

O'Brien, Conor Cruise. "The Future of 'The West.'" *National Interest* (1992–93): 3–10.

O'Hagan, Jacinta. *Conceptualizing the West in International Relations: From Spengler to Said.* New York: Palgrave, 2002.

O'Hagan, Jacinta. "'The Power and the Passion': Civilizational Identity and Alterity in the Wake of September 11." In *Identity and Global Politics: Theoretical and Empirical Elaborations,* edited by Patricia M. Goff and Kevin C. Dunn, 27–45. New York: Palgrave Macmillan, 2004.

Olson, Mancur. *The Logic of Collective Action: Public Goods and the Theory of Groups.* Cambridge: Harvard University Press, 1965.

Onuf, Nicholas. "Constructivism: A User's Manual." In *International Relations in a Constructed World,* edited by Vendulka Kubálková, Nicholas Onuf, and Paul Kowert, 58–78. Armonk, NY: M. E. Sharpe, 1998.

Parsons, Talcott. "The Present Position and Prospects of Systematic Theory in Sociology." In *Essays in Sociological Theory,* 212–37. New York: Free Press, 1954.

Parsons, Talcott. *Talcott Parsons on National Socialism.* Edited by Uta Gerhardt. New York: Aldine de Gruyter, 1993.

Paterson, Thomas G. *Meeting the Communist Threat: Truman to Reagan.* New York: Oxford University Press, 1988.

Patomäki, Heikki. "How to Tell Better Stories about World Politics." *European Journal of International Relations* 2, no. 1 (1996): 105–33.

Patomäki, Heikki, and Colin Wight. "After Postpositivism? The Promises of Critical Realism." *International Studies Quarterly* 44, no. 2 (2000): 213–37.

Patterson, James T. *Mr. Republican: A Biography of Robert A. Taft.* Boston: Houghton Mifflin, 1972.

Pettit, Philip. *The Common Mind: An Essay on Psychology, Society, and Politics.* New York: Oxford University Press, 1993.

Podell, Janet, and Steven Aszorin, eds. *Speeches of the American Presidents.* New York: H. W. Wilson, 1988.

Pogue, Forrest. "George C. Marshall and the Marshall Plan." In *The Marshall Plan and Germany,* edited by Charles Maier and Günter Bischoff, 46–70. New York: Berg, 1991.

Pollard, Robert. *Economic Security and the Origins of the Cold War, 1945–50.* New York: Columbia University Press, 1985.

Price, Richard. "Reversing the Gun Sights: Transnational Civil Society Targets Land Mines." *International Organization* 52, no. 3 (1998): 613–44.

Przeworski, Adam. *Capitalism and Social Democracy.* Cambridge: Cambridge University Press, 1985.

Richter, Melvin. "Introduction." In *Essays in Theory and History,* edited by Melvin Richter, 1–37. Cambridge: Harvard University Press, 1970.

Riker, William H. *The Strategy of Rhetoric: Campaigning for the American Constitution.* New Haven: Yale University Press, 1996.

Ringer, Fritz. *The Decline of the German Mandarins.* Cambridge: Harvard University Press, 1969.

Ringer, Fritz. *Max Weber's Methodology: The Unification of the Cultural and Social Sciences.* Cambridge: Harvard University Press, 1997.

Ringmar, Erik. *Identity, Interest, and Action.* Cambridge: Cambridge University Press, 1996a.

Ringmar, Erik. "On the Ontological Status of the State." *European Journal of International Relations* 2, no. 4 (1996b): 439–66.

Risse, Thomas. "'Let's Argue!' Communicative Action in World Politics." *International Organization* 54, no. 1 (2000): 1–39.

Risse-Kappen, Thomas. "Ideas Do Not Float Freely: Transnational Coalitions, Domestic Structures, and the End of the Cold War." *International Organization* 48, no. 2 (1994): 185–214.

Risse-Kappen, Thomas. "Collective Identity in a Democratic Community: The Case of NATO." In *The Culture of National Security,* edited by Peter Katzenstein, 357–99. New York: Columbia University Press, 1996.

Roberts, Priscilla. "The Anglo-American Theme: American Visions of an Atlantic Alliance, 1914–1933." *Diplomatic History* 21, no. 3 (1997): 333–64.

Rogers, Daniel E. *Politics After Hitler: The Western Allies and the German Party System.* New York: New York University Press, 1995.

Rorty, Richard. "The Ambiguity of 'Rationality.'" In *Pluralism and the Pragmatic Turn: The Transformation of Critical Theory,* edited by William Rehg and James Bohman, 41–52. Cambridge: MIT Press, 2001.

Roth, Guenther. *Max Webers deutsch-englische Familiengeschichte, 1800–1950.* Tübingen: Mohr Siebeck, 2001.

Rousseau, Jean-Jacques. *The Basic Political Writings.* Indianapolis: Hackett, 1987.

Ruggie, John Gerard. "International Regimes, Transactions, and Change: Embedded Liberalism in the Postwar Economic Order." In *International Regimes,* edited by Stephen D. Krasner, 195–231. Ithaca: Cornell University Press, 1983.

Ruggie, John Gerard. "Multilateralism: The Anatomy of an Institution." In *Multilateralism Matters,* edited by John Gerard Ruggie, 3–47. New York: Columbia University Press, 1993.

Ruggie, John Gerard. "Epistemology, Ontology, and the Study of International Regimes." In *Constructing the World Polity,* 85–101. London: Routledge, 1998a.

Ruggie, John Gerard. "Interests, Identity, and American Foreign Policy." In *Constructing the World Polity,* 203–28. London: Routledge, 1998b.

Ruggie, John Gerard. "Introduction: What Makes the World Hang Together?" In *Constructing the World Polity,* 1–39. London: Routledge, 1998c.

Ruhm von Oppen, Beate, ed. *Documents on Germany under Foreign Occupation, 1945–1954.* London: Oxford University Press, 1955.

Russett, Bruce. *Grasping the Democratic Peace.* Princeton: Princeton University Press, 1993.

Said, Edward. *Orientalism.* New York: Vintage, 1979.

Sander, Evelyn. 1993. Squaring the Circle. *Geometry Forum.* http://www.geom.uiuc .edu/docs/forum/square_circle/ (accessed 13 March 2005).

Schäfer, Wolf. "Global Civilization and Local Cultures." *International Sociology* 16, no. 3 (2001): 301–19.

Schimmelfennig, Frank. "Rhetorisches Handeln in der Internationalen Politik." *Zeitschrift für Internationale Beziehungen* 4, no. 2 (1997): 219–54.

Schimmelfennig, Frank. "NATO Enlargement: A Constructivist Explanation." *Security Studies* 8, no. 2/3 (1998–99): 198–234.

Schimmelfennig, Frank. "International Socialization in the New Europe: Rational Action in an Institutional Environment." *European Journal of International Relations* 6, no. 1 (2000): 109–39.

Schischkoff, Georgi. "Spengler und Toynbee." In *Spengler-Studien,* edited by Anton Mirko Koktanek, 59–75. Munich: C. H. Beck, 1965.

Schmid, Carlo. "Germany and Europe." *Foreign Affairs* 30, no. 4 (1952): 531–44.

Schmidt, Gustav. "'Tying' (West) Germany into the West—But to What? NATO? WEU? The European Community?" In *Western Europe and Germany: The Beginnings of European Integration, 1945–1960,* edited by Clemens Wurm, 137–74. Oxford: Berg, 1995.

Schoeps, Hans Joachim. *Vorläufer Spenglers.* Leiden: E. J. Brill, 1955.

Schulte Nordholt, Jan Willem. *The Myth of the West: America as the Last Empire.* Grand Rapids, MI: Wm. B. Eerdmans, 1995.

Schumacher, Kurt. *Reden-Schriften-Korrespondenzen, 1945–1952.* Edited by Willy Albrecht. Bonn: Verlag J. W. H. Dietz Nachf. GmbH, 1985.

Schwabe, Klaus. "German Policy Responses to the Marshall Plan." In *The Marshall Plan and Germany,* edited by Charles Maier and Günter Bischof, 225–81. Providence: Berg, 1991.

Schwabe, Klaus. "The United States and European Integration: 1947–1957." In *Western Europe and Germany: The Beginnings of European Integration, 1945–1960,* edited by Clemens Wurm, 115–35. Oxford: Berg, 1995.

Schwartz, Thomas A. *America's Germany: John J. McCloy and the Federal Republic of Germany.* Cambridge: Harvard University Press, 1991.

Schwartz, Thomas A. "Reeducation and Democracy: The Policies of the United States High Commission in Germany." In *America and the Shaping of German Society, 1945–1955,* edited by Michael Ermarth, 35–46. Providence: Berg, 1993.

Schwarz, Hans-Peter. *Vom Reich zur Bundesrepublik. Deutschland im Widerstreit der außenpolitischen Konzeptionen in der Jahren der Besatzungsherrschaft, 1945 bis 1949.* Neuwied and Berlin: Hermann Luchterhand Verlag, 1966.

Schwarz, Hans-Peter. "Adenauer und Europa." *Vierteljahrsheft für Zeitgeschichte* 27, no. 4 (1979): 471–523.

Schwarz, Hans-Peter. *Konrad Adenauer.* 2 vols. Providence: Berghahn, 1995, 1997.

Schweller, Randall L., and David Priess. "A Tale of Two Realisms: Expanding the Institutions Debate." *Mershon International Studies Review* 41, no. 1 (1997): 1–32.

Schweller, Randall L., and William C. Wohlforth. "Power Test: Evaluating Realism in Response to the End of the Cold War." *Security Studies* 9, no. 3 (2000): 60–107.

Scott, James C. *Domination and the Arts of Resistance: Hidden Transcripts.* New Haven: Yale University Press, 1990.

Searle, John. *The Construction of Social Reality.* New York: Free Press, 1995.

Seidel, Michael. *Streak: Joe DiMaggio and the Summer of '41.* New York: Penguin, 1988.

Sewell, William H. "A Theory of Structure: Duality, Agency, and Transformation." *American Journal of Sociology* 98, no. 1 (1992): 1–29.

Sheetz, Mark. "Exit Strategies: American Grand Designs for Postwar European Security." *Security Studies* 8, no. 4 (1999): 1–43.

Sheetz, Mark. "Exit Strategies Redux." *Security Studies* 11, no. 3 (2000): 200–205.

Sheetz, Mark. "France and the German Question: Avant-garde or Rearguard?" *Journal of Cold War Studies* 5, no. 3 (2003): 37–45.

Shotter, John. *Conversational Realities: Constructing Life through Language.* Thousand Oaks, CA: Sage, 1993a.

Shotter, John. *Cultural Politics of Everyday Life.* Toronto: University of Toronto Press, 1993b.

Sieferle, Rolf Peter. *Die Konservative Revolution.* Frankfurt am Main: Fischer Taschenbuch Verlag, 1995.

Singer, J. David. "The Level-of-Analysis Problem in International Relations." In *The International System,* edited by Klaus Knorr and Sidney Verba, 77–92. Princeton: Princeton University Press, 1961.

Skinner, Quentin. *Visions of Politics.* Cambridge: Cambridge University Press, 2002.

Smith, Rogers M. *Stories of Peoplehood: The Politics and Morals of Political Membership.* Cambridge: Cambridge University Press, 2003.

Smith, Tony. *America's Mission.* Princeton: Princeton University Press, 1994.

Smith, Woodruff D. *Politics and the Sciences of Culture in Germany, 1840–1920.* New York: Oxford University Press, 1991.

Snyder, Jack. *Myths of Empire: Domestic Politics and International Ambition.* Ithaca: Cornell University Press, 1991.

Sofsky, Wolfgang. *The Order of Terror: The Concentration Camp.* Princeton: Princeton University Press, 1997.

Southern, R. W. *Western Views of Islam in the Middle Ages.* Cambridge: Harvard University Press, 1962.

Spengler, Oswald. *The Decline of the West.* Vol. 1, *Form and Actuality.* New York: Alfred A. Knopf, 1926.

Spengler, Oswald. *The Decline of the West.* Vol. 2, *Perspectives of World-History.* New York: Alfred A. Knopf, 1928.

Spengler, Oswald. *Man and Technics: A Contribution to a Philosophy of Life.* New York: Alfred A. Knopf, 1932.

Spengler, Oswald. "Pessimus? (1921)." In *Reden und Aufsätze,* 63–79. Munich: C. H. Beck, 1938.

Starobinski, J. "The Word Civilization." In *Blessings in Disguise,* 1–35. Oxford: Polity, 1993.

Steel, Ronald. *Walter Lippmann and the American Century.* Boston: Little, Brown, 1980.

Steininger, Rolf. *The German Question: The Stalin Note of 1952 and the Problem of Reunification.* New York: Columbia University Press, 1990.

Stephanson, Anders. *Kennan and the Art of Foreign Policy.* Cambridge: Harvard University Press, 1989.

Stephanson, Anders. *Manifest Destiny: American Expansion and the Empire of Right.* New York: Hill and Wang, 1995.

Stephanson, Anders. "Fourteen Notes on the Very Concept of the Cold War." http://www.h-net.msu.edu/~diplo/stephanson.html (accessed 24 August 2003), 1996.

Stephanson, Anders. "Kennan's Abendland: On Nationalism, Europe, and the West." Manuscript, Department of History, Columbia University, n.d.

Sterling-Folker, Jennifer. "Realism and the Constructivist Challenge: Rejecting, Reconstructing, or Rereading." *International Studies Review* 4, no. 1 (2002a): 73–97.

Sterling-Folker, Jennifer. *Theories of International Cooperation and the Primacy of Anarchy: Explaining U.S. International Monetary Policy-Making after Bretton Woods.* Albany: SUNY Press, 2002b.

Stern, Fritz. *The Politics of Cultural Despair.* Berkeley: University of California Press, 1961.

Stimson, Henry L. "The Challenge to Americans." *Foreign Affairs* 26, no. 1 (1947): 5–14.

Sylvan, David, and Stephen Majeski. "A Methodology for the Study of Historical Counterfactuals." *International Studies Quarterly* 42, no. 1 (1998): 79–108.

Taft, Robert A. *A Foreign Policy for Americans.* Garden City, NY: Doubleday, 1951.

Thomas, Russell. *The Search for a Common Learning: General Education, 1800–1960.* New York: McGraw-Hill, 1962.

Tilly, Charles. "To Explain Political Processes." *American Journal of Sociology* 100, no. 6 (1995): 1594–1610.

Tilly, Charles. *Durable Inequality.* Berkeley: University of California Press, 1998a.

Tilly, Charles. "International Communities, Secure or Otherwise." In *Security Communities,* edited by Emanuel Adler and Michael Barnett, 397–412. Cambridge: Cambridge University Press, 1998b.

Tilly, Charles. *Stories, Identities, and Political Change.* Lanham, MD: Rowman and Littlefield, 2002.

Tiryakian, Edward A. "The Civilization of Modernity and the Modernity of Civilizations." *International Sociology* 16, no. 3 (2001): 277–92.

Todorov, Tzvetan. *The Conquest of America.* New York: Harper and Row, 1984.

Toynbee, Arnold. *Civilization on Trial and The World and the West.* New York: Meridian, 1958.

Trachtenberg, Marc. *A Constructed Peace: The Making of the European Settlement, 1945–1963.* Princeton: Princeton University Press, 1999.

Turner, James. *The Liberal Education of Charles Eliot Norton.* Baltimore: Johns Hopkins University Press, 1999.

Vandenberg, Arthur. *The Private Papers of Senator Vandenberg.* Boston: Houghton Mifflin, 1952.

Verdery, Katherine. "Whither 'Nation' and 'Nationalism'?" *Daedalus* 122, no. 3 (1993): 37–46.

Wala, Michael. *The Council on Foreign Relations and American Foreign Policy in the Early Cold War.* Providence: Berghahn, 1994.

Wallander, Celeste A. "Institutional Assets and Adaptability: NATO after the Cold War." *International Organization* 54, no. 4 (2000): 705–35.

Wallerstein, Immanuel Maurice. *The Modern World-System: Capitalist Agriculture and the Origins of the European World-Economy in the Sixteenth Century.* New York: Academic, 1974.

Waltz, Kenneth. *Man, the State, and War.* New York: Columbia University Press, 1959.

Waltz, Kenneth. *Theory of International Politics.* New York: McGraw-Hill, 1979.

Wapner, Paul. "Politics Beyond the State: Environmental Activism and World Civil Politics." *World Politics* 47, no. 3 (1995): 311–40.

Weber, Alfred, ed. *Unteilbarkeit des Friedens und Unteilbarkeit Deutschlands.* Heidelberg: Verlag Lambert Schneider, 1947.

Weber, Katja, and Paul Kowert. "Agency and Structure: Divergent Normative Views of Postwar German Politics." Paper presented at the American Political Science Association, Boston, 2002.

Weber, Max. *From Max Weber: Essays in Sociology.* Edited by H. H. Gerth and C. Wright Mills. New York: Oxford University Press, 1946.

Weber, Max. *Economy and Society.* Translated by Guenther Roth and Claus Wittich. Berkeley: University of California Press, 1968.

Weber, Max. *Wirtschaft und Gesellschaft.* Edited by Johannes Winckelmann. 5th ed. Tübingen: J. C. B. Mohr, 1976.

Weber, Max. *Wissenschaft als Beruf und Politik als Beruf.* Edited by Wolfgang J. Mommsen and Wolfgang Schluchter. Tübingen: J. C. B. Mohr, [1917/1919] 1994.

Weber, Max. "Kritische Studien auf dem Gebiet der kulturwissenschaftlichen Logik." In *Gesammelte Aufsätze zur Wissenschaftslehre,* edited by Elizabeth Flitner, 215–90. Potsdam: Internet-Ausgabe, http://www.uni-potsdam.de/u/paed/Flitner/Flitner/Weber/index.html, 1999a.

Weber, Max. "Die 'Objektivität' Sozialwissenschaftlicher und Sozialpolitischer Erkenntnis." In *Gesammelte Aufsätze zur Wissenschaftslehre,* edited by Elizabeth Flitner, 146–214. Potsdam: Internet-Ausgabe, http://www.uni-potsdam.de/u/paed/Flitner/Weber/index.html, 1999b.

Weber, Max. *The Protestant Ethic and the Spirit of Capitalism.* Translated by Stephen Kalberg. Edited by Stephen Kalberg. Los Angeles: Roxbury, 2002.

Weigert, Hans. "The Future in Retrospect: Oswald Spengler, Twenty-Five Years After." *Foreign Affairs* 21, no. 1 (1942): 120–31.

Weldes, Jutta. *Constructing National Interests: The United States and the Cuban Missile Crisis.* Minneapolis: University of Minnesota Press, 1999.

Wellman, Barry. "Structural Analysis: From Method and Metaphor to Theory and Substance." In *Social Structures: A Network Approach,* edited by Barry Wellman and S. D. Berkowitz, 19–61. Greenwich, CT: JAI Press, 1997.

Wendt, Alexander E. "The Agent-Structure Problem in International Relations Theory." *International Organization* 41, no. 3 (1987): 335–70.

Wendt, Alexander E. "Anarchy Is What States Make of It: The Social Construction of Power Politics." *International Organization* 46, no. 2 (1992): 391–425.

Wendt, Alexander E. "On Constitution and Causation in International Relations." In *The Eighty Years' Crisis: International Relations, 1919–1999,* edited by Tim Dunne, Michael Cox, and Ken Booth, 101–17. Cambridge: Cambridge University Press, 1998.

Wendt, Alexander E. *Social Theory of International Politics.* Cambridge: Cambridge University Press, 1999.

Wight, Colin. "They Shoot Dead Horses Don't They? Locating Agency in the Agent-Structure Problematique." *European Journal of International Relations* 5, no. 1 (1999): 109–42.

Wighton, Charles. *Adenauer: Democratic Dictator; A Critical Biography.* London: Frederick Muller, 1963.

Wilkinson, David. "Civilizations, World Systems, and Hegemonies." In *World System History: The Social Science of Long-Term Change,* edited by Robert A. Denemark, Jonathan Friedman, Barry K. Gills, and George Modelski, 54–84. London: Routledge, 2000.

Williams, Phil. *The Senate and U.S. Troops in Europe.* London: Macmillan, 1985.

Wittgenstein, Ludwig. *On Certainty.* Edited by G. E. M. Anscombe and G. H. von Wright. New York: Harper and Row, 1969.

Wittgenstein, Ludwig. *Philosophical Investigations.* Translated by G. E. M. Anscombe. Oxford: Blackwell, 1953.

Wolf, Eric. *Europe and the People Without History.* Berkeley: University of California Press, 1982.

Wolfers, Arnold. "National Security as an Ambiguous Symbol." In *Discord and Collaboration,* 147–65. Baltimore: Johns Hopkins University Press, [1952] 1962.

Woller, Hans. "Germany in Transition from Stalingrad (1943) to Currency Reform (1948)." In *America and the Shaping of German Society, 1945–1955,* edited by Michael Ermarth, 23–34. Providence: Berg, 1993.

"X" [George Kennan]. "The Sources of Soviet Conduct." *Foreign Affairs* 25, no. 4 (1947): 566–82.

Index

The letter *f* following a page number denotes a figure.